### Researching a Classroom Pet: An Example of a Scaffolded Web Project

Imagine you are a second-grade student, and your teacher decides that she will allow you and your classmates to purchase a class pet. She will contribute $30, and you will be allowed to help make the selection. But there are some issues beyond cost that you have to consider. Some pets are dangerous, and some students are allergic to certain animals. (You understand this because you have a cat at home, and your aunt says it makes her sneeze.) The pet will have to stay in a container of some sort and remain at school over weekends. There is one more thing: your teacher says the decision will be

***A Story*** **sections have extended narratives describing actual classroom projects and applications.**



made by the entire class. You have to gather information and then explain to other students what kind of pet you would like the class to buy and why.

Does this sound like a good project? Ellen Knudson, a second-grade teacher at Solheim Elementary in Bismarck, North Dakota, thought so. Mrs. Knudson has a history of keeping pets in her classroom. She also likes to involve her students with technology projects—particularly ones in which the students are in control and make their own decisions. It seemed natural, then, to let her students research possible classroom pets on the World Wide Web.

#### Preparing for the Project

To prepare for this project, Mrs. Knudson had a lot of work to do. To keep the students' research focused and efficient, she decided to ask them to consider just three potential classroom pets: a budgie (a type of bird, more formally known as a budgerigar or parakeet), a sugar glider (a marsupial), and a leopard gecko (a reptile). Even for just these three animals, finding Internet resources appropriate to second graders was a challenge.

Certain factors, such as the use of scientific nomenclature (*Melopsittacus undulatus* for budgie), did not bother her because she felt her students should learn to cope with real-world information. But she was concerned that the web resources be concise, contain the specific details students would be asked to locate, and be presented in a form that young readers could understand.

Sometimes, she discovered, a single Internet page provided all the information needed for an animal, and sometimes a page provided a great opportunity to investigate a particular issue. She made a careful selection of both types of sites. The varied experiences would be good for her students, she thought.

#### Introducing the Project

Mrs. Knudson used class discussion to introduce her students to the project. Then she directed them to a series of Internet pages she had created. The following information appeared on the introductory page:

**Class Pet**

Mrs. Knudson wants to buy a new pet for the classroom. She needs help in selecting the right one. Click on the pet names below to find out more about each animal. As you are reading, keep these guidelines in mind:

- It must not be a mammal because of allergies to animal hair and fur.
- It must be $30 or less in price.
- It must be able to live in the 10-gallon aquarium or bird cage in our room.
- It must be easy to feed. Food must be easy to get and fairly inexpensive.



After you have read through the information, write out y[…] ing the price, the cage or equipment the animal needs, [...] mal belongs to, and the animal's diet. Also explain why [...] would be interesting to study and care for.

Links from this introductory page connected students to the potential pets. Each of these pages then provided links sources Mrs. Knudson had located. In addition to the links, t comments suggesting what students should attempt to lear "This page tells about the budgie's diet," "This page has a p on. In this way Mrs. Knudson carefully scaffolded the projec

#### The Project Develops

The classroom had just one computer connected to the Int[...] Knudson could take her class to the school's computer lab [...] was necessary. During this project, students worked on the [...] pairs and took notes they would use in their discussions.

After the initial information-gathering phase, students [...] discussion back in the classroom. Because the students sat [...] than individual desks, each table of three to four students [...] nient discussion group. The course of discussions was unp[...] Mrs. Knudson listened to each group, asked questions, and answered some of the students' questions. When the students puzzled over scientific names, she reviewed general strategies for dealing with unfamiliar words. One group attempting to estimate food costs wanted to know how large a teaspoon was. Students at each table were asked to write out their group's recommendation before the entire class discussed the issue. Figure 4.3 illustrates the recommendation of one table of students.

**FIGURE 4.3** The classroom pet project: the recommendations of one group of students after their web research and discussion.

BEST PET by Table 3
We recomend the Budgie because it costs 10 dollar to
20 dollars.
They eat green vegtables. And they eat 2-3 teespons
of seeds a day.
They need a cage.
The budgie is in the bird family.

# Dedication

As the development of this book draws to a close, I cannot help thinking about how different my present experiences have been from experiences at a comparable point in the writing of our first technology book. As we worked to finish our other book, Cindy was diagnosed with cancer. I wrote parts of that book with a laptop while sitting in the corner of her hospital room. By the time this book is in your hands, it will be more than five years later and she will be considered a survivor. If you receive an e-mail from Cindy, notice her signature block (see Chapter 3, p. 68). There is a single sentence that reads "Appreciate every moment, you never know when they might be taken away." It is a simple message, but very good advice. This book is dedicated to my wife.

# Integrating the Internet for Meaningful Learning

**MARK GRABE**
*University of North Dakota*

**CINDY GRABE**
*Technology Facilitator, Grand Forks Schools*

HOUGHTON MIFFLIN COMPANY
BOSTON NEW YORK

Senior Sponsoring Editor: Loretta Wolozin
Associate Editor: Lisa Mafrici
Project Editor: Aileen Mason
Editorial Assistant: Jane Lee
Senior Production/Design Coordinator: Jennifer Meyer Dare
Senior Manufacturing Coordinator: Priscilla Bailey
Marketing Manager: Pamela Laskey
Associate Marketing Manager: Jean Zielinski DeMayo

Cover Image: Vicky Rabinowicz



Printed in the U.S.A.

Library of Congress Catalog Card Number: 99-72013

ISBN: 0-395-90958-9

123456789-CRS-03 02 01 00 99

# Brief Contents

# Contents

# Preface

This is our second book about learning with technology. We began writing about how technology might be used to enhance content-area instruction nearly seven years ago, and the result was our first book about the general use of technology in classrooms: *Integrating Technology for Meaningful Learning.*

When we wrote the second edition of that book (Grabe & Grabe, 1998), we responded to the growing interest in the Internet as an information resource and communication tool for students. We added a chapter titled "Learning with Internet Tools," and we supplemented our chapter on student projects with material on student web authoring. Yet our experience in working with teachers told us this was simply not enough. The prominence of the Internet in our society; the spending of schools, states, and the federal government on the infrastructure needed to connect schools to the Internet; the learning potential inherent in the Internet—all these demanded a more extensive approach. There is a tremendous need for practical, understandable information about integrating the Internet in K–12 classroom instruction.

## THE INTERNET IN EDUCATION

Does the Internet represent a powerful and practical vision for educational improvement? Schools are rushing to provide access to the Internet. Counting the number of "wired" classrooms within schools has become a method for quantifying a commitment to its use. In many venues—research, journals, presentations, daily newspapers—the Internet is held up as a means of achieving educational reform. Internet tools nicely lend themselves to a greater emphasis on student-centered learning, authentic tasks, and performance-based assessment.

Yet, it's important to acknowledge that we've just started on this journey, and we have a long way to go! The opportunities and the promise of the

Internet are very real, but extensive and meaningful use of the Internet to accomplish fundamental educational change is not all that common.

Our purpose in writing this book is to help you understand the vision of the Internet as a vehicle for change on a massive scale—but it is important to do so in ways likely to influence what happens in your classroom. Our objective is to help you see the many roles the Internet can play in education and why so many educators are excited about its potential for teaching and learning. Toward that end, you might want to turn now to Part One, "Why Use the Internet?", which has basic information on "The Internet in Education Today" (Chapter 1), and the nature of student learning in "Meaningful Learning in an Information Age" (Chapter 2). Throughout this text we use examples from classrooms and teachers familiar to anyone who knows "a place called school." We do so as a way to help you understand how ideas about using the Internet in education look in actual practice.

## USING THE INTERNET AS A TOOL FOR MEANINGFUL LEARNING

You will note that we frequently refer to *technology as a tool.* This metaphor has been carefully selected because it provides a very important perspective for educators. The value of developing proficiency in the use of any tool is realized only when the tool is applied in accomplishing a meaningful task. Education is partly about helping students acquire skills for the meaningful tasks they must accomplish throughout their lives. However, the use of technology tools does not need to be reserved exclusively for the future. Our emphasis is on the very important work students do in their present daily lives—students must be immediately invested in the productive work of learning. Our intent is to show you how to help students use the Internet to learn the skills and knowledge appropriate to the content area you teach. As you read, you will recognize our focus on three recursive themes. The Internet can provide (1) Tools for Communication, (2) Tools for Inquiry, and (3) Tools for Construction.

### THE INTERNET AS A TOOL FOR COMMUNICATION

This first theme focuses on how Internet systems can provide learners with an efficient method for exchanging information and communicating with others. Chapter 3, "Learning with Internet Communication Tools," provides detailed descriptions of e-mail, mailing lists, chat, and videoconferencing systems, along with examples of the types of Internet projects that can be accomplished with these tools.

## THE INTERNET AS A TOOL FOR INQUIRY

This theme focuses on how the Internet can provide students with opportunities for seeking the information needed to solve problems. Chapter 4, "Learning with Internet Inquiry Tools," shows how learners can make efficient use of the major Internet tools that promote student inquiry (e.g., the web browser and the World Wide Web). Chapter 5, "Integrating the Internet into Inquiry-Based Projects," builds on Chapter 4 and details the way students can incorporate the Internet into authentic problem-solving projects, and how teachers can develop and structure activities.

## THE INTERNET AS A TOOL FOR CONSTRUCTION

This final theme shows the Internet as a vehicle for presenting products students create to summarize a learning activity. Part 3, "Learning by Constructing Internet Resources," focuses on the constructive process of design with chapters on "Constructing Content-Area Web Projects" (Chapter 6) and "Designing Web Pages: Principles for Students and Teachers" (Chapter 7).

In other words, Internet tools can be integrated in classrooms to support some of the most fundamental and essential processes for meaningful learning.

## THIS TEXT'S GOALS AND PERSPECTIVE

Our general purpose in writing this book is to aid your classroom practice by bringing together current theory on meaningful learning and the development of critical thinking skills, short tutorials on Internet tools and resources, and a variety of suggestions for classroom activities. Our primary goals are

- To acquaint you with models of meaningful learning, information problem solving, and critical thinking that can establish useful goals for instruction.
- To present the different roles the Internet might play in facilitating meaningful learning, information problem solving, and critical thinking.
- To explain how to use essential Internet tools and resources to accomplish your instructional goals.
- To suggest how you can initiate and facilitate particular categories of classroom activities with your own students, and to demonstrate these possibilities with a variety of classroom examples.
- To promote your thinking and reflection about the best uses of the Internet in your classroom.

What we have to offer is a combination of stimulation, information, and encouragement. That is,

- We hope to stimulate you to think deeply about the processes of teaching and learning. What are the most important educational goals, and what roles do teachers and learners play in accomplishing these goals?
- We will provide you with information that includes concrete descriptions of Internet tools, online information resources, and classroom activities you can use to accomplish your goals. The book should help you answer questions such as: What software will I need, and how does this software work? What should my students and I do with these tools? How have other teachers used such tools and activities in their classrooms?
- Finally, we intend to help you develop the confidence necessary to implement Internet-supported activities in your classroom.

We hope that as you read this book you will not assume that school experiences as you know them must remain fixed, and that technology must somehow fit within this existing framework. Fitting technology and the Internet within existing models of educational practice is certainly possible. However, such a perspective closes off many unique opportunities. Some educators are urging that we drastically revamp our educational system. Criticism of educational practices is not new, of course, and whether massive changes occur, continual scrutiny of educational practices is healthy. We feel that computer technology and the Internet have served as catalysts for the examination of educational goals and methods and, in some cases, have encouraged valuable changes.

As you think about considering classroom applications of the Internet, you will likely find yourself examining broad educational issues. Just remember: in most cases effective teaching with technology is effective teaching by any means.

## OUR APPROACH IS ANCHORED IN EVERYDAY CLASSROOM LIFE

We want very much to assure you that what we propose would be practical for you to implement. Our strategy for doing this has been to rely primarily on our own experiences within our local school district.

We decided that it would be unfair for us to piece together a picture of Internet use based on grant-subsidized schools, high-tech demonstration sites, or what we have gleaned about the latest and greatest applications from the conferences we attend and the journals we read. Yes, the theory and research we describe in this book draw on contributions from a wide range of educational researchers and policy advocates. In contrast, however, most of the classroom examples we include come from teachers we know personally.

We both work and live in Grand Forks, North Dakota, and we anticipate that few of our readers have ever visited our community or have more than a vague notion of where it is located. What might be more relevant is that the technology in our schools is present largely because of the investment of local taxpayers. Thus the applications of technology we describe result from the decision making of the school board, local administrators, and teachers. Our resources for technology are above average: all schools and most classrooms have Ethernet connections to the Internet, and perhaps more important, teachers have access to support personnel assigned to help them use the available technology resources. But how and whether teachers make use of these resources is pretty much up to them. Our district is certainly not at the extremely sophisticated level of a demonstration site.

What we have done in writing this book is draw examples from some of the more involved and creative teachers we know. We do not claim that these teachers are typical, but rather that they work in fairly typical schools under typical conditions. For them the Internet is a valuable tool, and it contributes to practical and productive activities for their students.

## THE AUTHORS' COMPLEMENTARY EXPERIENCES

A few comments about our own backgrounds may provide a context for what we emphasize. The topics and theoretical perspective of this book result from a blend of the orientations, experiences, and individual interests of the two authors.

Mark Grabe's background is in educational psychology—he is a professor in the Psychology Department and the Instructional Design and Technology program at the University of North Dakota. He brings to this collaboration the theoretical perspectives and research experiences more typical of a university faculty member. Mark has been developing instructional software for approximately fourteen years in support of his own research activities. Originally trained to teach high school biology, he continues to pursue his interest in science education. Some of his first Internet activities involved designing instructional web sites to promote the outdoor educational programs of the North Dakota Department of Game and Fish. This work, which you will catch glimpses of throughout the book, has encouraged an interest in hands-on science and the role technology might play in it.

Cindy Grabe's original certification was as an elementary teacher; she later earned a master's degree as a learning disabilities specialist. After she had worked for many years as a reading specialist, her interest and experience in using technology in instruction led her to a full-time technology position with the Grand Forks, North Dakota, school district. She has been a technology facilitator, a position that in some districts may be described as a computer coordinator, for nine years. Her position requires that she provide training to district teachers, administrators, and staff members, collaborate on curriculum projects, and conduct demonstration activities with students. She is involved in providing continuing educational experiences for teachers in area schools, and she teaches courses for preservice teachers. Cindy deals directly and continuously with the very practical issues of integrating the Internet in classrooms. Her own work with students and her association with many gifted classroom teachers are responsible for most of the classroom examples we provide in this book. Cindy has been recognized as an Apple Distinguished Educator by the Apple Computer Corporation.

## LEARNING FEATURES OF THE TEXT

Embedded in the chapter content are special features to help you better understand important concepts and use them in your own classroom.

### SOURCES IN REAL CLASSROOMS: STORIES, PROJECTS, INTERVIEWS

Descriptions of actual classroom events can provide a powerful way to "see" in action many of the ideas we present. *Stories* of classroom events and descriptions of actual student *projects* are embedded in many chapters as demonstrations of teacher or student behavior. We have also included some *interviews* we conducted with people who work directly with teachers or students.

We have tried to remain true to the comments of the professionals we interviewed and to the stories that teachers and students actually related to us. In a few cases, such accuracy required that we include statements that are not in perfect agreement with suggestions we ourselves might make. We assume you understand that this is a field in which diverse and sometimes contradictory opinions exist.

### SCREEN IMAGES AND PROGRAM EXAMPLES

The graphics in this book are mostly images captured as they appear on the computer monitor. You may not always have immediate access to the computer tools or the Internet resources we describe, so these images are a convenient way to help you understand what the text explains. Visual examples are one of the best ways to explain topics such as web page design and to present samples from actual student projects.

### "FOCUS" AND "KEEPING CURRENT" FEATURES

The features that appear under the general titles "Focus" and "Keeping Current" allow us to break away from the main thrust of a presentation and consider a topic in more detail. The topic might involve a deeper explanation of how a particular software program or form of technology works; an extended discussion of an important issue or theory; or the presentation of an instructional strategy. Setting these discussions apart allows the reader to consider the topics independently from the main discussion. If we were presenting this material using hypermedia, we could use some great techniques for linking the central ideas to interesting details. A book is not hypermedia, but these features are the next best thing.

### ACTIVITIES

Following the text of each chapter, we include several activities that we suggest you try. These activities are our attempt to get you to think more actively about important issues presented in the chapters. We have attempted to generate activities that can be accomplished either with or without direct access to computer resources, so you should be able to complete most of the brief tasks we propose. We believe that reading about the application of the Internet will not be enough to prepare you to use the ideas in your classroom. We trust that this book will not be the only resource at your disposal and that you will also learn a great deal from teachers and colleagues.

### RESOURCES TO EXPAND YOUR KNOWLEDGE BASE

Each chapter ends with annotated lists of resources that offer further information about the topics and software tools covered in the chapter. Although we include resources of different types, we have decided to emphasize web sites. We feel that carefully selected web sites will provide you with the most immediate and current access to software information and examples of Internet applications—and increasingly to scholarly information as well.

Listing web sites has one limitation: web addresses may change or disappear. Our solution is to host our own web site so that you can keep up on changes that come to our attention. Please visit us at **http://ndwild.psych.und.nodak.edu/book** or connect to our site via the main Houghton Mifflin web page (**http://www.hmco.com/college** and select "Education"). From there you should be able to locate current resources related to this book.

Most of the Internet addresses from the text have also been collected in the "Teachers' Handy Reference" at the end of the book. We hope that you find this collection to be a valuable resource.

## ACKNOWLEDGMENTS

A book is a great example of a cooperative project. The authors get to put their names on the front cover, but many people make essential contributions. We owe many individuals our gratitude for helping to bring you this book. Loretta Wolozin, senior sponsoring editor at Houghton Mifflin, saw in the proposal for our first book the germ of a unique idea and made the trip to North Dakota to talk with us and examine student projects. Focusing on the curriculum and putting students in control of powerful tools were not typical themes at the time we began writing about technology, yet Loretta supported our belief that these themes should be at the core of what teachers learn about the classroom applications of technology. She has continued to support these themes as we have turned our attention to the Internet.

Doug Gordon was the developmental editor on this project. His patience and skill were very helpful as we explored the structure for this book and the way our ideas would be presented. Doug is very knowledgeable in the general area of technology, and several topics and resources were added at his suggestion. Most of all, he has a great way of shaping prose so that it reads easily. We hope you will find our arguments and explanations clear and our style friendly.

Aileen Mason, our project editor, was responsible for the tedious task of putting the finishing touches on this book. The more we learn about design, the more we appreciate that structure and presentation make important contributions to what a learner gains from any medium. Aileen also handled many details such as making certain there is a citation for each of our references—details that the reader takes for granted and that writers are never quite careful enough to guarantee.

Other people from Houghton Mifflin also made an important contribution to this project. Lisa Mafrici, our point of contact with Houghton Mifflin throughout the project, kept us aware of our responsibilities as different stages unfolded. Betsy Peterson from the Houghton Mifflin legal department provided valuable information relevant to our comments on fair use and copyright issues in Chapter 9. Houghton Mifflin was one of the publishing companies involved in the Conference on Fair Use that established some of the guidelines we discuss in that chapter.

Finally, we owe a giant debt to the many students, administrators, and teachers who provided the authentic examples and interviews we have included to ground the ideas of this book in real schools and classrooms. The individuals identified throughout this book represent a wider circle of people who have influenced our thinking about teaching and instructional applications of technology. Thanks to all who have allowed us to draw on their creativity and experience.

# PART ONE

# Why Use the Internet?

# Chapter 1
# The Internet in Education Today

## ORIENTATION

In this chapter you will get to know the Internet. You'll learn about its brief history, how it functions, and the options for connecting computers to it. You'll find out about the major Internet tools that both students and teachers can use, and you'll learn what you need to start using the Internet with your own students.

The text opens with a narrative that illustrates the many roles the Internet can play in education and in society at large. When you see all the possibilities, you'll begin to understand why the Internet has become such a vital force in our society—and why many educators are so excited about its potential for teaching and learning.

As you read, look for answers to the following questions:

**FOCUS QUESTIONS**

- How does the Internet work?
- What major opportunities does the Internet offer for students and teachers?
- What are the basic hardware and software needs for anyone who wants to connect to the Internet?
- How might Internet projects change the traditional role of a classroom teacher?
- What are the present Internet capabilities of a typical school?

## Life, Learning, and the Internet: The Red River Flood of 1997

In the spring of 1997, a massive flood swept up the Red River Valley in the northern Midwest. When it reached Grand Forks, North Dakota, the home of this book's authors, it submerged much of the metropolitan area. For those of us who lived in Grand Forks at the time, it was the kind of profound experience that now serves as a shared marker in our lives. It linked us with generations of people before us who had struggled with natural disasters in the region. But we had a key resource our forebears lacked—the Internet. In various ways, the Internet proved to be a lifeline for individuals, for schools, and for the community at large.

### Before the Flood: Using the Internet to Prepare and Learn

The winter of 1997 was one of the harshest on record. A total of eight blizzards dumped snow on the valley, and as spring approached, projections from the National Weather Service indicated that flooding was likely. As communities prepared for the river to rise, the educational process was often disrupted. Parents and teachers were severely stressed by their personal situations. School attendance declined, and classroom routines were altered.

Partly as a response to these problems, the Grand Forks Schools created a World Wide Web site on the Internet devoted to the impending flood. The web site was the brainchild of Darin King, the school district's network administrator, and several of his colleagues. The site was used to circulate flood-related curriculum ideas so that teachers could engage the preoccupied students in ways that would provide educational benefits. The lesson suggestions included these:

- Use a computerized spreadsheet to chart the rise of the river, based on data from the U.S. Geological Survey.
- Conduct an experiment to investigate changes in melt rate created by sprinkling sand on ice blocks. (Helicopters were being used to sand areas of the river in an effort to speed up the melt rate and increase the flow.)
- After reviewing web sites that offer safety tips, create flood safety posters.
- Contribute personal comments to an online flood journal.

One of the most dramatic applications on the web site was Darin King's "flood-cam." This in fact was the original idea that sparked the further development of the site. Darin worked in the district's four-story office building, which is located only a couple of blocks from the river. He took an old video camera, a mailbox, and a piece of transparent Plexiglas and fashioned an observation station that he positioned on top of the building (Figure 1.1). The video feed from the camera was brought into the building by

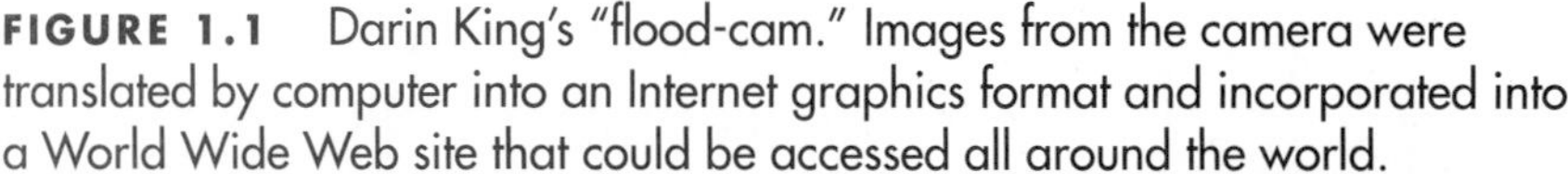

**FIGURE 1.1** Darin King's "flood-cam." Images from the camera were translated by computer into an Internet graphics format and incorporated into a World Wide Web site that could be accessed all around the world.

cable, and the images were "captured" by an old Macintosh computer. The computer generated a still image every fifteen minutes, and this image was automatically incorporated into the web page (Figure 1.2).

As the river rose, the flood-cam proved enormously popular. The site was listed as a *USA Today* web site of the day. Encouraged by this response, Darin and his colleagues created further web pages to reflect what they learned as they worked to protect their own homes and their community. The web site became a resource for the community at large, as well as for teachers and students. Here are some of the topics the web site addressed:

- What is a "sump," and how does a sump pump work?
- Why should you plug the drains in your basement, and exactly how can you do this?
- What does a sandbag machine look like, and how does it work?

In addition, the school's web site incorporated "links" to other web sites that provided important information related to the impending flood. Students or community members—or anyone else around the world—could access these sites simply by clicking on the links with the computer mouse. The linked sites included these:

- The U.S. Geological Survey site, which provided real-time river-level data from multiple locations as well as information about the hydrology of the Red River basin.
- The Federal Emergency Management Agency site, which contained an assortment of disaster-related resources, such as "Flood Preparedness Information."
- The U.S. Army Corps of Engineers site, which displayed the latest "Ice Reconnaissance Data." (Because the Red River flows from south to north, ice in the northern regions can cause the water to back up and thereby increase the flooding.)
- The Regional Weather Data Center, which offered weather data, satellite images, and the latest projected date and level of the river's crest.

As the potential magnitude of the disaster became more apparent, the school's flood pages were accessed more and more frequently by people in far-flung locations. In the short time the flood site existed, it was accessed

**FIGURE 1.2** The World Wide Web page containing the last picture taken by Darin King's flood-cam.

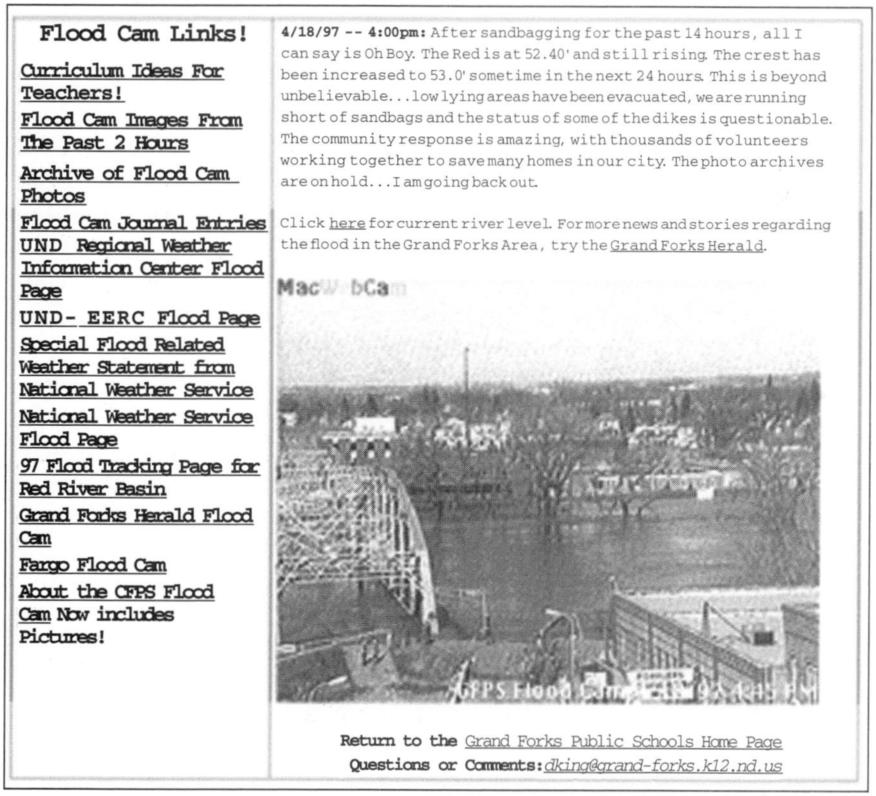

**Flood Cam Links!**

Curriculum Ideas For Teachers!
Flood Cam Images From The Past 2 Hours
Archive of Flood Cam Photos
Flood Cam Journal Entries
UND Regional Weather Information Center Flood Page
UND- EERC Flood Page
Special Flood Related Weather Statement from National Weather Service
National Weather Service Flood Page
97 Flood Tracking Page for Red River Basin
Grand Forks Herald Flood Cam
Fargo Flood Cam
About the GFPS Flood Cam Now includes Pictures!

**4/18/97 -- 4:00pm:** After sandbagging for the past 14 hours, all I can say is Oh Boy. The Red is at 52.40' and still rising. The crest has been increased to 53.0' sometime in the next 24 hours. This is beyond unbelievable...low lying areas have been evacuated, we are running short of sandbags and the status of some of the dikes is questionable. The community response is amazing, with thousands of volunteers working together to save many homes in our city. The photo archives are on hold...I am going back out.

Click here for current river level. For more news and stories regarding the flood in the Grand Forks Area, try the Grand Forks Herald.

**Return to the** Grand Forks Public Schools Home Page
**Questions or Comments:** *dking@grand-forks.k12.nd.us*

nearly 100,000 times. In response to what they saw on the web site, many people used the Internet to send electronic mail—e-mail—to Darin and the Grand Forks schools. Some were community members writing to describe their own experiences; some were ex-community members who sent notes of encouragement and consolation; some were individuals who had endured a disaster in their own community; and some were students in other schools who had begun to follow the flood.

As the e-mail messages poured in—from places like Owasso, Oklahoma; Battle Ground, Washington; Keller, Texas; Misawa, Japan—many of them were incorporated into the online flood journal. Grand Forks students also answered some of the e-mail from students in other areas, using the correspondence as an opportunity to discuss their experiences.

## During the Flood: The Internet as Lifeline

During the evening of April 18, the dike protecting Grand Forks from the river overflowed. Soon a state of emergency was declared, and about 40,000 people had to leave their homes.

Although we ourselves live several miles from the river, we had to evacuate our neighborhood. About two in the morning, we packed a few belongings and our dogs in the car and drove to a temporary shelter at a nearby Air Force base. The next day we drove back, parked a couple of blocks from our home, because the water was now blocking the street, and carried our computers back to the car. We had little time to rescue other possessions because more streets might soon become impassable.

Once the state of emergency was declared, people were told they would not be allowed to return to their homes until the water receded—likely a week or more. Because this part of the country is sparsely populated, there were few facilities nearby to accommodate so many displaced people. Community members scattered far and wide, throughout the country and in some cases throughout the world.

We first drove several hundred miles to a friend's cabin in western Wisconsin, but it had no telephone and scarcely any TV reception. We felt too isolated and anxious about our home, friends, and jobs. Soon we went instead to stay with Cindy's brother in northeastern Minnesota.

Imagine, if you will, the communication needs and difficulties created by these circumstances. You and most of the members of the community leave your homes in the middle of the night. Many phone connections are dead, and what remains of the system is severely taxed by emergency calls. You may not have the opportunity to call your friends or your boss, and at the time you are probably too consumed with your personal situation to do so. There is no time to establish a plan for how you will keep in contact, participate in group decisions, or obtain information about what might be expected of you.

As it turned out, technology became our lifeline, and the Internet played an especially vital role. The cable TV, of course, brought daily information about the flood's progress. A better source, however, was the World Wide Web site maintained by the *Grand Forks Herald* newspaper. Information from this site turned out to be more reliable than many of the televised reports from national news agencies, which, in their haste to cover the story, made some grievous (and sometimes ridiculous) errors.

### *The Saga of the* Grand Forks Herald

During the flood, a fire broke out in downtown Grand Forks, and with the streets underwater there was no way to use traditional firefighting equipment. As the fire advanced from one block to the next, the offices of the *Grand Forks Herald* fell victim. Although the building and one-hundred-plus years of photo and newspaper archives were destroyed, many of the employees relocated to the small community of Manvel, North Dakota, a few miles north of Grand Forks.

There they set up shop in an elementary school and continued to publish the paper. They edited and laid out the paper on the computers in the school's computer lab and sent the electronic files by Internet to St. Paul, Minnesota, where the paper was printed. For this effort—which would have been impossible without the Internet—the *Herald* won a Pulitzer Prize for service to the community.

### *The Community Reconnects*

The Internet also became a priceless means of personal communication. Many displaced people began to search out ways to connect to the Internet and then tried to access their e-mail accounts. Sometimes they were able to connect through the phone lines where they were staying. Sometimes it meant a special trip to a community or university library. When they did connect, people often found that their e-mail accounts were still available. The e-mail "server" for the K–12 system, for example, was located in another part of the state, undamaged by the flood. And the computer equipment responsible for the university e-mail systems was loaded on a truck, moved to another university, and reconnected to the Internet.

We have since talked with many people who shared the same experience: Turn on the machine. Activate a program such as *Telnet* and try the address for my old account. "What do you know, it works! I have mail!"

It's hard to describe the feeling of being connected again. There was the sense that a community—one that many of us had seldom thought about—still existed. Energized by this sense, we found excuses to write e-mail to many people—sometimes to people we barely knew.

For people who were not regular e-mail users, the experience was different, but the Internet still helped many of them reconnect with each other. Several web sites likely to be visited by people from the community established links to web "locator" pages. Visitors to a locator page were encouraged to provide information about themselves by filling out a simple form. Our entries were something like this:

> **Title—Mark and Cindy Grabe**
>
> **Message—**We are presently staying in Hinckley, Minnesota, with relatives. Jeff Holm and family made the trip with us and have gone on to Michigan. We are using our old e-mail accounts.

In this way people's names and messages were added to the locator pages. The name or message description became a link that would take a visitor to the associated message. Because more links could be added to these new message pages, chains of correspondence emerged. Although there was no privacy—and everyone pretty much read the messages from anyone they recognized—this Internet resource became a major means of keeping in touch with friends, colleagues, and family members.

## The Aftermath: Internet Learning Projects

We ended up returning to Grand Forks earlier than most residents, because Cindy was asked to help with another Internet project. To provide a positive experience for students during this time, Apple Computer decided to make a sizable donation of equipment to the schools of Grand Forks. Apple's intention was to create a technology-rich learning environment that students could use while their parents were involved in the early stages of rebuilding the community.

Apple apparently assumed that much of the community was still living at the Air Force base that had first been used to shelter evacuees. There Apple provided computers, digital cameras, and connections to the Internet, with the idea that students would continue communicating with others about their flood experiences. Actually, like us, most of the displaced community members had moved on to other parts of the country. Nevertheless, once the computer equipment became available, it was quickly put to use.

All of the public schools in the system had been closed for the year nearly six weeks early. But now the Air Force base schools were reopened on a limited basis so that interested students could have something constructive to do with their time. Using the new equipment, students and teachers began a number of learning projects.

### *"Faces in the Flood"*

One project at the Air Force base was a web publishing effort called "Faces in the Flood." Groups of students learned about some aspect of the flood recovery effort and then created web pages to communicate what they had learned.

First, the students and teachers worked together to identify interesting issues, people, or community activities they might investigate. The teachers then attempted to arrange interviews and a community site visit for each student group. When a field trip was possible, the group of students took a video camera and their notebooks and set off to learn what they could. One group of students visited the Humane Society to find out what was happening to pets abandoned in the flood. One group interviewed the "Flood Jocks," the radio announcers responsible for the around-the-clock emergency talk program simulcast by the local radio stations that were still functioning. One group told the story of the *Grand Forks Herald.*

### *The "Flying Kitchen"*

As part of "Faces in the Flood," Angela, Victor, Spencer, and Alex, fourth-grade students from the Carl Ben Eielson elementary school, decided to concentrate on the emergency food distribution system that was now providing 10,000 meals a day to those working in the community. The food was prepared in a hangar on the Air Force base, using mobile kitchen facilities that had rolled in on several trailer trucks. Southern Baptist volunteers from Texas operated the mobile kitchen, dubbed the "Flying Kitchen" because of the many trips it had made to disaster sites.

**FIGURE 1.3** A portion of the "Faces in the Flood" web site.

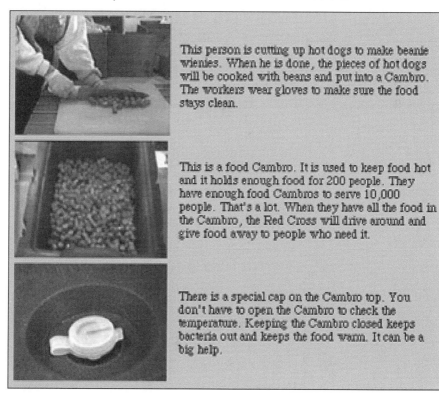

This person is cutting up hot dogs to make beanie wienies. When he is done, the pieces of hot dogs will be cooked with beans and put into a Cambro. The workers wear gloves to make sure the food stays clean.
This is a food Cambro. It is used to keep food hot and it holds enough food for 200 people. They have enough food Cambros to serve 10,000 people. That's a lot. When they have all the food in the Cambro, the Red Cross will drive around and give food away to people who need it.
There is a special cap on the Cambro top. You don't have to open the Cambro to check the temperature. Keeping the Cambro closed keeps bacteria out and keeps the food warm. It can be a big help.

Before the students visited the hangar, they developed a list of questions they wanted to ask and decided the specific duties each group member would take on. One student would operate a video camera and a second the digital camera. One would handle the tape recorder, and another would take notes. The students were amazed to see food prepared in such huge batches. They found many things to photograph and to discuss with the volunteers.

After the field trip, the students viewed the videotape and captured the images they wanted to use on their web page. While the other group members turned to a related project, Angela wrote comments to explain the images. When the students were ready to present their work, parents were asked to sign permission forms, and the story of the "Flying Kitchen" became part of the "Faces in the Flood" web site (Figure 1.3).

You can see that this project, and others like it, offered many opportunities for learning. The Internet was in many ways the "link" for all of these projects—the resource that made them feasible.

One final note on the Internet's role in the flood: Angela's grandmother in California, who learned about the web site from Angela's parents, sent Angela a congratulatory message—by e-mail.

## THEMES OF INTERNET USE IN EDUCATION

Our story about the Red River flood illustrates the rich variety of Internet applications that can promote learning for K–12 students. In our community the Internet became especially important because so many aspects of traditional schooling broke down. But you do not need to wait for a flood in your school district; you can take advantage of the Internet in your daily classroom activities now.

One way of describing the Internet is to say that it provides access to a suite of *tools* that offer great promise for education. The fundamental purposes of this book are to

*Purposes of this book*

1. Familiarize you with the learning tools the Internet offers.
2. Outline significant educational tasks to which these tools might be applied.
3. Help you apply Internet tools in a skillful manner.

Although we emphasize classroom applications that any teacher can use, some of the information will seem technical in nature. We believe that anyone who wants to make use of online resources should have a basic understanding of how the Internet and Internet applications work. If at first you feel overwhelmed by the topic, we hope you'll find our explanations clear enough so that you can relax and enjoy thinking about creative ways to apply what you are learning. If, on the other hand, our explanations seem too brief or lacking in specific detail, we urge you to spend some time with the additional information sources listed at the end of each chapter in the book.

Let's get one other warning out of the way. It is very difficult to provide

*Technology always changing*

*current* information about technology applications. Educational technology is constantly changing. The Internet tools available to you when you read this book may be later versions of the ones we describe, and they may have some new features. On the other hand, the setting where you work may not yet allow access to all of the tools we mention. In either case, the instructional strategies offered in this book can be adapted to your particular classroom needs and the resources you have available.

As we develop these instructional strategies, you'll find that certain key themes come up again and again:

### Key Themes

- The integration of technology tools into content-area instruction.
- A multidisciplinary or integrated-curriculum approach.
- An active role for learners.
- A facilitative role for the teacher.
- Cooperative learning.

The sections that follow introduce these themes. The rest of the chapter will then begin examining how the Internet works and what you as a teacher can do with it. Our goal is to provide you with the knowledge and strategies you will need to help your students use Internet tools in meaningful learning.

## INTEGRATION OF TECHNOLOGY TOOLS INTO CONTENT-AREA INSTRUCTION

The title of this book summarizes our first and foremost theme. Our focus is on applying Internet tools to the development of content-area knowledge and skills.

*Learning in context*

> *Learning about technology itself is important, but we feel it is most effective to learn about the Internet within the context of learning other subjects such as biology, history, or composition.*

*Helping you reach your own goals*

Our intent is to help you find ways to incorporate uses of the Internet that are consistent with your own instructional goals and philosophy. In your daily work in the classroom, you may be helping students learn to read and write, to be knowledgeable of and sensitive to different cultures, or to apply the processes and principles of mathematics and science to the solution of meaningful problems. Whatever content area you are teaching, Internet tools can play a significant role in achieving your goals.

## A MULTIDISCIPLINARY OR INTEGRATED-CURRICULUM APPROACH

In the "Faces in the Flood" project, you saw students investigating various facets of the flood-recovery effort and creating web pages to communicate

*Mingling traditional disciplines*

their learning. Their work involved several traditional content areas or disciplines—social studies, science, reading, writing, and art, to name a few. The same will be true of other examples of classroom projects you find in this book.

The student projects we emphasize seldom fall within a single content area or focus on a single skill. Instead, just as they integrate the Internet into content areas, they also tend to integrate the content areas with one another, creating a multidisciplinary approach to learning. Students explore authentic issues or problems, drawing on information from multiple disciplines and using a variety of information processing and communication skills.

## AN ACTIVE ROLE FOR LEARNERS

*Active = mentally engaged*

When we refer to active learners, we do not mean physical activities. Granted, the Grand Forks students were physically active when they took a trip to interview the people working in the emergency food kitchen. In our usage, however, the word *active* describes the *mental* behavior of the students. In the "Flying Kitchen" example, the external activity of gathering information and then generating a web page encouraged the learners to be active thinkers.

In later chapters, you will see this type of student activity described with terms like *constructive learning* (Chapter 2) and *knowledge as design* (Chapter 6). Overall, this book takes a cognitive approach, emphasizing the student's mental activity.

## A FACILITATIVE ROLE FOR THE TEACHER

In the flood story there are examples of teachers functioning in a variety of instructional roles. For instance, Darin King and his colleagues prepared some web pages to present information to students. Although this method of communication may be new to you, the role of presenting information to students is familiar. After reading this book, we think you will have the skills necessary to create your own online instructional materials.

*Adapting teaching to encourage active learning*

But we would also like to encourage you to take a different role—one closely related to the goal of encouraging active learning by students. When students play a more active role in their own learning, the teacher's behavior must be adjusted accordingly. The teacher becomes less of a "dispenser of information" and more of a "facilitator of learning." That is, teachers try to motivate, question, and evaluate in ways that encourage productive mental behaviors among the students. In Chapter 2 we will explore some of the assumptions behind this shift in role.

## COOPERATIVE LEARNING

*Does the Internet isolate?*

One charge consistently leveled against the Internet is that it isolates individuals. For example, a recent study concludes that the Internet reduces social involvement and increases the possibility of depression because Internet communication tends to be shallow and exploration of the World Wide Web takes the place of social activities (Kraut et al., 1998). We will directly address some of these issues in Chapter 3. Here, we simply want to point out that technology tools can be used in many different ways, and the ways we recommend are certainly not those that isolate students.

*Emphasis on cooperative projects*

The role of technology in education is strongly influenced by the teacher, and applications are isolating only when the teacher requires that students work on projects or assignments alone. In some cases independent work may be appropriate, but in other cases cooperative work is desirable. This book puts particular emphasis on Internet projects by cooperative groups. The "Faces in the Flood" projects were all cooperative, each of them involving a small number of students and an adult. These projects also brought students into contact with members of the community at large, and they generated some very unique conversations.

## WHAT IS THE INTERNET?

We hope that our introductory comments have started you thinking about the many different ways in which the Internet can be useful to educators and learners. Now let's tackle the most basic questions: What is the Internet, and how does it work?

*The Internet defined*

The **Internet** is an international collection of computer networks, with an estimated 150 million users in 200 nations—a number that continues to increase daily (Global Reach, 1998; Maddux & Johnson, 1997). People use the Internet to communicate with one another, to find and offer information, to exchange computer files, to advertise their services, to sell products—in fact, the number of ways to use the Internet is multiplying almost as fast as the number of users. Thus the Internet is not a single application providing a single service to a single group of people. Even when we narrow our focus to educational applications, the Internet still provides a wide variety of opportunities.

To begin to understand the Internet, you need a bit of background on how it evolved.

### A SHORT HISTORY OF THE INTERNET

The term *Internet* comes from "Internetting"—originally a research program of the U.S. Defense Department. Beginning in 1969, an early experimental network was established to link university-based research centers, the military, and defense contractors. This network was called ARPANet (Advanced Research Projects Agency Network of the Department of Defense).

The basic objective of the ARPANet project was to design a system by which many users could remain in contact despite unreliable channels of communication. An original concern, as you probably realize from coverage of the Internet in the popular press, was that a nuclear attack might destroy part of the country's conventional communication systems. The early researchers were also interested in such problems as how radio signals might be improved to overcome blackouts caused by such situations as the sender or receiver passing through a tunnel or behind a hill. Out of this basic research came applications based on two concepts: (1) networks and (2) sending information in packets.

*The original goals*

*What is a network?*

*Networks* connect multiple sites in multiple ways. The significance of this arrangement is that there are alternate pathways between any two points, and the flow of information is not terminated when any particular link is unavailable.

*What is a packet?*

The process of sending information in *packets* requires a more extended explanation. First, information sent in packets must exist in a digital form. This means that text, sound, and images must be converted to the digital form of representation—essentially strings of 1's and 0's. Luckily, most of us never actually see or work directly with this type of information. We can rely on computer hardware and software to convert nondigital inputs (for instance, the sound coming into a microphone, or video from a camcorder) into the digital format.

Second, individual packets contain a relatively small amount of digital information. Thus large files (like a large image or a video segment) must be broken down into many separate packets. This approach was created to minimize the effect of transmission errors. Remember, the original goal was to design a system that could recover from errors. It was assumed to be more efficient to resend the specific packets that become corrupted or lost than to resend an entire large file.

The nature of a packet is also very ingenious. A packet contains (1) some information and (2) information about this information. The information might be part of a picture or a segment of an e-mail message. The information "about" this information helps the packet reach the correct destination and helps the system recover when a packet does not arrive.

*Evolution of the Internet*

As the Internet moved beyond the developmental phase, ARPANet's functions were taken over by the National Science Foundation (NSFNET) and other special-purpose networks. More recently, as federal subsidies for research networks have been withdrawn and as the Internet has attracted users from the commercial sector, networks have been taken over largely by commercial providers. This evolution has created the highly popular—and increasingly commercial—Internet that we know today.

## DOMAINS AND PROTOCOLS

You may be wondering how so many computers manage to talk to one another. Even though computers share a basic digital language of 1's and 0's,

Keeping Current

## Issues for the Internet's Future

In the Internet's transition from government to private sponsorship, there are a couple of important issues for the education community:

- The Internet is a shared resource, and some tolerance is required in this collaborative environment. Some resources available on the Internet are not what many educators would prefer, but the Internet is not the exclusive domain of educators and students.
- The Internet is not free. Maintenance and the continued expansion of the Internet to meet higher and higher expectations require substantial revenue.

Some educators see a possible danger in these circumstances. Services that generate greater revenue and interest from the general public (video on demand, for example) may crowd out less lucrative educational applications of the Internet. Branscomb (1995) makes this kind of historical argument in evaluating the television industry. Early on, television seemed like a medium with potential to have a dramatic impact on education. However, as interest in commercial programming began to dominate, educational programming was relegated to the poorer-quality and limited-range UHF channels. A number of people worry that the same thing may happen with the Internet.

On this and other matters, educators at all levels will have a great deal to say about the future of the Internet and the roles it will play. Understanding where the Internet came from and some of the factors affecting its development can help you act wisely as an advocate for Internet proposals that can benefit teachers and students.✷

they must agree on how to express those digits and on what specific sequences of digits mean.

*What is the TCP/IP protocol?*

In computer terminology, the set of rules for expressing and understanding information is called a "protocol." For the Internet, the protocol in common use is the **TCP/IP protocol** (transmission control/Internet protocol). The TCP rules control the flow and recovery of the individual packets. The IP rules establish a system for addressing and forwarding the packets.

*What is a domain name?*

Every computer with a permanent connection to the Internet has a unique IP number. Mark Grabe's connection happens to have the number 134.129.172.88. Because strings of numbers are difficult to remember, a **domain name** (more accurately, a Fully Qualified Domain Name) is established as equivalent to the IP number. Mark's domain name is grabe.psych.und.nodak.edu. A special computer, a *domain name server (DNS),* keeps track of the domain names corresponding to the various IP numbers. One of the tasks someone has to complete in setting up a new computer or new Internet software is to enter the IP number and domain name and to tell that computer where to find the DNS (Leiner et al., 1997). Once you learn how, you

Focus

## Why Study Technical Matters?

When our discussion becomes somewhat technical, you may object that you manage to use telephones and television without learning their scientific details. Why should Internet technologies be any different?

Certainly you can manage to use a few standard Internet tools, such as e-mail software, without worrying about technical matters. As you teach, however, you will find an endless stream of new tools that offer your students authentic opportunities for adventure and collaborative learning. These tools often require a bit of tinkering, experimentation, and risk taking—and a bit of a technical background.

Most classroom teachers will not have to be technology experts, but as in many other fields, a familiarity with the basic concepts and vocabulary will help you. Even if you do not have to solve many technical problems yourself, you will need to know how to work well with your support personnel.✱

can easily do this yourself. However, in most educational institutions, there will be someone available to take care of this task for you.

### CLIENTS AND SERVERS

Often hardware and software components related to the Internet are described as "clients" and "servers." What do these terms mean?

*Two basic terms*

To put it simply, any computer that makes a resource available to other computers is known as a **server,** and the software it uses for this purpose is called server software. Another computer that connects to the server to gain access to the resource is known as the **client,** and the software it uses in the process is known as client software.

For example, imagine that a friend of yours connects to America Online (AOL) to send you an e-mail message. AOL provides this resource through its e-mail server. Your friend's computer is the client computer, and to compose and send her message she uses client software (the e-mail function in AOL's software package).

## WHAT ROLES CAN THE INTERNET PLAY IN EDUCATION?

There are many ways of categorizing the possible roles of the Internet in education. Researchers and educators have created schemes based on content areas (such as language arts or science), grade levels (elementary, secondary), or categories of software (web browsers, e-mail, FTP). Information on all these areas is included throughout this book. To help you understand the most essential issues for classrooms, however, we want to use a classification system based on the concept of *tools* that we mentioned earlier.

*Three types of tools*

You can think of the Internet as providing three basic types of tools for you and your students (adapted from Bruce & Levin, 1997):

### *Internet Tools*

- Tools for communication.
- Tools for inquiry.
- Tools for construction.

These categories are summed up in Table 1.1, and in the following sections we look at each of them in turn. As you read, think back to the story of the Red River flood and try to identify examples of these kinds of tools in use.

## TOOLS FOR COMMUNICATION

*Rapid, wide-reaching communication*

As you probably already know from using e-mail or talking with friends who use it, the Internet provides a remarkable tool for rapid communication. During the Red River flood, it allowed widely dispersed people to keep in touch, and it gave students the opportunity to share their experiences with peers in other areas. In more ordinary educational circumstances, the Internet allows students to communicate with their peers, with their teachers, or with members of the outside community. Similarly, teachers can communicate with each other or with experts in many different fields.

*Synchronous vs. asynchronous*

The communication can take many forms. It can include text (that is, words), still or video images, sound, or any combination of these elements. It can be *synchronous* (the sending and receiving take place at the same time) or *asynchronous* (a message is sent at one time and received at a later time). It can be person-to-person or person-to-group. It can be interactive, as when two people "chat" online, or noninteractive, as when a person publishes a document on a web site for others to read.

**TABLE 1.1**
Internet Resources for Teachers and Students: Three Basic Categories of Tools

| *Tools for Communication* | *Tools for Inquiry* |
|---|---|
| E-mail | The World Wide Web (WWW) |
| Mailing lists | File Transfer Protocol (FTP) |
| Newsgroups | Streaming audio and video |
| Chat | *Tools for Construction* |
| Videoconferencing | Content-area web projects |

*Essential component of teaching*

We all recognize that developing communication skills is an educational priority and that communication is an absolutely essential component of effective teaching and learning. Later chapters of this book, especially Chapter 3, will show how Internet communication tools can make unique and powerful contributions in your classroom. For now, we'll begin with a quick survey of the most common types of Internet communication tools.

## E-mail

*Phenomenal growth of e-mail*

Sending electronic mail—**e-mail**—was one of the earliest uses of the Internet, and it remains one of the dominant Internet applications. In 1997, it was estimated that 2.7 trillion e-mail messages were sent, and the volume of e-mail was predicted to grow to 6.9 trillion messages by the year 2000 (Moran, 1997). Standard e-mail consists of simple text messages. It is becoming more common, though, to include **attachments**—appended images or other file types—with text messages.

To use e-mail, you must first obtain an account on a computer with e-mail capabilities. Most Internet service providers offer this service. If you are presently a student, you probably have an account on a machine owned by the college or university you attend, and you connect to your account on that computer to send and receive e-mail.

Exchanging e-mail messages sounds simple, and it is. You probably do not need to be convinced that e-mail provides a convenient and inexpensive method for communicating. What may not be apparent is how e-mail might be useful in your classroom for content-area instruction. Think of these possibilities, which are already in use in many classrooms:

*How can you use email in the classroom?*

### *Classroom Examples*

- To learn about a different culture or to practice foreign language skills, your students could exchange e-mail with students from other regions or other countries.
- To examine a problem—say, the water quality in your city—your students could use e-mail to help them collect and integrate data from many different locations.
- As part of a writing project, your students could use e-mail to share their work with those in other classes or other schools.

This list is only a small sample of possible e-mail projects. E-mail and its classroom uses will be described in greater detail in Chapter 3.

## Mailing Lists

*Messages to many recipients*

**Mailing lists** are closely related to e-mail. Instead of a message's being sent to a single individual, however, the message is made available to many recipients. The message usually contains plain text only, without attachments.

Mailing lists exist on a huge variety of topics. As a teacher, for example,

*Focus*

## Intercultural E-mail Connections

Since 1992, St. Olaf College in Minnesota has hosted a service designed to help teachers and classes link with e-mail partners in other countries. This service began when professors from St. Olaf who were interested in the educational potential of e-mail had difficulty locating collaborators to fit specific interests. Realizing that others probably shared their difficulties, the St. Olaf faculty members started an electronic mailing list dedicated to establishing e-mail partnerships. At first they concentrated on college and university partnerships, but when their initial efforts attracted considerable attention from the K–12 community, the focus of the service was broadened.

Known as Intercultural E-mail Classroom Connections (IECC), the service has now distributed over 20,000 requests for e-mail partners. Nearly 7,000 individuals in approximately 70 countries are members of at least one mailing list sponsored by IECC. As it expanded its services, the IECC introduced a World Wide Web site (**http://www.stolaf.edu/network/iecc**), which lists requests from K–12 and higher education teachers for partner classrooms, reports specific e-mail projects, and announces survey projects (projects requesting a single contribution of information). Through the web site, the IECC also moderates an open discussion of the use of e-mail in intercultural class projects.✷

you might be interested in a mailing list on subjects relating to educational reform or one that offers information about Internet use in the classroom. These and other lists are discussed in more detail in Chapter 3.

### Newsgroups

*Browsing a collection of messages*

**Newsgroups** take a somewhat different approach from mailing lists. Instead of distributing messages by e-mail, as a mailing list would do, a newsgroup maintains its messages on a newsgroup server. Generally messages (usually referred to as *articles*) can be "posted" (submitted) to the server by anyone who has registered to join the group. To browse these messages, you use a special client application called a **newsreader.** In contrast to a mailing list, the messages do not automatically come to your account; instead, you make the effort to visit the newsgroup server.

### Chat

In the terminology we introduced earlier, mailing lists and newsgroups are asynchronous access systems—a message is sent at one time, received at another. Online chat rooms, in contrast, offer synchronous access to group conversation.

Keeping Current

## Using the Internet for Professional Development

How can practicing teachers keep up on the different issues that affect them as professionals? Many participate in continuing education workshops and subscribe to magazines and journals. Mailing lists and newsgroups can provide a valuable supplement to these options, offering teachers the opportunity to actively participate in sharing knowledge and experiences.

Consider how a high school biology teacher interested in using technology in her classroom might use newsgroups. She might participate in discussions of science education through the newsgroup called *k12.ed.science*; she might also investigate applications of technology at *k12.ed.tech*, keep up with her scientific specialty at *sci.bio.ecology,* and follow developments related to her favorite computer system at *comp.sys.mac.announce.* As these examples show, Internet resources can make a valuable contribution to the process of lifelong learning.✷

*Real-time communication*

A **chat** room is a virtual area where people meet and communicate online. Communication primarily takes the form of brief text messages submitted by multiple participants and then relayed by a server to each participant's chat client. The messages are accompanied by a name for each participant—either the person's real name or (often) a pseudonym. What appears on the computer monitor is a rolling series of names and messages.

**Internet relay chat (IRC)** is a chat format that can be used by anyone with Internet access and IRC client software. Commercial online services also provide their own chat rooms, which are a popular source of entertainment for adult and adolescent members. In some cases, use of chat communication becomes inappropriate, and in a few known cases it has been criminal (see Chapter 9's discussion of responsible use of the Internet). So this is an Internet communication tool that requires supervision in K–12 settings.

*Rise in educational applications*

Probably one of the most common educational applications of chat sessions is as part of online courses. More and more higher education institutions are offering complete courses over the Internet. The chat sessions allow students to participate in discussions and help them learn from each other. Applications of chat in K–12 classrooms are less well developed, but they are growing in number and significance. Students from several K–12 institutions may participate in chat sessions as part of their common involvement in a large-scale online project: for instance, following a group of scientists as they explore the Antarctic. In such projects, the chat sessions allow students to share observations with one another and ask questions of the scientists or other participants.

## Videoconferencing

*A developing technology*

For many years, Internet users have heard that **videoconferencing** was the Internet application of the future. The popular image was of a device that would allow interactive voice-and-image communication. Videoconferencing is here, but it would probably be fair to place this tool in what we refer to as our "adventurous teaching" category—that is, it works, but it is still in the developmental stages, and users can expect some problems in implementation. This technology is explored further in Chapter 3.

# TOOLS FOR INQUIRY

*A wealth of information*

As you are probably well aware, the Internet offers incredibly vast amounts of information. It allows students and teachers to access informative texts, images, video, and databases. Many of these resources are free to the general public, though there is a growing trend to offer instructional resources at a cost. Less numerous at present, but of great potential for the future, are sites that allow users to acquire *real-time* data, such as current weather statistics from cities around the globe or live video feeds from remote sites. In some cases, users can even manipulate remote scientific instruments to accomplish specific tasks (an application known as *telerobotics*).

To make any of these data sources meaningful, of course, students must *act* on the data, analyzing and interpreting them. That is,

> ▶ *Students must move beyond mere information gathering to genuine inquiry.*

*Defining* inquiry

As we use the term, **inquiry** involves finding sources of information appropriate to a task, working to understand the information resources and how they relate to the task, and then, in those cases for which some action is expected, applying this understanding in a productive way.

The Internet provides a number of different information exploration and delivery systems. The following descriptions will acquaint you with the major ones, and you will learn a great deal more in later chapters.

## The World Wide Web

*A user-friendly "killer application"*

Although the Internet has existed since the mid-1970s, it has been a practical source of information only since the mid-1990s. For many years, the information resources available on the Internet were disorganized and accessible only by individuals with fairly advanced technical skills. The **World Wide Web (WWW)** has changed all that. With an understandable organizational system and a user-friendly method for navigating, it has made Internet resources attractive to a much greater number of users. The WWW has been the "killer application" responsible for attracting millions of users to the Internet.

*Multimedia*

Part of the popularity of the WWW stems from the fact that it uses both multimedia and hypermedia. **Multimedia** roughly translates as "many formats." Multimedia is a communication format that integrates various different media—such as text, audio, video, and still images—into a single product. For example, when a computer user visits a web site, the screen image may contain both text and a video segment, and the computer may produce narration as the video plays.

*Hypermedia*

**Hypermedia** allows multimedia to be experienced in a nonlinear fashion. Unlike a book, which is read in a linear fashion, front to back, hypermedia allows units of information (text segments, images, video clips, and so on) to be connected to each other in multiple ways. When you are working within a hypermedia environment, you have a high degree of control over the order in which you experience the elements of information and even over which elements you experience.

*Pages and links*

The World Wide Web implements multimedia and hypermedia as interconnected **pages.** Each page consists of multimedia elements (text, images, video clips) and **links.** A link is a text segment or graphic element that the user can click with the mouse, causing another web page or element of information to appear (see the "Flood Cam Links!" in the left-hand column of Figure 1.2). The multiple links that branch from any particular web page are what qualify the Web as hypermedia. A link may take the user to more information prepared by the same author or to information on a completely different server prepared by a different author. As you saw in the flood example, links become a way to bring together the resources prepared by many different people.

The World Wide Web has generated a tremendous amount of enthusiasm. It has been promoted for its potential applications in business, entertainment, and—last but not least—education. Please note our use of the word *potential.* We intend to explore both the limitations and the strengths of the Web as it exists. How effectively World Wide Web experiences inform and stimulate student thought will be the real test of the Web's effectiveness as an important new tool in educational practice. You will find examples of classroom use of web resources in Chapters 4 and 5.

## File Transfer Protocol

*Transferring electronic files*

**File Transfer Protocol (FTP)** allows the transfer of a file from a remote computer to a personal computer. Companies, museums, special interest groups, and many individuals have been willing to collect and organize resources and offer them in this fashion to the general public. The file might be a picture, recipes, a computer program, information needed to prevent a new virus from infecting your computer, or the text content of *Moby Dick.* The educational applications of FTP are as many as you can imagine.

*Project Gutenberg*

One massive FTP application, known as Project Gutenberg, has created a mechanism for the inexpensive distribution of public domain literature, such as the works of William Shakespeare. The stated goal is to make available

*Focus*

## Push and Pull Technology

The Web is sometimes called a **pull technology.** This means that the user continually selects the next information source to be experienced by entering the address of a web page or clicking on a link to move from one resource to another. That is, the user "pulls in" the information.

A **push technology** works differently. At one level, push technology is something like cable television. You select a specialized channel, and resources appropriate to the theme of that channel start rolling in. But imagine that you could customize the channel to reflect your particular interests. For example, you might ask the weather channel to provide you with information about specific cities. You might ask the CNN channel to provide only U.S. news. That is how a push technology works on the Web. Various web news services, for example, will deliver you news customized to your stated preferences.

Push technology may offer some speed advantages. As long as you have an active connection to the Internet, your push client can be working. While you work with a word processing program or other computer application, the push client can continue to retrieve the most recent information of the type you have requested. When you want to view the information, it is already instantly available in your machine.

Educast is a push application designed for educators. Its channels allow access to lesson plans (by grade level or subject area), education news, professional issues, *USA Today,* ideas for community involvement, and the education marketplace. Information about Educast is available at **http://www.educast.com/**.✱

10,000 of the most frequently used books by the year 2001. This organization is not big on frills; the books are provided as plain-text computer files, with no embellishments. But text in this format is very inexpensive to distribute and very easy for the most inexpensive computer systems to display and search. Users are welcome to **download** books from this collection—that is, transfer the files to personal computers. (See the Project Gutenberg web site at **http://promo.net/pg/**.)

### Streaming Audio and Video

One of the visions of Internet entrepreneurs has always been to provide programming on demand. For example, if you want to view a particular television program, you must now either be in front of your television set when the program is scheduled to begin or have your VCR set to record the program. Many believe the Internet may eventually provide a solution to this inconvenience. Because most programs are actually stored on tape, wouldn't it be great if there were a way to ask the network to roll the tape when you were ready? And if this were possible, why not also deliver movies in this fashion? No more trips to the video store on cold winter nights!

*Audio and video when you want them*

Early forms of such technology have emerged in the form of **streaming audio** and **streaming video,** which allow a computer user to experience the sounds and images in real time. While streaming applications are in their infancy, there are already some interesting classroom applications. Nearly 600 radio stations send out their signals as streaming audio. Students of a foreign language might find it interesting to listen to a radio station broadcasting in that language. News programs can also be useful. National Public Radio (NPR) archives some of its news programs (such as "All Things Considered"), and streaming audio would allow all members of a class to review an assigned news story in preparation for class discussion.

*News programs available*

Real-time audio and video feeds associated with special events, such as the launch of a NASA shuttle mission, may also have important classroom uses. To explore the possibilities, see "Resources to Expand Your Knowledge Base" at the end of this chapter, where we list some web sites that provide links to streaming video and audio sources.

### TOOLS FOR CONSTRUCTION

We see the Internet not just as a means of communication or a source of information, but also as an outlet for authentic student work. The "Faces in the Flood" project in our opening story is an example. As a culmination of their learning activities, the Grand Forks students created web pages that presented their work to others.

*Constructing a product promotes meaningful learning*

Expressing personal understanding by constructing a product, such as a web page, gives students a reason for learning. It also requires that they use what they have learned in a meaningful way. Because web pages can incorporate written documents, pictures, video, sound, links to reference materials, and more, they are an excellent final product for many learning activities.

*Content-area web projects*

In Chapter 6, describing what we call *content-area web projects,* we explain how you can think of both personal knowledge and concrete products as the result of a "design" and "construction" process. For now, keep in mind the basic idea that students can construct their own web pages as a means of summarizing and presenting their learning. And for you as a teacher, the most important realization is that you *can* implement such projects within your own classroom.

## WHAT DO I NEED TO START?

After hearing about the multitude of Internet tools and resources, we hope you are eager to begin using the Internet for your teaching. But if you have never used the Internet before, you may be nervous about it, unsure what you need to do to get started. This section should answer some of your questions.

## MAKING THE CONNECTION

*Components of the system*

To understand how a computer on your desk can connect with the Internet and with resources on thousands of other computers throughout the world, it helps to think of the system as involving several components (Figure 1.4). These components include: (1) the Internet backbone, (2) the Internet service provider, (3) the transfer line, (4) the hardware device connecting your computer to the transfer line, and finally (5) your computer and its software.

### The Internet Backbone

*Trunk lines and access points*

The major trunk lines making up the backbone of the Internet are owned by large telecommunication companies such as Sprint and MCI. Major network access points (NAPs) located in San Francisco, Chicago, New York, and Washington provide high-speed switching centers. Various national and regional branches meet at these points.

### Internet Service Provider

*ISPs, small and large*

An **Internet service provider (ISP)** is a company or organization that connects multiple users to the Internet backbone. Some of the largest ISPs include companies whose names you probably recognize (MCI and AT&T) and others whose names are less familiar (UUNET). A local ISP may be operated by your university or a small private company in your community (check the phone book under "Internet"). An Internet connection may also be provided through an online service provider such as America Online (AOL), Microsoft Network (MSN), or Prodigy. These companies offer proprietary information resources that are available only to members of the service, but they also connect members to the Internet at large.

### The Transfer Line

*Types of connections*

To get from your school or home to the ISP, digital information must travel over some kind of *transfer line*. This link may be a regular copper phone line—a setup often referred to as a **dial-up connection** or dial-on-demand connection. A faster and higher-quality signal is provided by an **ISDN (integrated services digital network)** connection, which uses a device called a "repeater" to boost the signal on the phone line if the distance between you and the switching office is more than 3.5 miles. (This is one reason why ISDN connections are not available on all phone lines in all locations.)

For even higher-speed connections, many schools and other institutions rely on leased fiber optic lines, sometimes called **dedicated connections.**

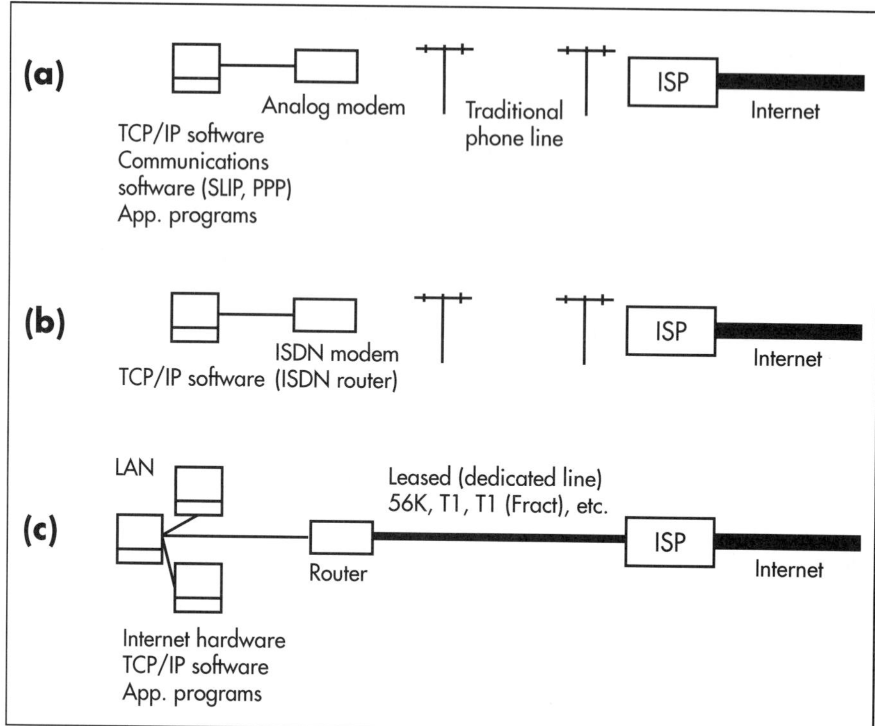


**FIGURE 1.4** Alternative configurations for connecting a personal computer to the Internet. (a) Connection using an ordinary modem and regular telephone lines. (b) ISDN connection. (c) Connection via a dedicated line.

*Variations in bandwidth*

These come in different bandwidths. The **bandwidth** indicates the amount of information that can be moved in a fixed amount of time. Some common fiber optic lines transmit information at 56/64 Kbps (kilobytes per second). T1 lines (1.5 megabits per second) are also common. Schools sometimes lease part of a T1 line, known as a fractional T1. Many school districts using a leased line also use a service called "frame relay," which allows multiple buildings to connect to a single leased line.

Other options are available now and may be used more heavily in the future. One approach makes use of the cable connections presently intended to bring a signal to your television set. Another less common option relies on satellite technology. At one level, these various options are in competition, and it is hard to predict how much success the backers of these different approaches will have in popularizing their particular visions for the Internet.

## Hardware Devices for Connecting to the Transfer Line

To send data through the transfer line, your computer needs a device to connect to that line. The type of device varies depending on the nature of your connection.

*Modems*

A **modem** is a hardware device connecting the computer to a copper phone line. A modem is necessary because a computer and a telephone communicate using different types of signals. A computer uses a digital signal and a telephone, an analog signal. An analog signal is continuous, and a digital signal is discrete (either 1 or 0). An *analog modem*, the most popular type at present, functions by converting the computer's digital signal into an analog signal that can be sent over a standard phone line. The term *modem* stands for "modulate/demodulate," which represents the processes of changing a signal back and forth between the digital and analog forms.

Most analog modems today offer transfer rates of at least 28.8 Kbps. ISDN lines, which use an all-digital technology, are capable of transfer rates up to 128 Kbps, but they require a different type of modem and supporting hardware when the distance to the ISP is several miles.

*Ethernet and LANs*

For a still faster connection using fiber optic cable instead of standard phone lines, your computer must have a special hardware device called an **Ethernet card.** This card is installed in the computer itself. But it would be very unusual for a single computer to be connected to one of these more expensive fiber optic lines. Usually, several computers are first joined together in a **local area network (LAN)**, and then the LAN is connected to the dedicated transfer line through a device called a "router." The computers in a school lab or in different classrooms would likely be connected in this fashion.

The speed of the modem and of the transfer line affect the performance of many Internet applications. But you can still do a great deal with a relatively low-cost connection to the Internet.

## The User's Computer and Its Software

*What your computer needs*

Several different types of software must be installed on the computer you use to access the Internet. First, your computer must have TCP/IP software. This software allows each computer to conform to the common protocol that allows all computers to share resources over the Internet. Second, your computer must have application software appropriate to the type of work that you or your students want to do on the Internet. That is, if you want to send and receive e-mail, you need e-mail software. If you want to browse the World Wide Web, you need a web browser.

*Modem protocols*

If you are connecting through a modem, the modem requires its own software. Most Internet applications operating over a modem require *SLIP (Serial Line Internet Protocol)* or *PPP (Point to Point Protocol)* software. A computer running SLIP or PPP effectively becomes part of the Internet. A more primitive type of connection would allow your personal computer to manipulate a remote computer on the Internet, but you would not be able to use today's advanced applications, such as multimedia web sites.

*How powerful a computer should you have?*

Not every school computer is adequate for Internet applications. Working with most of the applications described in this book requires a relatively fast central processing unit (CPU) and a significant amount of RAM (random access memory). We hesitate to say how fast or how much because new applications always seem to work best on machines of greater power. Suffice it to say that, if the machine is greatly outdated, you are likely to experience some frustration in using Internet applications.

## GETTING APPLICATION SOFTWARE

In our brief orientation to the Internet we have described a fairly large number of different tools and resources. To use all these different systems, you could probably acquire a dozen or so different computer programs. But that is not necessary. World Wide Web browsers (such as Microsoft Internet Explorer and Netscape Navigator) now offer many other applications in addition to web access.

*Helper "apps" and plug-ins*

Often the developers of web browsers create what are called **helper applications**, which are actually independent programs. When the browser downloads a specific category of information (such as streaming audio), it automatically launches the helper application to present that information. Browsers can also be enhanced with plug-ins. A **plug-in** is a special type of software developed to function within another software application. Many programs that started as helper applications have now been converted to plug-ins. Plug-ins perform their roles *within* the browser—for example, by presenting a video within the browser window itself.

The companies developing browsers keep adding more and more functions to attract more users. Plug-in and helper applications are also developed by other companies, and they can usually be downloaded from those companies' web sites. When web authors offer information in a format that is new or fairly unique, the author will usually provide a link to the location where the helper or plug-in can be obtained.

*Get it for free!*

For educators, one of the great things about the client software described here is that most of it is free. You simply connect to a server sponsored by the company that developed the product and download it. We present the Internet addresses for these companies throughout this book. Other sources include books and computer magazines that come with CDs containing free software. Often, the most common software applications are also given away by university computer centers and by computer specialists in K–12 institutions.

As you read this book, become familiar with these Internet applications and the Internet sites offering educational resources. Try locating the resources we have listed in this chapter and in the rest of the book. Then you'll be ready to begin thinking about how your students can take advantage of these resources.

## TRENDS IN INTERNET ACCESS

If you are already a teacher or plan to become one, you are probably interested in what typical schools and classrooms have in the way of Internet resources. The media sometimes focus on glamorous but atypical examples, and it is easy to get the wrong impression. We can offer some statistics on recent developments, but bear in mind that Internet use is changing so quickly that numbers become outdated almost as soon as they are available. Moreover, the government has not created any unified data collection process regarding Internet use. Nevertheless, the available statistics can help you see the general trends.

*Statistics on computers in schools*

First, the number of computers in schools is increasing at a rapid rate. The ratio of students to computers improved from 21:1 in 1990–1991 to 6:1 in 1998–1999. That is, by the 1998–1999 school year, there was one computer for every six students in U.S. schools. But schools have been investing in computers for almost two decades, and the computers acquired over this time period differ drastically in capability. Many schools still have a large number of older computers.

For that reason, some statistics focus on the number of "multimedia computers"—that is, Macintosh computers or PCs with a 386 or higher processor. For that type of computer, the student-to-computer ratio stood at 13:1 in 1998 (Figure 1.5). Because the comparable ratio from 1997 was 21:1, modernization is proceeding at a very rapid pace. Still, many of the machines classified as "multimedia computers" are actually old by technology standards; for some of the applications we have already described, they would have insufficient memory or too slow a central processor speed. Overall, however, it is clear that schools are purchasing computers at a rapid rate, and the general trend indicates a commitment to improving the resources available for learning and instruction.

*Schools with Internet connections*

The trend toward connecting schools to the Internet shows even more spectacular improvement. The percentage of schools with an Internet connection changed from 35 percent in 1994 to 85 percent in 1998. Again, however, these statistics should not be interpreted to indicate that large numbers of students have ready access. Only 44 percent of individual classrooms are actually connected, and the majority of schools still do not have high-speed Ethernet connections (Jerald, 1998b; Market Data Retrieval, 1998; National Center for Educational Statistics, 1997).

Of course, the averages we have been talking about do not address the great variability that exists among different schools and classrooms—and sometimes among different groups of students. In Chapter 9 you will find a discussion of some of the differences in Internet access and how they relate to issues of equity.

This brings us to the end of our brief introduction. From this point, our goal is to help you develop the knowledge and skills necessary to make the Internet a valuable resource in your classroom. Many specific instructional

**FIGURE 1.5**
Trends in computer resources and Internet connections in U.S. schools.

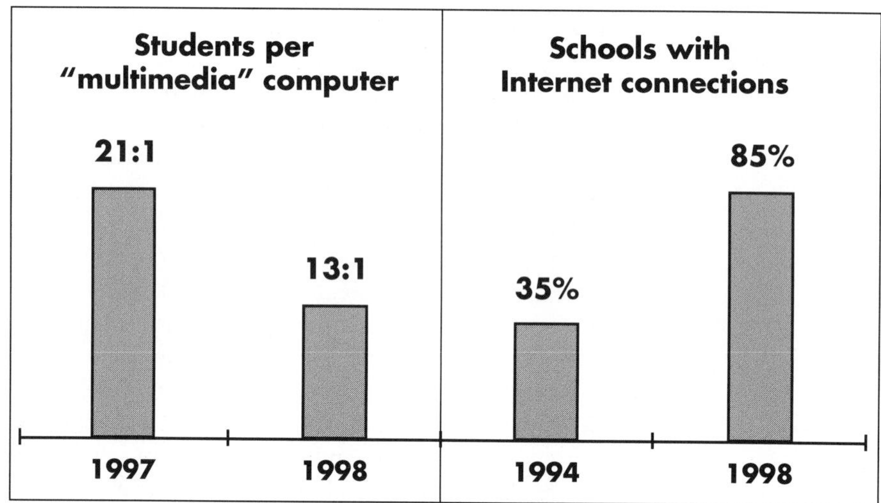


*Source:* Based on data from Jerald, C. (1998b). By the numbers: Student access to classroom technology is increasing dramatically. *Education Week, 38*(5), 102–105. Market Data Retrieval (1998), and National Center for Educational Statistics (1997).

strategies and classroom examples are included in the following chapters. Let's get started.

## SUMMARY

◆ This book presents Internet applications as versatile tools for content-area instruction. We give priority to applications that place students in an active role and that emphasize collaborative, multidisciplinary activities. In implementing the kinds of Internet projects we describe, the teacher acts more as a facilitator of learning than as a dispenser of information.

◆ The Internet is based on the concepts of a network and a packet transmission system. Small amounts of information (packets) are sent across a complex international system of interconnected computers (a network) to a computer with a unique identity (a designated IP number). The rules governing this transmission (TCP/IP protocol) allow the packets to take alternate pathways through the network and to be resent if they do not arrive. The computer receiving the packets (the client) assembles them into the information resource that is then made available to the computer user.

◆ The educational uses of the Internet can be categorized as communication, inquiry, and construction. The tools for communication include e-mail, mailing lists, chat, and various other means of putting students and teachers in contact with each other, with peers, and with outside experts. Tools for inquiry include, first and foremost, the World Wide Web, but also such applications as FTP and streaming audio and video. By tools for construction, we mean primarily content-area web projects in which students create web pages as a product of their learning activities.

◆ Connecting to the Internet requires Internet and application software, the use of special hardware to connect the computer to a transfer line, and the participation of an Internet service provider (ISP) to connect the transfer line to the Internet backbone. Different software, hardware, and transfer line options are available.
◆ Access to both computer equipment and the Internet has improved very rapidly in U.S. schools. Still, the majority of classrooms do not provide direct access, and the more advanced hardware necessary to run the newest multimedia Internet applications must typically be shared by many students.

---

## REFLECTING ON CHAPTER 1

### Activities

1. Consider how Internet technology has influenced you as a student. Are there examples from your own experience that would qualify as communication, inquiry, or construction?
2. Inquire into the Internet resources available in a local school district. Do elementary, middle school, and secondary school students have Internet access? If so, what kind of Internet connection do they have?
3. Assume you could not connect to the Internet through your college or university. How would you go about acquiring access? See if you can find at least two alternatives. Compare your options and the associated costs with what others in the class suggest.

### Key Terms

attachment *(p. 18)*
bandwidth *(p. 26)*
chat *(p. 20)*
client *(p. 16)*
dedicated connection *(p. 25)*
dial-up connection *(p. 25)*
domain name *(p. 15)*
download *(p. 23)*
e-mail *(p. 18)*
Ethernet card *(p. 27)*
File Transfer Protocol (FTP) *(p. 22)*
helper application *(p. 28)*
hypermedia *(p. 22)*
inquiry *(p. 21)*
Internet *(p. 13)*
Internet relay chat (IRC) *(p. 20)*
Internet service provider (ISP) *(p. 25)*
ISDN (integrated services digital network) *(p. 25)*
link *(p. 22)*
local area network (LAN) *(p. 27)*
mailing list *(p. 18)*
modem *(p. 27)*
multimedia *(p. 22)*
newsgroup *(p. 19)*
newsreader *(p. 19)*
page (on the World Wide Web) *(p. 22)*
plug-in *(p. 28)*
pull technology *(p. 23)*
push technology *(p. 23)*
server *(p. 16)*
streaming audio *(p. 24)*
streaming video *(p. 24)*
TCP/IP protocol *(p. 15)*
videoconferencing *(p. 21)*
World Wide Web (WWW) *(p. 21)*

### Resources to Expand Your Knowledge Base

The following World Wide Web addresses will allow you to examine some of the resources mentioned in this chapter.

*@Home.* A system for delivering Internet content using a cable TV connection. Information about this access method can be found at **http://www.home.net**.

*Educast.* **http://www.educast.com/** This site describes an example of push technology intended for educators.

Newsgroups: These sites provide lists of newsgroups.

*Cyber Fiber.* **http://www.cyberfiber.com**

*The Lizst of Newsgroups.* **http://www.liszt.com/news**

*Project Gutenberg.* **http://promo.net/pg/** Project Gutenberg is the effort to provide free access to a large body of literature.

Streaming video and audio: These sites offer access to streaming media.

*Real Guide.* **http://www.realguide.real.com**

*Audionet.* **http://www.audionet.com**

*National Public Radio.* **http://www.npr.com**

# Chapter 2

# Meaningful Learning in an Information Age

## ORIENTATION

This chapter considers some key ideas related to the goals of education and the nature of learning. These subjects are important, because the way you attempt to use the Internet in classroom situations will be determined by the goals you have for your students and your understanding of how students learn.

This chapter approaches these topics by looking at key themes in recent discussions of school reform and at some major models of learning. Then we examine what these ideas mean for the daily practice of teaching, learning, and using the Internet.

As you read, look for answers to the following questions:

**FOCUS QUESTIONS**

- What types of change are being advocated by those promoting educational reform?
- What does it mean to be an "active learner," and how do theories of learning support this approach?
- What are "authentic activities," and what would be necessary for classroom experiences to be more "authentic"?
- What are some of the elements involved in the social context of learning?

This chapter will help you develop a deeper understanding of how students learn and how the Internet can facilitate that learning. You'll notice that, compared to other chapters, this one is less focused on the Internet itself and more concerned with general ideas about learning. There is a good reason for that.

You've heard the old warning about putting the cart before the horse. For the purposes of this book, we could update it to read:

▶ *Never put the technology before the learning!*

In other words, we believe that the significant and long-term integration of technology into classrooms depends on applying technology in ways that *meet educational needs.* This is a different task from simply finding ways to "use" technology.

*Avoiding a backlash*

We fear a backlash if educators do not give serious consideration to what they are trying to accomplish with technology (see Oppenheimer, 1997). Technology, especially when applied wisely, involves a significant investment in human resources as well as in hardware and software. Classroom applications of technology often substitute for more conventional learning tasks. Why, then, should educational institutions make these changes, and why should the community support them?

*Questions for educators to ask themselves*

To answer such questions, educators need to confront some basic issues. They need to ask themselves about their fundamental goals—what they expect students to learn and how that learning can best be realized. There is little point in spending money on technology if it does not promote effective learning experiences. This chapter considers basic questions about the purposes and nature of learning by looking at some of the issues involved in the current movement toward school reform and in prominent models of learning. With that background, we can then talk about ways in which the Internet may serve the purpose of effective learning. As you'll see, we feel that Internet technology can play an important role in responding to reformers' concerns.

Throughout the chapter we emphasize a *cognitive* approach; that is, we try to understand the mental activities of learners and how learning tasks influence student thinking. Why a cognitive approach? Theoretical models in the cognitive tradition suggest that educators can establish learning environments that help students

*Possible gains from a cognitive approach*

- Learn more effectively.
- Apply what they have learned.
- Become more excited about learning.
- Continue learning throughout their lives.

We encourage you to actively evaluate our suggestions. You will eventually have to make your own decisions about the issues we discuss, taking into account the circumstances of your teaching environment, your personal philosophy of instruction, and what you have learned about learning and the classroom uses of technology.

## SCHOOL REFORM IN AN INFORMATION AGE

*"The industrial age has been replaced by the information age. A knowledge of facts is no longer as critical as the ability to creatively solve problems and continue learning throughout life."*

(Knapp & Glenn, 1996, p. 9)

*"However noble its aims, any movement that deprecates facts as irrelevant injures the cause of higher national literacy."*

(Hirsch, 1988, p. 133)

*"It is now almost universally acknowledged that science education must be rejuvenated to serve the needs of American society. . . . Although discovery learning is inefficient for imparting large amounts of information, it is potentially the best approach for helping students gain metareasoning skills and deep understanding."*

(Linn, 1986, pp. 155, 183)

*"The most effective learning environments meld traditional approaches and new approaches to facilitate learning of relevant content while addressing individual needs."*

(International Society for Technology in Education [ISTE], 1998, p. 2)

*Controversy about purposes of schooling*

These varied remarks from prominent educators—some of them contradictory—demonstrate what you probably already know: there is now, as there has always been, considerable controversy focused on our schools. Much of the controversy involves fundamental notions of what students should learn and what learning experiences they should have. Such disagreements are magnified in an era like ours, when we expect so much from our educational institutions.

*What must schools do?*

Think about what we ask our schools to do. First of all, students must acquire the basic knowledge and skills we expect of an "educated person," prepare for work or more advanced education, learn to function as responsible citizens, and develop personal interests that bring richness and meaning to life. As if that were not enough, we also expect schools to "fix things." That is, schools must somehow play a role in addressing the inequities in society, help future citizens appreciate the rising diversity of cultures and languages they are likely to encounter, reduce slippage in our international economic dominance, head off new health risks, and generally help citizens adjust as the world changes around them. This is a great deal to ask of schools.

The many special interest groups that look to schools for solutions can be unrealistically critical. Often, extreme and pessimistic positions are taken to gain public attention. Educational institutions can serve the role of scapegoat for other frustrations with society or help critics gain an advantage for a particular political agenda.

*An opportunity to reconsider*

For us, a more productive and positive approach is to see the debate over the future of education as an opportunity rather than a crisis. We think of *reform* and *restructuring,* two terms often used to describe the process of change, as opportunities to consider and possibly readjust goals and priorities. We value the chance to think seriously about the purposes of education and to ask whether certain types of learning experiences are likely to achieve these goals. And we believe that the power, reach, and resources of the Internet may help educators think about learning in a broader way.

Although you may wish that this book or other books would ignore differences of opinion and just tell you what you must do to be a successful teacher, we think such an approach would be inappropriate. It would seriously understate the actual complexity of teaching practice, and it would not serve our purpose of helping you integrate Internet technology effectively into your classroom. So let's examine some of the issues in the current debate about our schools.

## PRESSURES OF TECHNOLOGICAL AND SOCIAL CHANGE

*New skills required*

As this chapter will show, Internet technology can play a prominent role in responding to the priorities raised by school reformers. It is also true, though, that technology is partially responsible for some of the *need* for school reform. Information and communication technologies have helped create new types of jobs and demands for new skills, which in turn have led educational critics to ask how our schools can be more effective in meeting these needs.

## LIFELONG LEARNING

Besides altering the nature of the jobs we do, the rapid changes in technology mean that we cannot master a subject once and then simply apply that knowledge for the rest of our lives. Rather, we must continually learn new skills. It has been estimated that today's students will experience four to five different occupations during their lifetime (see, for instance, Naisbitt, 1984).

*Need to keep learning throughout life*

> *As a basic condition of employment, not to mention social and cultural awareness, we must engage in* ***lifelong learning****—that is, learning continuously over the years as life presents us with new challenges.*

The recognition that learners cannot be defined in terms of a particular age period has a number of implications:

### *IMPLICATIONS OF LIFELONG LEARNING*

- The boundaries between school and work begin to break down. Learning cannot be confined to formal institutions.
- Learners need to be prepared to take greater responsibility for their own learning.
- Educators, for their part, will work with different categories of students under different circumstances.
- Even with "traditional" students, educators will be attempting to develop nontraditional skills.

As an educator, you will personally exemplify these trends. You will have to be a lifelong learner, and you will have to learn many important skills on your own. In fact, you may already be a practicing teacher, reading this book because integrating technology in your classroom is a new vocational skill expected of you.

## THE INFORMATION EXPLOSION

*Incredible increases in information*

Another characteristic of our age for which technology—especially the Internet—is partly responsible is the "information explosion." Six to seven thousand scientific articles are authored daily in the United States alone. The amount of information available in print format doubles every 5.5 years (Naisbitt, 1984), and the pace is still increasing. The information available on the World Wide Web is mounting so fast that any statistic would be out of date before we printed it (see "Keeping Current: Internet Statistics").

With so much raw information available, the question of what and how students should learn—and how teachers should attempt to teach—becomes ever more pressing. Can educators teach the same way they used to? Are the skills needed in an information-packed environment the same as they always have been, or are they significantly different?

## KEY THEMES IN REFORM: ACTIVE LEARNING AND MEANINGFUL EXPERIENCES

Despite the many disagreements among educational reformers, some proposals have drawn a great deal of support. One response to changes caused by technology has been an increasing emphasis on teaching technology itself—for instance, educating students in how to use computers, keyboards, and other technological tools (see, for example, ISTE, 1998).

*Call for major revisions in teaching and learning*

For many educators, however, the question of reform goes much deeper. They believe that developments in the understanding of how students learn, plus the changing conditions of our society, demand some dramatic modifications in traditional teaching and learning practices. Often you will see a

## Keeping Current

### Internet Statistics

The Internet changes moment by moment. In contrast, the process of distributing information in print can take months and even years. Thus current statistics about the Internet can really be obtained only from the Internet itself.

The very nature of the Internet presents additional challenges to any effort to provide accurate information about it. Users of the Internet have tremendous freedom, and they are required to provide little information about how they make use of this resource. This is true for both individual users and large corporations. Therefore, questions such as How much information is available on the Internet? and How many sites are providing information? are challenging to answer.

In the mid-1990s, the Netcraft company (Netcraft, 1998) began conducting an online survey of World Wide Web servers. In 1996, Netcraft was able to locate 342,000 servers. In late 1998, this survey located over 3,500,000 servers—an astonishing rate of growth.

Although the Netcraft survey provides one way to follow the growth of the Web, it does not indicate just how much information web servers make available. Recently, however, two researchers generated an ingenious estimate of the total number of web pages (Lawrence & Giles, 1998). The authors began with the number of web pages that had been indexed by popular search engines (see Chapter 4). But when they compared the databases of the different search engines, it was obvious that each of the search engines had missed many web resources. Therefore, the authors took the size of the largest database, combined it with an estimate of the frequency with which this search engine had missed web pages, and arrived at a total estimate of 320,000,000 items on the searchable Web.

These figures will all be out of date when you read them. However, they should give you some feel for what we mean when we talk about an information explosion. In the "Resources to Expand Your Knowledge Base" at the end of this chapter, we list web addresses where you can look for more current information.✱

summary table, such as Table 2.1, that contrasts "conventional," or "traditional," education with a "reformed" or "restructured" school setting (for instance, Brown, 1992; Knapp & Glenn, 1996; Means et al., 1993).

Although charts like Table 2.1 oversimplify complex issues, they help us identify critical dimensions. Look at the table carefully. What do you think are the common themes of the "restructured" school setting as opposed to the "conventional" setting?

To us, there is a basic commonality that you will see emphasized throughout the book:

*A shared principle*

▶ *A major principle of the reformed school is that students have greater experience with learning tasks that are* active *and* meaningful.

**TABLE 2.1**
A Comparison of Traditional and Restructured Schools

| | CONVENTIONAL SETTING | RESTRUCTURED SETTING |
|---|---|---|
| Student Role | Learn facts and skills by absorbing the content presented by teachers and media resources. | Create personal knowledge by acting on content provided by teachers, media resources, and personal experiences. |
| Curriculum Characteristics | Fragmented knowledge and disciplinary separation. Basic literacy established before higher-level inquiry is encouraged. Focus on breadth of knowledge. | Multidisciplinary themes, knowledge integration and application. Emphasis on thinking skills and application. Emphasis on depth of understanding. |
| Social Characteristics | Teacher-controlled setting with students working independently. Some competition. | Teacher functions as facilitator and learner. Students work collaboratively and make some decisions. |
| Assessment | Measurement of fact knowledge and discrete skills. Traditional tests. | Assessment of knowledge application. Performance of tasks to demonstrate understanding. |
| Teacher Role | Present information and manage the classroom. | Guide student inquiry and model active learning. |
| Possible Use of Internet | Source of information for absorption. | Source of information for interpretation and knowledge creation. Outlet for original work. |

You may wonder exactly what those terms *active* and *meaningful* mean. That is what we are about to explore. Our goal is to get you to think about the student's mental behavior as a learner and how, as a teacher, you can influence this behavior.

## MODELS OF SCHOOL LEARNING

One effective way to understand learning and thinking is to represent the student as a processor of information. The issue differentiating learning in conventional and restructured settings is not whether or not students will process information, but what the nature of that processing should be. Many educational reformers emphasize that students not only *receive and store information,* but must also *construct personal knowledge* on the basis of that information.

*Models with a common emphasis*

In this section we look at some models of learning that have contributed to current efforts at school reform. Although they arose in different historical periods, from different philosophical perspectives or out of different research traditions, all of these theories stress that the role of teacher and instructional resources is to engage each learner in ways that encourage the active integration of new ideas or skills with the existing knowledge of the learner. After examining the models in turn, we will come back again to their common themes.

## MEANINGFUL LEARNING

According to Ausubel (1963), **meaningful learning** occurs when new experiences are related to what a learner already knows. It can be contrasted with **rote learning,** which Ausubel describes as the learning of a sequence of words with little attention to meaning, as in simple memorization. In both cases, learners are processing information, but their mental activities are quite different.

Meaningful learning assumes that:

*Assumptions of meaningful learning*

- Students already have some knowledge that is relevant to their new learning.
- Students are willing to do the mental work required to find connections with what they already know.

Learning tasks can contribute to the establishment of these connections by encouraging the student to recognize personal experiences that are relevant or even by providing new life experiences as part of the learning activity.

*Importance of student motivation*

Because meaningful learning takes work, student motivation is important. Student motivation can be subverted by a reward structure that provides too many incentives for rote learning, by a lack of confidence in the ability to learn meaningfully, or by disinterest. The teacher's role is to provide an optimal environment that makes the learner feel capable and presents the learner with tasks he or she regards as personally relevant. In other words, the student should feel there is some payoff for learning rather than merely memorizing. At a practical level, this might mean that the assessment of learning should require the learner to demonstrate understanding and the ability to apply knowledge as well as recall facts.

### Reception versus Discovery

In addition to meaningful and rote learning, Ausubel differentiated between reception and discovery learning. In **reception learning,** the ideas to be learned are presented directly to students, ideally in a well-organized fashion. In **discovery learning,** in contrast, the student must work to uncover, or discover, what is to be learned. Typically, a large proportion of what is learned in school is acquired through reception learning, and much of what is learned through everyday living is acquired through discovery learning.

*"Discovery" not necessarily "meaningful"*

Ausubel warned educators not to equate reception with rote learning, or meaningful learning with discovery learning. We agree with this warning. The activities connected with discovery are more concerned with generating the ideas to be learned than with relating these ideas to existing knowledge. Rote discovery learning is quite possible, and you can find it in the "cookbook" activities used in some science laboratories. In such activities, a student follows a detailed set of instructions to complete an experiment or task. Technically, the student is using a discovery framework, but because the student makes few decisions and does not have to understand the processes involved to move from one part of the activity to the next, meaningful learning may not occur.

To raise this issue, we sometimes ask the question: How much chemistry do you learn from baking bread? The point is that physically manipulating objects and completing activities does not necessarily mean that a student is mentally manipulating ideas. This is one of the dangers when teachers think only in terms of classroom activities and not in terms of how effectively and efficiently the assignments engage the learner.

## Characterizing Typical Learning Activities

*Applying the two dimensions*

Using the dual dimensions of rote/meaningful learning and reception/discovery learning, we can construct a chart that shows how typical learning activities compare with one another. Figure 2.1 offers an example of such a chart. School tasks, such as "Math facts," are positioned as proposed by Ausubel (1963). We have added some Internet-related activities, in brackets, based on our own perceptions of how these activities engage students. These activities will become more familiar to you in later chapters.

Of course, Figure 2.1 requires assumptions about how the typical student will respond to the activities. Not all students will respond in the same way. Nevertheless, you may want to test the concept by considering where you would place other learning activities on the graph. Where would a spelling test fall on these two dimensions? What about a book report assignment?

Ausubel and later reformers have stressed the need for activities that would be positioned toward the upper right of the graph—high on both discovery and meaningfulness. This does not mean, however, that rote-reception activities (those at the lower left of the graph) should always be avoided. The issue is more complicated than that. For example, rote learning may be a reasonable way to approach the learning of basic number facts, but not the historical antecedents of World War II.

*The teacher's decision process*

Part of a teacher's decision-making task is to determine what types of mental activities are desired in specific learning situations, and then to decide if the learning experiences actually result in the intended behaviors. If a school science laboratory experiment is intended to promote meaningful

**FIGURE 2.1** Learning activities categorized by two dimensions: rote learning versus meaningful learning, and reception learning versus discovery learning. Internet-based activities appear in brackets.

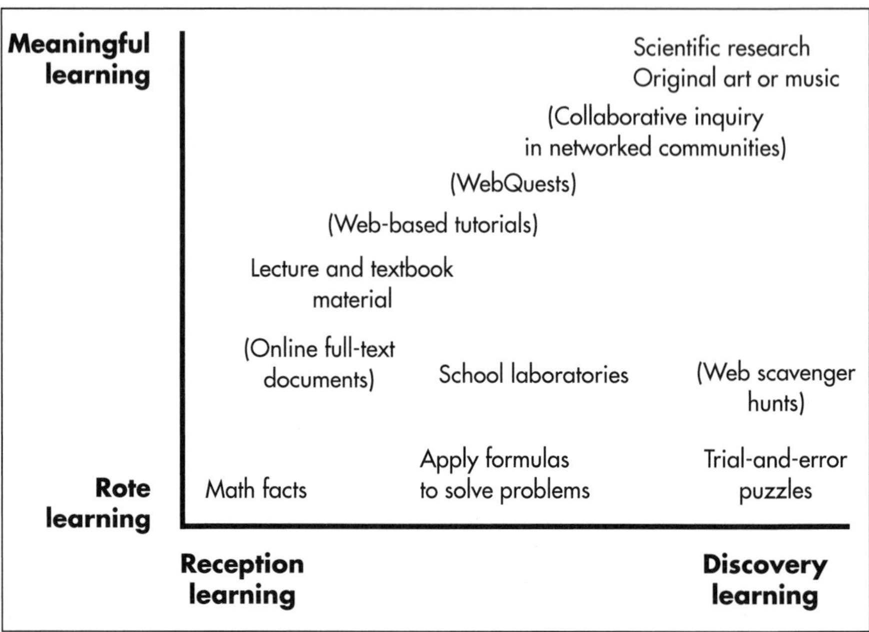


learning and original thinking, but instead it becomes a mindless, rote-discovery chore, then this is cause for concern.

## GENERATIVE LEARNING

*Creating a personal explanation*

Like Ausubel, Wittrock (1974a, 1974b, 1989, 1992) argues that students should establish connections with their existing knowledge rather than store isolated elements of information. In Wittrock's model of **generative learning,** a student selectively attends to events and generates meaning for these experiences by relating them to existing knowledge or by drawing inferences. That is, the active learner creates a personal model or explanation to account for new experiences within the context provided by existing knowledge.

In some cases, old ideas can assist a student in interpreting new experiences. In other cases, new experiences require the student to modify existing beliefs. In either case, the process of forming connections is distinct from simple storage of information. The generative model also assumes a motivated commitment from the student. The student must assume responsibility for expending the effort necessary to construct meaning.

Focus

## Scaffolding

Although discovery learning techniques use authentic approaches to learning, early attempts to implement them were frequently criticized because the techniques did not focus the learners. Many learners were not effective in managing their own efforts when working independently. Modified approaches, often called *guided discovery,* were regarded as more productive (Kersch, 1978). Essentially, educators found that the teacher can take a more purposeful approach, helping the student push through the limits imposed by personal knowledge and skill.

Today, assisting students in this way is often called **scaffolding,** an idea proposed by Russian developmental psychologist Lev Vygotsky (1978). Scaffolding, sometimes known as assisted learning, involves doing some of the work for students until they develop the capability or capacity to do it for themselves. Some examples might include:

- Offering reminders.
- Pronouncing or explaining words students do not understand.
- Giving clear, step-by-step instructions.
- Demonstrating tasks to be performed.

One important form of scaffolding related to the Internet would be locating task-appropriate Internet content for younger learners so they do not flounder about searching for material on their own. In Chapter 5 you will see how scaffolding is used in Internet inquiry projects known as WebQuests.

A key to understanding scaffolding is this: the purpose is not simplifying the task, but simplifying what the learner has to accomplish. Scaffolding serves an important motivational and strategic role by focusing the learner on immediate and attainable goals.✷

*Generative activities*

Although the generative effort Wittrock describes is mental and internal, it appears that external tasks can play a role. The area of reading comprehension offers many examples of improving understanding through the use of generative activities (Wittrock, 1989). Such tasks include writing paragraph summaries, developing and answering questions, creating paragraph headings, drawing pictures, or creating analogies or metaphors to encourage interpretation, organization, and storage. Generative activities applied in a nontrivial way have been consistently found to improve comprehension and retention.

*External tasks affect internal processing*

Although this book proposes some learning activities quite different from those mentioned by Wittrock, the basic idea that internal processing can be influenced by external tasks is quite consistent with our approach. In discussing Internet activities throughout this book, we emphasize the importance of what is done with information, not just how to access information.

## CONSTRUCTIVISM

Even a cursory reading of proposals for school reform will quickly acquaint you with the term ***constructivism*** (see, for instance, American Psychological Association, 1995; Knapp & Glenn, 1996; Means et al., 1993). There is no single, official explanation for what constructivism represents. The term has been used to address a wide range of issues, from the psychology of individual learning to philosophical reflections on science as a mechanism for pursuing knowledge (Loving, 1997).

Some extreme constructivist positions may be disruptive to those of us attempting to bring practical suggestions to classroom teachers, and we are in agreement with those who advocate a balanced approach (see Loving, 1997). Like Ausubel's meaningful learning and Wittrock's generative learning, constructivism generally argues that learners build personal understanding and that this constructive process can be facilitated by appropriate learning activities and a good learning environment.

*Basic principles of constructivism*

Probably the most generally accepted principle of constructivism is this:

- *What a person knows is not passively received, but* actively assembled *by the learner (Jonassen, 1991; Wheatley, 1991).*

A second principle can be stated in this way:

- *In most circumstances, learning serves an* adaptive *function. That is, the role of learning is to help the individual operate within his or her personal world.*

What are the practical implications of these principles? The following sections outline four important ways in which constructivism influences the practice of teaching and learning.

### Responsibility for Learning

*The learner's own responsibility*

One practical implication of constructivist principles concerns the responsibility for learning. Learning is accomplished by the student and results from mental work. Learners must mentally *act* on the information they receive in order to create personal understanding. Therefore, a large part of the responsibility for what happens rests with the learner.

### Role of the Teacher

*Teachers as models, guides, facilitators*

Teachers must recognize that the presentation of information by itself may not result in the generation of knowledge. Teachers cannot directly control the mental behaviors that result in learning, but they may, as Table 2.1 suggests, act as models and guides. That is, they can model effective learning behaviors for students, and they can guide students by engaging them in activities that encourage productive mental activity.

Teachers therefore play an important but indirect role. In Chapter 1 we described this as the role of a **facilitator** of learning, as opposed to a dispenser or transmitter of information. The term *coach* is often used in a similar way.

## Importance of Context

*Context influences knowledge integration*

Another practical implication relates to the context of learning. Context has a lot to do with what the learner perceives as useful knowledge and how the learner integrates new experiences with his or her existing knowledge. In the most critical sense, does the student see connections between the part of his or her world identified as "school" and the part sometimes referred to as "real life"? If the student perceives little or no connection, constructivists argue, he or she will not build much personal knowledge. Later, we discuss "authentic activities" as one way to establish a meaningful context for learning.

## The Approach to "Truth"

*Differences in "truth"*

A final implication of constructivist principles is that the primary purpose of education is not the acquisition of universal truths. Because each person has different experiences and is assumed to construct an individual interpretation of these experiences, each person's reality is slightly different. Learning means acquiring not abstract general truths, but useful, adaptive personal knowledge.

Focus

### Are We Abandoning Truth?

You may be concerned by the constructivist suggestion that universal truths are not the goal of student learning. But before making up your mind, consider a couple of points.

First, most of us have held beliefs that we learned at a later time were not truths. Some of these beliefs resulted from faulty information or naive concepts, but some were the official truths taught as part of a particular discipline, such as chemistry, physics, or history. Our ideas that passed for knowledge had to be modified later to handle new findings. Can you think of any such examples from your own education? science "facts" or theories? historical interpretations?

Second, we obviously do not end up with widely different views of our world. Education is pretty much a social process, and one adaptive purpose of the social context is to confront and negotiate differences in personal perspectives. When others explain their beliefs, we have new information to test against our personal views. Throughout this book, you'll see that we emphasize both learning tasks involving collaboration and tasks that require learners to represent their understanding in ways that allow others to react. Both types of activities are important.✷

## METACOGNITION

In the early 1980s, cognitive psychologists added a new component to their models of thinking and learning. This component, metacognition, sought to explain how learners control their own mental behaviors. **Metacognition** is demonstrated in planning, regulating, and evaluative behaviors (Paris & Lindauer, 1982):

*Types of metacognitive behavior*

- *Planning* refers to the decisions you make before beginning a learning task.
- *Regulating* involves adjustments while working on the task.
- *Evaluating* has to do with decisions you make once the task has been completed.

*Metacomprehension*

Metacognitive control functions play an important role in any form of independent learning or thinking. For example, *metacomprehension* describes the ability to evaluate your understanding while reading and to take action when comprehension failures occur. As you read this book, you may encounter sections you find confusing and as a consequence decide to reread the sections or ask a colleague for assistance. Your awareness of your own confusion and your subsequent efforts to achieve understanding demonstrate metacomprehension—that is, metacognition applied to the process of comprehension.

*Study behavior*

Similar metacognitive skills are involved in many other areas of student performance. Thomas and Rohwer (1986) describe study behavior as effortful, private, self-managed activities, often operating with little in the way of external guidance regarding what is to be accomplished or what level of mastery is required. If you think carefully about what is (or was) expected of you as a college student, you will note just how much responsibility advanced students must take for their own learning. Should I spend more time reviewing Chapter 1 or Chapter 3? If I quit studying now, what grade am I likely to receive on tomorrow's exam? In other words, it is not enough to be active; you must also decide what form this activity should take and evaluate when a different direction is required.

Metacognitive skills related to academic performance often need improvement. Deficiencies in these skills are usually most obvious in students who are having the greatest difficulty learning in the first place. Study behavior in less able students, for example, is often passive (rereading textbook assignments), and even when course material and evaluation procedures vary, students frequently use the same study approach. Likewise, students frequently are unaware of failures in their comprehension of material they have read (Baker, 1985; Markman & Gorin, 1981), and they seem unable to predict accurately how they will do on tests (Pressley, Snyder, Levin, Murray, & Ghatala, 1987).

Focus

## Testlike Events: The Potential of Online Review Activities

Students' awareness of how well they are prepared for an upcoming examination can be improved by presenting them with testlike events (Glenberg, Sanocki, Epstein, & Morris, 1987; Pressley, Snyder, Levin, Murray, & Ghatala, 1987). Teachers would probably describe what these researchers have been evaluating as "practice tests." The results of a practice test help students identify specific areas of weakness and understand how much more work they have to do. In this sense, practice tests can help stimulate metacognition.

One body of research suggests that free access to computer tests may provide an efficient way to provide students with this type of nongraded feedback (for instance, Anderson et al., 1975; Grabe, Petros, & Sawler, 1989). As instructors have begun to incorporate the Internet into their instruction, one fairly common application has been to provide online practice tests. Some textbook companies have offered similar opportunities as part of an online study guide made available as a textbook supplement.

When you complete this book, you should be capable of generating web pages that offer your students a simple practice test. Even better, you might teach your students these web page authoring skills and have them develop online tests for each other.✱

## SELF-REGULATION

**Self-regulated learning** proposes that, to be effective, learners must be capable of analyzing requirements and setting goals; applying appropriate strategies to reach the goals they have proposed; and modifying their approach when necessary (Butler & Winne, 1995; Pressley, 1995). Although this description may sound very much like the definition given for metacognition, self-regulated learning originated as part of social learning theory (Bandura, 1977) and thus has roots in a different theoretical tradition.

*Analyzing and adjusting one's own behavior*

Again, it is not necessary to become immersed in the details of the theory to appreciate certain key themes. Learning and thinking are complex processes. To achieve skilled performance, learners must be capable of analyzing their own behavior and must take responsibility for adjusting it as circumstances warrant.

It is clear that self-regulation often fails. Becoming a proficient learner, even within a specific field, takes a great amount of time (Pressley, 1995). Difficult or not, helping students improve the ability to plan, regulate, and evaluate their own thinking and learning behaviors is essential.

## REVIEWING THE COMMON THEMES

Rather than get caught up in one particular theory or another, we prefer to focus on the common themes of these various educational theories—themes that have frequently been emphasized by educational reformers. Let's reiterate these key ideas.

### *KEY IDEAS*

*Active learners*

- All the theories we have discussed describe the fundamental nature of the learner as *active.* **Active learners** seek to build an understanding of their personal world that will allow them to function productively. This process requires that learners make the effort to build on what they know in order to interpret and respond to new experiences.

*Purposeful behavior*

- The true active learner does not just drift along, but functions in a purposeful manner. He or she is capable of establishing personal goals, developing strategies for addressing these goals, and monitoring whether the strategies have been successful.

*Meaningful experiences*

- By taking such a purposeful, active approach, students make their learning experiences *meaningful.* That is, their new learning relates to their previous knowledge and is relevant to their personal lives. It is deeper than mere rote learning or memorization, and it can be applied not just in school but also in "real life."

Now let's turn to the question of what these theories mean for your classroom practice and how the Internet can help you apply them.

## FROM THEORY TO PRACTICE: TEACHING, LEARNING, AND THE ROLE OF THE INTERNET

Despite the many different approaches that educators take, ideas about school reform and theories about the nature of learning have tended to converge in certain recommendations for classroom practice. Consider the following general suggestions (Duffy & Bednar, 1991; Means et al., 1993):

*Recommendations for classroom practice*

1. The catalyst for changing the learning experience at a fundamental level will be centering more of the learner's time on *authentic, challenging tasks.* Students need richer contexts for learning that reduce the emphasis on fact mastery and isolated, discrete component skills and increase the emphasis on *multidisciplinary* tasks that require students to apply and create personal understanding.
2. The social environment should support learning in different ways:

a. Students should have *access to domain experts* who model the skills appropriate to the domain and provide insights into the culture of the domain within what has been described as an *apprenticeship* relationship.
b. Teachers should view their roles differently. The facilitation of thinking and problem solving must accompany the transfer of information. Teachers may guide student work related to unfamiliar content and acquire new knowledge along with their students.
c. Students should spend a greater amount of time working in *cooperative relationships* with other students to explore alternative perspectives and evaluate ideas. These relationships will help provide learning experiences that encourage communication and access to real-world examples.
d. The collective application of these changes in the social context of learning might be said to establish **learning communities.**

3. A greater emphasis should be placed on *reflective thinking* and *productivity*. The fundamental goal should be the ability to perform relevant tasks with the understanding that not every student will perform the tasks in the same way or acquire the same task-relevant skills.

We see Internet technology as providing an extremely useful set of tools for achieving these goals. Later chapters will explore particular uses of the Internet in greater depth. Here, we want to isolate a few of the important ideas for more detailed consideration.

## AUTHENTIC ACTIVITIES

Research shows that, when learning is accomplished as part of an authentic activity, it is more relevant and more likely to be used in future situations (Brown, Collins, & Duguid, 1989). But what, then, is an authentic activity?

*What is an authentic activity?*

According to one interesting perspective, **authentic activities** are the ordinary practices of a culture (Brown et al., 1989). The term *culture* here refers to what might best be understood as ordinary people doing the ordinary things that readers or writers, biologists, users of mathematics, or speakers of Spanish do. Language is a good example that we can understand from personal experience. Users of a language apply their knowledge as a tool to complete tasks within their everyday environment. By this definition, our use of language is authentic because it has great utility in our daily lives.

*The effect of classroom culture*

Searching for authentic activities in classrooms reveals an interesting insight. In each room there is a recognizable classroom culture, and there are identifiable authentic activities at work within this culture. The problem is that authentic classroom tasks may not be what teachers really intend. The goals, values, and activities of the classroom culture and the subject matter culture can be very different (Brown et al., 1989). The student functioning in the culture of a fairly typical classroom uses knowledge to solve problems relevant to the school domain, such as getting the most points possible on the next quiz or pleasing the teacher. But knowledge the student acquires for the school domain may not transfer to any domain beyond the school walls. To state the problem another way, the knowledge students acquire in school is too often inert.

## Inert Knowledge

*Knowledge limited to certain contexts*

**Inert knowledge** is knowledge students have learned but fail to use (Whitehead, 1929). More exactly, it is knowledge that is available in a restricted set of contexts rather than in all of the contexts in which it might apply. Often, the restricted context is extremely narrow. Students may activate knowledge for classroom examinations and then fail to recognize the valuable role the same knowledge could play in other situations. For instance, a student who does well on an arithmetic test may have little practical understanding of prices in a supermarket.

*Naive theories*

An interesting example of inert knowledge can be found in naive science conceptions. We all function somewhat like scientists in our everyday lives. People develop a wealth of knowledge from their unsystematic and uncontrolled daily observations of the world around them (Glover, Ronning, & Bruning, 1990). We form opinions, or *naive theories,* about all kinds of things based on our observation of daily phenomena. Sometimes these naive theories are simply incorrect and contradict more appropriate theories we have learned through formal education. Yet we can maintain incompatible academic and naive theories at the same time (Champagne, Gunstone, & Klopfer, 1985; Champagne, Klopfer, & Anderson, 1980; Clement, 1983; McCloskey, 1983). The academic theories seem to be applied in the classroom, and the naive theories, in the real world. The presence of incompatible knowledge means that, at any given time, one knowledge source or the other must be inert.

*Teachers' own naive theories*

Teachers themselves, like everyone else, are prone to naive theories and inert knowledge. For example, most teachers have passed examinations in college that focused on the theory of reinforcement and the value of praise for outstanding work. But in actual classroom practice, some teachers rely almost totally on criticizing student work that does not meet their standards; they seldom mete out praise. Have these teachers decided that reinforcement principles are incorrect or impractical? Or were these the teachers who performed poorly in college when reinforcement principles were taught? In most cases, the answer to both questions is probably no. Often, these teachers have simply not thought about how their knowledge of reinforcement applies to what they do in the classroom. The approach they take, providing critical feedback, may reflect their own naive theory of how classroom consequences affect student behavior.

## Hands-on Projects

How can naive theories be changed? For change to occur, people need to confront the discrepancies between their naive theories and more accurate models of the world. They must be made aware of both ideas at the same time. In the classroom this is often done through hands-on projects (Shipstone, 1988).

*Projects that convey relevance*

Hands-on projects can provide an element of realism that prevents the student from escaping to a purely hypothetical way of thinking. The student sees not just the academic relevance of certain ideas, but also their relevance to other aspects of life. When they serve this function, these projects meet our definition of authentic activities—the types of projects this book will emphasize.

## Authentic Activities and the Internet

The Internet can provide many of the resources necessary for authentic activities. We would describe the fundamental requirements for authentic activities as (1) the culture of practice and (2) primary information sources.

*The Internet and the culture of practice*

- The *culture of practice* provides the social contact and the purpose for authentic tasks. Previously, we described authentic activities as the ordinary practices of a culture—the practices, for example, of biologists, historians, and Spanish speakers. When used as a model for a learning environment, a culture of practice would mean applying content-area knowledge to the practice of tasks appropriate to the content domain. That is, students would take on some of the tasks of biologists, historians, and Spanish speakers.

  The Internet can help establish or provide access to such a culture by connecting interested teachers, students, parents, and practitioners who might rally around a particular project. These individuals might be active partners in implementing projects; sources of information, guidance, and feedback; or the audience for which projects are developed.

*The Internet and primary sources*

- *Primary sources* represent information or data on which learners act to produce personal knowledge. Using primary sources is an important component in authentic activities, and the Internet offers a vast amount of such information. The sources may exist in digital form (documents, images, sounds); in the form of people willing to provide their opinions or knowledge; or in some cases in the form of equipment that provides a stream of data (such as weather data or images from remote cameras).

With its connections to a wealth and variety of sources, the Internet can provide an excellent resource for constructing challenging projects that lead students to confront their own preconceptions and modify their thinking. See "Focus: Using the Internet for Authentic Activities" for a few specific examples. Chapters 5 and 6 will address this topic in more detail.

*Focus*

## Using the Internet for Authentic Activities

We will be providing examples of authentic activities throughout this book. However, a few examples here may help you start thinking about classroom applications.

- *Life of a One-Room School Teacher.* In this project, eighth-grade students are asked to develop a description of what it was like to teach in a northern prairie one-room school in the late nineteenth century. This description should provide some insights into who these teachers were and what their working conditions were like. For primary source materials, students are asked to use the searchable document and image collection provided by the Library of Congress American Memory Digital Library (**http://memory.loc.gov/ammem/**).
- *Spanish-Speaking Keypal.* In another project, students in a freshman Spanish class exchanged e-mail with students from Spain to develop their written language skills. The teacher, who had spent a semester in Madrid during college, was particularly interested in locating a companion class from that city, and she was able to do this using Keypals International (**http://www.collegebound.com/keypals/**).
- *Winter Bird Feeder Study.* Students in a sophomore biology class positioned a bird feeder outside their classroom window and made periodic observations of the birds. These data were entered into a web form and submitted to the Cornell Laboratory of Ornithology. The students have joined Project FeederWatch, a group of 13,000 amateur scientists who are gathering and sharing data in an effort to understand changes in bird populations (**http://birdsource.cornell.edu/features/pfw/**).✷

## THE SOCIAL CONTEXT OF LEARNING

Learning, particularly learning within educational institutions, is a social phenomenon. While the learning theories we have emphasized assume individual responsibility for learning, the social environment in which learners function can be essential to the process.

The social context includes the roles of the teacher, other students, and the community beyond the school. In this section, we will discuss these roles in terms of three major concepts: cognitive apprenticeship, cooperative learning, and learning communities.

### Cognitive Apprenticeship

Educational reformers who want to increase the emphasis on thinking or inquiry skills have tried to develop strategies for teaching such complex mental

*The learner as apprentice*

behaviors. The notion of **cognitive apprenticeship** is one such strategy. It places the learner in the role of apprentice to a more expert practitioner, who would typically be either the teacher or an outside authority.

*Reciprocal teaching*

Probably the most frequently cited example of cognitive apprenticeship is *reciprocal teaching,* which was designed to teach students how to comprehend written material (Palincsar & Brown, 1984). In this approach, the teacher works with a small number of students. Initially, the teacher takes the most active role and models important cognitive behaviors. Because cognitive behaviors (mental processes) cannot be observed directly, important behaviors are defined in terms of behaviors that can be demonstrated: asking questions, summarizing content, identifying and clarifying difficulties, and making predictions.

In reciprocal teaching, the group reads a paragraph together. The teacher then models the target behaviors: asks the students a question, comments about something that seemed difficult to understand, or makes a prediction. Individual students then attempt these activities under the teacher's supervision. Eventually, the individual is expected to get to the point of performing all external behaviors and then only the internal equivalents.

The goal of cognitive apprenticeship is to help inexperienced practitioners acquire essential thinking skills. The social environment provides the opportunity to learn from a more skilled colleague and to share responsibility so that a demanding task does not overwhelm the learner. Critical to the approach are opportunities to externalize mental behaviors.

*Externalizing mental behaviors*

- Teachers and students describe what they are trying to do as they work on tasks that involve the essential thinking behaviors.
- The descriptions provide less experienced learners with something to consider and emulate.
- The descriptions allow the more skilled practitioners to evaluate and offer advice.

*Opportunities to model learning behaviors*

The group Internet projects described in Chapters 5 and 6 provide great opportunities for this kind of interaction. Internet projects are, by nature, less predictable and more exploratory than many other projects. Because of these qualities,

> *Authentic Internet projects allow teachers frequent occasions to model learning and problem-solving behaviors.*

Teachers who are flexible and open to new experiences will have the opportunity to explore and learn along with their students. In the process, they will be modeling mature approaches to communication, information gathering, information integration, and problem solving.

## Cooperative Learning

*Fundamentals of cooperative learning*

In **cooperative learning**, students work together to accomplish a learning task. They may accomplish this goal by motivating, teaching, evaluating, or engaging each other in discussions that encourage reflection. When all students contribute, cooperative approaches encourage active learning.

In many cases, cooperative learning is used to accomplish other goals as well. Cooperative methods typically encourage inclusion and promote participation regardless of ability, gender, ethnic group, or disability. The nature of the cooperative task can vary. It may be as simple as working together to prepare for an examination. One student may serve as a tutor to a younger or less experienced peer. Or, as we emphasize in this volume, students may work in groups to complete a classroom project.

*Carefully structured methods*

We use the phrase *cooperative learning* in a formal way. Because not every situation in which small groups of students work together will be productive, the details of how cooperation is structured and how it proceeds are important. Some methods of student collaboration have been purposely structured according to specific and clearly identified principles and have been thoroughly evaluated (for instance, Johnson & Johnson, 1999; Slavin, 1991, 1996).

Experts in classroom cooperation suggest that three tasks must be accomplished to ensure productive groups (Johnson & Johnson, 1999; Johnson, Johnson, & Holubec, 1991).

### *ESSENTIALS FOR COOPERATIVE GROUPS*

*Three needs for productive groups*

- Teachers need to help students understand what the desired skill would look or sound like. For example, the teacher may need to explain that a basic principle of working together is learning to criticize ideas and not people. As you will discover in Chapter 3, students often forget this when communicating through e-mail.
- Students need the opportunity to practice the skill. Role playing, for instance, is an effective way to learn social skills. Again, if the task were to learn e-mail etiquette, the teacher might propose a scenario and have students send her a tactful message as a reply.
- Students new to cooperative projects need to reflect on their use of cooperative skills. In fact, all students can benefit from the opportunity to discuss process skills. Did the group encounter conflicts as it worked on the project? Were anyone's feelings hurt because someone misinterpreted the intent of an e-mail message?

There is no single cooperative learning method. Some methods are designed to help students master a body of factual material. There are certainly classroom situations in which this is an important goal, and cooperative methods that use group competition to push all group members to achieve have demonstrated value (Slavin, 1991). But the cooperative methods of greatest relevance for this book are those that involve students in group tasks requiring both the acquisition and the application of knowledge and skill. One such method, group investigation, is discussed in greater detail in Chapter 6.

*Learning from discussion*

As students work together on a project, they must discuss course content related to the project. Not only do students acquire knowledge from one another, but they also learn from the process of trying to put their ideas into words in order to allow someone else to understand them. Others in the group may see a problem differently or have a different explanation for some phenomenon. The group process naturally produces a level of cognitive conflict that challenges the personal understanding of group members and encourages more active, self-regulated learning.

*The Internet and cooperative groups*

How does the Internet relate to cooperative groups? In many ways it provides exciting new options for cooperative learning. The Internet might be used as a convenient communication tool, allowing students from different schools to work together. It can also serve as an inquiry tool that helps groups of students gather information for a project. Or it can be a construction tool that provides student groups with an outlet for their creative work. Many of the Internet activities we discuss throughout this book involve at least some cooperative activities.

## Learning Communities

We might define a *community* as a social organization created by people who share common goals, values, and practices. If you try to apply this description to the city or town in which you live, you might find it excessively idealistic. We would agree that most cities and towns fail miserably in meeting this standard. But a *functional* community can be any collection of people who have identified themselves with a set of goals, values, and practices. Our interests are in understanding how such communities are formed and in using these mechanisms to build learning communities.

*School-based learning communities*

Communities come together when some form of search process acquaints people who share goals, values, and practices *and* this group begins to act on their common interests. *School-based learning communities* are formed when teachers and students join together to work on long-term projects. The idea is to select authentic and challenging tasks that can be productively approached in a collaborative fashion. The social environment surrounding the project encourages learners of all ages to learn from and teach one another. The task goals of the project shape what knowledge and skills must be acquired, and the nature of authentic tasks usually requires that the learning experiences cross disciplinary boundaries (Gordin, Gomez, Pea, & Fishman, 1997).

Educators do not have to limit themselves to learning communities formed within school walls. Some have argued, in fact, that schools have become distanced physically, emotionally, and intellectually from the core of

Focus

## National Educational Technology Standards

Although some commentators emphasize learning about technology for its own sake—because so much of our world now relies on technological devices—many educators focus, as we do, on the contributions technology can make to effective learning in many different content areas.

The National Educational Technology Standards for Students (ISTE, 1998) are a case in point. Here are the "foundation standards," which specify the skills and types of knowledge students may be expected to master. Although these standards begin with the "basic operations" of technology, they then proceed to the use of technology as a tool for other, more conventional purposes, such as collecting information, solving problems, and publishing results. Note how the various points stress collaboration, lifelong learning, and solving problems in the real world—topics you have read about extensively in this chapter.

1. Basic operations and concepts
   - Students demonstrate a sound understanding of the nature and operation of technology systems.
   - Students are proficient in the use of technology.
2. Social, ethical, and human issues
   - Students understand the ethical, cultural, and societal issues related to technology.
   - Students practice responsible use of technology systems, information, and software.
   - Students develop positive attitudes toward technology uses that support lifelong learning, collaboration, personal pursuits, and productivity.
3. Technology productivity tools
   - Students use technology tools to enhance learning, increase productivity, and promote creativity.
   - Students use productivity tools to collaborate in constructing technology-enhanced models, preparing publications, and producing other creative works.
4. Technology communications tools
   - Students use telecommunications to collaborate, publish, and interact with peers, experts, and other audiences.
   - Students use a variety of media and formats to communicate information and ideas effectively to multiple audiences.
5. Technology research tools
   - Students use technology to locate, evaluate, and collect information from a variety of sources.
   - Students use technology tools to process data and report results.
   - Students evaluate and select new information resources and technological innovations based on the appropriateness to specific tasks.
6. Technology problem-solving and decision-making tools
   - Students use technology resources for solving problems and making informed decisions.
   - Students employ technology in the development of strategies for solving problems in the real world. (Reprinted with permission from *National Educational Technology Standards for Students* (June, 1998, pp. 5–6), published by the International Society for Technology in Education (ISTE), NETS Project.)✱

our traditional communities (Riel, 1997). Students have few experiences directly connecting what they learn with the world outside the school. Moreover, by focusing on the learning needs of citizens of a narrow age range, schools fail to support lifelong learning. For these reasons, many educators are beginning to create *work-based learning communities,* which allow students to participate in the practices of a discipline or profession.

*Work-based learning communities*

This brings us back to what we described earlier as the culture of practice surrounding authentic activities. For a student, it is the essential difference between learning about what biologists or historians have produced as information and having the opportunity at some meaningful level to *function* as a biologist or historian in order to construct personal knowledge (Gordin et al., 1997).

*Culture of practice: participating in a discipline*

## Learning Communities and the Internet

The Internet can serve a role in creating both school- and work-based learning communities. The Internet offers opportunities for engaging students in collaborative tasks and can involve them in extended and authentic communities of practice.

Clearly the Internet allows an expansive view of a learning community.

*Virtual learning communities*

▶ *On the Internet it is possible to create **virtual learning communities,** and the participants can be defined by interest and expertise rather than by their generational, temporal, cultural, geographical, or institutional distribution.*

The opportunity to broaden the distribution of participants has some important benefits. As we have mentioned, students who are studying a foreign language or culture can converse by e-mail with students from the other country. In this case, the Internet provides a way to overcome cultural, geographic, and temporal constraints.

Even within the physical community, the reach of the Internet can be valuable. Working parents or community members willing to serve as content experts may find it difficult to get away from work and make the trip to the school. Class field trips are also fairly rare events. The Internet can help overcome these obstacles by allowing the convenient exchange of messages and announcements, "virtual" tours of museums, and so forth.

*Overcoming obstacles of time and distance*

We hope that our message is never interpreted as advocating the replacement of face-to-face meetings and visits to museums, forests, or business establishments with computer experiences. In fact, you will discover as you proceed that we feel technology-based activities can increase and improve the use of field experiences. We see virtual experiences and field experiences as complementary. For example, a field trip to a local pond generates an added benefit when students prepare a web page to share their observations with a class that is making a similar trip to a pond in a different region of the country.

*Technology as support (not replacement) for field experiences*

The concept of the virtual learning community allows one other interpretation. Internet technology has allowed colleges, secondary schools, and various other organizations to pursue alternative methods for instruction and learning. Learning experiences—in some cases, entire courses—are being delivered totally via the Internet. These experiences—a form of what is often called **distance learning** or *distributed learning*—involve many complex issues that you will find discussed throughout this book. Without getting into the complexities at this point, we can say that Internet delivery of learning experiences increases access by overcoming problems of distance and time.

*Distance learning*

## RESEARCH ON LEARNING WITH TECHNOLOGY

In this chapter, we have developed the theoretical framework for the concepts and practices addressed in the rest of the book. This framework is supported by current research on how learning happens and how it deepens (Bransford, Brown, & Cocking, 1999). We have indicated that purposeful Internet use offers an excellent way for teachers to put these powerful ideas into practice. Yet you may be wondering: How much direct evidence is there that Internet projects do provide effective and meaningful learning experiences?

*Studies of computer-based instruction*

Although the Internet itself is a new technology, there have been hundreds of studies of computer-based instruction. When a number of studies in a particular domain amount to a critical mass, we can apply a special statistical procedure called *meta-analysis* to combine the data and formulate general conclusions. Such meta-analyses have consistently found that there are indeed benefits in computer-based instruction (for instance, Christmann, Badgett, & Lucking, 1997; Fletcher-Flinn & Gravatt, 1995; Kulik & Kulik, 1991).

*Emerging research on cognitive applications*

Much of the early research focused, however, on use of computers for drill and practice or for tutorials—the prevalent applications at the time. Given the relatively new convergence of cognitive perspectives and higher-level technology applications (such as multimedia and hypermedia), there has been little research so far on the use of computer technology for cognitive learning applications (Panel on Educational Technology, 1997). But promising studies of this type have begun to emerge (Cognition and Technology Group, 1992; Wenglinsky, 1998). As for the Internet, as you might guess, it is simply too new to have given rise to a substantial body of research on educational applications. Overall, for the emerging uses of computer technology, the issues are complex, the research methods are controversial, and the data are sparse. Yet the resources being invested in educational technology are substantial, as we indicated in Chapter 1.

In this situation there are many differences of opinion regarding what should be done in schools. One position (expressed, for instance, by Oppenheimer, 1997) is to stop spending so much money on new technology until studies exist to support particular applications. This position argues that the federal government, many state governments, and many schools should back away from programs they have already initiated. Another position (Panel on Educational Technology, 1997) is to continue the commitment to technology and the Internet, relying on general theory and smaller-scale studies to guide development and expenditures. Those who take this second approach also recognize the need for additional research, but they argue that only a major commitment at the federal level will allow the type of studies needed to provide definitive answers.

*Opposing stands on technology*

Now, where does this controversy about the benefits of technology leave you as an educator? For the moment, it probably leaves you with access to a moderate collection of technology resources, local expectations that you use these resources productively, and personal responsibility and considerable flexibility for what will happen in your classroom. Specific recommendations for what you should do with technology may be lacking. There are, however, general standards for the integration of technology into classroom teaching, published by various states and associations (for instance, ISTE, 1998). You can also draw on a large body of knowledge concerning effective teaching and learning, some of which we have reviewed in this chapter.

*General guidelines for teachers*

We believe that, with the theoretical base you have gained from this chapter, plus a general foundation in instructional methods and a good deal of common sense, you can guide your students in Internet-based experiences that promote meaningful learning. The following chapters examine how the Internet can be used as a classroom tool for communication, inquiry, and construction. As we discuss each type of application, we will continue to present a combination of theory, research, and suggestions for classroom activities. Our intent is to help you explore a number of options so that you can make your own decisions and feel comfortable implementing them.

*This book's position*

## SUMMARY

- Before investing heavily in hardware, software, Internet access, and support services, educators should consider what they want classroom applications of technology to accomplish. This chapter therefore asks you to contemplate instructional goals and the nature of learning from several interrelated perspectives.
- Advocates of educational reform point out the rapid pace of social and technological change that requires a commitment to lifelong learning. They also underscore the current explosion of information resources. In this context, many reformers stress two basic needs for the education of today's students: active learning and meaningful experiences.
- The theoretical models of learning examined in this chapter can help you understand these concepts. Both meaningful learning and generative learning stress

the active role of the learner, who creates personal knowledge by establishing links between new ideas and what is already known. Current constructivist models also place the learner in the role of creating a personal understanding of experience. Theorists who study metacognition and self-regulation further bring out the need for independent, self-governed learning and thinking.

◆ The school reform movement and the various theories of learning tend to converge on certain recommendations for classroom practice. This chapter examined two types of recommendations in detail: (1) the call for authentic activities, and (2) ideas about improving the social context of learning through cognitive apprenticeship, cooperative learning, and learning communities.

◆ The Internet—with its tools for communication, inquiry, and construction—can support these vital concepts of schooling. As yet, few research studies exist to prove the effectiveness of Internet projects. But we feel confident that the Internet applications described in this book can help you engage your students in the kind of active mental work and authentic, cooperative activities that form a basis for meaningful learning.

## REFLECTING ON CHAPTER 2

### Activities

1. Provide an example of inert knowledge. What knowledge or skill was involved? Under what circumstances was this knowledge or skill available, and when was it not available?
2. For your content area of interest, generate an example of an activity that satisfies the definition of *authentic activity.* Explain what makes this activity authentic.
3. Students are sometimes surprised by the scores they earn on course examinations. Propose a practical method that students might use to evaluate their strengths and weaknesses before taking a test.

### Key Terms

active learner *(p. 48)*
authentic activity *(p. 49)*
cognitive apprenticeship *(p. 53)*
constructivism *(p. 44)*
cooperative learning *(p. 54)*
discovery learning *(p. 40)*
distance learning *(p. 58)*
facilitator *(p. 45)*
generative learning *(p. 42)*
inert knowledge *(p. 50)*
learning community *(p. 49)*
lifelong learning *(p. 36)*
meaningful learning *(p. 40)*
metacognition *(p. 46)*
reception learning *(p. 40)*
rote learning *(p. 40)*
scaffolding *(p. 43)*
self-regulated learning *(p. 47)*
virtual learning community *(p. 57)*

### Resources to Expand Your Knowledge Base

**Estimated Size of the World Wide Web**

Netcraft (1998). The *Netcraft Web Server Survey* [online]. Available at **http://www.netcraft.com/Survey**.

Net Wizards (1998). *Distribution by top-level domain names* [online]. Available at **http://www.nw.com/zone/WWW/dist-byname.html**.

### Books on Key Chapter Topics

Hogan, K., & Pressley, M. (1997). *Scaffolding Student Learning.* Cambridge, MA: Brookline Books.

Johnson, D., & Johnson, R. (1999). *Learning Together and Alone.* 5th ed. Boston: Allyn and Bacon.

Jones, B., & Maloy, R. (1996). *Schools for an Information Age.* Westport, CT: Praeger Publishing.

Meichenbaum, D., & Biemiller, A. (1998). *Nurturing Independent Learners.* Cambridge, MA: Brookline Books.

Wilson, B. (Ed.) (1996). *Constructivist Learning Environments.* Englewood Cliffs, NJ: Educational Technology Publications.

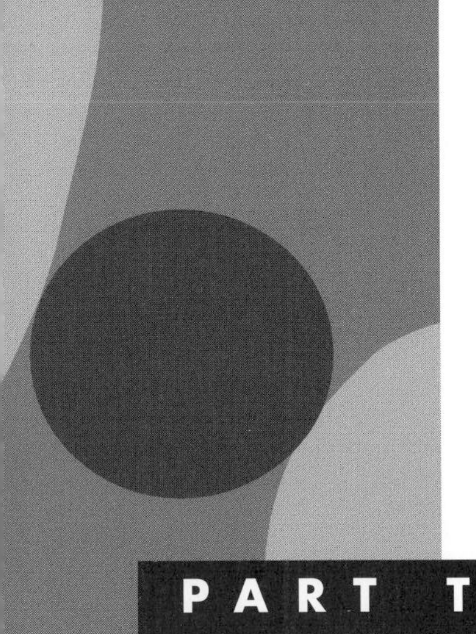

# PART TWO

# Learning with Internet Resources

# Chapter 3 Learning with Internet Communication Tools

## ORIENTATION

In this chapter you will become acquainted with Internet systems that allow learners to communicate with others. The chapter expands our previous descriptions of e-mail, mailing lists, chat, and videoconferencing systems and describes types of Internet projects that can be accomplished with these tools. As you read, look for answers to the following questions:

**FOCUS QUESTIONS**

- What are the advantages of e-mail, mailing lists, chat, and videoconferencing as communication tools for students? Are there disadvantages?
- How can teachers use Internet communication tools so that students reap the most benefit?
- What are some e-mail activities that can be adapted for the content area you plan to teach?
- What considerations should guide teachers in implementing an online project?

## USING E-MAIL

**E-mail** is an Internet access system for sending, receiving, and storing messages. As we noted in Chapter 1, e-mail was one of the first Internet applications, and it remains the most frequently used.

*Reasons for e-mail's popularity*

The popularity of e-mail probably stems from its familiar, efficient, and versatile applications. We are all used to communicating through letters or memos. E-mail can be used to ask a question, post a simple reminder, or transmit a lengthy report. It can serve as a substitute for traditional mail, faxes, telephone messages, and voice mail. Depending on the communication system to which it is compared, e-mail can be much faster, less expensive, and more efficient in reaching multiple parties with the same message. Collectively, these factors have resulted in the widespread adoption of e-mail as a practical system for personal and business correspondence.

*E-mail in education*

What about educational applications? Many of the advantages we have just described are also important in the classroom, and there is one overriding benefit as well:

> *Because the processes of questioning and communicating are essential to learning, e-mail has much to offer teachers and learners.*

At this point, we would like to familiarize you with some of the basics of e-mail use. E-mail systems are easy to learn. Later in the chapter, we will take a closer look at some of the strengths and weaknesses of Internet communication and examine how e-mail and other Internet communication systems can play a fundamental role in projects that emphasize active and meaningful learning.

## E-MAIL ADDRESSES

*Components of an address*

Like a traditional letter, an e-mail message contains an address for the person to receive the message and a return address for the sender. Each address consists of two components: a name for the person and the domain name where the user has an account. The two components are separated by the @ symbol; for example, Mark Grabe's e-mail address is grabe@plains. nodak.edu.

Domain names commonly end in a three-letter identifier that describes the organization sponsoring the mail server. In the United States the typical identifiers are these:

*Common domain identifiers*

| | |
|---|---|
| .edu | an educational institution |
| .gov | a government agency |
| .net | a network source |
| .org | a nonprofit organization |
| .com | a commercial organization |

Recently, K–12 schools with direct connections have adopted a convention that results in an address terminating in "k12," the state, and the country. For example, Cindy Grabe's e-mail address at the Grand Forks Schools in North Dakota is grabe@grand-forks.k12.nd.us.

E-mail addresses must be entered *exactly,* or your message will not arrive. There is no friendly human mail carrier to interpret your error and make the necessary corrections. In the event of an erroneous address or some type of system problem, your e-mail will **bounce;** that is, appear back in your account,

*What to do if a message bounces*

usually with a brief message explaining why the message did not go through. Often, if the error was a simple one, you can fix it and resend the message. Sometimes, too, if the server to which the message was sent was down, the message can simply be resent. If your e-mail does not bounce, you can be fairly certain it has arrived, but unless the person responds, you will never really know if the message was opened and read.

*Finding someone's e-mail address*

How do you find the address for someone you want to contact? You might think that there is some kind of giant directory in which you can look up the person you want to contact, but this isn't the case. There are Internet directories, such as **http://www.people.yahoo.com**, but if you're trying to locate a friend you met on summer vacation, you will probably be unsuccessful even if she or he has a valid account. Internet directories typically require that users apply to have their address included, and many e-mail users don't bother. If the person you want to contact is affiliated with an educational institution (college or school district) and that institution sponsors a web site, you may find that a directory is included as part of the web site. This is a fairly reliable way to find college students or faculty, as well as many K–12 faculty. You do have to know the person's institutional affiliation. See "Focus: Tips for Locating an E-mail Address" for more details.

## PARTS OF A MESSAGE

An e-mail message usually has three main parts: the header, the body, and the signature. It can also include other components, such as information about an attached file. For an example, see Figure 3.1 (p. 68), which shows an e-mail message from Cindy Grabe to Mark Grabe. Let's look at the parts of this message one by one.

### The Header

The **header** in Figure 3.1 includes the following information:

*Elements of the header*

- The date and time the message was sent: Saturday, December 27, 1997, at 17:23:41. The time is specified on a 24-hour clock, and in this case it would translate to 5:23 P.M. plus 41 seconds.
- The name of the sender (Cindy Grabe) and her e-mail address.
- The address of the person who is to receive the message (in this case, Mark's address, grabe@plains.NoDak.edu).
- The subject of the message: "Proposal Outline."

If other e-mail addresses received the same message, these usually show in the header as well, labeled "CC:" (for "carbon copy," a term that survives despite the absence of carbon paper).

When you compose a message, the e-mail program automatically fills in your address and the time and date. You must either enter the address of the re-

## Tips for Locating an E-mail Address

Here are three ideas for finding someone's e-mail address. We have used all of these methods successfully at one time or another.

- If you know the person's institutional affiliation, you can search for the institution's home page on the World Wide Web (see Chapter 4 for web search procedures). If it has a web site, you can explore the site to see if it offers a link to a directory. Universities in particular often provide student and faculty e-mail addresses through the web site.
- You can also use a web search engine to check directly for a reference to the person you are seeking. If that person has a web home page, it probably contains the e-mail address. Similarly, if the person participates in an electronic mailing list, the search engine may turn up an archive of the mailing list's messages, indicating return addresses for the participants.
- Finally, the simplest way to find addresses is the most obvious: ask the person you want to contact, using the telephone or a regular letter.✷

cipient manually or retrieve it using an address book function (explained later in this chapter); the same is true for people who receive a CC of the message.

*Importance of the subject field*

The phrase in the **subject field** is intended to identify or summarize the message. There are some situations in which you should carefully consider what you enter here. This phrase is particularly significant when sending an important message or a message to someone you do not know well. Many people who receive a large number of messages will first open messages from people they recognize and then open messages with subjects that capture their attention. On particularly busy days, messages that don't fall into either category may be deleted or ignored. The subject heading may also be important if the person decides to archive the message after reading it. The message may be added to hundreds of other saved messages, and the heading may then provide an important retrieval cue.

### The Body

E-mail messages can be long or short, simple or complicated. Because an e-mail message generally costs nothing to send and arrives almost instantly, people often use e-mail for short but timely messages. In Figure 3.1, Cindy's message to Mark ("I finished the outline. . . .") was short and to the point.

*Unformatted text*

The e-mail message body usually contains only unformatted text; that is, no bold or underlined words, no columns of numbers, and no pictures. This situation exists because e-mail systems were developed to accommodate the lowest common denominator in types of computers and software. Newer e-mail systems allow more elaborate multimedia (see the description of

**FIGURE 3.1** Parts of an e-mail message.

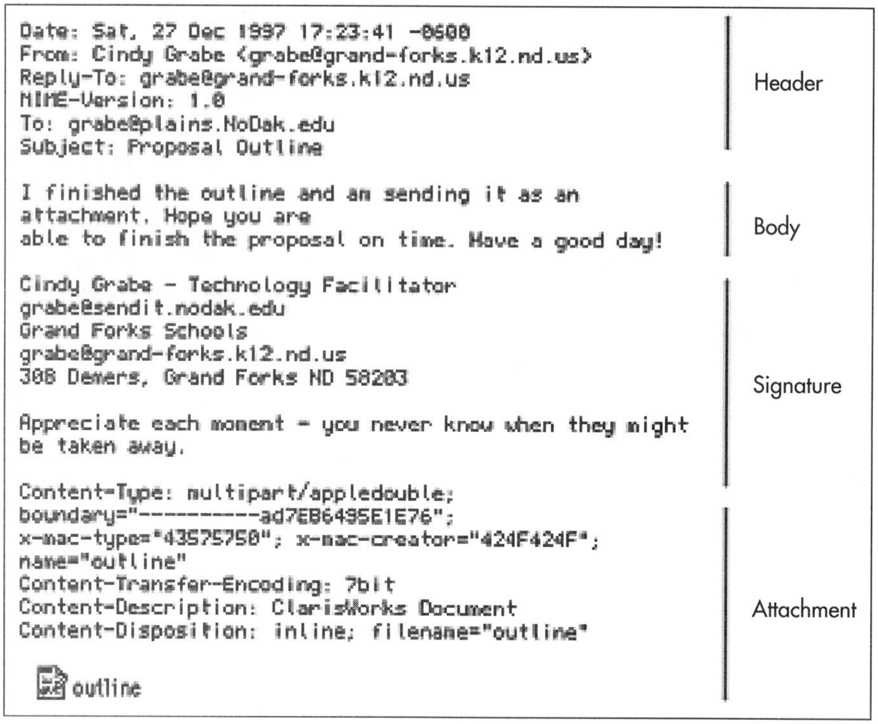

```
Date: Sat, 27 Dec 1997 17:23:41 -0600                          Header
From: Cindy Grabe <grabe@grand-forks.k12.nd.us>
Reply-To: grabe@grand-forks.k12.nd.us
MIME-Version: 1.0
To: grabe@plains.NoDak.edu
Subject: Proposal Outline

I finished the outline and am sending it as an                 Body
attachment. Hope you are
able to finish the proposal on time. Have a good day!

Cindy Grabe - Technology Facilitator                           Signature
grabe@sendit.nodak.edu
Grand Forks Schools
grabe@grand-forks.k12.nd.us
308 Demers, Grand Forks ND 58203

Appreciate each moment - you never know when they might
be taken away.

Content-Type: multipart/appledouble;                           Attachment
boundary="----------ad7EB6495E1E76";
x-mac-type="43575750"; x-mac-creator="424F424F";
name="outline"
Content-Transfer-Encoding: 7bit
Content-Description: ClarisWorks Document
Content-Disposition: inline; filename="outline"

outline
```

HTML-coded multimedia in Chapter 6), but it is best to send such documents to individuals only after you know for certain that they use the software capable of presenting multimedia.

## The Signature

*Elements of a signature*

E-mail programs commonly allow the inclusion of a **signature** after the message body. As long as it is created in text, you can put whatever you want into your signature. Besides your name, as Figure 3.1 shows, it can also include information such as your postal address, e-mail address, web home page, and phone and fax numbers. Some people include funny or inspirational quotes (as Cindy did in our example) or simple graphics created from text symbols. The signature is stored as a text file by the e-mail software and is added automatically each time your e-mail program sends a message.

*Concerns about student signatures*

For students, the information they provide about themselves in a signature is sometimes a safety concern.

> *As a teacher you will want to establish a policy about signatures, if your school or district does not already have one.*

Younger students might identify themselves in the following manner: Mark G., 3rd grade, Central Elementary. This information would provide some context for the reader but wouldn't reveal too much personal information.

### Attachments

As we explained earlier, the e-mail message body usually consists of unformatted text. There are obvious limitations to working at this level. A picture or diagram would often make a written comment much easier to understand. Numerical data in the form of a spreadsheet page might be essential for a science project. Most e-mail programs address this situation through the attachment function.

*Attaching various types of ffles*

**Attachments** allow fully formatted word processor files, graphics or sound files, or any other file format to accompany an e-mail message. Attachments just ride along with the e-mail message to the intended destination. As the attachment section in Figure 3.1 indicates, Cindy sent an attached file called "outline," created in ClarisWorks (a program now known as AppleWorks).

## FUNCTIONS OF E-MAIL CLIENT SOFTWARE

All e-mail software is designed to allow users to create, send, receive, and read messages. Most software allows other functions that can increase productivity and perhaps improve the value of e-mail as a learning activity. The following comments briefly outline these functions and explain how they are implemented.

### Reading a Message

*A two-step process*

Mail client software first displays a list of all messages received, using information from the message header (usually creation date, author, and subject) and then allows the user to select one message at a time to display fully for reading. This two-step process is especially useful for people who receive large numbers of e-mail messages. Again, we reiterate the importance of the subject phrase entered in the header. Your e-mail address and the subject phrase are what your potential reader will use to decide whether or not to read your message.

### Deleting a Message

The *delete* function allows you to remove unwanted messages. You can use it either at the level of the message header or after displaying the full message.

### Creating a New Message

This function allows the user to author messages. More sophisticated e-mail software contains many of the features of word processing software, allowing easy editing of the text, the insertion of segments of text copied from some other source, and even spell-checking.

## Replying to a Message

The *reply* function offers a convenient opportunity to use e-mail for the purpose of discussion. You can use this function to respond to the message of another person in a way that links the messages together.

The reply function automatically addresses your reply to the original message's author. It also fills in the new message's subject field by using the subject line from the original message preceded by "Re:."

*Reply options*

The reply function also allows users the option of including a copy of the original message. The original message is marked in some way (usually, each line begins with the symbol >) and is prefaced with a comment such as "At 02:26 PM 2/2/99–0600, you wrote:." In responding, you can edit this original material in any way you like. You might delete most of the original message with the exception of the specific comments you want to address. After each of the comments, you might insert your own reaction or position. The message would then consist of a mixture of the comments you received and your reaction to each. Before or after this section of message, you could also add whatever other comments you might want to make.

*Using the reply function for teacher comments*

Imagine using this feature in an instructional setting. Some instructors ask that students submit written assignments by e-mail. As a teacher you could use the method just described to insert your own comments on each passage of the student's assignment. For short suggestions, you might insert a comment in capital letters within the original text. The version with your comments would then be e-mailed back to the student.

*Sorting threads*

Replying to a reply creates what is called a **thread,** a series of linked messages. E-mail software often can sort the messages available in various ways, such as by date, address, or subject. Sorting by subject allows the reader to follow a thread to read a series of interrelated messages.

## Forwarding a Message

The *forward* function is intended to redirect a message to a third party. You can do this with or without adding your own comments to the original message.

*Ease of forwarding*

There will frequently be times when you receive information that you feel others will also find useful. Perhaps it is a great idea for a classroom activity or a list of useful web sites for a topic you know other teachers in your district emphasize. Perhaps someone has written a persuasive argument that you want a colleague to see.

*Caution: be careful what you forward!*

Carefully consider, however, the implications of sending someone's message on to others. Was the original message intended for general distribution? Are there personal comments in the message that the author might have intended only for you? Sometimes it is worth the time to ask the author if he or she would care if you forwarded the message to some of your colleagues.

## Saving a Message

As an e-mail user, you will encounter messages you want to keep. E-mail clients usually have a mechanism allowing you to establish and label multiple

*Multiple mailboxes*

storage places for mail (sometimes called "mailboxes"). Mail downloaded from the server comes into a particular mailbox, usually called the "In Box." This is where you open and read your mail. Then, if you want to store the mail for some other time, you can move it to one of the other mailboxes.

If you are working with e-mail on the server rather than on your own computer, the process of storing your mail may be slightly different. Perhaps you will convert your messages to data files to store them on the server. If you must transfer messages to your personal computer to store them, the e-mail client will probably make this easy to accomplish.

## Keeping an Address Book

*Automatically inserting an address*

Most e-mail clients allow users to create address books. An **address book** is a list of e-mail addresses that is usually organized alphabetically. New addresses can be added manually or captured from incoming e-mail. The address book is extremely useful when sending messages. An address from the address book can automatically be transferred to the message being prepared. There is no need to risk an error in addressing a message.

*Creating a list in the address book*

Some address books also allow the creation of lists. A list consists of a number of e-mail addresses with a single list name. When the list name is used to address an e-mail message, the message is sent to each of the addresses on the list. This feature is very convenient for anyone who regularly sends the same message to the members of a particular group. You could use it, for instance, for messages to everyone in your class or in a professional organization. Your students might use it to e-mail all their partners on an Internet project.

## Attaching a File

Sending an attachment using an e-mail client is an easy procedure. Usually, you use a button or menu option to indicate that you want to attach a file and then indicate the particular file to be attached. Once this has been done, when the e-mail message is sent, so is the attached file.

*Considerations in attaching a file*

Although the preparation is easy, there are some things that can go wrong. Attaching a file assumes that the recipient uses an ISP that allows file transfers, is prepared to transfer the file to his or her personal computer, and can use the file once it arrives. Each of these assumptions may be inappropriate.

### *Cautions for File Attachments*

- Not all ISPs allow e-mail attachments. Attached files tend to be much larger than e-mail messages, and the companies have to set aside much more space in the accounts of individual users.
- Many e-mail users work with e-mail on the server rather than transfer it to their personal machines. They may not be prepared to take the additional step to transfer an attached file to their personal computer.
- If the file format is not appropriate to the kind of computer and software the person has available, he or she may not be able to use the file. For example, if you send a file created in a Windows application to someone

Focus

## E-mail in Labs or Other Multi-user Settings

Most e-mail clients were developed with the assumption that they would be used consistently by the same person on the same personal computer. As a consequence, certain functions are built into the software. For example, most e-mail clients are set up to enter your e-mail address automatically when you create a message. They also store your saved messages on your personal computer according to the system of mailboxes you have created.

But students' use of e-mail in a school environment does not conform to these expectations. How do schools handle e-mail when several students use the same computers, either in a classroom or in a school computer lab? What can be done when the same student must complete assignments using different computers in different locations? It would certainly be inappropriate to mix different students' messages together in the same mailbox at the same address. It is also problematic if students are limited to doing e-mail assignments on a specific machine.

In this situation, students may use a program (such as *Telnet*) that connects them to the mail server. Then they use e-mail software on the server to create and read their mail. This can be rather cumbersome, however. There are also e-mail client programs designed to address some of the multi-user, multimachine problems just described, allowing the user to do the work on a personal computer rather than manipulate a program on the server. Using client software on a personal computer is easier and allows much greater flexibility, and thus is the preferred option for students. One example of this type of software, POPmail/Lab, was developed at the University of Minnesota to provide an e-mail client for use in computer labs.

Here is the way POPmail/Lab solves some of the problems we have described. When POPmail/Lab is launched, each user is asked to supply an e-mail address and password. This is a convenient method for allowing different students to use the same machine and the same software to access their own individual accounts. Second, when messages are sent to the personal computer, they are not automatically removed from the e-mail server. The messages are deleted from the server only when the user decides to do so. Thus a student can keep messages on the server indefinitely, in an account that he or she can access from different machines in the school. If the user wishes to store a copy of e-mail messages, any message or attachment can be transferred to a personal disk.

There are other ways to accomplish some of the tasks just described, using other client software. The important point is that you consider some of the special circumstances that may be involved in using e-mail in a K–12 environment.✱

who uses only a Macintosh, there may be translation problems, depending on the particular software.

None of these problems is catastrophic. The recipient will at least receive a valid e-mail message and will realize that an attempt was made to send an attached file. The recipient will likely reply and inform you that the file did not transfer properly. However, it is probably best to discuss potential problems ahead of time.

## MAILING LISTS: E-MAIL FOR GROUP COMMUNICATION

A **mailing list** is essentially a system for relaying an e-mail message to all of the e-mail addresses on a membership list. The site from which the list originates is called the **list server,** and you may encounter mailing lists referred to as **listservs.**

*Benefits for teachers*

Mailing lists provide the opportunity to participate in or simply observe an ongoing group discussion. For teachers or learners interested in specific topics, mailing lists provide a way to communicate with others who share similar interests. There are opportunities to ask questions, to offer advice, and generally to benefit from serious discussion of the topic.

*Types of mailing lists*

*Messages combined in a digest*

Mailing lists differ drastically in size and scope. There are very large mailing lists that cover broad areas of interest, such as teaching in middle school. These lists may have hundreds of members, a list administrator, rules governing members' behavior, and special options that require sophisticated server software (for instance, receiving a week's worth of messages as a single large file called a "digest"). But mailing lists can also be small, focused, and run with much less sophisticated hardware and software. For example, a college instructor may decide to set up a mailing list as a way to extend the discussion opportunities in a single course.

It is always difficult to tell if a list you subscribe to will be useful until you have tried it for a while. The purpose of the list may turn out to be something other than what you anticipated. You may also find that a particular mailing list generates simply too many messages, of which you will find only a small proportion interesting. In that case, you can simply unsubscribe from the list.

### MAILING LIST PROCEDURES

*Two different addresses*

Mailing lists have two addresses: a submission address and an administrative address. When you want to send a message to the membership of a mailing list, you send the message to the **submission address.** When you want to join a mailing list or perform other administrative functions, such as removing yourself from the list or suspending mail from the list for a short time, you send a message to the **administrative address.**

*How to subscribe and unsubscribe*

To join a mailing list, the message you send should have nothing on the subject line. It should include a simple statement in the form *subscribe listname firstname lastname* as the body of the message. For example, to subscribe to the educational web discussion list WWWEDU, the coauthor of this book would enter as the body of the message: subscribe WWWEDU Mark

Grabe. Similarly, you would typically remove your name from a mailing list by sending the message *unsubscribe listname* to the administrative address.

If you are an e-mail user, participating in a mailing list does not require that you learn a new type of software. The e-mail software you have become comfortable with will work just fine. There will be some new skills to learn, however. To get the most from participation in a mailing list, you will need to understand how a list functions.

## Following Instructions

When you first subscribe to one of the larger lists, you will usually be sent a summary of the procedures that apply to that list. Often these procedures will explain how to unsubscribe when you decide to leave the list, what to do if you plan to take a summer vacation and will not access your e-mail, how to have mail sent as a digest, and other user options. *Save this list of instructions.*

*Keep track of the addresses!*

One of the major problems with mailing lists is that users frequently forget the administrative address. It is fairly common to see someone try to unsubscribe several times using the wrong address, the submission address, often adding comments to the requests as they grow more and more frustrated. At some point a list member often complains about this person's lack of understanding of how a mailing list works, and an online argument may develop.

## List Conventions

*Conventions of particular lists*

Messages sent to a mailing list may be expected to follow certain conventions in the use of the subject heading. These conventions help subscribers categorize the many messages they receive from the list. For example, some educators have found it useful to ask members of the list to send an e-mail message to a certain address on a certain day. Often this is done to impress a group such as the school board with just how useful the Internet can be in reaching out to other schools. When this type of request is made by many schools, members of the mailing list may become annoyed. As a compromise, many lists ask that schools requesting this kind of assistance use a standard subject phrase such as "Request for Greeting." Members of the list who are in a hurry can then delete such requests without opening the actual message. Because list members can appreciate the purpose of such requests, they are also more likely to reply when the person making the request follows the conventions of the list.

## Using the Reply Function

*Responding to the entire list*

Using the reply function with a message originating from a mailing list sends the reply to all list members. When you want to respond to an ongoing discussion and present a personal perspective to the entire list, this is a very useful way to establish the desired context for the message. Some e-mail software indicates the presence of related mail in your account and provides an active link to these messages, helping you follow the threads of the discussion.

## LEARNING FROM PARTICIPATION IN A MAILING LIST

*Professional development for teachers*

Teachers see mailing lists as a form of continuous professional development. You can subscribe to mailing lists that address your academic discipline, the academic level of the students you teach (elementary, middle school, secondary, college), or professional issues concerning teachers. See "Keeping Current: Finding Useful Mailing Lists" for some examples of mailing lists that you may find helpful.

*K–12 lists in student projects*

Mailing lists organized for K–12 students are probably less common than those for teachers. Many of the K–12 mailing lists that do exist have been established as part of special projects that require the collaboration of students from several schools. Often such projects are sponsored through an agency with the resources necessary to coordinate the projects and run the list server. One good example is the use of learning circles, which we will describe in some detail.

### The International Education and Resources Network Learning Circles Project

*Learning circles as virtual communities*

A good example of using e-mail and mailing lists within the classroom curriculum is the International Education and Resource Network (I*EARN) Learning Circles project. **Learning circles** are groups of about eight to ten classes (and their teachers) that collaborate for approximately a semester. The classes forming a particular learning circle are purposely selected by the organizer to create a virtual community of learners with diverse backgrounds. This diversity may include students from different parts of the United States and schools from the most rural and urban settings. The diversity may also involve schools from other countries; in fact, as of 1998, more than thirty countries had participated in learning circle projects.

Learning circles come together to investigate a theme that appeals to all participants. Working within the framework provided by the general theme, individual classes develop more specialized topics that have particular relevance to them. Then they help each other learn about the topics they have proposed.

Learning circle projects go through a series of stages:

*Classes get acquainted*

1. *Opening the circle.* Classes begin interacting with each other in a get-acquainted phase. Each teacher sends an introductory message to the other classes, and students complete a survey related to self, school, and community. Classes also prepare and mail welcome packs to each other; the pack typically includes some physical objects to reflect each group, such as pictures, maps, homework examples, and other small items that may tell about themselves and their community.

*Students plan multiple, interrelated projects*

2. *Planning learning circle projects.* Classes in a learning circle engage in a number of interrelated projects related to the common theme. Each participating class takes primary responsibility for planning a project that involves participants from the other classrooms in a small way. The host

Keeping Current

## Finding Useful Mailing Lists

Most days we all have discussions that draw on the knowledge of our colleagues. Such coffee-break conversations allow us to request help from experienced associates and to check out what others might think of our new ideas. Imagine having similar access to hundreds of experienced colleagues, and you can begin to appreciate the potential of mailing lists.

Below are a few mailing lists you may find helpful. Lists do change address or simply go out of service, but the ones listed here have been around for a while. In addition, the web site at **http://www.liszt.com** maintains a database of approximately 85,000 lists. Another useful directory is maintained at **http://www.tile.net/listserv/alphabetical.html**.

| *List Name* | *List Topic* | *Administrative Address* |
|---|---|---|
| BGEDU-L | Forum on Educational Reform | listserv@lsv.uky.edu |
| EDTECH | Topics in Educational Technology | listserv@msu.edu |
| IECC | International Classroom Connect | iecc-request@stolaf.edu |
| INCLASS | Internet in the Classroom | listproc@schoolnet.carleton.ca |
| ITS | Integrating Technology in Schools | listserve@unm.edu |
| K12ADMIN | Educational Administration | listserv@suvm.syr.edu |
| MIDDLE-L | Middle School Topics | listserv@postoffice.cso.uiuc.edu |
| SIGTEL-L | Telecommunications in Education | listserv@unmvma.unm.edu |
| WWWEDU | Educational Web Discussion | listproc@kudzu.cnidr.org✱ |

class functions as "primary investigators" for the issue it has proposed for study. For example, under the general theme of "Society's Problems," individual middle school classrooms might focus on specific topics such as AIDS, gangs, and teenage pregnancy.

One of the fundamental goals for each class is to develop a project that will fit comfortably with the curriculum and represent an authentic issue. The development of the project within each classroom is a joint effort of teacher and students.

*Students share information*

3. *Exchanging student work.* As the projects are implemented, students in each class gather information and send it via the Internet to the class sponsoring the project. The information exchanged varies with the nature of the project; it might include surveys, data collections, or essays. Teachers are urged to divide their classes into groups for such interaction and to involve students most heavily with tasks that are most relevant to local curriculum needs. With older students, schools sometimes involve

other teachers when a project fits particularly well with the content that these teachers address (for instance, science or languages).

*Students summarize and publish results*

4. *Creating the summary publication.* Each sponsoring class is responsible for summarizing and presenting the results of its investigation. The collective publication of these summaries represents the product of the learning circle's work.

*All reflect on the experience*

5. *Closing the circle.* The final phase of each learning circle allows students and teachers to reflect on their work, on the experiences of working together, and on the relationships they have developed.

*Advantages of linking projects*

What makes learning circles different from many other online projects is that they allow for multiple interrelated investigations. Linking multiple projects provides a practical way to gather information necessary to complete them all. Even more important, it creates an interactive social structure in which each teacher and student functions in multiple roles. This can lead to a collective excitement in the processes of creating and sharing knowledge. Learning circles combine a focus on authentic local problems and the gathering of local information with a broader perspective provided by the participation of the larger virtual community of collaborators.

*Developing a community of teachers*

Learning circles were designed to operate on several levels. In addition to using Internet communication tools to promote theme-based projects within the classroom curriculum, learning circles also help develop a community of teaching professionals. Teachers become involved with each other through the class projects. Gradually, each teacher develops an expanding network of professional contacts with other teachers who are interested in finding ways to use the Internet to improve classroom instruction. Teacher networking is promoted by the limited duration of the projects and by the reorganization that occurs when teachers involve their classes in additional projects.

Information about present learning circle projects can be obtained on the World Wide Web at **http://www.iearn.org/iearn/circles/lc-home.html**. I*EARN, the sponsoring agency, is a nonprofit, international organization, and schools are expected to join I*EARN to participate in the projects it sponsors. Our description of the learning circle approach is based on a paper by Margaret Riel (1993), who is presently the Learning Circle Coordinator.

## CHAT

As we mentioned in Chapter 1, **chats** allow synchronous—that is, real-time—text-based interaction. When chat participants type in comments, these comments are sent to the chat server and then relayed immediately to all connected to the chat session. Sophisticated chat servers offer a choice of multiple *channels*, with each channel serving a particular group of participants.

*Differences between chats and mailing lists*

Chats differ from mailing lists in a number of ways:

- Only those participants actually connected view the messages that are exchanged.
- Chat reduces the steps involved in the communication process. Usually, incoming messages scroll through one screen field, and the participants type in messages in another field (see Figure 3.2). The messages are available immediately, with no need to find and open e-mail.
- The messages in a chat session are more like the messages in a phone or face-to-face discussion. They tend to be short, and the pattern of communication is intended to be interactive.

## PROS AND CONS OF CHAT SESSIONS

*Potential for confusion?*

Careful reading of the short chat sample provided in Figure 3.2 reveals one possible problem with chat conversation. In this example, a student asks the

**FIGURE 3.2** Screen image from a chat conversation.

**Ray** - Tuesday, January 27, 1998 17:04:54
Dr Grabe, You mentioned Hyperstudio. Is there a PC program that will also work?
*205.183.42.66*

**lois** - Tuesday, January 27, 1998 17:07:29
I have no idea how to submit chapter activities! What kind of activities do we have to do? I have never used hyperstudio before. *205.183.42.66*

**Grabe** - Tuesday, January 27, 1998 17:09:12
HyperStudio is supposed to be cross-platform. I must admit that I have not worked on Windows version. My plan is to contact company to arrange for demo disks. I do need an accurate count of how many of each type to order. *134.129.172.88*

**To add to the discussion above use the form below**

Your Name:

Your Response:
(you may include HTML formatting or links, but keep them simple please!)

Post | Clear the Form

instructor a question, and before the instructor can read and respond, another completely unrelated comment has been added to the conversation. In many chat sessions, you end up with several pairs of participants trying to carry on simultaneous conversations with many intervening messages.

*Pluses for online courses*

Despite such difficulties, chat sessions have become an important component of most online courses. In such settings, chat sessions provide opportunities for class discussion and group interaction. Although text-based interaction may not be ideal, chat communication is very economical and can be implemented even over slow Internet connections. For these reasons, chat sessions may be used as an alternative to group long-distance phone discussions or videoconferencing among multiple sites.

At present, few K–12 students take entire courses on line. Chat sessions are being used, however, as components of particular K–12 online projects. Such projects have an established agenda, and when project goals fit with the curriculum needs of particular classrooms, the projects can provide valuable interactive experiences.

Focus

## Chat Opportunities for Students

On a technical level, there are at least two kinds of Internet chats. The more traditional chats, Internet relay chats (IRCs), make use of special client software that participants have to download and install. Typically, IRCs offer a sophisticated chat environment with multiple channels and the opportunity to arrange for private conversations.

An alternative approach that works within a traditional web browser is sometimes called a *web chat.* Participants type and send messages in a manner similar to the IRC format. Viewing the accumulation of messages works a little differently, however; it is similar to loading a web page. Some versions require that reloading be accomplished manually, and users have to click a button periodically to see recent messages.

Although they are in some ways less sophisticated than IRCs, web chat environments have the advantage that the software is less expensive and easier to operate. If schools have a web server, adding the software to host web chats can be done very reasonably (see the information on web chat software in the Resources at the end of this chapter). With this software, individual classrooms can easily create and implement projects that involve synchronous conversations.

Here are some sites that host web-based chats:

Apple Learning Interchange. **http://ali.apple.com**

Talk City EduCenter. **http://www.jamz.com/**

Teacher Chat. **http://www.realkids.com/tlchat.shtml**

Women in NASA. **http://quest.arc.nasa.gov/webchat/won-chat.html**✱

### KIDLINK: A CHAT APPLICATION

*Matching students from around the world*

Kidlink provides an interesting example of a sponsored online project. The Kidlink organization (**http://www.kidlink.org**) matches students from all over the world for e-mail and chat. The chat areas are organized by language, so that students can choose to chat in one of several different languages. The interactive sessions provide authentic opportunities to work on second-language skills.

*Adult supervision*

Kidlink also tries to provide a protected environment for young learners. Students must be preregistered and use a password to participate in chat sessions. Adult assistants monitor the sessions. The concern that some adults may use the anonymity of the Internet and student naivete to engage students in inappropriate conversations is drastically reduced in this protected environment.

## VIDEOCONFERENCING

**Videoconferencing** allows participants to communicate using both video and audio. It can be accomplished in a number of ways and, as is often the case, the amount of money you have to invest will influence the quality of the video and audio.

*Connection speed matters*

In particular, the speed of the connection to the Internet has a major influence on the quality of the visual signal that learners experience. A 28.8 Kbps or better connection is required for minimal-quality full participation, and even at this speed the image changes infrequently. The experience is more like a series of still images than like true video. Sometimes, too, the sound is garbled beyond recognition. Faster connections increase the number of video frames sent per second and make it less likely the audio will break up.

The technology continues to improve. Already, despite its current limitations, there are many educational opportunities possible on typical K–12 budgets. CU-SeeMe, an economical and very useful product for teachers, is described in the next section.

### CU-SEEME: VIDEOCONFERENCING IN PRACTICE

**CU-SeeMe,** free software originally developed by Cornell University (see the Resources at the end of the chapter), allows anyone to participate in videoconferencing with the following minimal equipment:

*Equipment needed for CU-SeeMe*

- An Internet connection.
- A computer equipped with video and audio digitizing hardware.
- A video camera.
- A microphone.

*Simple and deluxe versions*

CU-SeeMe was developed to provide a useful conferencing environment at minimal cost. Special black-and-white video cameras, specifically designed to feed a video signal into computers, can be obtained for under $100. Color cameras and a commercial color version of CU-SeeMe are also available. The commercial software, available at a special rate to educational institutions, offers significant enhancements (see the Resources at the end of the chapter).

## Two Types of Connection

*Point-to-point connections*

There are two basic ways to use CU-SeeMe. First, two appropriately equipped computers running the CU-SeeMe software can achieve a direct or **point-to-point connection,** as illustrated in Figure 3.3. One user simply enters the IP number or address of the second user to request a connection. The second user is informed of the request, consents, and a connection is established. If you are working in a school computer lab and want another user to connect to you, the most difficult part will likely be determining the IP number for your computer so you can share this identifier with the other user (ask your lab technician for help).

*Reflector sites*

The second method allows multiple users to connect to a single source. For example, NASA provides a live feed during space shuttle missions, which

**FIGURE 3.3** CU-SeeMe screen images for host and remote.

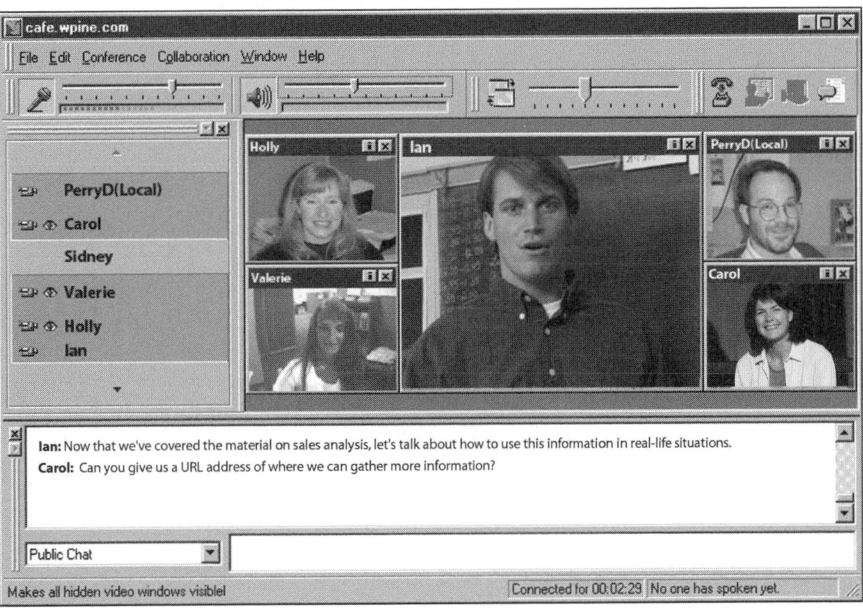


Reprinted with permission of White Pine Software, Inc.

many users like to watch and listen to. In this situation, the NASA feed comes into what is called a **reflector site,** and multiple users connect to this one site.

## Classroom Applications

*Current limitations*

Finding ways to use CU-SeeMe in the classroom requires teachers and students who enjoy the excitement of exploring something new and a little unpredictable. Classroom videoconferencing is not like tuning in to a television news program or like the interactive television you may have experienced in your college classes. Both the sound and the image will be garbled from time to time. The image may freeze completely for a time if the network is congested. Consider CU-SeeMe as a way to place powerful technology in the

Focus

### Screening Reflector Sites for CU-SeeMe

Cindy was recently conducting an after-school in-service program, helping teachers learn to use CU-SeeMe. A group of teachers working in a laboratory setting had the opportunity to use CU-SeeMe to connect to each other (point to point) so they would later feel comfortable making arrangements for their students to connect to another school. Cindy also distributed a list of IP numbers for reflector sites so that the teachers could explore the information resources that are available.

Cindy was moving about the room, making certain the individual teachers were able to get the software to work, when a teacher in the corner waved her over. As Cindy walked up, there on the teacher's screen was a close-up of male genitalia in a very aroused state.

A situation like this has a way of quickly attracting attention, and soon a crowd formed. The list of IPs Cindy had distributed was supposed to be for a general audience, but there are no guarantees with Internet content. Some consenting adults use CU-SeeMe to exchange explicit images, and it is possible to stumble into this kind of material.

Cindy decided this was a good time to point out that the Internet provides access to a great diversity of content, and it is possible to accidentally encounter content that is inappropriate for an educational situation. This is something teachers need to understand. Clearly, IPs should be screened before use, even when the list of IPs comes with a description of the expected content.

What would you do if, despite precautions, one of your own students came across such material? When unsuitable content is encountered in a classroom situation, Cindy suggests that the teacher:

- Ask the student to quit the program.
- Take a moment to remind all the students that inappropriate content does exist on the Internet and may be encountered accidentally.
- Reiterate school policy, which normally requires that students leave such sites immediately.

Chapter 9 will address the subject of inappropriate material in more detail.✷

hands of students at a reasonable price—and approach the entire experience as an adventure.

*Adding authenticity to a project*

CU-SeeMe technology may be effective in any situation in which a visual or audio signal would add to the authenticity of an online project. For example, questioning an expert is likely to be more spontaneous in real time. We encourage you to locate reflector sites and explore what is available. Look first for opportunities in science (active volcanoes, zoo and aquarium exhibits, shuttle missions) and foreign languages (a variety of experimental formats including simple news programs). For a cautionary note, however, see "Focus: Screening Reflector Sites for CU-SeeMe."

The Global SchoolNet Foundation maintains a list of international and U.S. schools using CU-SeeMe (**http://www.gsn.org/cu/index.html**). More ideas for classroom use of videoconferencing are available through periodicals (e.g., Andres, 1996) and are often shared on the Internet.

## ADVANTAGES AND PITFALLS OF COMPUTER-MEDIATED COMMUNICATION

At this point you may be evaluating the advantages of the types of electronic communication described in this chapter. You may wonder: Couldn't most school projects be handled just as well in a low-tech environment? On the other hand, you may worry that some pitfalls are lurking beneath the apparent ease and simplicity of electronic communication.

In this section we look directly at the benefits and problems of **computer-mediated communication (CMC),** as it is often called. What characteristics of CMC seem to be beneficial in educational settings, and what characteristics are cause for concern? Are there strategies that can be employed to avoid or compensate for the problems?

Most of the existing research has focused on the use of text-based systems (e-mail, chat) in higher education. You will have to consider carefully whether the information generalizes to the type of use you may be considering.

### ADVANTAGES OF CMC

Some advantages of CMC are obvious. For instance,

*Independent of time and place*

- All CMC is place independent—that is, the parties do not have to be in the same location to communicate.
- Certain forms of CMC, such as e-mail, are also time independent—the parties do not have to participate in the exchange of information at the same point in time.

*A practical solution*

For these reasons, CMC may offer a practical solution to some educational problems relating to time and location. There are situations in which face-to-face communication is nearly impossible. We teach a graduate course that deals with technology. Some teachers in our state who want to take the course live more than a hundred miles from us or from any other university with similar courses. We started teaching an Internet version of our course because this is sometimes the only practical option for these students.

As another example, some of our university colleagues are involved in a graduate program in space studies that operates entirely as a distance education program. Because the program enrolls students from several countries, as well as many people in industry or the military, CMC again represents a practical way for the students to gain access. CMC plays a further valuable role in this program. Because graduate space studies programs are rare, it is not an easy matter for any university to assemble a suitable faculty. The program here uses experts from NASA, industry, and other educational institutions to extend the faculty expertise available on campus.

*K–12 applications*

A K–12 teacher can use CMC in a similar manner. Through CMC, students can communicate with professionals who cannot take the time or are unable to make the trip to meet with students face to face. Thus CMC can create opportunities for communication that may not be possible otherwise.

The issues of time and place come into play in some other important ways. Class time is precious, especially time devoted to student participation, and it turns out that CMC may have a significant positive impact in that area.

## CMC'S IMPACT ON STUDENT PARTICIPATION

*Who dominates discussion?*

For a long time, educational researchers have studied the question of who tends to dominate classroom discussions. When classes are involved in discussion, teachers speak between 40 and 80 percent of the time, and most communication is between the teacher and a student rather than among students (see, for example, Dunkin & Biddle, 1974; Flanders, 1971).

*Who gets recognized?*

The nature of classroom discussion also has some startling characteristics. Traditional instruction tends to involve rapid questions and students who are good at developing quick responses. This situation may exist because students must compete for the attention of the teacher and group within a time-dependent environment (Althaus, 1997). Quick responses are also rewarded because most teachers pause after asking a question for less than 2 seconds before speaking again to call on another student, rephrase the question, or provide an answer (Tobin, 1986, 1987).

Reviews of CMC research indicate that the properties of CMC change some of these patterns of interaction (Althaus, 1997; Harasim, 1990; McComb, 1994; Olaniran, Savage, & Sorenson, 1996). It appears that CMC facilitates greater and more diverse participation. One research group found that

*How CMC promotes more complex messages*

student comments in the classroom averaged 12 words, but contributions to an e-mail discussion averaged 106 words. The greater length may be due to the greater complexity of the e-mail messages, which itself may reflect the greater amount of time students have to construct their messages. Students observed during an online session spent an average of 47 of 65 minutes composing their contributions. Besides being longer, e-mail messages are more complex than classroom comments and tend to address multiple topics rather than follow the thread of a very focused discussion. As you might expect, however, message complexity in chat sessions is more similar to that found in face-to-face classroom comments (Black, Levin, Mehan, & Quinn, 1983; Quinn, Mehan, Levin, & Black, 1983).

Reviews of the research literature also indicate that CMC reduces the proportion of the discussion dominated by the teacher and involves more students in providing comments (Althaus, 1997; Harasim, 1990; Olaniran, et al., 1996). Several factors may contribute to this situation:

*How CMC broadens student participation*

- Submitting a CMC comment does not require that you first be recognized. With the possible exception of a moderated mailing list, anyone with something to contribute has access to the other discussion participants.
- In both chat and e-mail discussions, students can work on the preparation of their comments at the same time and can be assured that the comments will eventually be added to the discussion. The first student to hit the "send" button does not block out other participants.
- Finally, CMC reduces a variety of classroom cues (sounds and visual information) that may signal authority or inhibit some students. For example, the physical presence of the teacher signals authority, and students defer, are inhibited, or perhaps take less initiative when the presence of an authority figure is so obvious. CMC also reduces some of the cues that would be produced by other students in a face-to-face situation. The lack of cues provides a separation that may be beneficial for some students.

In summary, CMC may change what might be described as the discussion component of learning by increasing the number of active student participants and the overall proportion of the discussion contributed by students. It can help involve those students who cannot think as quickly as others, who may not be as proficient in using the language, or who may be apprehensive of sharing within a physical group (Althaus, 1997).

*CMC and meaningful learning*

In all of these ways CMC can help create the *active, meaningful* learning experiences that we discussed in Chapter 2. Even for students who have no difficulty expressing themselves in class discussions, the writing activities involved in e-mail and mailing lists can be extremely beneficial. "Writing to learn" has been proposed as a general technique to encourage active and self-regulated learning (McGinley, 1992; Zinsser, 1988), and CMC is a good way to stimulate writing in multiple areas of the curriculum.

## POTENTIAL PROBLEMS WITH CMC

Despite the advantages of CMC, there are some difficulties that are important to recognize. Often these difficulties stem from the same basic attributes as the advantages.

### Student Behavior

*May students get out of hand?*

One of the most consistently recognized characteristics of CMC is the reduced number and variety of visual and auditory cues that are available. Some researchers, as we have just seen, feel that fewer cues encourage greater student participation. But others feel that the lack of cues can be associated with immature, insensitive, and unproductive behaviors. There is some indication that CMC results in more evaluative comments, including comments that are too critical (Kiesler, Zubrow, Moses, & Geller, 1985; Smilowitz, Compton, & Flint, 1988). Participants sometimes retaliate in an insulting manner, and then the conversation can degenerate into what in the online world is called a **flame war,** an exchange of angry or derogatory remarks.

*A code of online behavior*

As a teacher, you should be aware that CMC messages can be misinterpreted and exchanges can become negative. Students involved in CMC can be sensitized to these limitations, learning to become more careful in the construction of the messages they send. Schools frequently provide students with a code of on-line conduct, often called **netiquette.** (See "Focus: Netiquette Guidelines" for further discussion.)

### "Connectedness" of Messages

*Are messages too disconnected?*

In the preceding section, we described research indicating that CMC can increase student participation in discussions by allowing various students to work on their contributions simultaneously and to contribute them when finished. But other researchers note that this situation also has the disadvantage of disrupting the anticipated "connectedness" among messages. In face-to-face group conversations, it is more apparent which participant has the floor, and it is easier to follow how one comment relates to the next. CMC may hinder patterns of interaction in which a progression is supposed to unfold over time (McGrath, 1990). The purpose of the conversation may be an issue here. CMC may be helpful in getting ideas out but make it more difficult for a group to work toward an agreement or solution.

*The teacher's role in minimizing problems*

There are strategies you can use to minimize this type of problem. As you saw earlier, the reply function in e-mail makes it easy to include fragments of a previous message, providing a link between an earlier comment and the one you are making. As a teacher, you can encourage student participants in CMC to use such links, including comments that indicate the person and the idea that prompted their response. You can also head off difficulties by playing an active facilitative role in organizing the online group communication and bringing closure to it.

Focus

## Netiquette Guidelines

Internet etiquette, commonly referred to as netiquette, consists of conventions for proper online behavior. Conventions are important in facilitating group interaction and allowing groups to function efficiently, fairly, and in ways that allow individuals to feel good about their participation. By following these guidelines, both in personal communication and in class work with your students, you will minimize problems and show others that you are knowledgeable and caring.

### Monitor Your E-mail Account

If you intend to communicate with e-mail, you should monitor your account on a regular basis and respond to messages promptly. Responding promptly is courteous and lets the sender know the message has been received.

### Watch Grammar and Spelling

Proper grammar and accurate spelling should be an obvious expectation for educational applications of CMC. Online messages are often informal, but they still offer students the opportunity to practice good habits. For you, too, spelling and grammar are important; your words leave an impression, especially important in the absence of other cues. So take the time to reread your messages before you send them, and encourage your students to do the same with their messages. Some e-mail software comes equipped with a built-in spell checker, and software can also be purchased that will monitor text as you type.

### Create a Context for Your Comments

"Go ahead, George. I think it is a good idea." If you walked up to your friend George on the street and said this, he might be pleased, but he would probably have no idea what you were talking about. This exact thing happens frequently online. Someone makes a comment or asks a question. Someone else reads the comment or question and replies. But the passage of time increases the likelihood that the person asking the question will forget what was asked or who was asked to respond.

The easiest way to establish the context for a reply is to connect your reply to the original message. Usually the best approach is to retain only the sections of the original message that are relevant to your reply and to merge your comments with the original comments you are attempting to address. You can preface this section of combined material with a short introduction and explanation.

### Compose the Subject Line Carefully

The subject line is the first thing the recipient of your message sees. If the subject or your e-mail address does not attract attention, the recipient may delay reading the message or even delete it. The subject line also provides context for the rest of the message. With people you do not know, the best policy is to write a subject line that accurately describes the content or purpose of the message. "Question about PEP Grants" is better than "Important Question." While you can enter a long phrase for the subject, short phrases are generally preferable because the e-mail client may display only the first few words.

### Ask Yourself: Would You Say It Face to Face?

One way to evaluate messages for appropriateness is to consider whether you could make the same comments in a face-to-face setting. If you would not, because the comments would be considered unnecessarily harsh, the message should be rewritten in less offensive language.

### Be Careful with Sarcasm and Humor

Without the benefit of the cues present in face-to-face communication, sarcasm and poking fun at another person can easily be misinterpreted as criticism.

### Remember That CMC Messages Can Be Permanent

Once your message is sent, it continues to exist, no longer under your control. The recipient may save it indefinitely or may forward it to others. While forwarding without permission is considered inappropriate, you should recognize the possibility that almost anyone may see what you have written. If you would not be willing to make your comments public, carefully consider sending them over the Internet.

### Listen Before You Speak

You might think that the Internet would be a great setting in which to ask whether you should purchase computer brand X or computer brand Y. True, but don't assume that this question would be welcomed in many settings. Ask this kind of question on the wrong mailing list and you will immediately set off howls of protest. Computer users are very loyal to brands, and many lists have tired of the debate over which brand is better.

Another good example involves making recommendations for commercial products. Some lists and chat rooms encourage the exchange of information about books, programs, and services, and some actively oppose it. How do you know what behavior is appropriate? Sometimes the only way to know is to observe before you participate. This behavior, often called **lurking,** will allow you to become familiar with the topics and communication styles that are allowed.

### Reply to the Proper Person

This guideline sounds obvious, but it is still commonly abused. Sometimes the problem results from a simple mistake. Often mailing list participants forget that an e-mail message came from the list and not from the person authoring the message. Attempting to reply to the author results in a message sent to all members of the list. Many e-mail users have been embarrassed by unintentionally sending a very personal or insensitive message to a mailing list. A similar problem can be created by overuse of the CC function. Do not send a message to many people just because you can.

See Virginia Shea's book *Netiquette* for additional ideas (San Francisco: Albion Press, 1994).✷

## Skills Needed

Another potential problem with CMC has to do with the skills it demands. CMC, particularly those forms that rely exclusively on text, requires that users be proficient in keyboarding, writing, and general computer skills. Those who do not have these skills may struggle.

*Adapting CMC projects to students' skill levels*

As a teacher, you will want to make sure that CMC projects are adapted to the keyboarding and writing abilities of your students. As far as general computer skills are concerned, the ones necessary for e-mail and chat are reasonably easy to master when students are working in a reliable technology environment. With a coach and supportive student colleagues, even inexperienced students can meet class expectations (Ross, 1996).

### YOUR OWN EVALUATION

We expect that the area of CMC will attract even more attention from researchers. Our comments have been somewhat speculative, intended to make you think about this form of interaction. CMC has a down side, but perhaps some advantages you may not have considered.

*How can your own classroom benefit?*

Our discussion of the positive and negative aspects of CMC should not be misinterpreted. Teachers working with elementary and secondary students seldom have to view CMC and face-to-face discussions as mutually exclusive options. The question to ask yourself is how your particular classroom activities can benefit from each kind of discussion.

In general, we believe that, once students have learned the rudiments of courteous and clear communication, CMC experiences can provide valuable supplements to classroom discussions.

## STRUCTURING CLASSROOM PROJECTS

For the new teacher, or for an experienced teacher trying an Internet communication project for the first time, moving from the general idea to the actual implementation can be a challenge. One way to get started is to join an existing project.

*Existing online projects*

A great variety of projects exists (some web sites that serve as project clearinghouses are listed in the Resources at the end of the chapter). Some projects have been put together by national agencies with federal or private foundation support. Others have been proposed by classroom teachers who are simply seeking to partner with other teachers. Some proposed projects have a clearly defined focus and a well-developed course of study; others offer only a general description of what a teacher would like to try. Some may require a fee for participation.

Joining an existing project, especially one in which a lot of preplanning has been completed, may be a good strategy for your first attempt. But we would also like to encourage you to develop projects of your own, ones that are particularly suited to your own skills, your students' interests and skills, the equipment you have available, and the topics or approach you are emphasizing in class. You and your students may be especially motivated by a project you and they originate.

## TYPES OF PROJECTS

To help you understand the types of projects you can consider, here is a classification developed by Harris (1995, 1997), who refers to the different categories as "activity structures":

*Interpersonal exchanges.* "Talk" among individuals, between individuals and groups, and among groups.

*Types of projects involving interpersonal exchange*

- *Keypals.* Unstructured exchanges among individuals or groups, such as exchanges to develop cultural awareness or language skills.
- *Global classrooms.* Projects that combine different classrooms in study of a common topic and exchanges of accounts of what students have learned; for example, a cross-cultural study of common themes in fairy tales.
- *Electronic appearances.* E-mail or chat interaction with a guest, usually after some preparation; for instance, a local engineer could respond to questions from students in a physics class.
- *Electronic mentoring.* Ongoing interaction between a subject matter expert and a student, related to a specific topic, as when college education majors offer middle school students advice on class projects or when a college faculty member keeps in contact with a college student involved in student teaching.
- *Impersonations.* Participants interact "in character"; for example, students could correspond with a graduate student who is impersonating Benjamin Franklin.

*Information collections.* Groups working together to collect and compile information.

*Types of projects involving information exchange*

- *Information exchanges.* Accumulation of information on some theme, such as favorite playground games or recycling practices.
- *Publishing.* Publication of a document based on electronic submissions by group members, such as a district literary magazine of short stories submitted by elementary school students.
- *Tele-field trips.* Sharing of observations made during local field trips, such as visits to local parks.
- *Pooled data analysis.* Analyzing data collected from multiple sites; for instance, doing a cost comparison of gasoline prices and related factors in different regions.

*Problem-solving projects.* Projects in which the focus of interaction involves solving problems.

*Types of problem-solving projects*

- *Information searches.* Students collaborate to solve a problem based on clues and reference sources, such as identifying state landmarks or cities in response to a progression of clues.

- *Electronic process writing.* Posting of written works for critiques before revision; for example, allowing composition students to comment by e-mail on classmates' papers.
- *Parallel problem-solving.* Groups at different sites solve the same problem and then exchange and discuss their methods and conclusions; this procedure can lend itself to speculative questions, such as How can we improve school spirit?
- *Sequential creations.* Different groups work on sequential components of an expressive piece, as by adding new stanzas to a poem about friendship.
- *Social action projects.* Groups take responsibility for solving an authentic problem and sharing reports of their activities and the consequences; such a problem might involve cleaning up the local environment or caring for the homeless.

These basic categories can be a useful starting point for your own ideas. Don't feel bound by them, however. You may create a project that crosses the boundaries between categories or even produces a new category.

## PLANNING A PROJECT

In planning your own classroom projects using Internet communication tools, what factors should you consider? We think you'll find that planning for Internet projects is much like the lesson planning you already do. To get you started, the following sections comment on some of the main points you will need to ponder and offer questions for you to ask yourself. (This discussion is based to some degree on Oliver, 1997.)

### Resources and Skills

For any project you plan, you will need to determine the resources and skills necessary to implement it. Which of these skills can students learn during the project? Which skills must students have when the project begins? Overstepping the capabilities of students and resources can cause a good idea to fail.

If your project involves e-mail, for example, you should be able to answer the following questions, at a minimum:

*Questions about skills and resources*

#### *Questions to Ask Yourself*

- Do students have their own e-mail accounts?
- What software will be used to send and receive e-mail messages?
- Are students experienced in using this software?
- How many of the students in your class will be expected to send e-mail messages?

- How often will each student expected to send e-mail have access to a computer?
- Have the students been prepared to write effective e-mail messages?

Likewise, if the project makes use of student teams, as many Internet projects do, you will want to prepare for the special demands of cooperative learning. For some students, working in a cooperative team may be a completely novel experience. How will the teams be established? Are there skills students need to learn that will allow them to function more effectively as a team?

## Sources of Information

Most structured educational experiences begin by bringing learners into contact with information. Online projects generally expect students to play an active role in gathering information relevant to the project's goal. Think about how your project will use the many possible information sources, including these:

### *Possible Information Sources*

*Contacting online "experts"*

*Choosing web resources*

*Integrating offline experiences*

- *On-line communication with other people.* Your project might involve e-mail contact with a history professor who has agreed to answer questions posed by the class. Or you might establish contact with members of a local senior center who have agreed to answer questions based on their life experiences. In other cases, the "experts" your students contact may be other students—students of different ages, who live in different areas of the country or in different countries, or who live in different kinds of communities. A crucial part of your planning process will be choosing these other people, gaining their cooperation, and making sure they will be available during the time frame of the project.
- *Online research.* The most commonly used resources for students' online research are on the World Wide Web. You will need to decide how much to rely on such resources and how to direct students to appropriate ones. Chapters 4 and 5 will delve into this subject in detail.
- *Offline research.* Even in a project that uses Internet resources, students can gather information through activities that have nothing to do with the Internet: reading a novel, taking a field trip, conducting a lab experiment. The Internet does not have to be involved in every phase of the online project.

## Sharing, Organizing, and Communicating Information

*How will your students share information?*

We have talked about e-mail and mailing lists as efficient ways of sharing information, but the sharing can be accomplished in a number of different ways. For example, do you want to set up a mailing list so that all the project's participants automatically get all the contributions? Or do you want to name a project coordinator who will collect information from the participants and organize it in some way before sharing it?

For meaningful, self-regulated learning, it will be useful to have your students, as much as possible, do the organizing and communicating themselves, but you will need to decide how to guide and support their efforts.

### Analysis

*How will you prompt analysis?*

How will you encourage students to analyze the information they have gathered or generated? If the project involved testing a particular idea, was the initial hypothesis supported or not? If the project included a chat discussion, what do students think about the topic afterward? Ideally, your planning should include ways to prompt careful analysis, reflection, and further inquiry.

### Products

Projects often are structured to result in some kind of outcome or product. Summarizing their experiences through a specific product provides learners another opportunity to actively reflect on the information they have received. It also requires that they practice their written, verbal, or multimedia communication skills.

*What kind of culminating product?*

Ask yourself: What kind of product will be most appropriate for your project and for your students? A written product, such as an essay, report, poem, or play? An oral report or presentation? A web page? Again, an Internet project need not involve the Internet at every stage.

### Evaluation

*How will you assess students' learning?*

How will you evaluate what your students have learned? If you will base your evaluation mainly on their product or presentation, will you need a scoring rubric or template? What will your evaluation standards be, and how will you give useful feedback to your students?

Not all Internet projects contain all of these components, but the ones mentioned here are common. Considering these elements in the planning process should help you ensure that your students become active learners in their Internet communication experiences.

## SUMMARY

- Schools already use a number of computer-mediated communication (CMC) systems. Because it is so versatile and easy, e-mail is the most popular. E-mail systems are capable of storing and organizing messages you would like to keep, building an address book, and sending computer files as attachments. You can also use the reply function to respond to messages in a way that indicates the relationship between your comments and the previous message.
- Mailing lists are an adaptation of e-mail that allow an individual to communicate with a group. Participation in a mailing list first requires that you join the list

by sending a request to the list's administrative address. Once your e-mail address has been added to the list, all messages sent to the list server's submission address will be forwarded to your e-mail account. It is important to understand the difference between the administrative address and the submission address.

◆ Chat sessions offer a synchronous text-based communication format. Chat sessions have become a common feature of online courses because they provide an excellent opportunity for class discussion. For classes of K–12 students, the use of mailing lists and chat sessions generally involves large online projects sponsored by an agency outside of the school district.

◆ Videoconferencing offers a synchronous video and audio communication format. Inexpensive software allows an appropriately equipped computer to participate in (1) a two-way exchange with a comparable computer in another location or (2) a larger group coordinated through a reflector site.

◆ The advantages and disadvantages of computer-mediated communication (CMC) in educational settings are still being investigated. Two important factors are (1) the greater flexibility CMC allows one to think and compose messages in the time available and (2) the limited number of cues available from communication partners. Whether these factors result in positive or negative consequences is a matter of perspective. The more leisurely pace allowed by CMC and the limited number of cues available from other participants may allow more students to participate and shift the balance from a teacher-dominated discussion toward more equal participation. However, discussion may be less organized, without clear lines of authority, and perhaps less sensitive in addressing the comments offered by other participants. In most educational settings, CMC can be offered as an addition to classroom activity rather than as a replacement. CMC participants do need to learn the basics of online netiquette.

◆ CMC can provide opportunities to involve students in a wide variety of projects. Teachers new to the technology may want to begin with well-tested classroom projects, but we also urge you to create or adapt projects to the needs and interests of your own students and your particular curriculum. Planning such a project—like planning any other extended class activity—involves asking yourself a number of key questions about available resources, skills, and the particular tasks students will undertake.

## REFLECTING ON CHAPTER 3

### Activities

1. Subscribe to a mailing list appropriate to your instructional interests (see the suggestions in "Resources to Expand Your Knowledge Base"). Make sure you save the information that explains how to unsubscribe. After one week, summarize the volume of messages and the topics covered for your classmates.
2. Locate an existing communication project that might be relevant for your area of interest (see project sources in "Resources to Expand Your Knowledge Base"). Classify this project according to the scheme provided by Harris. Summarize the project for your classmates.
3. Conduct a WWW search (see Chapter 4 for search techniques) for CU-SeeMe reflector sites. Create a list of sites you feel may be of value to classroom teachers.

## Key Terms

address book (p. 71)
administrative address (p. 73)
attachment (p. 69)
bounce (p. 65)
chat (p. 77)
computer-mediated communication (CMC) (p. 82)
CU-SeeMe (p. 80)
e-mail (p. 64)
flame war (p. 86)
header (p. 66)
learning circle (p. 75)
listserv (p. 73)
list server (p. 73)
lurking (p. 88)
mailing list (p. 73)
netiquette (p. 86)
point-to-point connection (p. 81)
reflector site (p. 82)
signature (p. 68)
subject field (p. 67)
submission address (p. 73)
thread (p. 70)
videoconferencing (p. 79)

## Resources to Expand Your Knowledge Base

### Mailing List Directories

The following web sites describe mailing lists and provide a convenient method for subscribing.

Liszt, The Mailing List Directory. **http://www.liszt.com/**

Publicly accessible mailing lists. **http://www.neosoft.com/internet/paml/default.html**

Tile.Net Lists. **http://www.tile.net/listserv/**

### Sample Internet Communication Projects

The following web sites describe and in some cases provide access to Internet communication projects.

Global School Network Projects Page. **http://www.gsn.org/project/index.html**

Intercultural e-mail classroom connections. **http://www.stolaf.edu/network/iecc/**

Kidlink. **http://www.kidlink.org/**

NASA Internet in the Classroom Page. **http://quest.arc.nasa.gov/interactive/index.html**

Judi Harris's Network-Based Educational Activity Collection. **http://lrs.ed.uiuc.edu/Activity-Structures/Harris-Activity-Structures.html**

### Communication Software Resources

***E-mail clients.*** Here are addresses you can use to download free e-mail clients:

Eudora Light (Qualcomm). **http://eudora.qualcomm.com/products/**

Outlook Express (Microsoft). **http://www.microsoft.com/msdownload/**

***Free E-mail through the Web.*** Some companies provide a free e-mail account that can be accessed using a web browser. Why would a company provide such a service free of charge? Use of the e-mail system provides the opportunity to present advertisements.

Juno. **http://www.juno.com/**

Hotmail. **http://www.hotmail.com/**

***PopMail/Lab.*** We place PopMail/Lab in a unique category because it is designed specifically for an open laboratory environment. This product is freeware developed at the University of Minnesota and can be obtained from many Internet sources. One dependable source is **http://www.shareware.com/**.

### Web Chat Software

ConferWeb, developed for a Macintosh server by Brian Johnson, is available at **http://www.caup.washington.edu/software/**.

### CU-SeeMe

CU-SeeMe was originally experimental software developed by Cornell University. All rights are now owned by White Pine Software, Inc. (**http://www.wpine.com**). CU-SeeMe is available for both Windows and Macintosh platforms.

Older versions of CU-SeeMe are still available at no cost. A good general CU-SeeMe resource, which includes both access to the original software and descriptions of the new commercial versions, is CU-SeeMe Network (**http://cu-seeme.net/**).

The Global School Network CU-SeeMe Schools project is available at **http://www.gsn.org/cu/index.html**.

If you would like to observe an example of CU-SeeMe, try the following:

NASA Television on CU-SeeMe. **http://btree.lerc.nasa.gov/NASA_TV/**

Rice University, Ask the Scientist. **http://space.rice.edu/hmns/ask.html**.

# Chapter 4

# Learning with Internet Inquiry Tools

## ORIENTATION

In this chapter you will learn what you and your students need to know to make efficient use of the major Internet tools that promote student inquiry. The web browser and the World Wide Web are responsible for the tremendous surge of interest in the Internet. We will explain the techniques involved in operating the browser and searching for resources within the vastness of the Internet. We will begin to demonstrate how you as a teacher can increase the productivity of your students' web use. You will also learn about two additional formats for delivering Internet resources: file transfer protocol and streaming audio or video.

As you read, look for answers to the following questions:

**FOCUS QUESTIONS**

- What are the properties of the multimedia and hypermedia that characterize World Wide Web content?
- Can learners really become "lost" as they explore World Wide Web material?
- How can teachers and students keep track of valuable web resources they have located?
- How can learners take advantage of online services to locate needed information through the processes of browsing and searching? What can learners do to improve the efficiency of their searches?
- What tools besides the web browser allow access to Internet information resources?

In Chapter 1 we described one of the purposes of this book as helping you understand how the Internet can function as a tool for *inquiry.* This chapter and the next are part of our attempt to explain how the World Wide Web can be applied in this way.

This book would not exist without the World Wide Web. While the Internet offers experiences and resources that do not require the Web, it is the Web's potential and the promise of future implementations that have captured the imagination of so many. The World Wide Web has established the true educational potential of the Internet—a potential that translates into school interest and the commitment of school funds.

*The Web's importance for schools*

A concept from the computer industry may help you understand the enthusiasm the World Wide Web has generated. The term *killer app* (short for *killer application*) refers to a new application so powerful that it will eliminate earlier applications and so impressive that it will attract new users to the technology. Both the World Wide Web and the software that allows users to explore it are great examples of killer apps. The Web has encouraged schools to connect to the Internet like nothing that existed before. To a lesser degree, the presence of the Web has even encouraged schools to purchase more computers. Moreover, because the number of web users has increased so drastically, more information, educational and otherwise, is being created for the Web. Both the number of Internet users and the quantity of web resources are spiraling upward at a rapid rate.

This chapter will describe some important properties of the collective body of information available on the World Wide Web, explain how to use the main software tools necessary to explore the Web, and discuss how you can search the Web to locate information relevant to your classroom needs. A less detailed section at the end of the chapter will discuss File Transfer Protocol (FTP), an older technology for transferring information resources from a server to the computer of a user, and streaming audio and video, a more recent innovation for delivering extended audio and video content. These topics are intended to prepare you for our more detailed discussion of learning and problem solving with World Wide Web resources in Chapter 5.

## THE WORLD WIDE WEB: MULTIMEDIA AND HYPERMEDIA

The World Wide Web (WWW, or simply the Web) quickly attracted attention to the Internet because it allowed online multimedia and hypermedia. The properties of information offered as multimedia and hypermedia provide the power, ease of use, and appeal that make the Web so attractive.

### WHAT ARE MULTIMEDIA AND HYPERMEDIA?

You may remember the explanation of multimedia in Chapter 1.

*What is multimedia?*

▶ ***Multimedia*** *is a communication format that integrates several media categories, such as text, images, audio, and video.*

Many educational computer applications have involved multimedia for some time, but online versions of multimedia were not readily available until Marc Andreessen, a student at the University of Illinois, and colleagues developed the Mosaic browser for personal computers in 1993. Many from this development group later formed the company Netscape and are responsible for some of the most popular WWW software tools used in schools.

*Evolution of online multimedia*

Early WWW implementations were limited in the variety of multimedia formats that could be presented. They allowed text and still images, but nothing more. However, the tremendous interest in online multimedia, as well as improvements in the speed with which content could be transmitted over the Internet, led to rapid developments in both web servers and clients. The quality of online presentations does not yet approach the quality of multimedia software products you might load directly on your personal computer, but the diversity of media types has expanded greatly. In general, the properties of online multimedia—including quality, quantity, and cost—appear to be more than adequate for educational institutions to commit to the WWW in a big way.

As we mentioned in Chapter 1 (p. 22),

*What is hypermedia?*

▶ *The term* ***hypermedia*** *refers to applications that allow multimedia to be experienced in a nonlinear fashion.*

*Interactivity*

In hypermedia, units of information, such as portions of text, segments of audio, pictures, animations, and video clips, are connected to each other in multiple ways. Hypermedia environments are often described as *interactive* because the hypermedia user must direct the software and hardware to present the next unit of information. A student working with hypermedia can choose the order in which he or she will investigate different segments of information.

## NAVIGATING WITH LINKS

*Using links*

In hypermedia, many of the user's decisions are implemented by selecting one of several possible **links.** Most frequently, selecting a link means using the mouse to click on a specially designated segment of text or part of an image. Each link moves the user from the present information to a new source of information. Multiple links allow multiple choices of what information will be experienced next:

*Varied experiences*

▶ *Because control is vested in the user, different individuals may have very different experiences as they work in hypermedia environments.*

In addition, if the same student works with a hypermedia environment on several occasions, it is likely that he or she will explore the environment in different ways.

The World Wide Web is essentially hypermedia on a massive scale. The development of this worldwide hypermedia environment has had some exciting consequences. Before the Web, the resources available on the Internet existed in a very disorganized fashion, and individuals without a technological background found them difficult to access. The World Wide Web, along with the browser software developed for it, allows these same information resources to be connected through hypermedia links. The major advantage for educators and students is that someone else has already done some of the work of locating and organizing meaningful collections of Internet resources.

*The Internet organized*

A web author uses links to connect information elements in the web pages he or she prepares, and the author also typically provides links to relevant material elsewhere on the Web. Special indexing services create massive directories of web resources, allowing users to follow links to pages that seem relevant. Furthermore, search engines allow users to search the Web for pages with certain keywords. Although these options may sound complex, contemporary browser software offers easy methods of navigating through the hypermedia environment. The next section explores the basic features of a typical web browser.

## THE BROWSER: YOUR WEB CONNECTION TOOL

The web **browser** is the special software program you need to take advantage of web resources. Figure 4.1 shows a screen image from Netscape Communicator, one of the two major browsers available in most educational institutions. (Netscape Communicator incorporates Netscape Navigator, the web-browsing software that made Netscape famous.) We will refer to Figure 4.1 repeatedly as we explain how a browser operates. (For an explanation of how to obtain a free copy of browser software, see Resources to Expand Your Knowledge Base at the end of the chapter.)

*Appearance of a browser window*

In Figure 4.1, you will note that a central **content window** is surrounded on three sides by user controls of various types. The collection of user controls can be called the browser's *interface,* the conventional term applied to the mechanisms by which a user interacts with a computer program. Let's begin with the content window.

### THE CONTENT WINDOW

*Size of the content window*

The content window is the part of the browser used to display multimedia information. The content window in Figure 4.1 would cover an area of approximately 6 by 7 inches on a typical monitor. This is not a very large area when

**FIGURE 4.1** The Netscape Communicator browser.

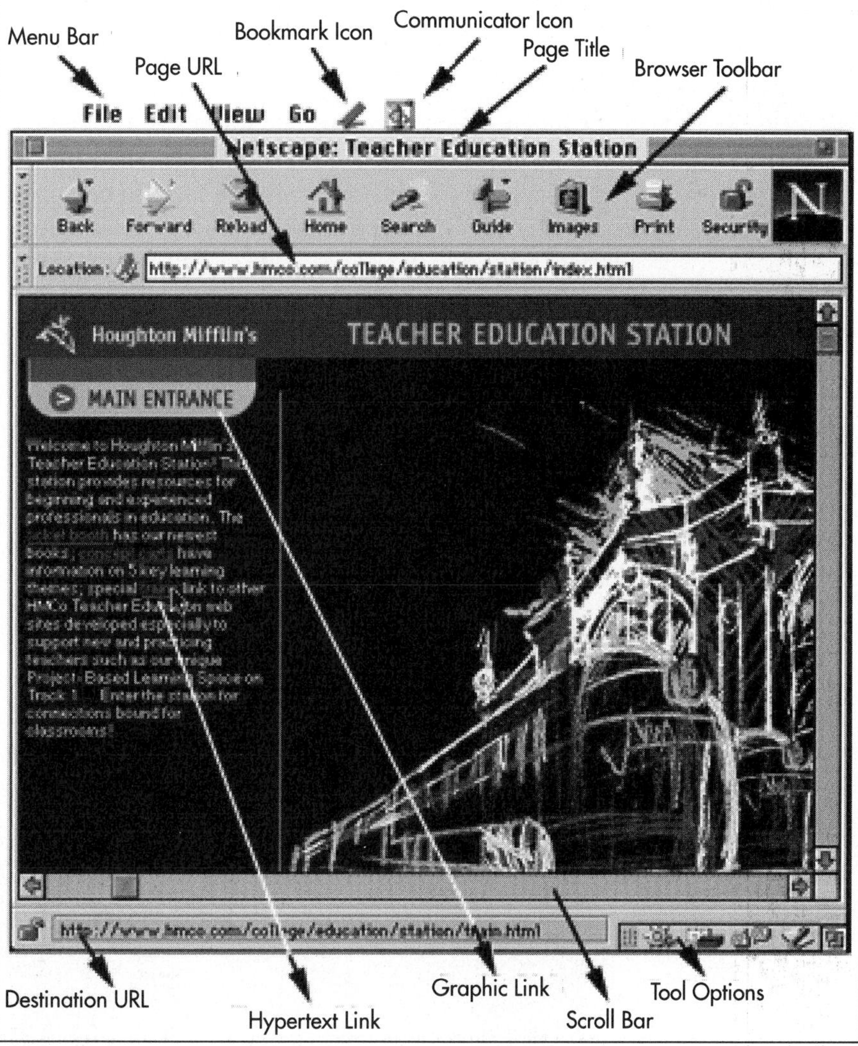




compared with the dimensions of an open textbook or magazine, a television screen, or even the entire area of a computer monitor. The size of the content window certainly influences how web pages are designed and the efficiency with which learners receive information. Browsers are designed so that some interface features can be eliminated to increase the size of the content window, and this option may prove useful in setting up browser software for students.

*Scroll bars*

## Scroll Bars

Because web pages are often larger than the dimensions of the content window, *scroll bars* along the bottom and right-hand sides of the window allow users to move to parts of a page that are not immediately visible (see Figure 4.1). Most designers of web pages do not expect users to scroll horizontally, but vertical scrolling is often necessary to see the entire page.

## Frames

*Common uses of frames*

Contemporary browsers allow the content window to be subdivided into multiple areas called **frames.** The content of various frames is independent, so that the content of one frame can be changed while other frames remain constant. A common application is to have users act on the contents of one frame to control what appears or happens in a second frame. For example, in Figure 4.2, selections made in the frame on the left control which image will appear in the frame on the right.

Frames can be a nuisance on smaller monitors because parts of the display can be hidden when a multiple-frame display is forced into a small area. For example, if the screen display in Figure 4.2 were forced into a smaller area, it might no longer be possible to see the full names of the toads and frogs. This problem can be more serious with more complicated designs.

*Resizing frames*

Some web sites offer two versions of web pages, with and without frames, as a convenience to those site visitors who find the frames inconvenient. In addition, sometimes users can resize frames. This is a property that some web

**FIGURE 4.2** The browser's content window divided by frames. Clicking with the mouse on one of the frog or toad names in the left frame will cause a picture of that kind of amphibian to appear in the right frame.

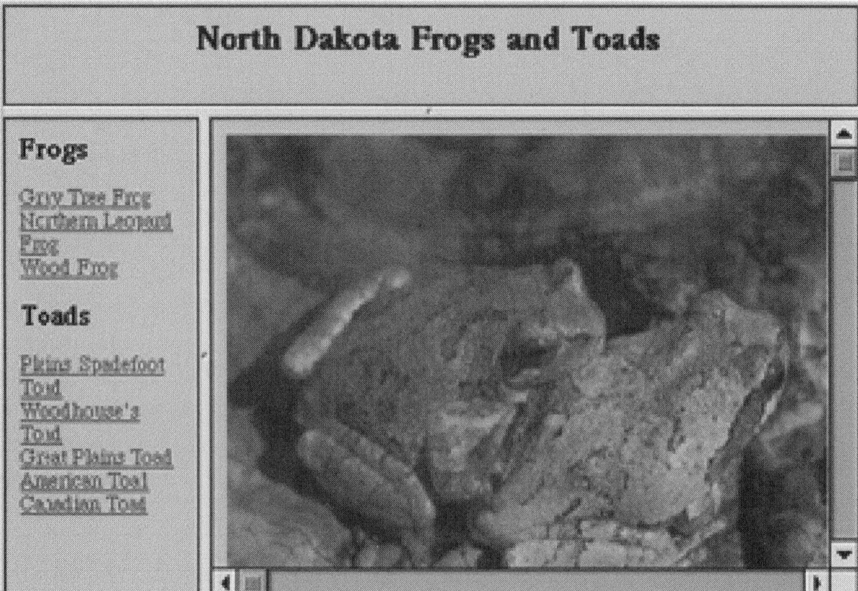

page designers insist on turning off, so it is not always available. You will know that a frame border is adjustable if your cursor turns into a double arrow when you move it over a border. By using the mouse to drag a frame border, you can reallocate the screen areas that the frames occupy.

## THE BROWSER INTERFACE

Browsers have a number of buttons and menu items that allow users to control the browser functions. Mastering a few of these controls and understanding a limited number of conventions will allow even young users to navigate the World Wide Web.

For the sake of brevity, we will review only one version of one browser (Netscape Communicator 4.0, Macintosh version). But the features we mention are fairly standard. A user interacts with all browsers by clicking buttons, typing information into fields, and selecting options from menus.

### The Location Window

*Entering a URL in the location window*

One of the most basic tasks is to connect to a distant web site. The easiest way to do this is to type the **Universal Resource Locator (URL)** into the *location window* (shown immediately under the browser toolbar in Figure 4.1). The URL is the Internet address for the desired site; it tells the browser which server needs to be located and then which page needs to be transferred from that server to the browser. As you can see from the location window, the web page displayed in Figure 4.1 comes from the URL **http://www.hmco.com/college/ education/station/index.html**. The server for this page was **www.hmco.com** (the server for Houghton Mifflin Company, the publisher of this book), and the page index.html was found on this machine within the directory college/education/station. The prefix "http" stands for *hypertext transfer protocol,* the basic protocol used in communication of web pages.

Typing in long URLs can be tedious and subject to error. Luckily, you do not have to do this for every page you visit. Once you get started, you can follow links within the content to move to new pages of material. You can also save useful URLs as bookmarks, which we will discuss later in the chapter.

### Toolbar and Menubar

*Options on the toolbar*

The browser *toolbar* allows you to perform common actions simply by clicking on buttons. For example, the Back button in Figure 4.1 allows the user to return to a web page viewed a little earlier during the same session of web exploration. The Print button prints a copy of the web page currently displayed.

*Options on the menu bar*

The *menubar,* above the toolbar, contains additional options, although they are a little more difficult to get at than those available as buttons. See "Focus: Browser Menus and Buttons" for a description of the menu commands as well as more details about the toolbar buttons.

Focus

## Browser Menus and Buttons

Here is a brief description of the browser buttons and menu items you are most likely to use.

### Toolbar Buttons

- Browsers keep track of the history of pages you have visited during each session. The *Back* and *Forward* buttons allow you to move within this sequence of pages. These buttons provide a convenient way to move back to a recently visited page without having to find and enter the address for that page.
- The *Reload* button asks the server to resend the present page. Sometimes the transfer of a page is interrupted or *times out* because the transfer is too slow, and Reload is a convenient way to ask for the page again.
- *Home* takes the user to the default **home page.** This page is originally a page sponsored by the company that developed the browser, but the default page can be changed with the Preferences command (see "Edit Menu") to any web page you desire. If your school has developed a web page, it would make sense to use that as your default home page. Students may also reset the default page, so it is useful to know how to change the preference back to one that you prefer.
- *Search* takes you to a search engine designated by the company responsible for the browser.
- *Images* is used in combination with a preference setting that substitutes a standard icon or placeholder for the actual images that are to appear on a web page. Some users, particularly those connecting with a modem, do this so they can examine pages without the delay required to download images. If it seems the images would be useful, clicking the Images button will transfer the actual pictures.
- The *Print* button sends the displayed page to the printer.
- The *Security* button brings up a page that deals with security options such as encryption. This information may be important if you want to do something like send credit card information over the Internet.

### Main Menus

Menu options can be confusing because they can change according to the application window that is active. You may remember that you want to do a particular thing, but not see the command to accomplish the task when you look under the appropriate menu heading. The options we discuss here are available when the browser content window is active.

### File Menu

- Under the *File* menu heading, you will find the commands allowing you to open a location or a file. The term *location* refers to an Internet location; that is, a WWW page or FTP site. The *Open Location* command will open a field into which you can enter the address for the site you want to access. Open Location provides an alternative to entering the address in the location window.
- *Open File,* on the other hand, is used to display the contents of a file that exists on your own computer. The files must be of the type that can be read by the browser

(text, for instance, or a graphic format such as GIF or JPEG).

There are some times when opening a file residing on your own computer or a local network can be very convenient. We often prepare presentations so the supporting material and illustrations can be viewed with a web browser. There are several advantages to this technique. The file containing the presentation can be easily transported on a disk and displayed by either Macintosh or Windows computers, using whatever browser happens to be available. The same material can be made available on the Internet for viewing by those who were not able to attend the original presentation. For example, the lecture notes from my college classes are immediately made available on the Internet for student review. You and your students may find similar applications.

- Like the Print button, the *Print* menu command sends the page that is displayed to the printer.
- *Page Setup* allows the user to manipulate attributes associated with the appearance of what is printed. For example, if your computer is connected to a color ink-jet printer, Page Setup would allow you to select grayscale or color output. Since color output is more expensive to produce, it would be wise to select grayscale for everyday classroom use.

  *Hint:* Students often forget to record the address for material they print. This address is necessary when referencing web resources (see Chapter 5). The information appearing in the location window is not part of the display and is thus not automatically printed. Page Setup allows the location field to be included as a header or footer (a line of text attached at the top or bottom of the page), and selecting this option automatically attaches the page address to any printed material.

## Edit Menu

- The *Preferences* command under the *Edit* menu allows the user to control many aspects of the way the browser will function. There are many options, and some require more technical background than we can provide here.
- For classroom computers, preferences that control the default home page, how frequently the cache is flushed (that is, how much content will be stored from past uses of the browser), and which helper applications or plug-ins will be used are probably most important. Web browsers are now typically part of a suite of applications providing access to e-mail and newsgroups, and preferences for these applications are set using the same menu option. For example, this would be where you would enter the Internet address for your e-mail account.

## View Menu

- Most of the commands in the *View* menu duplicate buttons available on the toolbar.
- *Document Source,* one of the nonduplicated commands on the View menu, opens a separate window displaying the source code responsible for the current web page. If you are trying to learn how to create web pages, you can discover a great deal by studying the source code.

## Go Menu

- The most recently visited sites are listed under the *Go* menu, and this list can be used to return directly to one of the sites on the list. This is a convenient device when you decide to take one more look at a web page you viewed a bit earlier.

### Bookmark Menu

- As you spend time with the World Wide Web, you will begin to find web sites that you know you will want to visit again. You could keep the addresses of these sites in a little notebook, but the web browser itself provides a much more convenient approach. The *Bookmarks* menu (identified in Figure 4.1 by an icon rather than a word) allows users to save links to important sites. The titles of these sites become part of the Bookmarks menu, and selecting a site name from the menu will return you to the site. Because bookmarks are very useful in educational settings, we will consider them in detail later in the chapter.

### Communicator Icon

- The final item on the menu bar in Figure 4.1 is the Communicator icon. This menu provides access to other tools in the Netscape suite, such as the e-mail program. One option from this menu opens the Bookmarks window. *History*, another command on this menu, opens up a window displaying the names and URLs for recently visited web pages. The number of days this information is maintained is set as a preference.✱

## HOW A BROWSER WORKS

*How the browser assembles a web page*

The browser accomplishes several important tasks. First, it assembles and then displays the multimedia information sent from a server. Loading a web page from the Internet is not like loading a file such as a word processing document from a disk. Web servers send individual components (text, images, video clips), and the browser integrates and presents the components as a display, according to instructions specified by the author. For example, if you look back at Figure 4.1, you'll see that it contains a segment of text and multiple images. The images include the "Teacher Education Station" banner, the "Main Entrance" graphic, and the large drawing of the train and the station.

The instructions that tell the browser how to assemble and display the pieces are normally hidden from view, but they can be accessed using the Document Source command. When you use this command, you find a plain text file; that is, a file without any large, headline-sized fonts, centered headings, or pictures. It does contain the text that appears on the web page.

*HTML tags*

This simple text document has one unique characteristic. Embedded within the text are the special tags making up the **hypertext markup language (HTML).** The tags are instructions to the browser. For instance, the tag set <I></I>surrounding text would cause the text to appear italicized. The IMG tag causes an image to be transferred and displayed at a specified location. The browser reads these tags and uses them to build the display that you see on your screen. Chapter 6 will explain some of these basic instructions that control page appearance.

## Helper Applications and Plug-Ins

A particular browser may not be able to present all of the information formats that the web offers. The variety of formats available is constantly expanding. We have already mentioned text, pictures, video, and sounds. More recent additions include 3-D virtual experiences based on VRML (virtual reality modeling language) or QuickTime VR; "live" video and audio; and small programs (**applets**) that are transferred to your computer and run within your browser.

*Function of helper applications*

Typically, new formats become available before a standard web browser is capable of handling them by itself. For this reason, developers create **helper applications** that function like a second program. The browser application downloads a data file (such as a three-dimensional explorable environment), and the helper application then presents the unique format.

*Function of plug-ins*

A more integrated approach takes advantage of browser plug-ins. A **plug-in** is a special type of software that is developed to add capability to a host program. Helper applications are often eventually converted to plug-ins. Plug-ins perform their role *within* the browser—for example, by presenting a movie within the browser window rather than in a separate window. As newer versions of browsers are developed, the more popular functions once provided by helper applications and plug-ins are sometimes incorporated into the browser itself.

Plug-ins and helper applications must be obtained independently of the browser. This usually means they must be downloaded from a different Internet source—a task that can often be accomplished using the browser. Sometimes, when a web author uses an uncommon multimedia element, such as a VRML scene, the author will point you to a web site where the appropriate helper application or plug-in can be found.

## Interactivity: Links

Another important function of the browser is to serve as an interface allowing the user, within certain limits, to interact with or respond to the information that is presented. The most basic such action is to select a link, causing a server to send new information. The server may be the same server that provided the present page or a different server entirely.

*Varieties of links*

Various types of links are possible: text segments, images, or parts of an image. In Figure 4.1, you should be able to locate both image and text links.

### *Types of Links*

- *Text.* Text links are usually underlined and appear in a different color from the surrounding text. In Figure 4.1, terms like *ticket booth* and *trains* serve as links.
- *Images.* In Figure 4.1, the graphic labeled "Main Entrance" serves as an image link. In some cases, image links will have a colored border.

*Image mapping*

- *Parts of an image.* Using a process called **image mapping,** a web page author can identify different parts of an image to serve as separate links. For example, the author might present a state weather map that allows the user to request additional information about different regions of the state. Clicking on a region would link you to data about that particular area. In this way, image mapping allows one image to serve as the source for several links.

When the cursor is positioned on top of a link, the destination for that link appears in a special window near the bottom of the browser. In Figure 4.1, the cursor is positioned over "trains," and the destination for this link is displayed at the bottom of the screen.

### Interactivity: Searches and Forms

Links limit the user to preestablished alternatives. But there are many applications that allow a more open-ended interactivity. For example, when you are working with an Internet search engine, the browser allows you to enter a word or phrase that defines the subject you want to research. The browser sends this information to the server, which then forwards it to another computer program that locates web pages indexed to keywords. In this situation and in others, the browser provides the connection with the program running on the other computer.

*Uses of online forms*

Web pages that accept input from the user and then transmit it to the server for some type of action are called **forms.** Common uses of forms include searching an online database; contributing to a database; taking online tests to determine what you know about a topic; ordering from an online catalog; and submitting text information to be added to existing web pages (such as when you offer comments on an issue or sign a site visitor's guest book). The server software itself does not act on the information you submit through the form; rather, it passes the information on to a second computer program for processing.

*Interactivity and learning*

This kind of interactivity is important for educational applications. It makes the Internet more than a static source of information. Interactivity allows Internet use to match many of the learning experiences available with the kinds of educational software that you can load on an individual machine.

## LEARNING IN AN ONLINE, HYPERMEDIA ENVIRONMENT

To understand the Web as a tool for inquiry, it is important to think about how web resources might differ from other resources you are familiar with. What are these differences, and how do they affect learning?

*Why not deliver this book on the Web?*

It is possible to take information prepared for a familiar format, such as a newspaper or textbook, and present it as extended web pages. The Internet could be an alternative delivery system for this textbook, for instance. Such a delivery system would avoid printing costs and still, perhaps, generate revenue for the authors and the publishing company. Then why don't we simply offer this book on the Web?

*Different design principles*

One answer is that it would be harder to read the web version than the version you are now using. Screens of solid text are difficult to read. But a more sophisticated answer is that books and web pages are created according to different design principles. A textbook provides a highly structured environment in which the author controls the order in which ideas will be experienced. In contrast, within a hypermedia environment, users make decisions about which links to follow and the order in which specific items of information will be examined. Users may avoid certain links entirely.

*The issue of control*

In educational settings, the opportunity for learners to control their own experiences is a major theoretical advantage. But some see this feature of hypermedia as a curse rather than a blessing. There is a popular notion that students begin moving from link to link with no real plan, ending up "lost in hyperspace" and functioning in a very inefficient manner. Is this really true? To answer this question, we will first examine some relevant research and then look at a classroom example of web use by very young students.

## LOST IN HYPERSPACE?

As yet, little research has focused on online hypermedia. But there is a body of research on computer-resident hypermedia and multimedia that provides some useful insights into the question of whether students may become "lost" online (Lawless & Brown, 1997; Locatis, Letourneau, & Banvard, 1990). Several studies have identified three recognizable categories of multimedia learners:

*Three categories of multimedia learners*

- *Knowledge seekers.* Learners who use a strategic approach, concentrating on the examination of material consistent with an assigned goal.
- *Feature explorers.* Learners who seem captivated by special effects and gravitate toward options such as movies and sound files.
- *Apathetic users.* Learners who spend very limited time interacting with instructional material, moving through what is available in a rapid and linear fashion.

These categories suggest that, when learners use hypermedia ineffectively, it may be for a variety of reasons. They may wander off, get lost, or simply lose interest.

*Importance of experience*

It appears that experience plays an important role in determining how effectively learners use a hypermedia environment. With poor background knowledge, learners have little insight into what might be important to examine carefully. They may be unaware of holes in the understanding they are creating. These learners with poor background seem to be more easily distracted by attractive but nonessential features and face greater danger of becoming lost and frustrated (Gay, 1986; Lawless & Brown, 1997).

When learners do have poor experiences with hypermedia, is the problem in the learning environment or in the learner? It is probably unfair to pose the question in such a simplistic manner.

*Limitations of the Web*

There are clearly better and poorer ways to design learning environments to help learners appreciate the structure of information and examine it systematically (Jonassen & Grabinger, 1990). The Web has some inherent limitations in this regard. Even when the structure of any individual web site follows sound principles of design, web designers usually work in isolation, and connections among web sites are nearly always unidirectional. Once a learner follows a link to a different web site, he or she must assume responsibility for keeping a sense of direction and navigating back to previously visited sites.

*Tools to help a learner stay focused*

Fortunately, web browsers have built-in tools and resources that can facilitate learner control or at least help students return to the main focus of their online exploration. As you have already seen, the Back and Forward buttons allow a user to retrace his or her pathway in a step-by-step fashion. The History available on the menu bar provides a list of web sites recently visited. Later in this chapter, we will look at some additional browser tools that help a user work efficiently. First, however, we should consider your role as a teacher.

*Scaffolding the students' experience*

When students are not experienced with web exploration and have a limited background in a content area, it is important to *scaffold* their web explorations. We introduced the idea of scaffolding in Chapter 2 (p. 43). For online learning tasks, scaffolding generally means that the teacher structures the project by finding useful web sites in advance, providing a convenient method for connecting to these sites and suggesting what students might search for when they examine each site. One excellent example is the project in Mrs. Knudson's class described in the next section.

## Researching a Classroom Pet: An Example of a Scaffolded Web Project

Imagine you are a second-grade student, and your teacher decides that she will allow you and your classmates to purchase a class pet. She will contribute $30, and you will be allowed to help make the selection. But there are some issues beyond cost that you have to consider. Some pets are dangerous, and some students are allergic to certain animals. (You understand this because you have a cat at home, and your aunt says it makes her sneeze.) The pet will have to stay in a container of some sort and remain at school over weekends. There is one more thing: your teacher says the decision will be made by the entire class. You have to gather information and then explain to other students what kind of pet you would like the class to buy and why.

Does this sound like a good project? Ellen Knudson, a second-grade teacher at Solheim Elementary in Bismarck, North Dakota, thought so. Mrs. Knudson has a history of keeping pets in her classroom. She also likes to involve her students with technology projects—particularly ones in which the students are in control and make their own decisions. It seemed natural, then, to let her students research possible classroom pets on the World Wide Web.

### Preparing for the Project

To prepare for this project, Mrs. Knudson had a lot of work to do. To keep the students' research focused and efficient, she decided to ask them to consider just three potential classroom pets: a budgie (a type of bird, more formally known as a budgerigar or parakeet), a sugar glider (a marsupial), and a leopard gecko (a reptile). Even for just these three animals, finding Internet resources appropriate to second graders was a challenge.

Certain factors, such as the use of scientific nomenclature *(Melopsittacus undulatus* for budgie), did not bother her because she felt her students should learn to cope with real-world information. But she was concerned that the web resources be concise, contain the specific details students would be asked to locate, and be presented in a form that young readers could understand.

Sometimes, she discovered, a single Internet page provided all the information needed for an animal, and sometimes a page provided a great opportunity to investigate a particular issue. She made a careful selection of both types of sites. The varied experiences would be good for her students, she thought.

### Introducing the Project

Mrs. Knudson used class discussion to introduce her students to the project. Then she directed them to a series of Internet pages she had created. The following information appeared on the introductory page:

> **Class Pet**
>
> Mrs. Knudson wants to buy a new pet for the classroom. She needs help in selecting the right one. Click on the pet names below to find out more about each animal. As you are reading, keep these guidelines in mind:
>
> - It must not be a mammal because of allergies to animal hair and fur.
> - It must be $30 or less in price.
> - It must be able to live in the 10-gallon aquarium or bird cage in our room.
> - It must be easy to feed. Food must be easy to get and fairly inexpensive.

After you have read through the information, write out your choice, listing the price, the cage or equipment the animal needs, the group the animal belongs to, and the animal's diet. Also explain why you think this pet would be interesting to study and care for.

Links from this introductory page connected students to pages for each of the potential pets. Each of these pages then provided links to the Internet resources Mrs. Knudson had located. In addition to the links, the pages contained comments suggesting what students should attempt to learn from each site: "This page tells about the budgie's diet," "This page has a price list," and so on. In this way Mrs. Knudson carefully scaffolded the project for her students.

## The Project Develops

The classroom had just one computer connected to the Internet, but Mrs. Knudson could take her class to the school's computer lab when group work was necessary. During this project, students worked on the lab computers in pairs and took notes they would use in their discussions.

After the initial information-gathering phase, students continued the discussion back in the classroom. Because the students sat at tables rather than individual desks, each table of three to four students formed a convenient discussion group. The course of discussions was unpredictable.

Mrs. Knudson listened to each group, asked questions, and answered some of the students' questions. When the students puzzled over scientific names, she reviewed general strategies for dealing with unfamiliar words. One group attempting to estimate food costs wanted to know how large a teaspoon was. Students at each table were asked to write out their group's recommendation before the entire class discussed the issue. Figure 4.3 illustrates the recommendation of one table of students.

**FIGURE 4.3** The classroom pet project: the recommendations of one group of students after their web research and discussion.

BEST PET by Table 3
We recomend the Budgie because it costs 10 dollar to 20 dollars.
They eat green vegtables. And they eat 2-3 teespons of seeds a day.
They need a cage.
The budgie is in the bird family.

### An Authentic Activity

You can see from Mrs. Knudson's example that carefully prepared web projects can serve as excellent, authentic learning activities even for very young students. We make frequent references to authentic tasks throughout this book and provide an extended discussion in Chapter 2 (p. 49).

In the case of Mrs. Knudson's class, the students learned about various animals, not just to store the information, but to accomplish a meaningful task. Each group needed to make a good case for a certain class pet in the hope of persuading classmates to agree.

## USING A BROWSER EFFICIENTLY

Mrs. Knudson's scaffolding of her classroom web project helped keep her students from getting "lost" or wasting their time online. Another way of reducing potential problems is for teachers and students alike to become familiar with additional tools and strategies for browser use. In this part of the chapter you will learn about browser bookmarks, search engines, and good search techniques that greatly increase the efficiency of the Web as a tool for inquiry.

### USING BOOKMARK OPTIONS TO INCREASE PRODUCTIVITY

When anyone is in the early stages of using the Web to solve an inquiry problem, there seems to be an exploratory phase. Various sites are examined briefly in search of information resources that most directly address the problem. Some sites are rejected, and some are identified as candidates for further study. The question is how to remember those sites you would like to visit again.

*Bookmarks and favorites*

Most experienced web users would suggest that you use the browser to save links to the useful sites as **bookmarks** (the term used by Netscape Navigator or Communicator) or **favorites** (the term used by Microsoft's Internet Explorer). By clicking on a bookmark, you can send the browser directly to that site, without typing in the site's long URL. Once you and your students begin using bookmarks, you will likely find them to be indispensable.

However, there are more and less efficient ways of using bookmarks. As you locate more and more valuable web sites, you will realize that a long list of site titles—which is what a raw list of bookmarks offers—is not exactly the best guide for research. Such a list is time consuming to search and has few contextual cues to aid you in interpreting the site titles. Fortunately, browsers offer other features that allow you to use bookmarks in a more productive manner.

Our brief discussion of these features will focus on the Netscape browser, but similar features are available within Internet Explorer. Each browser—and often each version of a browser—implements features in slightly different ways, so you will likely have to do some exploration on your own to become adept.

## Accessing the Bookmarks

In Netscape, the bookmark list and the mechanisms for modifying the list are separated. The bookmark list is available directly from the menu bar. This menu bar option allows you two functions: (a) selecting a bookmark, which returns you to the web site associated with the bookmark; and (b) selecting Add Bookmark, which creates a new bookmark for the site currently displayed by the browser.

*Editing bookmarks*

The advanced features for organizing and customizing your bookmarks are available within the Edit Bookmarks window. To open this window, select the Bookmarks option available from the Communicator menu (in earlier versions of Netscape, the Bookmarks option appeared under the Window menu). Actions taken within this window modify how the bookmarks appear within the bookmark list and also allow you to use bookmarks in ways that do not involve the list.

How can you use the Edit Bookmarks window to increase productivity for yourself and your students? The following sections explain several options.

*Customizing a bookmark title*

***Making bookmarks more informative.*** One of the long-term problems in working with bookmarks is interpreting the bookmark titles. The original bookmark takes on the title that the author has attached to the web site. But web authors sometimes fail to title their web pages, or they may provide a very generic name (such as "Home Page") that has little value when you see it on your bookmark list. The Get Info selection under the Edit menu allows the user to customize the bookmark title, so that you can replace the title provided by the author with a phrase you find more personally meaningful. This option also allows you to enter a description of the web site.

*Adding descriptive information*

The descriptive information you can enter provides one seldom-used advantage. "Find in Bookmarks" is a search function available from the Edit menu. This feature allows users to search bookmark titles and descriptions for a particular word. This can be a valuable tool to any teacher who has stored hundreds or thousands of bookmarks and now wants to locate the sites related to a particular topic. With some experience, you can learn to add descriptors based on your personal needs. For example, if you like to keep track of interesting lesson plans you find on web pages, you might begin to label pages with descriptors such as "Ecology Lesson Plan," "Cell Lesson Plan," or "Mitosis Lesson Plan." Searching for those terms would then lead you to all the bookmarks relating to the subject.

***Organizing bookmarks: Simple techniques.*** Browser users quickly find that a long, random list of bookmarks is difficult to use. One of the easiest ways to make a list more useful is to order the list by topic.

*Moving bookmarks*

When you add a new bookmark, it appears at the bottom of the list, but you can then move it. In the Edit Bookmarks window, you can simply drag a bookmark from one location to another. If you want, you can also "cut" a bookmark, select a different position in the list, and then "paste" the bookmark into that new position. In addition, browsers allow you to add *separators* (horizontal lines) to the bookmark list. The separators provide a visual break between categories of bookmarks.

*Setting up a filing system*

***Organizing bookmarks: Advanced techniques.*** With a large number of bookmarks, more powerful methods are required to provide adequate organization. Browsers allow the creation of a hierarchical filing system based on the concept of folders. Each folder can be assigned a title, and folders can be nested within other folders. Once you create a folder system, you can move bookmarks into the appropriate folders. In fact, since bookmarks can be duplicated, you can place the same one in several folders.

*An example of bookmarks organized by subject*

When this folder system is accessed from the Bookmarks menu, the hierarchical system shows up as a system of submenus. Figure 4.4 displays part of our own bookmark list. Part of this list organizes some of the online references we have been using in writing this book. We have labeled the top level of our hierarchy to identify chapters of the book. The next level represents major chapter topics (such as browsers and searching), and at the bottom level are the titles of web sites. The site titles you see here are the names of web search services, some of which are discussed later in this chapter. The multiple

**FIGURE 4.4** Part of a bookmark hierarchy.

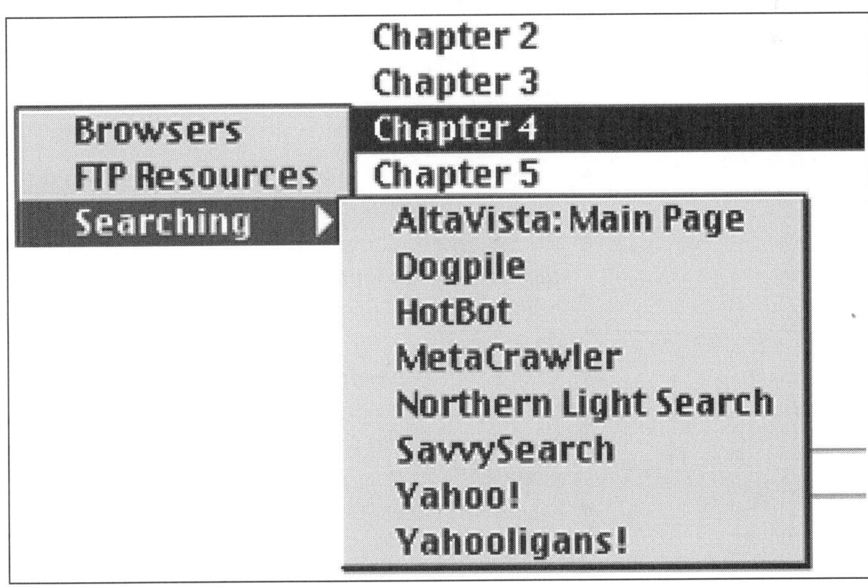

levels of the hierarchy become visible when each higher level is selected. That is, selecting Chapter 4 reveals the level containing Browsers, FTP Resources, and Searching; then selecting Searching reveals the list of search services.

*Copying bookmark files*

***Exporting bookmarks.*** Once you have spent time creating an organized system of bookmarks, you can make a copy of it. One of the most basic reasons for making a backup copy is to safeguard against some type of computer problem. Backup systems are always important when working with technology. Another reason—a very important one for teachers—is to transfer your bookmark collection to another machine or to make the bookmarks available to another person.

The Save As selection under the File menu will save the entire bookmark collection, including your bookmark descriptions, as an HTML file. (The original bookmark collection is actually stored on your computer as Bookmarks.html, and you can search for this file if you are curious.) The new file you create can be stored on a floppy disk, which you can put away for safekeeping or pass on to another person.

To add such a file of bookmarks to an existing set, select Import from the File menu. The Import command allows two bookmark lists to be merged.

## HINTS FOR PREPARING BOOKMARKS FOR STUDENT USE

Students should learn to use bookmarks themselves as an aid to their Internet research. However, we do not expect that most students will learn to apply *all* the techniques we have just described. You can assist your students with the basic bookmark functions. Beyond that, here are some suggestions to make their time (and yours) more productive:

*Ways to help your students get the most from bookmarks*

### *Useful Tips*

- After students have worked on projects, you may sometimes find it useful to clean up and reorganize the bookmark list.
- Bookmark lists targeted to specific content-area topics can be a valuable resource for students. That is, you can set up folders labeled with a topic-relevant name, and you can annotate the list with topic-appropriate descriptions.
- Using the Save As feature, you can distribute a topic-specific bookmark list to more than one student user.
- You can also post your bookmarks list as a web page, as discussed in Chapter 5.
- When multiple students need to save personal bookmarks on the same computer, see the techniques described in "Focus: Personal Bookmark Lists for Students."

*Focus*

## Personal Bookmark Lists for Students

How can students set up their own personal bookmarks when computers are shared by several students and when individual students often use several different computers over the course of a project? Ordinary browser software is not particularly well adapted to these situations. But here are some potential solutions:

### Solution 1: A Separate Folder for Each Student

You can create a specific bookmark folder for each student and label it with the student's name. Then the student can use that folder to store his or her personal bookmarks.

*Problems*: This approach provides no security. In a particular student's folder, other students may purposely or accidentally add or delete bookmarks. Also, this solution is not mobile; the student would have to complete all his or her work on a specific computer.

### Solution 2: Communicator User Profile Manager

Netscape Communicator comes with a program called User Profile Manager, which allows independent profiles for multiple users. This program creates independent bookmark lists and other useful features such as isolated storage of e-mail messages. When Communicator is launched, the names associated with the multiple profiles are displayed, and the user selects the appropriate option.

*Problems:* This approach, like the first, provides no security. There is no password or other device to prevent a user from using the wrong profile. This solution is also not mobile, so the student would have to complete all work on a specific computer.

### Solution 3: Multiple Bookmark Files

Netscape Communicator can create and save multiple bookmark files, which offers a better solution than either of our first two options. Here is a step-by-step description of the process:

- Under the Communicator menu, select the Bookmarks option. This step will open a window containing the existing bookmarks.
- Choose Select All and then Clear from the Edit menu. This combination of commands will remove all existing bookmarks. (If you have many existing bookmarks this probably sounds very scary. We would certainly use Save As first to make a backup. The original bookmarks continue to exist as a file called Bookmarks.html, which is automatically reloaded when you next launch Communicator. However, it always pays to play it safe.)
- Use Save As to create an empty bookmark file. Label this new file with the name of an individual student. Repeat this step until you have a file for each student—Sam, Sally, and so on.

Here is how students would manage their personal bookmark collections:

- After starting Communicator, a student would select Bookmarks from the Communicator menu. This would display the present (default) bookmarks and also open up bookmark menu options.

- The student would then use the command Open Bookmarks File under the File menu to open his or her personal bookmark file.
- Then, when the student uses the browser and adds bookmarks, they will appear in that student's personal bookmark file.

This is the most powerful and flexible solution among those we have listed. The personal bookmark file can be secured on a personal disk and moved from computer to computer as necessary. The most likely problem is that students may have some trouble learning how to make the transition from the default bookmarks to their personal bookmark files.✱

## LOCATING INFORMATION ON THE WEB: BROWSING VERSUS SEARCHING

Before the Web can be a useful resource, teachers and students must become familiar with the tools for locating information within the Web's vastness. Online services offer web users two basic approaches to locating resources: browsing and searching.

*What is browsing?*

The first approach, *browsing,* is based on a web index or web directory consisting of a hierarchical system of subject headings and subheadings. As you move down through this hierarchical system, you reach a level at which links to specific web sites are provided. The links have terse but descriptive titles and are sometimes accompanied by a sentence of additional information. This system is great when you are exploring a topic and trying to gain an understanding of its ramifications.

*What is a search engine?*

The second basic approach to locating web information is based on the use of a **search engine,** an online database that contains information about a large number of web sites. A search engine accepts a user's request or **query** and searches through its body of stored information to identify potentially useful web sites. Then a list of these web site addresses and brief content descriptions are returned to the user. Searching is most useful when you begin with a specific goal in mind and generate a query targeted fairly precisely to this goal.

Online services cannot be neatly divided into those offering browsing and those offering search engines. Because the online services are competing to attract as many users as possible, many commercial sites now offer a combination of methods. Let's look at some examples, both for browsing and for searching.

## AN EXAMPLE OF BROWSING

For a demonstration of how you might browse a directory to solve an information problem, we can use Yahoo!, one of the most popular web directories. Assume you want to research the topic you are now reading about; that is, locating information on the Web.

The Yahoo! home page offers fourteen basic subject categories. These initial categories are very broad: "Health," "Science," "Society & Culture," and so on. For our topic, the category "Computers and the Internet" is obviously the most relevant. This link leads us to a new page containing approximately thirty new subject headings. Several subject headings at this level seem potentially useful: "Information," "Internet," "World Wide Web." As this example shows, it is sometimes difficult to know which subject to select. You will sometimes have to try several different options. Let's assume we choose the category "World Wide Web."

*Moving through a hierarchy of subjects*

Selecting this link brings us to a list of thirty new subject headings. Among them is the promising topic "Searching the Web." Selecting this subject reveals three subheadings: "How to Search the Web," "Indices to Web," and "Search Engines." Each of these options finally produces a long list of links to individual web pages. The links are the titles from the web pages, such as "How to Search the World Wide Web: A Tutorial for Beginners and Non-Experts" (Habib & Balliot, 1998). Sometimes an additional sentence is added to provide a better hint about the site's contents. Sometimes, though, the title is not very helpful, and you have to take a look to see if the site will be useful.

Our browsing has taken us through four levels of subject headings, and we have ended up with three groups of links to web pages. To put what we have accomplished into perspective, Yahoo! is subdivided into approximately 25,000 categories that link to slightly over 500,000 web sites. The procedure we described did not require a great deal of time, and it located a large number of informative web sites. As you can see, browsing in a well-organized system can be quite productive, and we encourage you to try the process on your own.

The web address for Yahoo! as well as those for the search services described in the following section, is listed in "Resources to Expand Your Knowledge Base" at the end of the chapter.

## TYPES OF SEARCH SERVICES

There are many search engines bidding for your attention. Although a few experimental ones are maintained by universities as part of research projects, most are commercial. This does not mean that you have to pay to use them, though. As soon as you connect to a commercial search engine, you will realize that it is supported by advertising dollars. You have to maneuver around the colorful product displays to get your work done!

The major services all offer some form of searchable database, but they differ in how sites are added to the database and what information about each site is stored in the database:

*Basic differences among search engines*

- *Adding sites.* New servers and new web pages may become known to the online service through nominations received from the public (mostly from people who are themselves page authors). Alternatively, the service can identify new sites by using a software *robot* (also called a *bot, spider,* or *crawler*) that continually roams the Internet looking for new servers and new pages.

- *Generating information about sites.* The information stored in the database can be generated by web librarians—people who examine web documents and classify material they feel might be useful. Or, as an alternative, the service can use indexing software that automatically examines designated parts of web pages and identifies keywords. Some indexing software generates keywords by examining a limited amount of information, such as the page title and the first hundred words of text. Other indexing software reads and processes *all* of the text found in each web page.

*Pros and cons of different indexing methods*

The indexing process is especially important, and it accounts for some noticeable differences among the search services. For example, computerized indexing methods are less expensive than web librarians and generate larger databases. Also, indexing methods that use the entire web page will link more descriptive terms with each web page. Therefore, searching with a service that has built its database from computerized searches of entire web pages tends to generate a longer list of sites to examine. In some cases this may be an advantage. In other cases, however, you may find it much more useful to examine a list of 10 quality sites rather than a list of 100 sites that vary greatly in quality.

Because of such differences among search services, you will want to become familiar with several of them. The following sections offer some guidance:

### Search Engine and Directory Combinations

*Library-style catalogs*

Several search services are based on a cataloging system very much like that maintained by conventional libraries. Human editors examine web material and organize content within what they consider to be a useful classification system. You can browse the classification system or search the catalogued material using key terms.

*Combining browsing and searching*

You can also use a combination of browsing and searching to improve the quality of your search. The combination of browsing and searching is a unique advantage of this type of service. For example, assume you want to learn more about the type of spider that wanders about the web searching for new web pages. If you were to connect to Yahoo! and search for "spider" from the home page, you would find about 600 sites, including pages that address a cartoon character, a type of car, and eight-legged arthropods, as well as the Internet search robot. However, if you first select the Yahoo! subject heading "Computers and Internet" and then perform the same search, the return would be approximately 25 links, nearly all of which are appropriate to your topic of interest.

This type of search system provides access to less of the Web than do search services that rely on a computer-generated database, but it might be argued that their overall quality of material is a little higher. Examples of this type of search service include Yahoo! and Magellan.

## Index Search Engines

Index search engines rely on a computer-generated index of the contents of web sites. Thankfully, the techniques used are more sophisticated than a simple list of all the web pages containing a specific word. Some form of proprietary artificial intelligence system is used to determine which web pages are most relevant to your query. For example, search engines that index entire web pages use variables such as how many times keywords are mentioned in an article and how close to the top of a document a keyword appears. When the search engine responds to your query with a list of sites, the ones deemed most relevant appear at the top of the list.

*Index search engines: huge databases*

Index search engines tend to provide access to huge numbers of web pages. HotBot, the search engine with perhaps the largest database at the time this text was written, found over 200,000 sites for the search term "spider." Other examples of this type of search service are AltaVista and Northern Light.

## Meta-index Searches

*Combining results from several search engines*

Some search tools actually activate and cross-reference the results from several search engines. These meta-index searches take a little longer because various individual searches must be initiated, the results integrated, and duplicates eliminated. However, a meta-index search does not accumulate *all* the sites generated by all of the search engines. To keep things more manageable, the search tool takes only the top ten to fifty sites generated by each search engine.

You might suppose a meta-index search would always be the most productive. However, as you'll see later in this chapter, search engines offer certain advanced search methods that can help you in many situations, and these methods differ from one engine to another. For this reason, meta-index search tools can use only basic search procedures, consisting of combinations of keywords. Examples of this type of search service include MetaCrawler and SavvySearch.

## Which Type of Search Engine Should I Use?

Every experienced user of the Web seems to have an opinion about which search engine is most useful. From time to time, articles in computer magazines compare the different search engines on a standard set of search tasks. Despite authors' recommendations based on these analyses, examination of the actual search data shows that search engine effectiveness differs between assignments. If anything, reading such articles has caused us to try different search engines than we might normally employ.

We would suggest that you, too, take the time to explore several search

*Value of your own experience*

engines, just to gain some personal familiarity and make your own decisions. At the end of the chapter, we provide the addresses for the search tools we have mentioned. Whenever you feel the results from your favorite search engine are disappointing, it is worth trying both a different engine and a different combination of search terms.

Many people wonder just how much of the Web the index search engines actually cover. One recent investigation (Lawrence & Giles, 1998) estimated that the best search engine had catalogued only about one-third of the total number of web pages. The entire group of six engines used in the study generated 3.5 times as many pages as the single best search engine. So, if a comprehensive search is your goal, it may be necessary to use several search engines or a metasearch engine.

## CONDUCTING A SEARCH

Web search engines usually present users with a very simple and easy-to-use interface. An unfortunate consequence is that many users never really learn to take advantage of the powerful search features that are available. It is so easy just to type something into the little text field, click the Submit button, and see what you get. For serious research, however, it is important to learn at least some of the rules that govern searches.

### Narrowing a Search with Quotation Marks

*Problems of too broad a search*

Let's use the search requested in Figure 4.5 as an example. When we submitted this request for information on Civil War battles, we generated more than 600,000 sites—far too large a number for us to examine productively. But when we changed the request to "civil war battles" (that is, with the phrase en-

**FIGURE 4.5** The AltaVista search page, showing a query about Civil War battles.

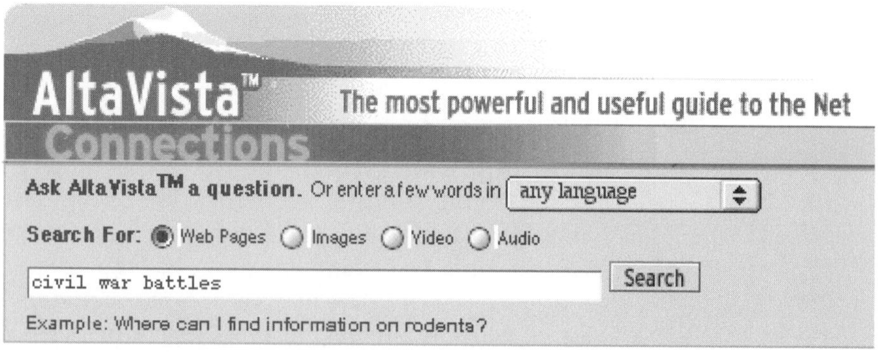

Reproduced with the permission of AltaVista. AltaVista and the AltaVista logo are trademarks of AltaVista Company.

closed in quotations), the search generated slightly more than 1,300 entries, still a large number but much more manageable.

Why did this happen? The search engine interpreted our two requests in very different ways:

*Comparing two search queries*

1. In the first situation, the search process located all web pages containing the word *civil,* the word *war,* or the word *battles.* Thus we might have found pages about battles between Athenians and Spartans, or between spiders and wasps.
2. In the second situation, the search engine found only those pages containing the entire phrase *civil war battles.*

Actually, the situation is a little more complicated. Because the search engine we used, AltaVista, lists documents containing several of the targeted terms before documents containing fewer of the terms, some of the links near the tops of the two lists were similar. Still, the difference between 1,300 and 600,000 was well worth the effort of typing in quotation marks.

## Boolean Searches

*Using Boolean operators*

Search engines are usually capable of conducting what are called **Boolean searches.** You probably learned the basics of Boolean logic in a high school math class. Boolean operators, such as AND, NOT, and OR, define ways in which sets are combined. Let's see what you remember. What could we accomplish with the following search request?

bat NOT baseball NOT computer

The answer is that we would generate a list of web resources about bats—the furry, flying kind.

In this example, you can probably guess the purpose of "NOT baseball." This excludes the large number of web pages containing information about baseball players who *bat* right- or left-handed, pages devoted to collecting baseball *bats*, and other pages focused on the game of baseball. The request to exclude pages about computers may stump you, but it has a similar explanation. Some computers utilize *bat files*, which list special instructions the computer is to follow, and various web pages contain information about such files. At any rate, excluding web pages about baseball and computers generates a list of resources containing a much higher proportion of sites on the topic we really want to review.

## Using Forms

*Forms that build in special operators*

As the Web evolves, search engines are changing to make it easier for users to conduct more complicated searches. Instead of requiring that users learn Boolean operators, several search engines now offer a form in which you can specify certain search techniques. After entering your keywords in a text field, you choose from menus the operators to be applied to these words, as shown

Focus

## Tips for Successful Searches

Here are some suggestions that should help you conduct more powerful searches with most search engines. To learn the unique techniques that apply with a particular search engine, look for a Help link somewhere on the search engine home page.

- *Use quotation marks when searching for a multiword phrase.* Quotation marks tell the search engine to return only those sites containing all the target words in the exact order—for instance, "acceptable use policy" but not "policy use" or "acceptable policy."
- *Use Boolean operators to require certain combinations of words.* The operator AND (in capitals) or the plus sign (+) will produce pages containing more than one targeted word. For instance, to find pages on spider monkeys, you could link the word *spider* and the word *monkey* with an AND or with a plus sign:

  spider AND monkey

  spider +monkey

- (In the second instance, there is a space before the +, but no space between the + and the second word.)

  Similarly, using OR between search terms will return documents containing at least one of the words: monkey OR ape. Using AND NOT or the minus sign (–) will locate documents containing one word but not the other:

  spider AND NOT monkey

  spider–monkey.

- You can create more complicated expressions by using parentheses with the Boolean operators. For example, a search for

  basketball AND (bulls OR jazz)

- should produce web sites about either of two basketball teams, the Chicago Bulls or the Utah Jazz.
- *Use a capital letter only when you really want words that contain a capital letter.* A lowercase request will find both lower- and uppercase matches. An uppercase request will find *only* uppercase matches:

  mark → mark or Mark

  Mark → Mark

  maRK→ (no matches at all!)

- *Take advantage of HTML tags to locate certain kinds of material.* You can use some HTML tags to search for words contained within the tags. This works with the tags "image," "title," and "text." You join the full word for the tag and the target word with a colon. The most useful application of this tip is probably in searching for images. For instance, by typing *image:frog,* you tell the search engine to look for pages that contain images labeled "frog." The databases generated by some search services do store the names of image files.✷

**FIGURE 4.6** Some of the search options available from the HotBot advanced form.

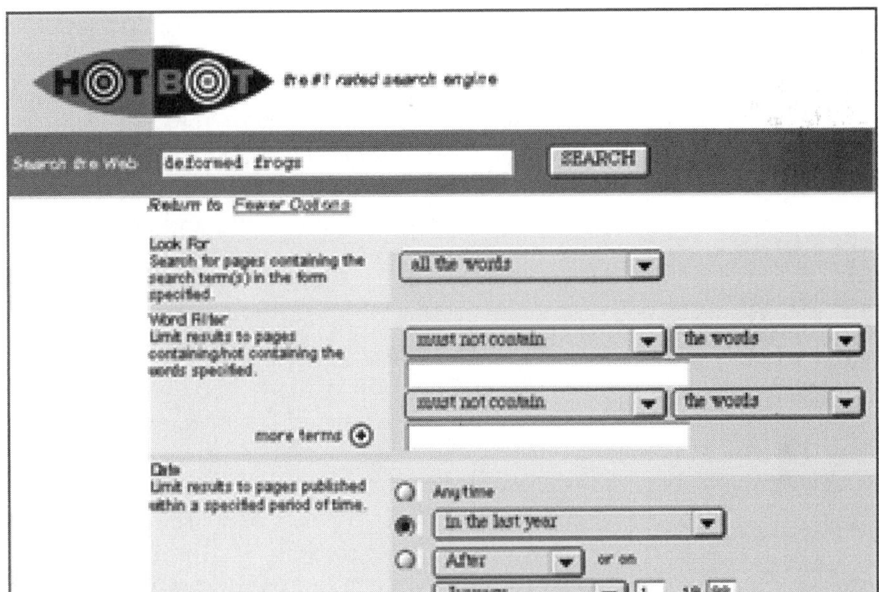




in Figure 4.6. Typical choices include "all the words," "any of the words," "exact phrase," "must contain," and "must not contain"—terms that can be understood without a lot of training.

HotBot, the search engine displayed in Figure 4.6, also allows users to define a search based on publication date, location of the server (by country or type of organization), and how deep within the web site the search is to be conducted. For example, on the topic of deformed frogs, a search of this type produced a list of eighteen web pages established within the past twelve months on K–12 servers in the state of Minnesota. Learning to apply techniques of this type can greatly improve the efficiency of your searches.

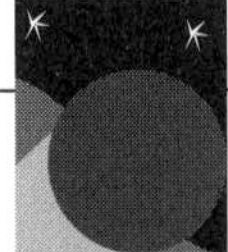

## ACCESSING OTHER FORMS OF INTERNET INFORMATION

Although accessing the World Wide Web with a standard browser is by far the most widely used method of obtaining information over the Internet, some other methods also have significant educational applications. In this section we will look at two of them: FTP and streaming audio/video.

## ACCESS TO FILES: USING FTP

Various commercial, public, and government institutions maintain archives of files that users can download to their personal computers. These files can be text documents, graphic images, sounds, or programs. If the archive has been developed specifically for educators or students, the files might be lesson plans for hands-on science activities, information about the latest shuttle mission, the text of *Moby Dick,* pictures from the Smithsonian, pictures of the presidents, or a virus protection program for your school computers.

It is important to understand and appreciate the various commitments individuals have made to provide these resources. One term with which you should be familiar is *shareware.*

*Shareware ≠ freeware!*

▶ ***Shareware*** *products are distributed free for evaluation, but the author has copyrighted the material and expects to receive payment if use extends beyond the initial evaluation.*

Some users of commercial services assume that the fees they pay for the service somehow cover the cost of shareware products they have downloaded. This is not the case; software and other resources designated as shareware come with the expectation that the author will eventually receive some compensation. You will learn more about shareware and other copyright issues in Chapter 9.

*Importance of your contributions*

It is also important for teachers to understand that file transfers are not a one-way process. Some resources, such as collections of lesson plans, would be greatly enhanced if more teachers took the time to contribute their best ideas. For certain archives, too, students' work is a welcome addition. Thus, when you download a file from such a source, you should think about ways you might contribute to maintaining or expanding that valuable resource.

*FTP*

The process of transferring files over the Internet is relatively simple once a user has gained access and knows a bit about establishing an active network connection. The transfer of a file to or from the remote computer is accomplished using **File Transfer Protocol (FTP).** The following demonstration illustrates how a picture from a collection generated by the Smithsonian Institution is transferred from the archives maintained by Apple Computer.

### An FTP Example

Most of the machines that make files available on a large-scale basis are large computers running on the UNIX operating system. To transfer a file from the UNIX machine to your desktop machine used to require that you know UNIX commands. Now, software has been developed to execute these procedures automatically. Often this can be done using a web browser. Our example, though, uses a separate program called Fetch.

Often you will hear about valuable downloadable files from magazines or

**FIGURE 4.7** Connecting to a remote host with Fetch.

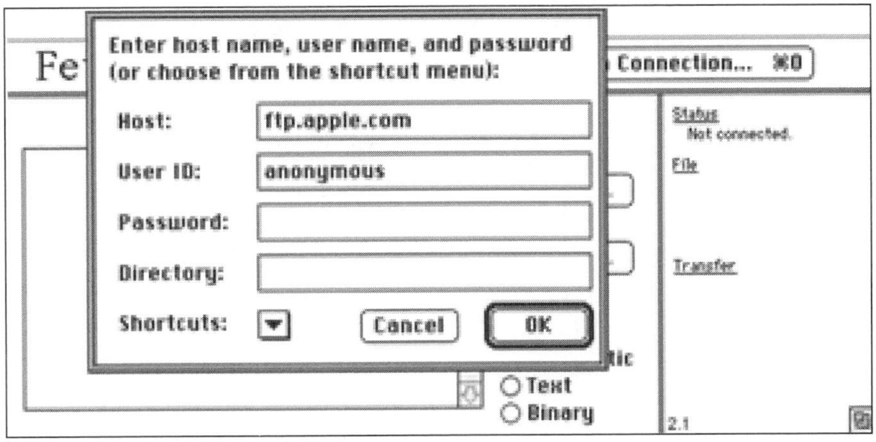

Reprinted by permission of the Trustees of Dartmouth College.

*Using Fetch to download a photo*

by e-mail. Let's assume that a colleague has told us by e-mail that interesting Smithsonian photos are available from Apple Computer's FTP site. To connect to the remote computer, we launch the Fetch program and enter the remote computer's address (in this case ftp.apple.com), as shown in Figure 4.7.

*Your password, please*

Like many sites allowing all interested users to access file archives, this site allows the user to log on using the name ANONYMOUS. Some sites will then expect a password (ftp.apple.com does not). This may seem a bit strange, if the files are available to everyone. But the desired password for anonymous logons is typically the user's e-mail address. This is a courtesy that allows the host site to gather data on how many different users take advantage of the services.

Now what? The next step is to see what files are available. The server stores files in a hierarchical system of directories. A directory is represented within Fetch as a folder, as Figure 4.8 illustrates. So what we have are folders stored within folders. We can distinguish individual files (what we are after) because they are not accompanied by the folder icon (the small picture of a folder), and they often have endings like .txt (a text file) or .bin (a binary file such as a program or picture).

At this point we need to know which directory we want. Our e-mail source has told us that the Smithsonian photographs are in alug/Smith/jpeg. This tells us that we should open the alug subdirectory, then the Smith (an abbreviation for Smithsonian) subdirectory, and finally the jpeg subdirectory. To open each directory, we double-click on the appropriate folder.

*File formats: ASCII versus binary*

As you know, files can be stored in various formats. The Internet transfers files in either **ASCII** or **binary** mode. Transferring a file as ASCII means that we will receive plain text, with no special attributes or images. The binary mode, in contrast, transfers the electronic information in 1's and 0's, exactly as it is stored

**FIGURE 4.8** Moving through a server's directories with Fetch.

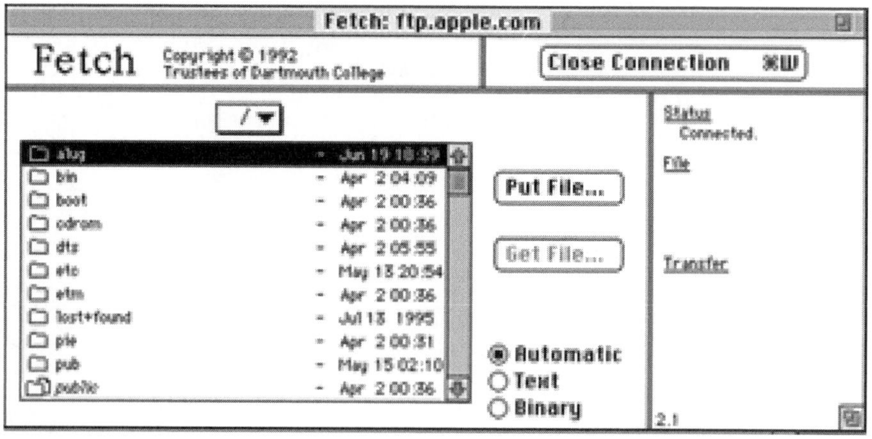

Reprinted by permission of the Trustees of Dartmouth College.

on the host computer. If the transfer mode is not consistent with the format in which the file has been stored, the file we receive will be unusable. The file format is one of those small details that is easy to forget, and it can easily create consequences that confuse novice users. Teachers or students with limited computer experience may need to seek a local resource person's assistance.

In our example, however, the format in which the photographs are stored is easy to determine because of the suffix attached to the file name. The ".bin" suffix indicates that the file is binary. Fetch, the software we are using, automatically recognizes the file type and makes the necessary preparations for a file transfer.

*The transfer completed*

Say we are especially interested in a picture of a gorilla for a project on African primates. To transfer the picture of a gorilla, we select the filename gorila.jpeg.bin and then click on the Get button. The results can be quite satisfying. Figure 4.9 shows an incredible image a student might use in a classroom report.

## STREAMING AUDIO AND VIDEO

At first, **streaming** audio and video was more a curiosity than a useful resource. As it develops, however, it may become one of the "killer apps" we described at the beginning of this chapter.

### Current Formats

The present applications of streaming audio and video allow fairly good-quality audio and poor-quality video to be delivered over the Internet. The main advantage of streaming technologies over more conventional applications of audio and video (such as educational programs on public television)

**FIGURE 4.9** The image file gorila.jpg.bin, downloaded with Fetch.

*Access on demand*

is that they can be accessed on demand. That is, a "program" can be accessed whenever a viewer/listener is interested, and the server can archive many programs indefinitely. The opportunity to have students connect at any time and to access a wide variety of useful information is a very appealing prospect.

There are presently several streaming formats (for example, RealAudio and QuickTime) available on the Internet. The "player" from RealNetworks is displayed in Figure 4.10. Note the small image size; this is used reduce the amount of data that must be sent over the Internet, an accommodation for the presently available transfer speeds.

## Educational Applications

*Use in distance education*

How is streaming technology presently being used to deliver instructional content? So far, classroom applications are largely experimental. Distance education programs are using streaming technologies to deliver minilectures or to add segments of audio or video to static web pages. And although this is not exactly an educational application, educational institutions are using streaming technologies to make live athletic events available to alumni.

**FIGURE 4.10** A screen image generated by RealPlayer.

If you are interested in trying streaming technologies in your own classroom, we would suggest you consider "repurposing" content developed for more general audiences. Here are some examples:

*What you might do with streaming audio or video*

### Classroom Applications of Streaming

- For foreign language instruction, you may want to access radio broadcasts from other countries. More and more are available via the Internet.
- For health topics, the Stanford University Health Library makes available 30- to 60-minute programs.
- A number of science and ecology sites offer streaming transmissions. The program being accessed in Figure 4.10 is a weekly two-and-a-half-minute segment on the North Dakota outdoors.
- There are real-time audio and video feeds associated with special events, such as NASA shuttle missions and various C-SPAN programs.
- For a wide variety of content areas, you may want to monitor the archives of programs such as National Public Radio's "All Things Considered."

You could access individual program segments and use them as background information or discussion starters.

## SUMMARY

◆ The World Wide Web is largely responsible for the surge of interest in the Internet, and it is one reason why schools are investing heavily in technology and Internet access. The quantity of information resources and ready access from classroom computers offer a great potential for using the Web as a tool for inquiry.

◆ The World Wide Web provides online multimedia and hypermedia. Web content qualifies as multimedia because it incorporates several media categories. Because web content and tools allow the user a relatively high degree of control over which information segments will be experienced and the order in which the segments will be presented, the Web also represents a hypermedia environment.

◆ The browser is the software application that provides access to web information as well as tools for navigating within this content, printing segments of the content, and saving information for future use. Teachers and students should learn to use these tools to improve the efficiency of their web explorations. Because hypermedia gives learners considerable control over their own learning experiences, students must take greater responsibility for their learning. Some students can become distracted, following links that take them away from their learning goals. To avoid such problems, it is important for teachers to scaffold students' web experiences. It is also important for students to learn to use browser features that help them get back on track.

◆ Bookmarks are one browser tool that teachers should master. While creating bookmarks is very easy, they may not be useful unless they are organized and annotated. Learning to create and export topic-specific bookmark lists is a useful technique for guiding your students' web exploration.

◆ Learning to locate useful web resources is another essential skill for web-based inquiry. Search services provide opportunities for both browsing and searching. Often it can be useful to use several services. Teachers and students should also try to master a few of the more advanced search techniques that allow targets to be pinpointed more accurately.

◆ FTP is an older but still useful Internet technique for transferring files. Streaming media offer a new and evolving format for sending audio and video over the Internet in real time. Although not as important as the Web, both of these formats have interesting classroom applications.

## REFLECTING ON CHAPTER 4

**Activities**

1. Investigate your browser's interface. Set the default home page to the home page for your college or school and see how that changes what happens when you open the browser. Next, investigate the History command. How long does the browser keep track of the last sites visited? Finally, select Document Source and look at the raw HTML for a web page. Can you figure out any of the codes?

2. Compare the productivity of several web search methods. Submit the same request to a browsing service such as Yahoo! and then to a searching service such as HotBot. What do you notice about the results? How many "hits" did you generate with each service? Did the same pages appear at the top of each list? Could you see any difference in the quality of the resources you generated?

3. Select a content-area topic and generate a bookmark list, complete with annotations appropriate to that topic. Export this list as an HTML file. Make certain you can then open this file using your browser.

## Key Terms

applet *(p. 107)*
ASCII *(p. 127)*
binary *(p. 127)*
bookmark *(p. 113)*
Boolean search *(p. 123)*
browser *(p. 100)*
content window *(p. 100)*
favorites *(p. 113)*
File Transfer Protocol (FTP) *(p. 126)*
form *(p. 108)*
frame *(p. 102)*
helper application *(p. 107)*
home page *(p. 104)*
hypermedia *(p. 99)*
hypertext markup language (HTML) *(p. 106)*
image mapping *(p. 108)*
link *(p. 99)*
multimedia *(p. 99)*
plug-in *(p. 107)*
query *(p. 118)*
search engine *(p. 118)*
shareware *(p. 126)*
streaming *(p. 128)*
Universal Resource Locator (URL) *(p. 103)*

## Resources to Expand Your Knowledge Base

### Books About Using Web Browsers

Books explaining how to operate the popular web browsers are available at nearly any bookstore. Because web browsers are continually being updated and enhanced with new features, we will not list any particular books here. Instead, we suggest you visit a nearby bookstore and see what is available.

### Sites for Downloading Internet Tools

The companies that have developed Internet tools want to make them widely available. Web tools are regularly distributed as part of the assortment of software you get when you purchase a new computer. Once loaded on the computer, this software can be used to download more recent versions.

Even when you are starting from scratch, the home page for a company's web site usually has a clearly identified link that takes you to a web page where you can download the most recent version of a browser or other tool. Here is a list of common web tools and the web sites where you can obtain them:

Internet Explorer (Microsoft): **http://www.microsoft.com/ie/**

Netscape Communicator and Navigator (Netscape):
**http://www.netscape.com/comprod/mirror/client_download.html**

RealPlayer (RealNetworks): **http://www.real.com/products/player/index.html**

### Search Engines

The number of search engines is continually expanding as both commercial and experimental services are added. Here are addresses for the search services mentioned in this chapter:

AltaVista: **http://www.altavista.com/**

HotBot: **http://www.hotbot.com/**

Magellan: **http://www.magellan.excite.com/**

MetaCrawler: **http://www.metacrawler.com/**

Northern Light: **http://www.northernlight.com/**

SavvySearch: **http://guaraldi.cs.colostate.edu:2000/**

Yahoo!: **http://www.yahoo.com/**

Chapter 5

# Integrating the Internet into Inquiry-Based Projects

## ORIENTATION

Building on Chapter 4, which explained the principal Internet inquiry tools, this chapter focuses on ways of incorporating the Internet into authentic problem-solving projects for students. You will learn how the Big Six, a model of information problem-solving skills, can be applied to Internet-related tasks. Then the chapter examines how you as a teacher can develop and structure activities, such as WebQuests, that involve your students with Internet resources.

As you read, look for answers to the following questions:

**FOCUS QUESTIONS**

- What are the differences between instructional resources and primary sources, and what roles do these resources play in a learning environment?
- What information problem-solving processes are emphasized in the Big Six model, and how do these apply to Internet inquiry tasks?
- What guidelines might students use to evaluate the information found on web pages?
- What are the components of a WebQuest? How can you use a WebQuest with your students?

This chapter continues our exploration of how Internet access can provide productive and stimulating opportunities for active learning in your classroom. From the beginning of this book, we have argued that learners are most productive when they take an active role in finding meaning in information. This is true even in such traditional tasks as reading a textbook. Here, we want to develop a related but somewhat different idea:

> *Learning in many contexts requires that we work with information that was not specifically prepared to educate us—at least not in the ways we had in mind.*

*Authentic problems*

This principle clearly holds true in our daily lives, and it is also true for some of the more challenging projects your students may undertake. Solving authentic problems requires that we understand the nature of the problem, identify the type of information that may be relevant, locate that kind of information, and only then begin to interpret the information, evaluate it, and apply it to the problem. This is a complex set of skills, and it is important for students to learn them within the context of meaningful classroom projects.

Later parts of this chapter examine how you can help your students build these skills through structured projects, such as WebQuests, which draw on the vast resources of the World Wide Web. First, however, we look in more detail at the different types of information resources as well as the kinds of skills needed to deal with them.

## INSTRUCTIONAL RESOURCES AND PRIMARY SOURCES

Although there seems to be general agreement that the Internet offers many resources, many educators are uncertain about how to use these resources in their classrooms. One step in reducing this uncertainty might be to relate Internet resources to other common resources used by students.

*"Preprocessed" resources . . .*

We like to use the term ***instructional resources*** for materials that have been "preprocessed" for students. That is, an educational expert such as a classroom teacher or textbook author has identified educational goals, carefully selected the ideas or experiences students should encounter to achieve these goals, organized the content in a useful way, and taken the trouble to explain the content in ways that are likely to fit with the background of students of a particular grade level. The information is presented so that it will build on existing knowledge and move learners forward in a systematic manner. Most likely, too, the materials make judicious use of examples to illustrate the most important issues and to maintain students' interest.

*. . . "raw" information sources . . .*

**Primary sources,** in contrast, are "raw" information sources, not necessarily developed to meet educational needs or even to provide a fair or unbiased treatment of a particular issue. The issue of biased and potentially dangerous sources will be covered in more detail in Chapter 9; for now, it is important to understand that raw information represents a very broad and varied category. Many sources of information we encounter daily fall into this group. Newsmagazine articles (*Newsweek, Time*) and encyclopedia entries would qualify, and so would interviews students might conduct with members of their community. Similarly, most library books—even many of those in school libraries—are not specifically packaged to meet educational goals.

*. . . and the Internet equivalents*

Just like print materials, Internet resources can be classified into these two categories. As the Internet develops, more and more complete instructional units and even entire courses are being delivered online. These are the equivalent of traditional, print-based instructional resources, carefully prepared for student use. On the other hand, online equivalents of encyclopedias and news sources are also becoming more common in school libraries (see "Keeping Current: Subscription Information Services"). Then, of course, there are the millions of free World Wide Web pages and downloadable files. Such raw information sources are typically developed independently of any curriculum standards and often not with the K–12 age group in mind.

*Value of using primary sources*

In our view, in order to develop their inquiry skills, students need more opportunities to work with information in interesting ways. To this end, we think students would benefit from more tasks requiring that they use primary sources rather than prepackaged instructional resources.

▶ *We strongly urge teachers to take advantage of primary sources, both through the Internet and through other media.*

From the perspective of lifelong learning, working with primary sources is extremely important. It is a constant requirement for professionals in any field and for any citizen who chooses to take an active role in community decision making. Our process of formal education needs to prepare students to use such sources of information to make carefully reasoned decisions.

*A continuum of teacher involvement*

Actually, we see primary sources and instructional resources as points along a continuum (Figure 5.1), differentiated in terms of the amount and type of involvement required of the classroom teacher:

- Working with primary resources (at the left side of Figure 5.1) is most demanding in terms of teacher time and creativity. In addition to locating useful information resources, teachers must develop learning activities that are likely to involve students with these resources in ways that are active and productive; then they must guide and evaluate student completion of these activities.
- Further along the continuum, teachers can take advantage of existing instructional resources, as shown by the middle point in Figure 5.1. Here the information sources have already been identified or developed and the activities have been prepared. The teacher can now focus on implementing the activity in the classroom and evaluating student learning.
- At the far right of the continuum is the online tutorial, the online equivalent of a computer-based tutorial. Online tutorials are designed for independent learning with well-integrated information sources, explanatory segments, and evaluation activities. Hence they usually do not require a great deal of time or creativity from the teacher.

Keeping Current

## Subscription Information Services

Online commercial information services are becoming more and more common. These services range from providers offering the online equivalent of a library (full-text versions of many books, magazines, and newspapers) to the online version of a single source such as a major newspaper.

Schools purchase access to such services because of the quantity and selection of materials, the search tools, and the reasonable cost. The quantity of information available is impressive. The resources available from each of the general services will vary, but it is common to have access to the full-text version of hundreds of magazines and newspapers, maps, and photo collections. Some sites provide access to newswire services. The resources are selected to meet the information needs of educational institutions, and the search features give students important aids in finding the information they need. Although schools must pay for access, the cost is typically less than that of subscribing to several newspapers and magazines.

You can find a list of several commercial services and related web addresses in "Resources to Expand Your Knowledge Base" at the end of this chapter. The web sites allow you a glimpse of the information sources that are available to subscribers.✱

Students can learn by working with any of the resources along this continuum and would probably benefit from a variety of experiences. This chapter deals mostly with the classroom use of primary sources and instructional resources. But online tutorials—self-contained learning experiences—are an option you may see more frequently in coming years.

*Information addiction?*

On the Internet, primary sources present a particular challenge because they come at us in a deluge, and the amount of information available is increasing at an ever-accelerating rate. Some critics claim that our society has become addicted to information. Our stress levels rise because resources that seem important are either constantly bombarding our senses or would be very easy to access (Murray, 1998). Self-help authors are now attempting to help professionals deal with this stress by suggesting techniques for managing job-related information (Shenk, 1997).

*Efficiency requires structure*

Given this information glut, on the Internet and elsewhere, we must address the issue of efficiency if we want students to work with primary sources. Time is always in short supply in educational settings, and any activities we propose must impose reasonable expectations on both teachers and students. Of course, when students are given the opportunity to work with raw online resources, it is important to structure their experiences and guide their interaction with the information so that they grasp the important underlying principles. Students need to be prepared to approach such sources carefully

**FIGURE 5.1** A continuum of Internet resources for learning.

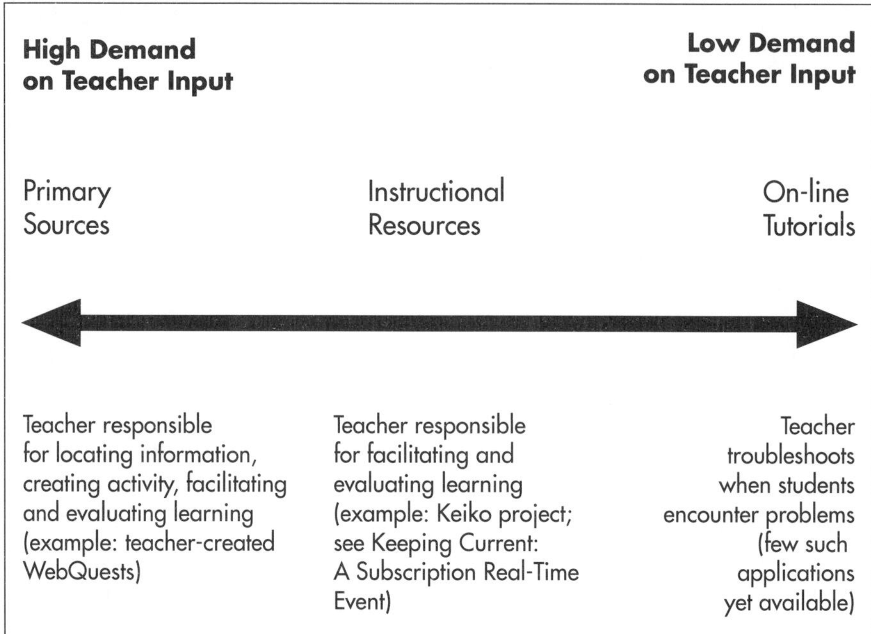


and to take personal responsibility for putting the information into a broader perspective. Later in this chapter we focus on web projects that offer structured problem-solving tasks in formats that are practical for teachers and students alike.

## THE BIG SIX: SKILLS FOR INFORMATION PROBLEM SOLVING

Besides understanding the types of information your students will encounter, you also need to understand the skills students will need to locate, interpret, and apply this information to authentic inquiry tasks. Some researchers have identified six such skills, and these have come to be known as the Big Six.

*A set of specific skills*

The **Big Six** is a clearly articulated and interrelated set of skills for solving information problems. Because of their concreteness, these skills provide an especially useful way of conceptualizing—and teaching—the skills necessary to use the Internet as a tool for inquiry. The individual skills comprising this approach enable a learner to identify the nature of an information problem; locate, process, organize, and apply information resources to the solution; and finally, evaluate the success of this solution (Eisenberg & Berkowitz, 1990).

At one time, such information problem-solving skills might have been described as "library skills." While interest in the Big Six has existed among school professionals for some years, library media specialists have probably been most aware of this approach and have taken the greatest responsibility for actively teaching such skills to students.

*Application to "real life"*

The originators of the Big Six have always argued that many life tasks require these skills. Problems such as figuring out how to get from one location to another using the subway system in a strange city or even determining which movie you might find most enjoyable on a Saturday evening are commonly solved through the acquisition and processing of information. To see why the Big Six is such a useful model, let's look in more detail at the skills it includes.

## WHAT ARE THE BIG SIX?

The following sections offer a brief summary of the Big Six. Each of the six skill stages involves specific information-processing skills. Under ideal circumstances, a problem solver would move through the stages in order. In practice, difficulty in completing the tasks at one level may reveal the inadequacy of a decision or process at an earlier stage, in which case the most productive thing to do is to cycle back.

*Skill stage #1*

### Task Definition

The initial information problem-solving skill is to recognize that you are in need of information and then to define what it is you need to know. In the school environment, recognizing you are in need of information is usually not a problem. You are typically given an assignment, and it is obvious that you are to take some action. A more likely difficulty is determining what information need the assignment has created. Students sometimes tend to launch prematurely into a project before they have taken the time to clarify exactly what it is they are searching for.

*Skill stage #2*

### Information Seeking

This is sometimes described as the brainstorming stage. What resources might provide information that will be useful? What is the likelihood that each of these resources will be available and current, and will provide unbiased and accurate information? It is important to recognize that different resources may be suited to different types of information problems. The encyclopedia is not the solution to every classroom assignment, nor is the Internet. The goal of this stage is to identify what seem to be the most practical and appropriate resources.

## Pat Henry, Middle-School Librarian

*Has the Internet changed how you see your role?*

The Internet has added another dimension. There is more volume—sometimes even too much. There is access to more current resources—many books are soon dated. I feel the Internet will continue to grow in importance in schools. And, as we continue to invest money in equipment and access, there will also be more pressure to learn to use the Internet more effectively.

*What new skills do you think are important?*

It seems easy for nearly anyone to put an Internet site together, so students can run into almost anything. I was working with students looking up information on Nazi Germany for a history project, and we ended up looking at skinhead propaganda. We talk to the students and to the teachers about the need to understand that some sites are going to be controversial. It can be a problem when students accept what they find too easily. However, getting students to think more carefully about the information they find is also an opportunity—for instance, we tend to accept things we read in the newspaper too easily. Students need to think critically about what they read, to compare sources before they reach conclusions, and to cite sources for the information they use. I don't think there will ever be a library without books, but we will need to learn to use all kinds of sources.

*You have access to commercial document services and to the "free" Internet. Do you have a preference?*

I think it is great to have access to both sources and would not want to give up either. The commercial services are better defined and more dependable. The money is well spent because we gain access to things we could not afford to purchase as paper sources. There is no way we could keep daily newspapers from around the country. The free Internet provides a sense of adventure, and that is also very important for learning. Quality varies a great deal, but there are many wonderful sites.

*Should students do their own Internet searches, or should teachers select sites they want students to visit?*

It depends on the purpose. Students do need to learn how to find things. However, students can spend a lot of time just looking. When efficiency is important, teachers can presearch a topic and save bookmarks for students. This takes time, but it really helps the students focus. Teachers spend more time out of class, but the efficiency of student work during class time is much greater, and more work gets done.

*Describe how you try to work with teachers.*

Sometimes teachers come to me for help in preparing a topic they want students to work on. Librarians are also aware of the curriculum and make suggestions from time to time. We can offer technical skills in searching for information, and our awareness of many different information resources can provide a different approach. I think we help teachers try something new and be a little more adventuresome. Our role requires that we can't anticipate exactly what we will be doing next. A teacher or student comes in with a problem or an idea, and it is a challenge to see what we can find to respond to that need.

*Skill stage #3*

## Locating and Accessing

At this third stage, the learner finds specific resources. If a student has decided to rely on books and journal articles, he or she must know how to use the bibliographic databases available in the library and then how to find the actual resources on the library shelves. If the student decides to make use of the World Wide Web, appropriate web pages would have to be located.

*Skill stage #4*

## Use of Information

Once they have accessed information, learners must process it (that is, read it or view it), decide what is useful, and then extract relevant elements for later use. These steps require that the learner determine both the quality of the information and the relevance of specific ideas to the task. Extracting useful information, which involves separating material (text, images) for later use, can rely on such traditional processes as note taking, highlighting, or using a photocopy machine. At this stage, students also need to document the source, using approved citation techniques, and they must understand their responsibilities with respect to intellectual property and copyright issues (see Chapter 9).

*Skill stage #5*

## Organizing and Communicating

This stage involves putting information together to solve the problem. A typical academic information problem-solving activity, such as the completion of a research paper, requires the synthesis of essential ideas and the generation of a product that communicates the task solution.

*Skill stage #6*

## Evaluation

The evaluation stage requires the problem solver to reflect on the quality of the solution and on the process used to arrive at it. Students usually do this by making judgments about the grade they are likely to receive. If a student feels the product will not receive a satisfactory grade, there is often time to return to an earlier stage and invest more effort. Students' perceptions about productive and unproductive resources and techniques are also likely to influence their future behavior.

### A Quick Review

Want a quick summary? The Big Six can also be expressed as a series of questions that provide a slightly different perspective on these skills (Jansen & Culpepper, 1996):

*The Big Six in question form*

- What needs to be done?
- What can I use to find what I need?
- Where can I find what I need?
- What information can I use?
- How can I put my information together?
- How will I know if I did my job well?

## THE BIG SIX AND THE INTERNET

As a general model, the Big Six is appropriate for understanding the application of Internet resources to information problems and for suggesting skills students may need to develop to take full advantage of the Internet. We will concentrate on the World Wide Web and other Internet services allowing students to access stored resources. However, the same considerations will often apply to other Internet tools, such as using e-mail and mailing lists (see Chapter 3, pp. 64–77).

### Information Seeking on the Internet

Let's begin with the second of the Big Six stages, *information seeking* strategies. We would want students to consider Internet resources among the various information sources that might be used to address a problem. Before they do so, they will have to know that their use of such resources will be respected by the teachers who evaluate their work. You might contemplate your own experience in this respect. When you receive a class assignment that requires you to seek information, do you include the WWW among other possibilities, such as visiting the library to search for relevant books or journal articles? Has your approach changed in the past few years? How do your instructors react to information that you indicate came from the Internet?

*Teacher respect for Internet resources*

Students will also need to achieve a certain familiarity with the various information resources available on the Internet. One obvious instructional approach to increasing student familiarity is to *require* that some problems be approached using Internet resources. However, after familiarity has been achieved, students should also be able to evaluate the strengths and weaknesses of online resources and use them whenever they are appropriate to the task.

*Guiding and preparing students*

In guiding your students at this stage, you will have to consider whether to point them toward commercial online services to which your school subscribes, or toward various free web sites, or toward a combination of these categories. The resources available from commercial sources are likely to be carefully selected. The resources available without cost are more diverse, sometimes more interesting, and possibly more biased or factually flawed. In our view, students need to be prepared to use both types of resources, and your role as a teacher will include helping your students become familiar with both types. For example, in the structured approach proposed by McKenzie (1997a), students first encounter and synthesize carefully selected commercial resources, then explore and synthesize carefully selected free Internet resources. In this way students gain a more formal and traditional background in a subject before considering resources that are not subject to the same editorial scrutiny.

## Locating and Accessing Internet Resources

*Developing computer literacy*

At the stage of *locating and accessing* resources, students need to develop basic computer literacy skills involved in operating a web browser, but they do not necessarily have to do their own searching for potential Internet resources. As you saw in Chapter 4, advanced search techniques take some skill and experience, and even the most experienced web user must often spend considerable time sifting through the many resources available to locate a few good ones. In a structured curriculum project like the WebQuests described later in this chapter, teachers do the initial searching for useful sites and then share their findings with students and with other teachers.

*Scaffolded tasks*

The intention in any scaffolded task is eventually to turn more and more of the responsibility over to the learner. You can recognize this process in grade-to-grade changes in traditional information-intensive projects. A third grade teacher who wanted students to complete a project on butterflies would likely go to the school librarian and locate appropriate resources that might then be brought back to the classroom for students to examine. A sophomore biology teacher, on the other hand, would likely send students to the library to locate their own resources. In the transition years, classroom teachers and librarians would work with students to develop the students' skills in using various research tools.

*Integrating skill building into authentic tasks*

The same kind of transition and continual instruction should be applied in the use of Internet information resources. Students need to be introduced gradually to various search tools and procedures. Although activities of this type can be taught in an isolated fashion (as in Internet treasure hunts, in which search skills are taught by requiring students to answer unrelated trivia questions), we prefer integrating instruction and learning within a more authentic task. As part of an inquiry project, students might be directed to explore the use of several search engines and different Boolean search strategies. Students would document their results and discuss with other class members the strategies they found most productive. Resources that seem particularly useful can then be added to the list of required resources the teacher has already identified. With experience, students should be expected to take total responsibility for some projects.

## Using Internet Information

*Processing information and extracting what is useful*

At the stage of *using information,* students carefully process the Internet resources they have located and then extract the information that is important to the problem-solving task. This part of the process is roughly equivalent to traditional reading and taking notes. Because the resources are Internet based, the skills involved can be slightly different, however. For example, web resources typically exist as hypermedia rather than in the linear format found in books. Working through material in which you can make decisions about the order in which you explore the content requires some experience. It can be helpful to have different students compare what they have learned from the same web site to assist them in evaluating how they processed the document.

Students can take notes from online resources using traditional paper-and-pencil methods. However, relevant information (text and images) can also be abstracted from online resources using technology. Students can learn to cut critical text segments and images from the online document and paste this information into a word-processing document to be saved or printed (Eisenberg & Johnson, 1996). Students do need to appreciate the copyright issues that govern this behavior, and they must provide proper credit to the original sources.

*Guarding against misuse of intellectual property*

Educators are legitimately concerned that the ease with which computers allow information to be copied will contribute to abuse. Some fear that they may be unable to detect when students simply use copied material in their projects. Probably the best defense against such abuse is to take a proactive approach—clearly explain how students are to make use of intellectual property they locate online and perhaps require that students demonstrate how they have used their notes and the material they have extracted to create their own products. Any project based on Internet material should require that students work to generate their own way of explaining the ideas they obtain from online sources.

Judging the quality of information obtained online is a special concern. If you have chosen the sites for your students, you probably will have weeded out those you consider unreliable. But as students do more of their own exploring, teachers must prepare them for what they will encounter. The freedom the Internet offers to express personal opinion and the common lack of editorial supervision make critical thinking skills essential.

*Need for critical thinking*

**Critical thinking** requires a combination of intentions, dispositions, and skills. Learners must be willing to reflect on information they encounter, have a desire to understand, and consider options and opinions with an open

Focus

## Citing Internet Sources

Research is one of the most common reasons secondary and elementary students make use of the Internet. Students need to learn to provide citations for Internet resources just as they cite the source for information taken from resources more familiar to them. Some educators feel that citing Internet sources is especially important because the nature of the Internet makes it so easy to copy and paste material. Providing accurate citations makes students aware of their responsibilities and offers teachers a way to follow up on the resources students have used (Li & Crane, 1996).

Here is the form of citation we find most useful, along with two examples:

**General Format**

Author/editor. (Year). *Title* (edition) [Type of medium]. Producer (optional). Available: Protocol (e.g., ftp, http): Site/Path/File. [Access date].

**Sample WWW Resource**

Li, X. (1996). *Electronic Sources: APA Style of Citation* [online]. Available: http://www.uvm.edu/~xli/reference/apa.html. [1999, March 22].

**Sample FTP Resource**

Smithsonian Institution. (1992). gorila.jpg.bin [online]. Available: ftp://ftp.apple.com/alug/Smith/jpg/gorila.jpg.bin. [1998, March 22].

Our inclusion of the access date in these samples warrants a comment. One of the frustrating things about Internet resources is that they have a tendency to disappear as host sites come and go. The access date indicates when the author citing a resource found that resource. This date may be helpful to someone following up on a large list of citations. Materials with more recent access dates are more likely to still be available at the listed site.✱

mind. Some of the skills that apply include the following (Beyer, 1988, p. 87; Ennis, 1987):

Analyzing arguments.

Differentiating verifiable facts from personal beliefs.

Evaluating the credibility of a source.

Identifying the perspective or bias of a source.

Identifying unstated assumptions.

Detecting critical ambiguities.

Evaluating the inductive or deductive logic used in reaching a conclusion.

The question of how to evaluate the quality of Internet information is important enough that we explore it further in the next section.

## EVALUATING WEB INFORMATION

Evaluating web pages can mean many things. Often the emphasis is on design and appearance issues; for instance, are pages well organized, attractive, and functional? These concerns are important both in attracting visitors and in communicating effectively, and we will come back to them in Chapter 7. Our interest here, however, is in evaluating the information itself.

*Issues of accuracy*

Because the Internet provides a nearly open environment for self-expression and publication, issues of accuracy and bias must be considered. Students are impressionable, and the lack of editorial intervention within the Internet community may expose them to questionable information. On the other hand, it can be argued that all information originates within certain biases and perspectives, and one goal of a sound education might be to encourage learners to recognize these influences. Many of the information sources we encounter outside the school environment are intended to persuade us to make certain consumer, political, or personal decisions, and there is no obligation of the individuals or organizations offering this information to be objective or fair.

For these reasons we see the variable quality of Internet information as both a concern and an opportunity. How can you maximize your students' opportunities for authentic inquiry while minimizing the risk that they will be seriously misled? Let's consider the tools and criteria you can use for screening web sources.

### EDITORIAL REVIEW AND SCREENING OF INTERNET RESOURCES

While it is true that there are few barriers to making information available on the Web, there are ways to screen or filter the information that students access.

*Filtering software*

Many schools have invested in filtering software (see Chapter 9). This software works primarily by refusing to allow browsers to access material from certain targeted sites. The companies selling this software continually update their lists of potentially offensive sites and make these revised lists available to schools that have purchased the software.

*Online reviews*

Another possibility is to take advantage of reviews generated by some of the companies that provide Internet search engines. Some of these companies use human editors to review and catalog web sites. When web users search for sites by using the search engine maintained by these companies, the search is really of the database of information the company has accumulated. In some cases, the user can draw directly on the reviews the company has generated. For example:

- Magellan's search service (**http://www.magellan.excite.com/**) allows users to search for key words in all sites in the Magellan database, all sites that have been reviewed (approximately 60,000), or all sites that have been reviewed and rated as "green sites" (containing no objectionable content). With the final two options, it would be possible to obtain some evaluative comments before visiting the actual sites.

- Lycos (**http://point.lycos.com/**) offers content and presentation-quality reviews of the most popular web sites.
- Yahoo!, one of the original and most popular Internet directory and search services, has taken an even more specialized approach. Yahoo! has created Yahooligans (**http://www.yahooligans.com/**), a specialized and separate directory of sites for younger web users.

## MAKING YOUR OWN DECISIONS

Reviews exist for only a small proportion of Internet sites, and for a typical project there will be many useful resources that are not reviewed. If we accept the premise that the Internet contains a great deal of useful information, mixed with some worthless information and a little that is dangerous, how can you as a teacher make best use of it?

For educational purposes, it seems appropriate to recognize and immediately weed out any dangerous or blatantly erroneous information. Further, you will want to be constantly sensitive to indicators of quality and objectivity. This type of healthy skepticism, which we might also describe as part of critical thinking, is an appropriate response to nearly any information resource.

*Healthy skepticism*

Although evaluating information is a subjective process, several criteria can be helpful:

### Who Is the Author?

The primary question in evaluating any resource is: Who is responsible for this information? A variant of this question, which all too often applies to web resources, is: Does *anyone* claim authorship of this information? The identity of the author is useful in establishing the credibility of the information.

*Background of the author*

Often, the author's name on a web page will also function as a link to the author's home page. Information on the home page or perhaps on the original document may indicate the author's affiliation with an institution or organization. This affiliation may reveal something about the author's qualifications or bias. Additional links or references may point to other work by the author. Authors with a body of work in a variety of sources, particularly sources requiring editorial approval, are traditionally regarded as greater authorities than those who have published less or more narrowly.

### Is There an Organizational Sponsor?

*Information about the organization*

If the information appears under the sponsorship of an organization, you may be able to draw some additional inferences. Is the organization an official academic or scholarly one? Is there a logical connection between the organization

**Focus**

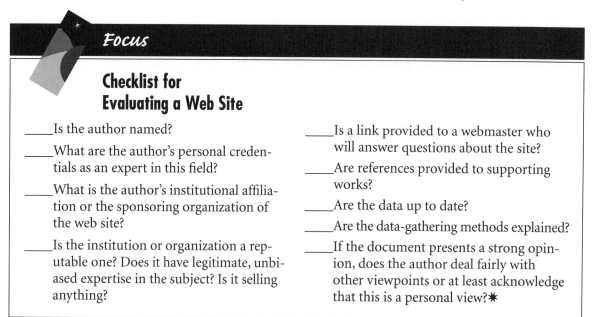

## Checklist for Evaluating a Web Site

____Is the author named?

____What are the author's personal credentials as an expert in this field?

____What is the author's institutional affiliation or the sponsoring organization of the web site?

____Is the institution or organization a reputable one? Does it have legitimate, unbiased expertise in the subject? Is it selling anything?

____Is a link provided to a webmaster who will answer questions about the site?

____Are references provided to supporting works?

____Are the data up to date?

____Are the data-gathering methods explained?

____If the document presents a strong opinion, does the author deal fairly with other viewpoints or at least acknowledge that this is a personal view?✱

and the type of information offered at the web site? Would such a connection indicate a possible bias or just a commitment to support work in a particular area? Does the organization advertise products or services related to the information provided? Does the site supply a connection to a webmaster who may be able to provide additional information?

Remember that sites ending in .edu or .gov are sponsored by educational institutions and government agencies, and sites ending in .org and .com are sponsored by other organizations or commercial entities.

### Additional Evaluation Criteria

Finally, some further criteria may be helpful in evaluating the verifiability, accuracy, and objectivity of the information provided (Descy, 1996; Kirk, 1996):

*Other signs of reliability*

- If the document is an attempt to summarize the findings from other sources, are the conclusions adequately referenced or linked to other work?
- If the document presents data, is there a clear description of how the data were gathered?
- If the document addresses issues or provides data that are time sensitive, does it include a publication date?
- If the document argues for a particular position, does it acknowledge other positions in an evenhanded manner?
- If the document is essentially an editorial, does the author acknowledge that it expresses a personal opinion?

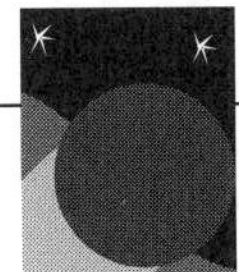

## SCAFFOLDING STUDENTS' WEB EXPLORATION

As you have seen, the Big Six model provides a useful description of the various skills that contribute to solving problems that students will face during inquiry tasks. Yet a very practical issue remains to be addressed. If teachers are willing to accept the challenge of integrating authentic, Internet-based, problem-solving tasks into their curriculum, what exactly might they have students *do?*

*A template for web projects*

In this section, we will use a concrete example as a general template that can be applied to many content areas and grade levels. Understanding this one approach will provide you with a framework for thinking about projects for your own classroom. We want you to feel confident in your ability to design and implement a problem-solving activity that uses information resources from the World Wide Web.

The general approach we propose is based on cognitive apprenticeship, scaffolding, and some of the other concepts introduced in Chapter 2. The basic ideas are these:

### *Keys to Scaffolded Inquiry*

- Present students with challenging tasks that are relevant to the curriculum they are expected to master.
- Engage students with online resources in efficient ways.
- Gradually ease students into inquiry tasks by creating a supportive structure to guide their work.

## THE SCAFFOLDING PROCESS

Here is how the teacher might create a scaffold to support novice students:

*A sample task*

Assume that you would like your students to write a position paper on a controversial topic, using resources from the web. If the student were working independently, he or she would have to find resources related to the topic, examine a number of the resources in an attempt to determine both the opposing positions and the basic arguments for and against each position, select a position to defend, find particularly good resources related to that position, carefully review the sources to obtain key data and develop sound arguments, and then write the paper. These activities essentially involve Big Six activities as they might apply to this particular task.

Consider just a few areas that might cause difficulty:

*Problems your students might encounter*

- Students may lack the experience to use a web browser in a sophisticated way, such as to conduct a sophisticated search or to bookmark potentially relevant resources.

- Students may be unable or unmotivated to find truly good sources among the many that are available, or they may lack the reading or inquiry skills to identify different positions or the arguments for and against these positions.
- Even when students are willing to spend a lot of time on their project, access to computers or the Internet may be limited, and they may not have the opportunity to search through hundreds of sites to find good sources.

Now consider how you as a teacher might participate to assist your students, using what you know about scaffolding and cognitive apprenticeship:

*Ways you might respond*

- You might begin by identifying interesting problems or tasks that are consistent with current curriculum goals.
- Then you might conduct an initial web search to identify resources appropriate to each problem.
- You could save and annotate URLs that provide relevant information and identify a small number of sites that students would find of greatest value.
- For each of these highly useful sites, you could offer guiding comments for the students, such as "This resource presents a good description of the general problem and outlines positions A and B" or "This site provides some very persuasive arguments for position B." (See "Focus: Annotating Web Sites.")
- You might also deal with some computer-skill issues by authoring a simple web page that presents this background material to your students, directly linking them to the most productive sites. If your students have even the most basic competence in using a browser, this web page would allow them to connect easily to the suggested resources.

*The apprenticeship process*

The cognitive apprenticeship model assumes that students will gradually take on more and more of these skills. Perhaps the process might begin by having students search for their own resources to augment those that you have provided. Or you could ask students to review key resources without suggesting specific things they should try to learn from each resource. Your students might also share some tasks with classmates. For example, each student might be required to submit one annotated URL, and these resources could be integrated into a web page to be shared among members of the class.

## WebQuests

Bernie Dodge (1995) has proposed that educators provide scaffolding through what he describes as WebQuests. A **WebQuest** is a document (usually prepared as a WWW page) consisting of

*Elements of a WebQuest*

1. A brief introduction to a topic.
2. The description of an inquiry task related to the topic.

*Focus*

## Annotating Web Sites

In Chapter 4 we mentioned that web browsers typically allow you to annotate your bookmarks. Exactly how might you use this feature to assist your students?

Assume you are going to use Netscape Navigator or Communicator to save a set of bookmarks as an HTML file and distribute it to your students. We described this process in Chapter 4. Annotating these bookmarks is simple. Select a bookmark you want to annotate (click on the bookmark so that it becomes highlighted), and then select Edit Bookmark from the Item menu (or, in some versions, editing is allowed when the Get Info option is selected). A dialogue box will appear, allowing you to enter information about the site, as shown in Figure 5.2.

In this dialogue box, the Name field contains the original name the author has given to the web page. You can change this name to be more descriptive for the purpose you have in mind. Then, in the Description field, you can enter the information you want students to read about the web site. Do not change the URL because this exact information is necessary to locate the site. Complete this process for all of the web sites you intend to present to students.✷

**FIGURE 5.2** Dialogue box for editing bookmark information.

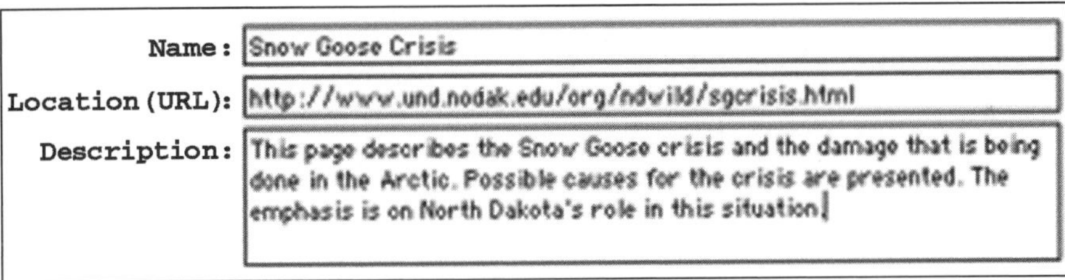


3. A set of primary WWW resources that students can use in performing the task.
4. A description of the specific processes students should employ in performing the assigned task.

The simplicity and practicality of the approach have encouraged many educators to create WebQuests, and Dodge has established a web page so that teachers can learn about WebQuests, share some of their best work with others, and find examples for classroom use (Dodge, 1998). (For relevant URLs, see "Resources to Expand Your Knowledge Base" at the end of the chapter.)

*Presenting a WebQuest*

WebQuests can be presented to students in a variety of ways. Probably the most common format is a four-part web page (Introduction, Alternative

Activities, Annotated Primary Internet Resources, Other Internet Resources). WebQuests are very convenient when made available as web pages. Students can move easily between the WebQuest page and the WWW pages containing information relevant to the activity they have chosen. Of course, a conventional paper document listing the actual URLs could be prepared for distribution to students, and this would work nearly as well.

In the following example, we demonstrate how you might use HyperStudio, a popular multimedia authoring tool widely used in K–12 classrooms, to present a WebQuest to your students.

## The Snow Goose Crisis: A WebQuest Example

Our sample project originated in a magazine article that described how a rapid increase in the population of snow geese was threatening the fragile ecology of Arctic tundra. The article went on to consider whether this was a situation biologists should attempt to address and, if intervention was appropriate, what possible actions might be effective. This seemed an interesting situation for a WebQuest for middle-school or high school students. Students could be asked to examine information related to the snow goose crisis and to propose what, if anything, should be done. The problem seemed complex enough that students might realistically argue for several different courses of action.

### Background on the Issue

To understand the situation, students would need the following background:

Because of the extreme climate, tundra vegetation grows very slowly. Geese use the tundra as a breeding ground, and the parents and young rip plants out by the roots as they feed around the nesting areas. Once an area has been destroyed in this manner, neither geese, other wildlife that feed on the vegetation, nor animals that feed on the plant eaters will be able to inhabit the area for many years. There is a very real threat of a population crash in which many birds and animals will die from malnutrition and related diseases.

One of the most basic issues in such a situation is whether humans should intervene to alter a process of nature. Noninterventionists argue that nature will find a solution even though the process may be harsh. In contrast, biologists favoring active management of natural resources assume that intervention can avoid extreme swings in populations. Those favoring intervention also argue that some of the causes for the present situation are the result of human actions. These human causes include changes in farming practices that leave a great deal of waste grain on the ground following harvest, making it easy for birds to feed during the fall and winter; and the development of a system of protected areas that allow geese to avoid hunters and predators during the fall and spring migrations.

If biologists choose to intervene, there are many possible, but untested, approaches. One interesting question is whether economic benefits should be considered. For example, a solution that extends the hunting season and increases the bag limit (the number of birds that can be shot each day) may attract more hunters and money to certain areas of the United States and Canada. Reducing food and habitat in areas in which geese overwinter would also reduce the population, but with no economic benefits. There is also the matter of expense and who pays for the intervention (taxpayers, nature lovers, hunters). Finally, there is a question of personal values regarding such issues as intervention and killing wildlife for sport.

## Instructional Tasks

A major part of creating a structured inquiry task of this type is locating task-appropriate Internet resources. The teacher takes responsibility for this job. But why not just make the assignment, you may ask, and allow students to find their own resources?

Assume that you are developing this activity for middle-school students. Students familiar with web searching might reasonably conduct a search on the phrase *snow goose.* We did our own search of this type, and we received over 4,200 "hits." Listed among the first four sites were the titles "Snow Goose with White Wine," "Snow Goose Hunting in Nebraska," and "Snow Goose Inn." Yes, you may say, but why not use Boolean search techniques as described in Chapter 4? Well, a search on the Boolean expression *"snow goose" +population* returned 427 hits, and a search on *"snow goose" +crisis* returned 115 hits. Even if middle-school students were experienced enough to generate these Boolean searches, the amount of material to examine would be formidable and would require a great amount of their time.

Thus, while students do need to learn to conduct their own web searches, you might decide in this case to locate useful web sites in advance so that your students could concentrate on the problem-solving process. You might also want to locate task-appropriate web resources simply to save the students' time.

In general, WebQuests are described as scaffolded because the teacher assists the student in ways that allow the student to address challenging problems with an acceptable level of effort and a reasonable opportunity for success. This is particularly important for younger students. As a teacher, you can set the stage for your students, allowing them to focus on key issues and encouraging them in their critical thinking and problem-solving.

### TheWebQuest Presentation

Figure 5.3 provides two sample screens from a WebQuest developed with the multimedia authoring tool HyperStudio. The first screen image—Figure 5.3 (a)—shows the WebQuest introduction, which is intended to establish a background for the activity and generate student interest. The photograph shows the devastation caused by the feeding habits of snow geese (note the difference between the fenced and the unfenced areas).

The second screen image provides an example of how students might be prompted to explore a particular web resource for a certain type of informa-

**FIGURE 5.3** Sample screen images for a WebQuest, developed in Hyper-Studio. (a) The WebQuest introductory screen. (b) A second screen that directs students to a particular web site (via the "click to open" icon) and guides them to find certain information at that site.

(a)

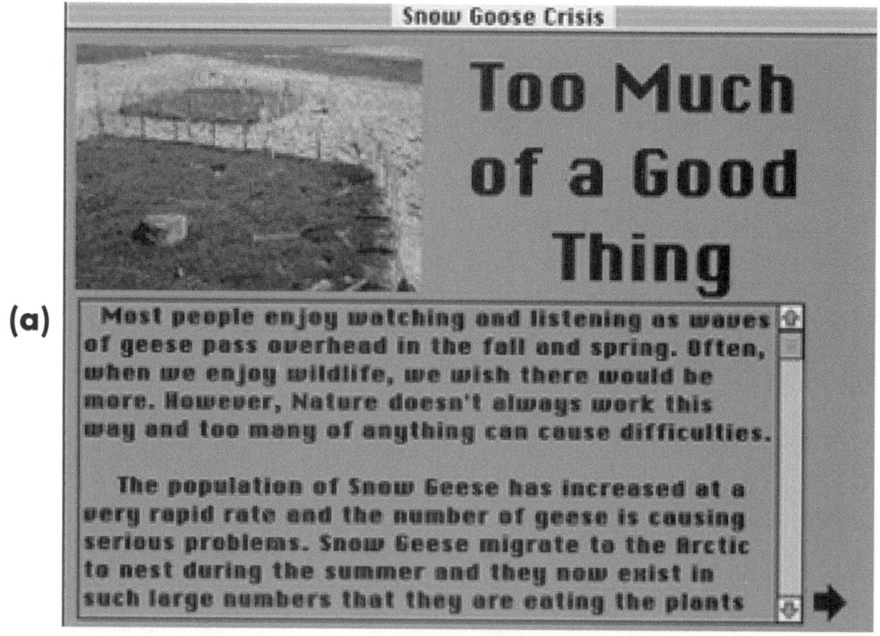

(b)

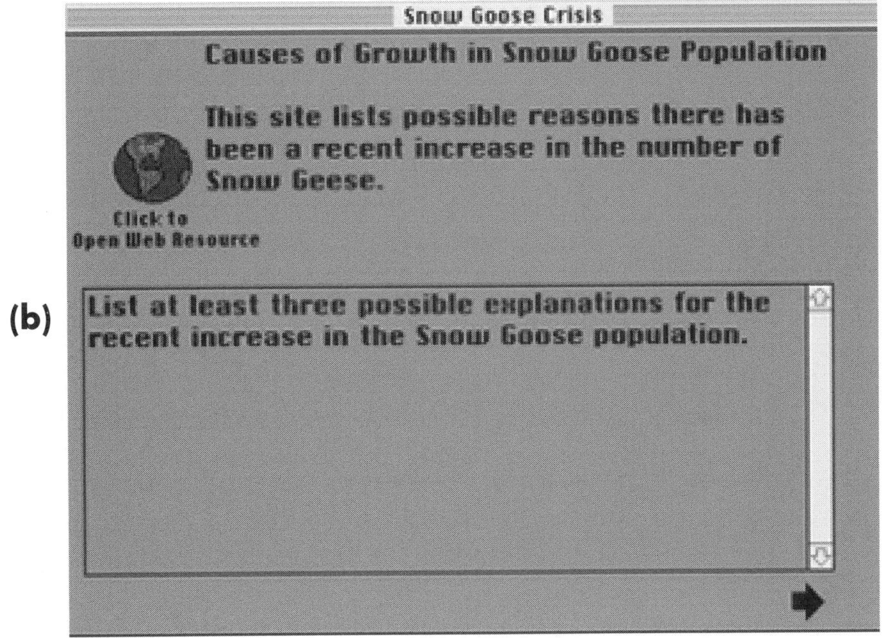


tion. As you can see from Figure 5.3 (b), HyperStudio has a very useful feature that allows a button (the world icon in this case) to launch a browser and send the user to a designated URL. In this instance, the user is encouraged to examine the information found at that web site and to record on the HyperStudio "card" (the bottom portion of the screen) several possible reasons for the rapid increase in the snow goose population.

Although WebQuests direct students to consider specific information at specific sites, they may also provide links to other Web sites that students can explore without such detailed guidance. Students can use all the information they accumulate, and they can return to the web resources as needed while they complete the activity.

Figure 5.4 shows a similar version of the WebQuest presented as a WWW page. Here you can see the four typical components we identified earlier: (a) introduction, (b) task or activity, (c) annotated primary sources, and (d) secondary sources. Some WebQuests provide multiple tasks and offer students a choice. Tasks can take a wide variety of formats, but we would urge more frequent use of tasks that emphasize decision making, problem solving, and information integration rather than mere fact reporting.

**FIGURE 5.4** The WebQuest as it might appear as a web page.

# Too Much of a Good Thing

The population of Snow Geese has increased at a very rapid rate. Snow Geese migrate to the Arctic to nest during the summer and they now exist in such large numbers that they are eating the plants faster than they can grow. The lack of plants threatens the survival of Snow Geese and all animals that live in this region. The basic question is what should be done. Some people believe we should allow Nature to take its course and others feel we should play a more active role. If we attempt to "manage" this problem, the question is what action or actions should be taken?

## The Task

Create a HyperStudio stack to express your view of what should be done about the problem. Provide a clear explanation of what has gone wrong, propose whether or not people should intervene, and if intervention is proposed, exactly what should be done. Defend your proposal based on the factors you discover from your review of web resources.

## Primary Web Resources

North Dakota Description of Problem: General introduction. Ideas about why population has increased. Description of problems created in the Arctic.
Ideas for Management: Some ideas that have been tried to control goose numbers. Some other ideas that might be tried.
Texas Parks and Recreation Description of the Snow Goose problem.

## Secondary Resources

http://www.bbc.co.uk/heading_south/snowmap.htm
http://ngp.ngpc.state.ne.us/wildlife/snowhist.html

## SHOULD TEACHERS CREATE THEIR OWN WEB PROJECTS?

We hope the WebQuest we have just described intrigues you. But you may be worrying that the preparation of a project on this scale is beyond your skills. Creating a scaffolded set of instructions and links with HyperStudio, and then presenting it perhaps via your own Web page—doesn't this require a high level of technological skill?

Not as much as you might think. Authoring tools make it relatively easy to learn to prepare web content. Producing functional, but not exceptional, web content is more like desktop publishing than like computer programming.

*You can create your own projects*

In some cases, obviously, schools may choose to budget money to subscribe to existing online projects rather than have their teachers spend time creating unique projects. Many subscription-based online projects already exist. (See "Keeping Current: A Subscription Real-Time Event.") Often, though, we think that teachers, both individually and in groups, can create their own web-based instructional projects with a moderate amount of effort. The key is to organize existing web content in ways that students of a particular school or classroom can put to best use.

Teachers in Bellingham, Washington, offer a good example. Teams of four to six Bellingham teachers work over the summer months to develop curriculum projects they call online research modules. These modules consist of a series of structured activities leading groups of learners toward an answer to an essential question. The questions are carefully selected to motivate the students and to require careful thinking and problem solving. Examples include "Which disease is most deserving of our research dollars?" and "What are the best ways to reduce teen smoking?"

*An example from Bellingham, Washington*

Students complete each module during approximately six visits to the computer lab. At each work session, web pages created by the teachers lead groups of students through a series of activities in which they are asked to:

- List the types of questions they will need to answer to respond to the larger "essential" question.
- Visit carefully selected pay-for-service and free Internet sites to gather information related to their questions.
- Sort through the information and ideas they have accumulated and attempt a synthesis of this information.
- Evaluate what information they still need and how to find it.
- Create a report that represents the group's shared conclusions.

In addition to the stage-by-stage guidance provided to students, the curriculum development teams also create evaluation guides and offer suggestions to assist classroom teachers with the project.

Keeping Current

## A Subscription Real-Time Event

Some companies use the Internet to offer subscription instructional resources. During the 1998–1999 school year, for example, several of our local middle-school classes participated in a multidisciplinary curriculum project offered by Classroom Connect (**http://www.classroom.com**). This project focused on the ongoing attempt to return the captive Keiko, star of the movie *Free Willy,* to life in the ocean. Keiko is an orca, the species better known as the killer whale.

Classroom Connect describes activities of this type as "RealTime Events" because the curriculum project is built around an actual evolving story. In this case, students followed the activities of scientists from the Jean-Michel Cousteau Institute and the Free Willy Keiko Foundation. In the autumn, the scientists transported Keiko from an aquarium in Oregon to a sea pen in the waters off Iceland. There, they conducted tests to determine how effectively Keiko acclimated over the winter. If things progressed well, they planned to follow Keiko when he was released to the wild. The curriculum materials associated with this project emphasized the study of the oceans, the environment, and issues of international governance.

Some of the activities were preplanned and made available to participating classrooms in the form of a manual and related online resources. For example, a class might choose to investigate the concept of habitat as it applies to marine mammals. Resources developed by project staff and links from the project site to other web sites might be used to address the following questions:

- What are the features of existing orca tanks and aquariums?
- What are the characteristics of oceans that affect marine mammals?
- Do you think any characteristics of Keiko's holding pen should be changed? Why?

The project web site offered multimedia updates, posed questions for classes to answer, and provided opportunities for communication with the scientists and other participating classes. There were also suggestions for helping students learn to search the Internet, cite Internet sources, and understand the responsible use of intellectual property.

Not all of the activities were focused on online experiences. The project attempted to draw connections to local issues, and it encouraged related hands-on activities such as water-quality assessment, searching for microorganisms, identifying sources of pollution, and more. The real-time nature of such an experience offers varied and not-always-predictable learning opportunities. There is no way to know what will actually happen as the experiment progresses.

In this case, the cost for a single class to participate was \$75, and the charge per class declined as more classes from a district became involved (ten classes for \$300). Both the class and the teacher were given a login and password (the teacher had access to additional instructional resources). In situations of this sort, what you end up paying for is the development and organization of instructional resources. It could be argued, of course, that a teacher could provide similar experiences for nothing. While this claim would be true for some experienced and creative teachers, educators need to consider the cost-effectiveness of having teachers spend their time on such activities.

A sampler of other online projects is included in "Resources to Expand Your Knowledge Base" at the end of the chapter. Be sure to investigate some of the projects and think about whether they would be appropriate in your classroom.✷

*A reasonable investment of time*

To pose a challenging essential question, identify appropriate Internet resources, outline a student project based on the question, develop evaluation techniques and teacher guidelines, and create the web pages necessary to present and organize the entire process, each member of the curriculum development team spent approximately 25 hours. This means that a total of 100 to 150 hours of teacher labor was required to create each curriculum project. Because this time was invested to create interesting projects that could be used in many classrooms, the time was considered a reasonable investment (McKenzie, 1997a).

*From small scale to large—your choice*

With this example in mind, we would suggest that teachers can indeed develop significant curriculum materials focused on web resources. The scale of the effort can depend on the situation. An annotated bookmark page may require only a couple of hours to create. Week-long research modules may take a hundred hours or more. But both approaches—and many others along this continuum—can involve students in active use of Internet resources, serving as a meaningful component of content area instruction.

In Chapter 6 you will learn more about constructing web sites and using authoring software. That chapter will also explore the use of web projects as *construction* tools—that is, as a way for your students to synthesize and present what they have learned.

## SUMMARY

◆ This chapter divides Internet resources into instructional resources, which have been prepared specifically to meet educational goals, and primary sources, which offer "raw" information. While instructional resources provide an efficient learning experience, students must also learn to process information for themselves. Even though primary sources can be biased and insensitive to the background of the learner, and even though they appear on the Internet in seemingly overwhelming quantity, working with them prepares students to solve authentic problems outside a classroom environment.

◆ The Big Six provides a model of the skills required to solve problems that rely on the gathering and processing of information. The six general skill areas involve

(1) task definition; (2) information seeking, or identifying possible resources; (3) locating and accessing those resources; (4) using the information (that is, processing it and extracting relevant ideas); (5) organizing the information and communicating the problem's solution; and (6) evaluating the solution and the experience of solving the problem. Applied to the Internet, the Big Six model helps us describe specific skills students need to acquire. For example, locating Internet information may require the development of skill in using search engines. Processing Internet information requires that learners know the basic skills of using a web browser and the unique properties of hypermedia.

◆ The WebQuest is a specific type of web-based inquiry task. WebQuests are scaffolded, which means that the developers have taken responsibility for organizing the process for students and completing some of the more difficult or time-consuming tasks. A WebQuest proposes a decision-making, problem-solving, or information integration task and then directs students to specific web pages that provide the necessary resources. WebQuests offer an excellent format for curriculum projects that teachers can accomplish within a reasonable amount of time.

---

## REFLECTING ON CHAPTER 5

### Activities

1. You live in a third-floor apartment and would like to purchase a dog or cat as a pet. You are not certain if this is a practical idea, and you don't know which type or breed of animal would be most appropriate. Apply the Big Six to solving this information problem. Outline what you would do in each step and how the Internet might be involved.
2. Design the "paper equivalent" of a WebQuest for a topic that interests you. That is, describe a problem, propose inquiry tasks, and identify key web resources.
3. Explore one of the subscription project sites listed in "Resources to Expand Your Knowledge Base" (under the heading "Sources for Structured Internet Activities"). Create a summary of the project, its intended grade level, the content areas it emphasizes, and its cost, and share this information with other students in your class.

### Key Terms

Big Six *(p. 138)*
critical thinking *(p. 144)*
instructional resources *(p. 135)*
primary sources *(p. 135)*
WebQuest *(p. 150)*

### Resources to Expand Your Knowledge Base

#### Internet Directory and Search Engines That Offer Reviews of Web Sites

*Magellan:* **http://www.magellan.excite.com/** *(Magellan home page)* and **http://www.magellan.excite.com/magellan/Reviews/index.magellan.html** *(for reviews)*

*Lycos:* **http://point.lycos.com/**

*Yahooligans:* **http://www.yahooligans.com/**

### Subscription Services That Provide Information Resources

#### *General Information Services*

*EBSCO Information Services:* **http://www.ebsco.com/**

*The Electric Library:* **http://www.elibrary.com**

*Encarta OnLine Library:* **http://www.encarta.msn.com/library/intro.asp**

*ProQuest Direct:* **http://www.umi.com/proquest/**

SIRS Researcher on the Web: **http://www.sirs.com/**

#### *News Services*

*Washington Post and Los Angeles Times:* **http://www.newsservice.com/**

*Wall Street Journal:* **http://www.wsj.com/**

*New York Times:* **http://www.nytimes.com/**

### WebQuest Resources

Dodge, Bernie. *Some Thoughts About WebQuests.* Available: **http://edweb.sdsu.edu/courses/edtec596/about_webquests.html**.

*The WebQuest Page:* **http://edweb.sdsu.edu/webquest/webquest.html**. Offers links to a wide variety of WebQuests.

### Sources for Structured Internet Activities

*GlobaLearn:* **http://www.globalearn.org/**. GlobaLearn conducts expeditions twice a year to places like Turkey, Black Sea nations, Brazil, and Africa, and facilitates classroom experiences related to these expeditions. The web site shares the discoveries of the explorers and organizes resources for teachers and students. (Fee for participation.)

*Global Grocery List:* **http://www.landmark-project.com/ggl.html**. This is an ongoing e-mail project, especially good for Internet beginners, that asks students to visit their local grocery stores and record the prices of items on the grocery list. Through sharing of this information, data are collected from students all over the world. (No fee for participation.)

*JASON Project:* **http://www.jasonproject.org/**. The JASON Project sponsors an annual scientific expedition to engage students in science and technology and to provide professional development for teachers in grades 4 through 8. Classes can participate individually or receive further services through statewide sponsored networks. (Fee for participation.)

*The Journey North:* **http://www.learner.org/jnorth/**. This yearly adventure engages students in a global study of wildlife migration and seasonal change. (No fee for participation, but there is a charge for associated curriculum materials.)

*KidChronicles:* **http://www.gsn.org/project/newsday/index.html**. KidChronicles encourages students to produce their own newspaper based on the news articles submitted to *Newsday* by student reporters all over the world. (No fee; two projects a year.)

*North American Quilt:* **http://www.online class.com/NAQ/NAQhome.html**. This is an interactive online project designed to bring an interdisciplinary approach to the study of geography. Students study their local geography and share their research on the WWW. (Sponsored by Online Class; fee for participation.)

*One Sky, Many Voices:* **http://onesky.engin.umich.edu/**. This project provides the opportunity for K–12 students to use technology tools to investigate environmental themes related to weather. Projects run from four to eight weeks. (Nominal fee for participation.)

*Online Interactive Projects:* **http://quest.arc.nasa.gov/interactive.html**. Sponsored by NASA, these projects allow students to share in some of the excitement of authentic scientific explorations in fields such as high-altitude astronomy, Antarctic biology, and robotics. Resources include television broadcasts and videotapes, printed workbooks, and online interaction. (No fee for participation.)

*ThinkQuest:* **http://io.advanced.org/ThinkQuest/**. This annual contest challenges students and teachers to create web projects that harness the power of the Internet. The archives form a library of Internet educational materials for use in the classroom or at home. Project competitions include an international division for students ages twelve to nineteen, a junior division for U.S. students in grades 4 to 6, and a teacher division for U.S. teachers. (No fee to participate, and contestants compete for cash prizes.)

# PART THREE

# Learning by Constructing Internet Resources

# Chapter 6

# Constructing Content-Area Web Projects

## ORIENTATION

In this chapter we explore a major concept in learning: design. It is typical to understand design as the process by which professionals construct useful products. Architects design buildings. Engineers design bridges and new cars. The process by which active and motivated students create personal understanding might also be considered a form of design. What these constructive processes have in common is the application of skilled behavior to the accomplishment of a meaningful goal.

Our focus here is on the learning opportunities that arise when students create their own web pages as part of a content-area project. As you read, look for answers to the following questions:

**FOCUS QUESTIONS**

- What is meant by the phrase "knowledge as design"?
- How can the design and creation of web pages facilitate the design of knowledge?
- What student and teacher activities typify the various stages in a cooperative group project?
- How does the teacher interact with students to make the creation of web pages a valuable learning experience?
- What tools can students use for constructing web pages?

## Following the Iditarod: A Multidisciplinary Project

The children strain at the ropes, their bootie-clad feet dig into the snow, and the sled begins to move. None of them speaks. None is supposed to speak.

The man on the sled barks out orders and the pace picks up. It is hard work, and the children have difficulty with the rough terrain. Finally the weary children catch a glimpse of civilization in the distance, but as the sled gains speed and rounds a curve, the group comes face to face with a mother moose. Precious time passes as the moose eyes the children. The man reaches under the blanket for his gun, but he knows this will be used only as a last resort. There would likely be severe penalties for discharging the weapon. The group waits and the moose ambles away. Now the dash to make up time begins.

At last the sled arrives at the rest area. Here the routine is strict. Each child has a personal drinking cup to avoid the transmission of disease. It will be a long journey and the strength of every child will be needed. Next comes the high-calorie food. Finally, there is a brief but welcome opportunity to rest while booties are checked for tears and garbage is picked up and stowed on the sled. Then, as the sun dips below the trees and the light begins to fade, it is back to the trail.

### The I-Kid-A-Rod

The foregoing scenario may puzzle you. It is a description of part of the I-Kid-A-Rod, the culminating activity in Mrs. Saiger's sixth grade theme unit focused on the annual Iditarod dogsled race in Alaska. Children and their parents build wooden sleds and race in a local park, following many of the rules of the great Alaskan race. Yes, the students are the dogs. They have been studying and participating in endurance training as well as learning about the nutritional ingredients in high-energy diets. The mother moose—well, it is really a student's mother. The gun is made of wood, but every sled has to have one.

Mrs. Saiger has used the Iditarod as the focus of a multidisciplinary unit for several years. The unit's activities are appropriate to math, science, language arts, and other elementary content areas. Over the years Mrs. Saiger has expanded her resource base to include books, videotapes, computer CDs, and, most recently, web resources. A scientist from a federal human nutrition research laboratory talks to the students about high-energy foods. A dad produced the design for the sleds. Mr. Holly, a middle-school industrial arts teacher, improved the design and created plans using a CAD (computer-assisted design) program. Student teams, actually the "dog teams," and their parents assembled the sleds.

There were some additional special circumstances. The students became acquainted with Brad Pozarnsky, the first North Dakotan to enter the Iditarod. The students had a contest to design a "Support Your Musher" button, creating their designs on the classroom computers. The best design was used on both buttons and T-shirts that were sold to raise funds to help support Brad. During the race, Mrs. Saiger would call Brad's wife, and the class learned some things about Brad's experiences that were not included in any published sources. After the race, Brad visited the school, autographed a T-shirt, and took a ride on one of the sleds.

### Integrating Technology

We offer this description of the I-Kid-A-Rod because we want you to understand what a cooperative, theme-based student project might involve. The Iditarod provided a complex environment involving many possible areas for investigation. Clearly, this project was not focused on technology, but as you will see, technology was used in many different ways and provided some unique experiences.

The activities involving technology and the Internet were truly integrated into the month-long project. Here is a list of some of the more technology-supported components:

- Students explored several CDs on Alaska, wolves, and other related subjects.
- Students studied several web sites devoted to the Iditarod and followed other web sites (such as the one sponsored by the *Anchorage Daily News*) that provided news during the race itself.
- Part of each student's task was to locate specific items of information on an individual musher. This information was gathered daily from web sites and organized with a computer spreadsheet.
- Each student wrote a daily journal in the first person, pretending to be a particular musher. (See "Focus: A Sample Student Journal.") The journals were written with a word processing program. Mrs. Saiger modeled this process by writing her own journal based on the experiences of Brad Pozarnsky.
- Students used a computer drawing program for their contest to design project logos.
- Students participated in an online chat with musher Martin Buser (sponsored by Scholastic Network).
- Students used a camcorder to document many of their experiences during the project.
- Finally, Mrs. Saiger and the students created web pages related to the project, incorporating the students' journal entries, selected images from the camcorder, a description of Brad's visit, and many interesting facts about the project.

Focus

## A Sample Student Journal

As an illustration of the motivating potential of projects like the I-Kid-A-Rod, look at the following entry from the journal of one of Mrs. Saiger's students.

**March 9, 1998**

Today I made it to Skwentna. I have been running sixteen dogs since the start of the race. I am currently in second place and I hope to pass Dee Dee Jonrowe so I can be first. So far I have been to Yentna and Skwentna. I checked into Skwentna at 7:03 PM and I checked out at 7:06 PM.

On my way through these first few checkpoints, I crossed the Little Susitna River. It was frozen most of the way across, but some spots were groggy. I was fearful of overflow, but it never happened. THANK GOD!

Besides Dee Dee Jonrowe, my main competition is Rick Swenson and Jeff King. I hope to finish the race in 9 days if possible. I am really excited because I am running this race for my sixteenth time! I hope that I will win so I can have my fourth victory. Someday I would like to beat Rick Swenson's record of 5 wins in the Iditarod. Maybe my Iditarod dreams will come true.✷

### The I-Kid-A-Rod Web Site

This chapter emphasizes the construction of web pages as a way to learn and demonstrate understanding. Mrs. Saiger's I-Kid-A-Rod web site (**http://www.grand-forks.k12.nd.us/~wilder/iditarod.html**) has become quite extensive, incorporating not only the students' work but also lists of the books, videotapes, and CDs she uses as part of the unit and descriptions of some of the specific activities she does in art, music, language arts, physical education, science, and math. Believing in the educational potential of large, theme-oriented learning projects, she uses the web site as a way to share her ideas with other teachers and classes. Because parents played a prominent role in the project, the web site also provides an important connection with parents.

Figure 6.1 is a small sample from Mrs. Saiger's web site. Part (a) reproduces a portion of a page explaining what happened during the chat with musher Martin Buser. Part (b) shows one of the sleds used in the I-Kid-A-Rod. In the rest of this chapter, we will explore projects of this nature from multiple perspectives, addressing questions like these: How can they contribute to your students' learning? How can students collaborate effectively on such projects? What do you and your students need to know about web authoring to begin such a project?

**FIGURE 6.1** Images from Mrs. Saiger's Iditarod web site. (a) Part of a page describing the online chat with musher Martin Buser. (b) One of the sleds used in the I-Kid-A-Rod, the children's own version of the race.

(a) The kids participated in the online chat sponsored by Scholastic Networt. Each student wrote down 3 questions they would like to ask Martin Buser. We then would type in their questions and wait patiently to see if ours was chosen to be answered by Martin. Although we asked a number of times about his strategy, he would not give out that information before the race.

(b) This is what a completed sled looks like. Each sled had 26 feet of rope to be used as gangline for pulling. Holes were bored into the front piece and knots tied into the rope to prevent it from pulling out of the sled during racing or practicing.

## MEANINGFUL LEARNING AND THE DESIGN PROCESS

We have organized much of the content in this book around the idea that the Internet can be understood as three sets of tools for learning: tools for communication, tools for inquiry, and tools for construction (Bruce & Levin, 1997). We are now focusing on the final set, the Internet as tools for construction. As the I-Kid-A-Rod example illustrates, the emphasis is both on the construction of a product (such as a web project) and on the construction of personal knowledge.

Think about this example in terms of the core concepts we introduced in Chapter 2:

*The core concepts revisited*

- A large-scale group project can represent an *authentic task* for a *school-based learning community.*

- As they work to complete such a project, learners must take considerable personal responsibility. They must function as *active and self-regulated learners* and usually as members of a *cooperative learning* group.
- In working to construct the product that is the focus of the project, students have an immediate and purposeful reason for learning. They share the knowledge they have generated with others in order to accomplish both personal and shared goals, and the acquisition and application of knowledge occur within a context that provides motivation and makes the learning *meaningful.*
- The teacher functions as *facilitator,* and in many projects that are truly authentic tasks, the teacher must also be a learner.

*The dual meaning of design*

Let's extend these ideas one step further, to include the concept of design. Following its traditional usage, **design** can mean the process of creating a physical product or object, such as a web page. But it can also mean the process of creating personal understanding.

> *Meaningful learning can be said to result from a student's personal and active cognitive process of design.*

In a project like the I-Kid-A-Rod, the two meanings of design come together. A challenging project to design a product like a sled or a web page usually requires the simultaneous design of personal knowledge.

The concept of design projects could apply to many classroom applications of technology: for instance, development of databases, projects requiring the analysis of data with a spreadsheet, various writing activities making use of word processing software, and video or multimedia projects (Grabe & Grabe, 1998). In fact, the idea of learning through design is very versatile and does not require technology at all. Our focus in this chapter, though, is on technology projects and specifically on Internet projects. You and your students will likely have many opportunities to create the kinds of projects described here.

## KNOWLEDGE AS DESIGN: LEARNING WITH A PURPOSE

*Views of knowledge . . .*

What is knowledge to you? What are the implications of your belief that you are knowledgeable about a particular subject? The way you answer these questions may be very important to your behavior as a student and a teacher (Perkins, 1986).

*(a) Knowledge as information*

You may equate being knowledgeable with the possession of a great deal of factual information about a particular topic. In that case, you probably think that the accumulation of such information is one of the basic purposes of education. Information is stored for the sake of knowing, under the assumption that the information will eventually prove useful. This view of knowledge is consistent with the metaphor of knowledge as "transmission." A more knowledgeable person passes knowledge on—transmits it—to a less knowledgeable person.

*(b) Knowledge as design*

**Knowledge as design** (Perkins, 1986) provides a different perspective. It is knowledge constructed by each individual student to accomplish some particular *purpose.* Some people, in fact, would argue that any *useful* knowledge is a design constructed by the learner. From this perspective, the learner with a purpose takes advantage of the information available to build personal understanding. A more knowledgeable person may help in this process—for instance, by modeling thinking behaviors and offering perspectives—but the ultimate act of knowledge construction must be performed by the learner.

> *Knowledge as design cannot simply be transmitted from one person to another. It is most likely to result from what we have called active learning.*

*Perkins's analogy*

Perkins (1986) uses the example of a familiar tool, a screwdriver, to demonstrate the logical connection between design and purpose. Consider how absurd it would be to create an elongated metal object with a flattened tip and then search for an application for it. In some ways, this is what educators ask students to do. Students frequently learn or memorize information on the assumption that it should be useful for something, but at the time the student really does not know exactly what.

It is important to understand that the distinction between knowledge as disconnected information and knowledge as design is not a function of the facts and experiences a learner encounters. The distinction focuses on *what the learner does in processing these inputs.*

## WORKS OF MIND

In addition to his screwdriver analogy, Perkins (1986) offers another strong justification for design projects. He points out that schools seldom allow students to do "works of mind." Schools teach students about history, biology, and mathematics, but students rarely get the opportunity to *do* history, biology, or mathematics. The one consistent exception seems to be art. Students at most grade levels do have the opportunity to create original works of art.

*Creative work: art versus other disciplines*

Why do educators make this division between art and other subjects? It seems that as educators we recognize that an artistic design can exist at many levels. The student is producing a creative work even when it is done in crayon or Play-Doh. But we often cannot think of what an elementary design in biology or history would look like. Perhaps we assume that learners must acquire a lot of background knowledge before they can do original work in these areas.

From the examples given in this book, you should realize the fallacy of this view.

*Focus*

## Two Views of Knowledge

*Knowledge as Information*

- Knowledge is information.
- Accumulating information is itself a sufficient purpose for education.
- Knowledge can be passed along—transmitted—from one person to another.
- Most disciplines of knowledge require considerable background information before a person can begin to create an original product or engage in a meaningful application.

*Knowledge as Design*

- Knowledge requires a personally constructed "design," not merely a collection of facts.
- Students will not truly learn unless they have a particular purpose for constructing their own meaning.
- Although knowledgeable people can aid a learner, knowledge itself cannot simply be transmitted.
- In most disciplines of knowledge, students at all stages can produce original products and learn from the experience.✷

> *Works of design and construction do not have to be completely novel or involve a large-scale problem. The important issue is that the activity challenge the learner's existing knowledge and inquiry skills and engage him or her in the design of new knowledge.*

Inquiry problems are indeed scalable, and the necessary background knowledge can be acquired. Students can act as historians, for example, by constructing histories of their own families. They can be ecologists when they study the ecology of the classroom aquarium.

## LEARNING COMMUNITIES AND COOPERATIVE DESIGN TEAMS

*Cooperative learning*

**Cooperative learning** is one of the basic themes of this book. As we noted in Chapter 2, the aim of cooperative learning is to create situations in which students help each other learn. They may accomplish this goal by motivating, teaching, or evaluating each other, or simply by engaging each other in discussions that encourage reflection. When all students contribute, cooperative approaches encourage active learning.

Our interest here is in cooperative methods that lend themselves to group design projects like Mrs. Saiger's I-Kid-A-Rod, helping to create a genuine

*Group investigation*

community of learners. One such method is **group investigation,** a task specialization model that guides students in group projects on a general theme proposed by the teacher (Sharan & Sharan, 1992).

The group investigation model is made up of six stages:

*Stages of group investigation*

*Stage 1: Identify the topic and form student groups.* After introducing the topic and letting students express their ideas, the teacher divides the class into groups on the basis of individual interests. The teacher continues to meet with each group periodically during the later stages, offering guidance as necessary.

*Stage 2: Team planning.* Members of each group devise a plan for the group's work, deciding how the information will be gathered, who will be responsible for which parts of the task, and so on.

*Stage 3: Team members conduct inquiry.* The group's members locate resources, gather information, and take notes to share with the rest of the team.

*Stage 4: Preparing the final report.* In each group the students integrate their information and prepare their report, dividing the tasks as they choose.

*Stage 5: Presenting the final report.* Each group presents its report in a way that allows the rest of the class to view it and ask questions about it. The class as a whole can decide how to integrate the various team projects. The project can then be shared with other classes or with parents.

*Stage 6: Evaluation.* Group members reflect on their methods, their successes, and their difficulties, and make suggestions for improving future projects.

Research demonstrates that group investigations result in significantly better performance than traditional learning activities, and a variety of examples already exist (Sharan & Shachar, 1988; Slavin, 1990). Although the original group investigations were intended to result in a written or oral "report," a web presentation can easily be substituted without altering the general nature of the strategy.

In the next two sections, we explore two other sets of classroom strategies that include the development of technology products. As you read, note how closely they follow the six stages of group investigation.

## GUIDED DISCOVERY

Ann Brown (Brown, 1992; Brown & Campione, 1994) offers some helpful instructional strategies for learning communities. Brown suggests that teachers attempt to create a middle ground between teacher-dominated direct instruction and pure discovery learning in which students work on their own with little guidance. The middle ground might be described as **guided discovery.**

Brown's procedure shares many features with the group investigation model. These are the elements that Brown proposes:

*Steps in guided discovery*

- The teacher establishes a general theme for investigation and identifies an initial set of stimulating resources. Students begin by exploring these materials.
- This exploration, in combination with group discussion and teacher suggestions, leads the students to identify some initial questions and define their subtopics. On the basis of their personal interests, students are then assigned to groups that will investigate these subtopics.
- Each research group thoroughly investigates its topic and prepares multimedia teaching materials based on its conclusions. Note that this use of student-authored multimedia is different from most methods we have described. Here students prepare instructional materials they will use to *teach each other.* The multimedia product is not the concluding activity, but an intermediary stage.
- Once the subtopic groups have completed their work, the students regroup so that each new group has an "expert" on each subtopic. This is the **jigsaw** strategy, a well-established method in cooperative learning. Each expert teaches his or her subtopic to the group and prepares questions for a final test.
- All children are responsible for mastery of all theme content.

## The Teacher's Role in Guided Discovery

As Brown indicates, the teacher's role requires considerable judgment. As a teacher in such a project, you want to allow your students some flexibility to pursue their own questions, while at the same time "seeding the environment" with interesting ideas.

*Learning with your students*

You may not always know where the learning process will take your students, and you may not have answers to all their questions. Frequently you will need to locate new resources along the way and even learn new ideas along with your students. In some cases, the new resources may include other teachers, contacts within the community, or experts reached through e-mail. In Brown's model, students should have the opportunity to observe the teacher doing research, reading, and working with technology.

## Ritualized Structures

Brown also emphasizes the use of *ritualized participant structures,* which are helpful in structuring class time and providing students a sense of what they should be doing. For example, students might agree to spend two class periods gathering and organizing information related to their different subtopics and then prepare a report to be read by others working on the same subtopic.

*Agreeing on specific joint activities*

Members might read these reports, ask questions, offer suggestions, and volunteer to investigate important questions that have been identified.

All of these defined, agreed-upon joint activities provide what Brown calls "ritualized structures." The jigsaw teaching activity also represents a ritualized structure, and short presentations by the teacher may be considered a type of ritualized activity as well.

## THE HYPERCOMPOSITION DESIGN MODEL

*Active learning through hypermedia design*

The **hypercomposition design model** (Lehrer, 1993; Lehrer, Erickson, & Connell, 1994) describes the use of hypermedia design projects as content-area learning experiences. A practical strategy for classroom application, this model applies the principles of active learning, cooperative learning, knowledge as design, and many of the other themes we have emphasized here and in Chapter 2. Although the model as the researchers described it did not involve the Internet, the principles can readily be extended from hypermedia to web page construction.

*Developed from a model of writing*

The hypercomposition design model was based on careful observation and interviews of students who were involved in the creation of hypermedia projects. The basic framework comes from a widely accepted model of the writing process (Flower & Hayes, 1981; Hayes & Flower, 1980) that has been successful in changing the way teachers understand student writing and the role they are to play in helping students write more effectively.

Perhaps the most essential insight is this:

*Design is not linear*

> ▶ *Both writing and project design are not linear processes that move forward in a series of smooth incremental stages. Rather, both involve a combination of construction and revision.*

Learners attempt to generate a product representing their knowledge, evaluate this product, and then make adjustments in both their understanding and their product. In both traditional writing and hypermedia authoring, students benefit from sharing "works in progress" with others. Information gathered from such interactions can improve both the product and the learner's understanding of the content area associated with the product.

To create guidelines for student hypermedia design projects, Lehrer extended the writing process model to include the following:

*Elements of Lehrer's model*

- An initial inquiry process, during which authors acquire the knowledge they will eventually present.
- Attention to the special features of hypermedia.
- The requirements of collaborative authorship. (Although a traditional writing process may involve interaction, it emphasizes the work of individual authors in developing their own products.)

This extended model, in combination with the insights gained from the observation of students working on hypermedia products, resulted in a general framework to help teachers facilitate hypermedia projects.

The model proposes that collaborative student projects incorporate the major stages of planning, transforming and translating, evaluating, and revising. The following sections look at each of these stages. The general model should provide you with principles, strategies, and ideas. Of course, your own experiences and the content area to be emphasized will determine how you implement this general framework in your own classroom.

## Planning

The general tasks in planning the project require the group to do the following:

*Tasks of the planning stage*

- Develop a major theme.
- Propose topics and the relationships among the topics.
- Propose a project—in our adaptation, a web project—appropriate to this organizational scheme.
- Establish responsibilities for team members.

Teachers usually initiate the project by proposing a broad topic. The intent is to allow students to explore a bit and then concentrate on what interests them. Student groups are given the freedom to define subtopics, establish the objectives for their hypermedia project, and determine the responsibilities for group members.

*Guiding students through difficulties*

Students may have difficulty with these tasks. Younger students may not have the information processing skills necessary to explore a completely novel area. Students of all ages may be inexperienced in working collaboratively. In such situations, the teacher must offer advice. You might give students a few key sources to help them get started. This would be a great opportunity to propose a WebQuest, as described in Chapter 5 (p. 150). Similarly, to help students function effectively in groups, you may have to establish simple guidelines and monitor student compliance.

## Transforming and Translating

This stage requires the collection of information and the generation of personal knowledge. Note the strong similarity between this stage of the hypercomposition model and the information processing skills of the Big Six (see Chapter 5, p. 138).

*Gathering information*

To collect information relevant to project goals, students must identify potentially relevant sources through the use of effective search strategies, locate the actual resources, and employ some process to store the information for later use. Clearly, the students could use Internet resources at this stage, applying the search, location, and storage skills described in Chapters 4 and 5. Students might also acquire information from their library or by asking community members or peers.

*Original discovery*

Further, students can generate their own information through original discovery. For example, they can conduct experiments of their own design or replicate established procedures to gather original data; they can develop and administer questionnaires; or they can conduct interviews. They can obtain information related to many fields (history, sociology, biology) by observing what happens in their own communities.

*Recording the information*

Data obtained from these resources can be retained in many ways. Students' note-taking skills are always important, but students might also use photocopying, audio recording, and video recording. Some of these skills are seldom used in school settings and may be novel for many students. Not all students will know how to operate a camcorder, for instance. Even the assumption that students know how to take good notes from text sources or during an interview may be incorrect.

*Helping students learn how to learn*

You will probably want to review samples of student work, such as their notes and their lists of sources, in order to provide feedback and offer suggestions. One advantage of the project approach is the opportunity to help students *learn how to learn* in a context where such skills can be immediately and authentically applied. Projects put more responsibility in the hands of students and also require them to engage in diverse self-guided activities. Be careful, however, that students are not left to drift aimlessly as they encounter situations that are unfamiliar to them.

*Organizing, summarizing, interpreting*

Once they have gathered their raw information, students will need to organize, summarize, and interpret it. These skills would include the fourth (using information) and fifth (organizing and communicating) stages of the Big Six, as described in Chapter 5 (p. 138). Depending on the nature of the project, you might introduce some specific academic skills at this stage. Students might benefit from instruction in how to generate an outline, a concept map, or summaries. Also, you might guide them in applying some basic statistical procedures to quantifiable data.

There are many technology tools that can contribute at this point. Special software for outlining and construction of concept maps can be helpful for organizing ideas within a group setting. Students might be introduced to spreadsheet software and the related data visualization capabilities.

The other major task of knowledge generation involves the publication of what has been learned. The design of web pages would be a perfect way for collaborative groups to present their findings.

To summarize, the transforming and translating stage guides students to:

*Tasks of the transforming and translating stage*

- Search for and collect information.
- Generate information through original discovery.
- Select and interpret information appropriate to the project.
- Author a product presenting what has been learned.

### Evaluating and Revising

Authoring is not a one-pass process. Many deficiencies may become apparent within the product itself or in the way the product conveys information to the online audience. Perhaps the web page looks awful when displayed on a different computer. Perhaps some of the links connecting project pages do not work. Maybe a student from another group says that the project lacks an adequate introduction or that it is not really clear what the project is about.

Evaluation involves the search for all of these difficulties and many more. Students need to learn to step back from their work and view it with an objective eye. They can also improve their evaluation skills and produce better products by evaluating each other's work. Here are some suggestions you may find productive:

*Suggestions for evaluating and revising*

- Students can ask people typical of their intended audience to try the completed product. For instance, if your students have designed their web pages to be used by younger students, they can visit an elementary classroom with an Internet connection and watch as a volunteer takes a look at what they have done. Does the volunteer become confused when moving about the site? What does the younger student say when asked if there are parts that are hard to understand?
- Ask a content-area expert to review the product. Commercial software developers do this all the time. The designer asks a biologist, historian, or other domain expert if the information is accurate. For many projects, perhaps the teacher can serve as the content expert. Or how about asking the teacher down the hall what she thinks? Maybe a classmate's parent has a relevant background and would be willing to offer some suggestions.
- Web projects should also be tried on different equipment and using different software, to test for compatibility problems. The arrangement of the page may shift when displayed on a different monitor or with a different browser. Image quality may deteriorate significantly when viewed on different equipment. Viewing a web project from a server is also important. There are some problems in linking pages that students may not detect when trying out the pages on the machine used to produce the pages.

## THE TEACHER'S ROLE IN THE DESIGN PROCESS

*Implications for you as a teacher*

To this point, we have considered design as a way of understanding individual learning and the process of creating useful products, and we have examined models you might use for structuring web-based design projects. Along the way, you have seen that there are implications for you, the teacher, as you attempt to implement these ideas. Now we want to look at those implications more closely.

Clearly, technology can provide an efficient way to engage students in

*Adjusting teaching methods*

stimulating projects. But incorporating design projects will require that many teachers make some adjustments in their teaching methods. In the early stages of a project, especially when working with inexperienced designers, the teacher may provide some direct instruction and demonstrate critical skills for gathering information or using technology. Yet students cannot truly function as junior biologists, historians, writers, or political advocates if teachers completely control the information resources, focus on learning tasks that require only shallow processing of information, and employ assessment methods that merely reward fact retention.

*Coaching small groups*

As you have seen in this chapter, one productive approach is to have students work in groups, using technology among themselves to explain or teach (Brown, 1992; Brown & Campione, 1994; Lehrer, 1993; Lehrer et al., 1994). In a typical classroom activity of this type, the teacher *coaches* small groups of students as they work first to learn and then to create their own instructional materials. To maintain a student focus, teachers must allow students some freedom. Rather than explicitly directing the students, the teacher tries to guide them—for instance, by asking leading questions.

*A "clinical skill"*

Working in this fashion takes considerable skill and experience. In some ways it is more demanding than exerting complete control over instructional content and student activities. Recognizing this, some researchers refer to teaching as a "clinical skill" (Brown & Campione, 1994). Allowing students the freedom to make some of their own decisions has also been described as "adventurous teaching" (Sheingold, 1991).

## The Cognitive Apprenticeship Method

*Initiation into the community of scholars*

One way to think of the teacher's role in student design projects is that teachers are initiating students into the community of scholars (Lehrer, 1993). To develop domain-appropriate learning and thinking processes, students engage in tasks authentic to that domain within an *apprenticeship* relationship with the teacher and perhaps with other domain experts in the community. In the Iditarod example at the beginning of this chapter, you saw examples of community participation. You saw the teacher, Mrs. Saiger, involved in some of the same activities as the students—for instance, when she created her own journal based on the Iditarod experiences of Brad Pozarnsky.

*Teacher's role evolves over time*

An approach in which less-experienced practitioners learn by modeling some of the key activities of more experienced practitioners is called **cognitive apprenticeship** (a term we introduced in Chapter 2, p. 53). In this approach, the role of the teacher shifts over time from modeling (demonstrating), to coaching the student, to a more passive role in which the teacher may observe and intervene only occasionally (Table 6.1).

*Externalizing cognitive behaviors*

The teacher must do more, however, than create her own version of the product expected of students. When the skills to be learned are cognitive, it is important to find some way to externalize the cognitive behaviors so that the less-experienced learners witness behaviors they can use as a guide. For in-

**TABLE 6.1**
The Teacher's Role in Cognitive Apprenticeship

| Project Stage | Teacher's Role | Teacher's Activities |
|---|---|---|
| Early | Modeling | The teacher offers students a model by personally demonstrating key activities, making a particular attempt to externalize conceptual behaviors so that students can observe and understand them. For instance, the teacher can describe what she is thinking as she performs a certain task, encouraging students to discuss these thoughts or ask questions about them. Tasks are distributed among several students. |
| Middle | Coaching | As students acquire the necessary skills, the teacher provides various types of support: offering reminders, describing conventions that apply to the task at hand, setting up constraints, and so forth. |
| Late | Fading | As learners become capable of working independently and integrating multiple tasks, the teacher gradually fades into the background, continuing to observe but intervening only on occasion. |

stance, the expert must often attempt to explain what he or she is thinking. Mrs. Saiger probably talked to students about her journal, explaining some of her thoughts and decisions as a guide for the students' own thinking. Group discussions are another way to externalize such cognitive behaviors.

## STUDENT HYPERMEDIA PROJECTS: CONSTRUCTING WEB PAGES

We want you as a teacher to feel fully capable of engaging your students in productive design projects. As you have seen, effective projects require you to create a learning environment focused on core themes, stocked with stimulating resources, and encouraging to student inquiry. You also need to exercise a sensitive clinical judgment so that your students can learn autonomously without experiencing too much frustration.

Of course, effective technology projects also require that both you and your students know how to use the technological tools. We have devoted the rest of this chapter to practical issues involved in creating web pages. An understanding of some web basics and the mastery of a couple of web authoring tools should give you the confidence you need to begin web design projects with your students. Chapter 7 will take you further by describing some specific principles of web page design.

*A minimalist approach*

We propose that you adopt a *minimalist* approach to web hypermedia

(D'Ignazio, 1996): to begin, learn as few new software tools and as few new technology skills as possible. If what you can produce is productive and exciting, there will be plenty of additional techniques and ideas you can explore later on.

## USING A WEB AUTHORING PROGRAM

Think of web pages as a combination of the following items:

*Basic elements of a web page*

1. Multimedia elements (text, graphics, movies, and such).
2. A special command language called **hypertext markup language (HTML),** which informs the browser how to organize these multimedia elements for display.
3. Links allowing access to other pages.

You have read about all of these elements in earlier chapters. One of the great things about web authoring is that what can be accomplished at the high end continues to expand in power and complexity, but what it takes to create basic web pages is, if anything, getting easier. If you have yet to prepare a web page, now is the time to learn.

### Commands Simplified

*Your previous experience*

At present, HTML is probably the part of web pages that is most mysterious. However, you probably already use a markup language on a frequent basis without realizing it. If you have written papers with a word processing program, you have underlined and bolded text, centered and enlarged a segment of text to serve as the title, and perhaps inserted a picture in your document. You did not type any commands to do these things, but the invisible commands were part of the data file you saved to disk.

One way to prove this to yourself is to save a word processing document containing some text enhancements (underline, bold, centered text) as a "text-only" file. As the phrase suggests, a text-only file contains no special characters or commands. When you open a text-only file with your word processing program, you will find that your text enhancements are gone. So a markup language is something you have probably used for years.

*Authoring via WYSIWYG*

You can now create web documents in nearly the same way. There are several readily available **web authoring programs** that allow you to create web pages by positioning multimedia elements on a blank page and then manipulating various aspects of these elements simply by clicking buttons or selecting menu items. These programs are sometimes described as **WYSIWYG** (an acronym for "what you see is what you get") because you can work at the level of visible objects rather than the underlying codes. (For a list of web authoring programs, see "Resources to Expand Your Knowledge Base" at the end of the chapter.)

**FIGURE 6.2** Button bar from FileMaker Home Page.

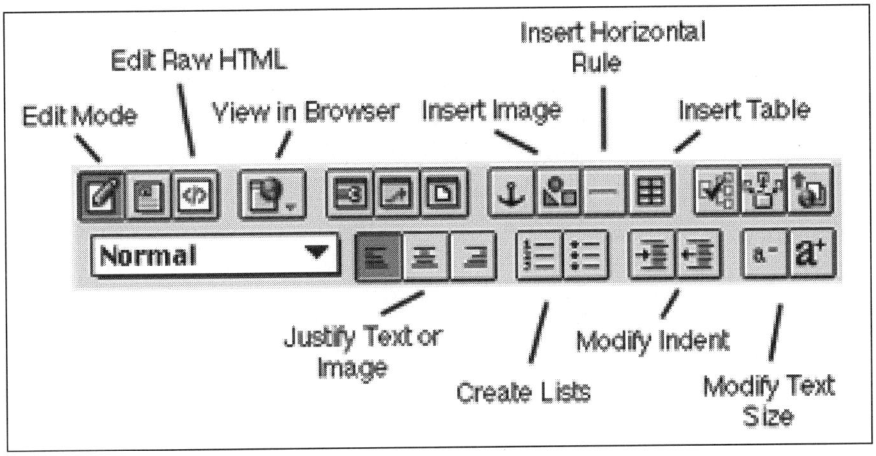

Screenshot reprinted by permission from Claris Corporation.

*A simple example*

As an example, look at the FileMaker Home Page button bar in Figure 6.2. To center a segment of text or an image on the page, you would first select the text or image and then click the center justification button. This button bar—in combination with the options available from the menu bar and special "object editors" that allow the author to control the attributes of objects (images, frames, tables, links)—makes it possible to create complex web pages without ever writing any HTML. Each web authoring program applies a slightly different strategy to the construction of web pages, but the basic approach is fairly standard from program to program.

*Invisible tags*

As we mentioned in Chapter 4 (p. 106), the HTML commands that control the appearance and function of the elements on the screen are called **tags.** When you construct a web page with an authoring program, you do not see these tags on the screen, but they are saved in the file that you eventually send to the machine that serves your web page.

*Viewing the tags*

Web authoring programs usually allow the author multiple options for creating web pages. If you look at the left-hand end of the top row of buttons in Figure 6.2, you can see edit-mode buttons that allow the author to toggle between the WYSIWYG and HTML views of a web page. If you want, you can view the tags and create a web page completely in text. Actually, you can create a web page using the simplest form of text editor or any word processing program. Some purists feel this is the most exact way to create web pages, because more options become available and the control of screen appearance is more precise, but the time required to learn the more obscure tags is probably not worthwhile for most students. You will want your students concentrating on the content and spending just a reasonable amount of time learning to use the tools. For that reason they will probably do most of their web authoring in the WYSIWYG mode.

## Web Page Components

One way to understand the possibilities and demands of authoring web pages is to review some of the basic building blocks from which web pages are constructed. Once students have learned to control these components, they will be able to combine them in different ways to construct a wide variety of projects.

The components in the following list are all basic ones that you should be able to create with any of the authoring programs listed in "Resources to Expand Your Knowledge Base" at the end of the chapter.

*Web page components available in authoring programs*

- *Background color.* The color of the web page can be set by selecting a menu option and then choosing the desired color from a color palette.
- *Text.* Text can be entered directly or copied and pasted from some other application.
- *Headings, text size, and other text characteristics.* You can select text with the mouse and then choose the appropriate attribute with a button or menu option.
- *Lists.* You can select multiple lines of text and then convert them into a list of a particular type by using a button or menu option.
- *Images, sounds, and movies.* Multimedia elements are inserted by using a button or menu option that automatically connects the appropriate file. Some authoring programs allow you to add such a file by simply dragging it onto the page with the mouse.
- *Link.* A text segment or graphic can be linked to another web page. You select the text or graphic to serve as the link, then use a menu option (or a link editor in some programs) to choose the destination file; for pages at other sites, you type in the URL for the remote page.
- *Horizontal rule.* You can use a button to draw a horizontal line separating areas of the page.

The techniques described here were used to create the page in Figure 6.3 from two graphics files and a text file. (*Note:* The image at the top of the page is actually rectangular in shape, but it appears as an oval because part of it is transparent.) Some labels have been added to the figure to point out noteworthy features. All the underlined text and the smaller graphic serve as links to other web pages. To make this page available to a web user, the HTML file and the two graphic files would have to be loaded to a server.

## Creating a Table

Once students have acquired a little experience, we feel they should become familiar with the use of tables. Web authoring programs make the generation and manipulation of tables a relatively easy matter.

*Tables: A simple and useful device*

Tables can be inserted with the click of a button, and attributes of the table (number of rows and columns, visibility of the table borders, justifica-

**FIGURE 6.3** A web page created from common components.

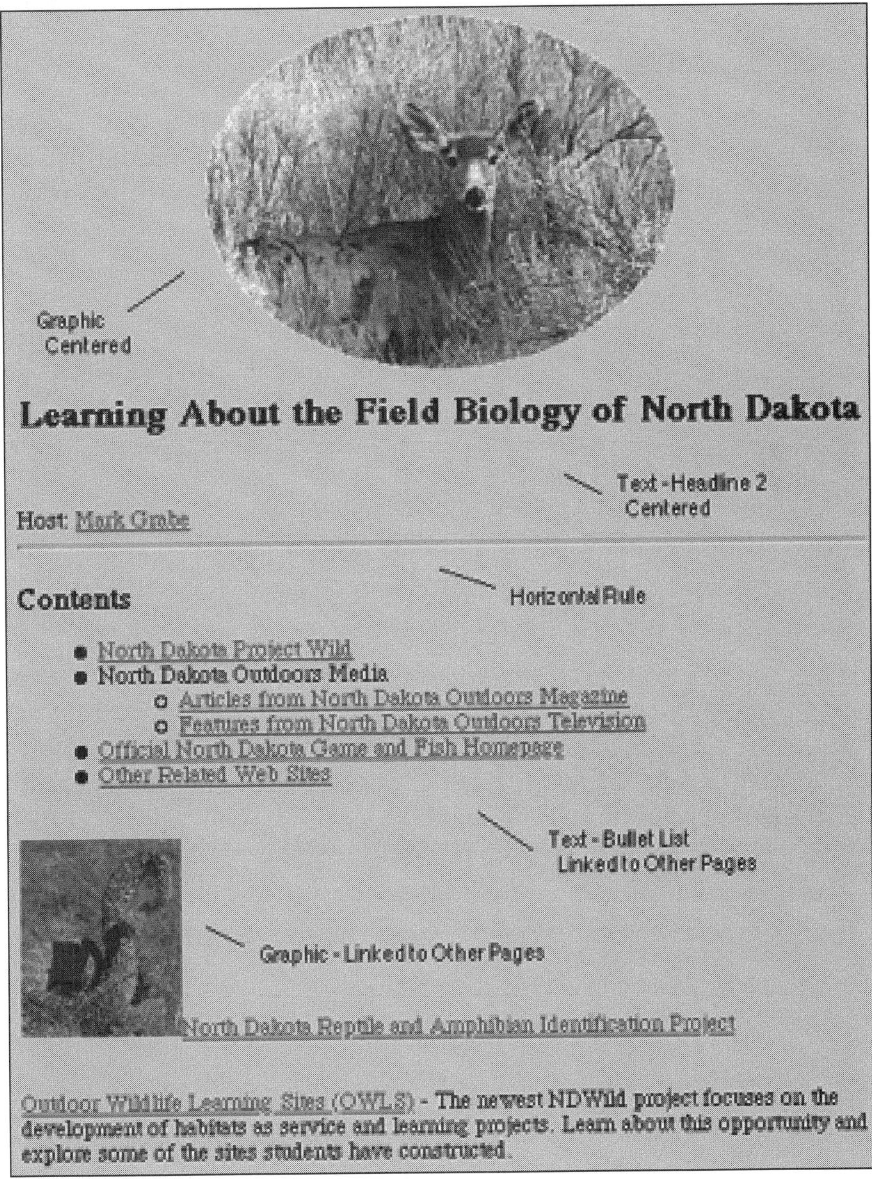


tion of text or images within cells) can be controlled by entering values in an editor. The dimensions of the table and of particular cells can be easily manipulated by dragging the borders. Figure 6.4 portrays part of a typical table editor and illustrates how cell boundaries can be dragged to change the appearance of the table.

Focus

## HTML Source Code

In case you're curious, the raw HTML document responsible for what you see in Figure 6.3 is shown here. At first glance it may seem more complicated than it really is. By looking back and forth from this document to the figure, you can probably determine what most of the tags mean.

```
<HTML>
<HEAD>
<TITLE>NDWild Home</TITLE>
</HEAD>
<BODY background="pics/slurry.jpg">
<P ALIGN=CENTER><IMG SRC="indexpic.GIF" WIDTH=233 HEIGHT=170
ALIGN=bottom></P>
<H2 ALIGN=CENTER>Learning About the Field Biology of North Dakota
</H2>
<P>Host: <A HREF="/dept/grabe">Mark Grabe</A><BR>
<HR ALIGN=LEFT>
<H3>Contents</H3>
<UL>
<LI>
<AHREF="http://ndwild.psych.und.nodak.edu/HTMLPages/projwildhome.html">North
Dakota Project Wild</A>
<LI>North Dakota Outdoors Media
<UL>
<LI><A HREF="media.html#anchor37399">Articles from North Dakota Outdoors
Magazine</A>
<LI><A HREF="media.html#anchor38708">Features from North Dakota Outdoors
Television</A>
</UL>
<LI><A HREF="http://www.state.nd.us/gnf/">Official North Dakota Game and
Fish Homepage</A>
<LI><A HREF="http://ndwild.psych.und.nodak.edu/HTMLPages/sites.html">Other
Related Web Sites</A>
</UL>
<P><BR>
<IMG SRC="rattleS.GIF" WIDTH=80 HEIGHT=95 ALIGN=bottom><A
HREF="keyhead.html">North Dakota Reptile and Amphibian Identification
Project</A><BR>
<BR>
<A HREF="http://ndwild.psych.und.nodak.edu/HTMLPages/owlshome.html">Outdoor
Wildlife Learning Sites (OWLS)</A> - The newest NDWild project focuses on
the development of habitats as service and learning projects. Learn about
this opportunity and explore some of the sites students have
constructed.<BR>
</BODY>
</HTML>
```
✷

**FIGURE 6.4** FileMaker Home Page table editor. (a) The editing window. (b) Dragging cell or table borders: by positioning the cursor on the border between two cells, you can use the mouse to drag it to a different position.

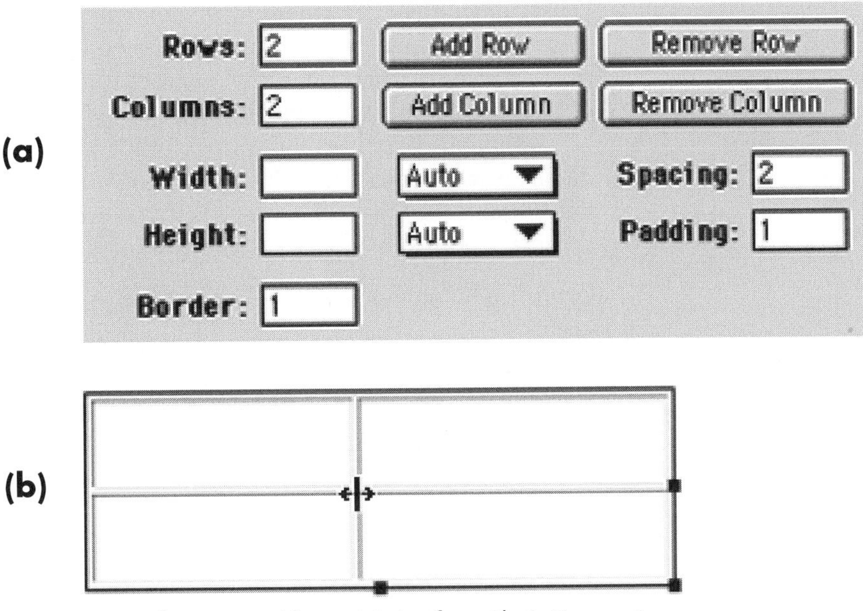


Screenshot reprinted by permission from Claris Corporation.

## ALTERNATIVE WAYS TO CONSTRUCT WEB PAGES

Content for the Web can be prepared in a surprising variety of ways. We have emphasized the use of general-purpose web authoring software, but there are some other approaches that are worth noting.

### Special Web Authoring Software for Students

Software companies, taking note of the potential for student web page authoring, have created products that attempt to simplify and focus the process of creating web pages.

*Web Workshop: A tool for young authors*

Web Workshop is a good example of an authoring environment designed specifically for young web authors. The author works by adding objects (images and text) within a window of a fixed size. The program comes with images (backgrounds and clipart), has some simple paint tools (lines, boxes, fill tool), and can import images created by another program. The text tool allows the addition and editing of text. Special tools allow the recording of sound segments and the creation of a link that launches a mail program preaddressed to a designated individual (the HTML mailto: tag). Any object (a picture, text selection, clipart) can be designated as a link and connected to another Web Workshop page or to an external URL.

Technically, Web Workshop stores this information in its own native file format. When saved, the file is also converted into an image map and an HTML document. The objects designated as links are converted into hot spots on the image map and also converted into text links that are displayed below the image map when the page appears in a browser. Both the HTML document and the image map are sent to the server.

Although developed for young authors, this program is capable of producing some impressive products, as shown in Figure 6.5. The most obvious limitation is that the web pages generated are intended to consist entirely of the image map and associated text links; this drastically limits web page size.

## Creating Web Pages with Tool Software

HTML pages were originally created with simple text editing programs, such as word processing software. These text-oriented programs were used to enter the HTML tags and text that would result in a multimedia web page when processed by a browser. Web authoring software emerged as a simpler alternative, allowing the author to create HTML tags without actually writing the HTML code.

**FIGURE 6.5** Web Workshop. (a) The authoring screen, showing a web page being created. (b) The finished web page when viewed with a browser.

**(b)**

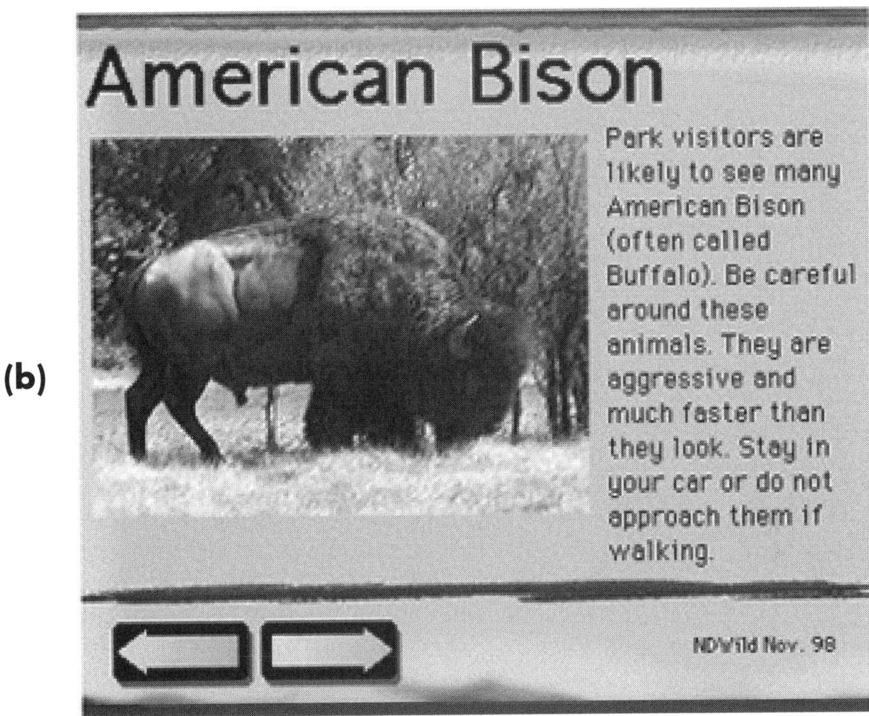


Screenshots reprinted by permission from Sunburst.

*Web authoring options in traditional software*

Now the distinction between traditional tool software and web authoring software is blurring. Many word processing, spreadsheet, and presentation programs offer options for saving files in HTML format. Even databases are being adapted so that they can interact with server software, though these adaptations are accomplished in different ways. To generate HTML files, tool software has been modified in two general ways:

*Conversion routines*

1. The software includes default conversion routines that translate properties of the standard file into HTML. For instance, a phrase that appears in bold type in a word processor is converted to HTML by surrounding it with the tags <B> and </B>. Similarly, the cell structure of a spreadsheet can be converted into a web table, and images are converted to JPG format.

*Incorporating HTML features*

2. The newer versions of tool software offer ways to incorporate HTML features directly into the original files. For example, many tool software programs offer some way to create links that branch to online web sites. These links may be activated directly from the tool software, which will launch a browser and attempt to connect to the designated web site, or

they can function as web page links when the document is saved in HTML format.

*Advantages of using traditional tool software*

These options in traditional tool software can be valuable to teachers and students for a number of reasons. One reason is access. The computers available in school settings probably already have tool software available, and the most recent versions of common packages like Microsoft Office, WordPerfect Suite, and AppleWorks will offer the HTML options we have just described. For you and your students, this familiar software also provides the advantages of convenience and familiarity. When your students want to create web pages from word processing documents, spreadsheet data, or a series of slides prepared with presentation software, they may find they can do so without becoming familiar with another program.

## Printing to the Web

*Myrmidon*

Still other products have emerged as companies find ways to help computer users convert their material for web presentation. An example well suited to classroom applications is a conversion program called Myrmidon, which functions by posing as a printer. Any program that can create a printed document can send the same document to Myrmidon through traditional print commands. Myrmidon accepts this input and automatically generates the HTML codes to produce a web page. For the classroom teacher, Myrmidon is an easy way to generate web pages.

Another advantage of Myrmidon is that it can translate products created by programs that do not have their own web conversion routines. For instance, HyperStudio and KidPix Studio, popular multimedia authoring programs for K–12 students (Grabe & Grabe, 1998), do not presently generate web pages. Myrmidon allows students to create projects using these tools and then "print" them to the Web.

*AppleWorks*

As another example, AppleWorks has a feature called "slide show," which allows a sequence of word processor or graphics pages to be presented as a series of full-screen images. The display shifts from image to image at the click of the mouse or after a preset delay. Because AppleWorks is a common multipurpose classroom tool, many teachers use the slide show feature for student projects. Although AppleWorks has a built-in web translation function, it would turn the slide show into a single long web document. Converting the same document with Myrmidon automatically creates a series of connected web pages that can be explored through the use of Forward and Back buttons.

## HyperStudio on the Web

HyperStudio is a popular multimedia authoring environment for educational applications. HyperStudio "stacks" are made up of individual "cards" that can incorporate text, images, animations, QuickTime movies, and sounds. Buttons can be added to stacks to control actions on a card (such as playing a movie or performing mathematical calculations) and to move between cards. Because even younger students can learn to construct impressive multimedia projects with HyperStudio, it has generated a loyal following among educators.

*Adapting HyperStudio for web pages*

HyperStudio stacks cannot be converted directly into interactive web pages. (Although Myrmidon can create web pages from individual HyperStudio cards, button actions and other programmable features are lost in the translation.) But HyperStudio's developers have added several interesting features to accommodate the tremendous interest in the Internet. First, a "button action" will launch a web browser and ask the browser to load a designated URL. Second, a browser plug-in will play HyperStudio stacks within the browser window.

What this means is that students can create a project in HyperStudio and then load this project on a school server. A link within a web page can request that this file, the HyperStudio stack, be sent to a browser. If the browser has the necessary plug-in (which can be downloaded at no cost; see "Resources to Expand Your Knowledge Base" at the end of the chapter), the stack appears within the browser and is fully functional.

*Impressive presentations*

The two enhancements we have just described can be combined to produce some very interesting and impressive presentations. A stack capable of card-to-card transitions, sound, animations, video, and many other interactive features—still very difficult to produce over the Internet—can operate within a browser and can also provide links to other web content.

The one negative factor we see in this approach is the issue of file size and transfer speed. Even relatively small HyperStudio stacks can be over a megabyte in size, and even with a direct connection, transferring this much information over the Internet can take a considerable amount of time. It may be worth the wait. Once the stack is on your machine, you can work with it intensively without additional waiting.

If you find yourself in a classroom where students have considerable experience with HyperStudio, it may be wise to take advantage of this experience rather than spending time developing the students' web authoring skills. The combination of a very basic web page and HyperStudio may offer an efficient way to generate a quality web product and encourage active learning.

## SUMMARY

◆ This chapter offers two views of design: design of products and design of personal knowledge. The common theme in each form of design is the commitment to purpose: both products and knowledge are structured to accomplish a purpose. The role of purpose in learning sometimes goes unrecognized in educational settings. Without purpose, learning becomes focused on the accumulation of information and not on its application.

◆ Student-authored web projects represent a concrete integration of the design of knowledge and the design of a public product. The online product provides a purpose for the students' construction of meaningful personal knowledge.

◆ Web design projects might be considered a special application of a cooperative learning model called "group investigation." In a group investigation, students identify aspects of a general theme that interest them and then join teams to study these individual topics. Each team identifies the essence of what it has learned and presents this information to the rest of the class. The guided discovery/jigsaw method proposed by Brown and Lehrer's hypercomposition design model represents strategies that use technology to implement cooperative group investigations.

◆ In cooperative design activities, the teacher takes a somewhat untraditional role. In the early stages of a project, the teacher might provide direct instruction, demonstrate critical information gathering or technology skills, model cognitive processes by externalizing thinking behavior, and stimulate cognitive behavior with leading questions. As students become more experienced, the teacher will play a less direct role.

◆ Web pages can be constructed in many different ways. Web authoring programs allow authors to manipulate the physical appearance of objects (text, graphics, tables), and the software will automatically add the HTML tags that produce the desired effects. Many traditional productivity tools (word processing, database, presentation software) also can convert their standard files to HTML pages. Many such productivity tools already exist in schools and are familiar to students, so the use of traditional tools may be a way to get started with web page authoring.

## REFLECTING ON CHAPTER 6

### Activities

1. Briefly outline a potential web project that students can work on in groups. How will your approach resemble the methods described in this chapter? Are there any significant differences between your approach and the models we have described?
2. Would the methods described in this chapter require any change in the way you see your role as a teacher? Why or why not?
3. Conduct a survey of the "tools" software in your computer laboratory. Which programs offer the option of saving files in HTML format?

### Key Terms

cognitive apprenticeship *(p. 178)*
cooperative learning *(p. 171)*
design *(p. 169)*
group investigation *(p. 172)*
guided discovery *(p. 173)*
hypercomposition design model *(p. 174)*
hypertext markup language (HTML) *(p. 180)*
jigsaw *(p. 173)*
knowledge as design *(p. 170)*
tag *(p. 181)*
web authoring program *(p. 180)*
WYSIWYG *(p. 180)*

### Resources to Expand Your Knowledge Base

**Cooperative Learning**

Johnson, D., Johnson, R., & Holubec, E. (1991). *Cooperation in the classroom.* Revised ed. Edina, MN: Interaction Book Company.

Koschmann, T. (Ed.) (1996). *Computer-supported collaborative learning.* Mahwah, NJ: Erlbaum.

Slavin, R. (1991). *Student team learning: A practical guide to cooperative learning.* 3rd ed. Washington, DC: National Education Association.

### Thematic Instruction and Classroom Projects

Fredericks, A., Meinbach, A., & Rothlein, L. (1993). *Thematic units: An integrated approach to teaching science and social studies.* New York: HarperCollins.

Katz, L., & Chard, S. (1989). *Engaging children's minds: The project approach.* Norwood, NJ: Ablex.

Nagel, N. (1996). *Learning through real-world problem solving.* Thousand Oaks, CA: Corwin Press.

Teachers might also review recent copies of *Learning and Leading with Technology* to find examples of student-generated hypermedia projects.

### Software for Web Authoring

*Adobe PageMill* is available for the Macintosh from Adobe Systems Incorporated, **http://www.adobe.com**.

*Filemaker Home Page* (formerly Claris Homepage) is available for the Macintosh and Windows operating systems from FileMaker, Inc., **http://www.filemaker.com/**.

*Microsoft Frontpage* is available for the Macintosh and Windows operating systems from Microsoft, Inc., **http://www.microsoft.com/frontpage/**.

*Netscape Composer* is available for the Macintosh and Windows operating systems from Netscape, **http://www.netscape.com/**.

### Other Software

*AppleWorks* (formerly ClarisWorks) is available for the Macintosh and Windows operating systems from Apple Computer, **http://www.apple.com/appleworks/**.

*HyperStudio* is available for the Macintosh and Windows operating systems from Roger Wagner Publishing, **http://www.hyperstudio.com** (the plug-in allowing HyperStudio stacks to appear within a web browser is available at **http://www.hyperstudio.com/lab/plugin.html**).

*Microsoft Office* is available for the Macintosh and Windows operating systems from Microsoft, Inc., **http://www.microsoft.com/office/**.

*Myrmidon* is a product for the Macintosh operating system from Terry Morse Software, Inc., **http://www.terrymorse.com**.

*Web Workshop* is a product for the Macintosh and Windows operating systems from Sunburst Communications, **http://www.sunburst.com**.

*WordPerfect Suite* is available for the Macintosh and Windows operating systems from Corel Corporation, **http://www.wordperfect.com**.

Chapter 7

# Designing Web Pages: Principles for Students and Teachers

## ORIENTATION

This chapter extends Chapter 6's discussion of constructing web pages as part of a content-area project. Here we concentrate on the design process involved in creating the final product. We will identify basic principles that contribute to effective communication and efficient navigation. Keep in mind, however, that the activity of designing a web page should also contribute to designing knowledge—that is, to the students' creation of their own personal understanding.

As you read, look for answers to the following questions:

**FOCUS QUESTIONS**

- What organizational, text, graphic, and navigational design principles should students be aware of as they develop web pages?
- What special issues must designers consider in preparing graphic images for the Web?
- How can you assess your students' performance on web design projects?

## The OWLS Project

The military Jeep rounds the corner of the school, drives off the pavement onto the grass, and parks in the middle of an area of tall plants growing between two wings of the building. An enlisted man gets out of the Jeep and disgustedly begins kicking at some heaps of dead branches overgrown with vegetation. Someone has complained about the "weeds" in this section of the Air Force base, and he has arrived to investigate. Just then the janitor emerges from the school.

"What are you doing?" the janitor yells.

Without bothering to answer, the young man yells back, "Look at this mess, they didn't even bother to clear out these old trees!"

"You better get that Jeep out of there," the janitor responds. "Those are rare plants the kids have been growing."

In a few moments, as his dilemma sinks in, the enlisted man is down on his hands and knees attempting to prop up the plants he has mangled.

Ted Hoberg, who teaches on an Air Force base in North Dakota, tells this story to illustrate the residents' general lack of familiarity with native vegetation. He, some of the other teachers, and many students at the school are trying to establish a natural habitat site, and it does look out of place among the carefully manicured lawns, shrubs, and trees of the Air Force base. Strict ordinances require that those living on the base keep their yards neatly mowed and free of weeds.

### Preparing the OWLS Site

The tall and sometimes scraggly plants of Ted's little patch aren't actually rare; they're just native plants growing naturally. The dead branches were hauled in and carefully placed about the site. The wood piles provide cover for rabbits. Some reptiles live under the logs. The snakes and toads are Ted's favorites.

Ted and his associates are developing an OWLS site. OWLS is an acronym for Outdoor Wildlife Learning Site. The basic idea is to take a small area of land near a school and create a natural habitat. It is hands-on work and it is dirty, but it is also real science. This isn't just reading about ecology; this is an opportunity for the students to create a habitat and then study it.

The students are actually trying to create several different habitats. One group has dug pits and lined them with plastic to create small pools. Another has tried to create a kind of lowland area. They dug out an area and planted marsh plants, and they try to keep the ground muddy. This group has taken to calling itself "the swamp people." Butterflies are a common elementary science unit, so a group of older students has planted milkweed and

**FIGURE 7.1** One sample web page from the OWLS project at Ted Hoberg's school.

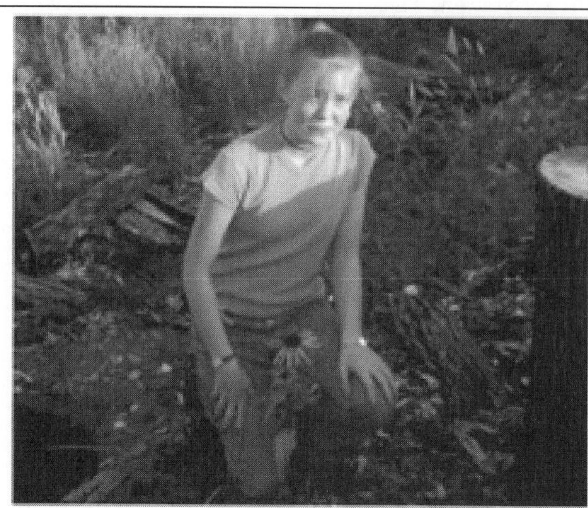

**Wildflowers (forbs)**

---

We have been trying to get wildflowers (forbs) started on our OWL site. The flower you see here is the purple coneflower (*Echinacea*). The coneflower is common in North Dakota. However, it is now thought that Echinacea has health benefits and may help the immune system. You can buy teas and pills made from this plant in health food stores. People have been digging the plants up and selling them. Taking plants from the wild is wrong and the plant should be grown on farms if we want to use it for medicine. We bought our plants at a nursery. Now we hope our plants will spread. We do not pick the flowers on our site.

---

OWLS | Wildflowers

other plants that attract monarchs and painted ladies. Several bird feeders have been added. Even the teachers enjoy watching the birds come to the feeders during the winter. Around the edge of the plot, Ted is adding some small plots of agricultural plants. Because the air base students come from all over the country, seeing what sugar beets, sunflowers, and wheat look like may help them understand how many locals make their living.

### Student Learning: Web Pages and Other Opportunities

Students have begun to create web pages to communicate with others about their projects. The OWLS program is supported by the State Department of

Game and Fish, and there are nearly twenty such sites being developed around the state, differing greatly in size, habitats, and upkeep methods. It isn't feasible for most students or teachers to visit other OWLS locations, but they share what they are developing by means of the Internet.

Figure 7.1 shows a student-created web page from the web site at Ted's school. Showing off their work this way is fun for the students, and it is also fascinating to see what similar groups at other schools are doing. To follow up their "virtual visits" to each other's web sites, the students and teachers can send questions and comments by e-mail.

Ted feels that the students' work on the OWLS physical site and on the web site offers a productive complement to traditional classroom activities. The same information can be approached in different ways. Students are motivated because the habitats and the web pages they create both provide a sense of ownership: "We did that!"

The group constructions allow a diversity of students to find particular activities that appeal to them. For instance, some students specialize in creating graphic images for the web site. One somewhat troubled student delights in beginning the day by watering the plants in the OWLS site with a garden hose. "It seems to relax him," Ted says.

The OWLS habitats and web projects are intended to develop together as students conduct observational research at the sites. What birds come to the feeder? Will native plants be able to squeeze out weeds? When do the monarchs appear? The students' web pages will summarize the data they collect and the conclusions they draw.

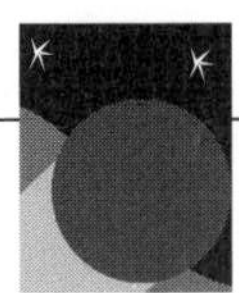

## THE DESIGN OF WEB PROJECTS

In this chapter we will explore what you and your students need to know about web design to incorporate well-made web pages into class projects. Like other design tasks, web page construction is based on certain priorities. But the priorities for teachers and students are somewhat different from those for most web designers.

*Educational vs. commercial purposes*

Our primary emphasis in this chapter is on structuring the web project as an effective learning opportunity for the student. Guidelines for commercial online hypermedia won't always be practical for students and teachers. For example, standard web design principles encourage concise text messages and small graphics. But what if your students' project involves writing short stories or creating watercolor paintings and sharing these original creations with another class focused on the same theme? Would you want the students to summarize their stories as bulleted lists or present their paintings as miniatures? Of course not. You and your students would give greater priority to the instructional task than to its presentation on the Web.

With these points in mind, look again at the OWLS page illustrated in

Figure 7.1. How does it differ from some of the commercial pages you've seen on the Web? Do you think it offers an appropriate combination of design and instructional content? In what situations would it offer benefits to site visitors as well as to the students who learned in the process of creating it? Keep thinking about these questions as you read the following sections, which summarize some of the more common design suggestions that seem appropriate to student projects.

*Gaining knowledge and pride*

In general, we want to emphasize the knowledge acquisition and inquiry activities encouraged by meaningful projects, but we also want students to be proud of the products they create. We think this combination of outcomes is realistic. As you read, keep in mind that you as a teacher will need to evaluate the issues we raise and make decisions appropriate to your specific classroom situations.

One further note before we begin. Our emphasis is on the development of a set of web pages that are the culmination of a particular content-area project. Such a web project typically represents just one of many resources available on a school's web site. The design principles we discuss here will not necessarily be applied uniformly to the entire school site. That does not seem a practical approach for school web sites, and it would prevent individual classes from working through the design process on their own. Chapter 8 will address some issues that apply to the overall operation of a school site.

## PLANNING A WEB PROJECT

*Initial decisions*

Before students begin assembling a web project, they need to make a few decisions that will guide their work. Without these decisions, the early stages of development will require a lot of fumbling, which may be discouraging. Even if some of the fundamental ideas change as students try them out, taking the time to develop guidelines will improve the efficiency of the process and the quality of the product.

In the early stages of designing a project site, you and your students should consider the nature of the content the web resources will address, the purpose to be achieved, and the audience likely to consider the material (Lynch & Horton, 1997, 1998). Let's look at these elements one by one.

### CONTENT

*Designing for content*

The *content* is the information or experience students have to offer. In theory, they should be designing web pages in response to the characteristics of the instructional content rather than creating content to fit within a design. Usually you will begin with a topic and learning activity appropriate to the curriculum and then extend the learning experience by requiring your students to document or teach what they have learned in the form of a web project.

## PURPOSE

*A continuum of purposes*

*Purpose* refers to the intended experience for the individuals who will examine the web project. In one way or another, the web project should allow those who connect to learn something. Figure 7.2 shows one interesting way to think of the range of such experiences: a continuum including the categories of training, teaching, education, and reference (Lynch & Horton, 1997). These categories differ in how much control the designer attempts to exert over the learning process.

### Potential Purposes of a Web Project

*Training in specific skills*

- *Training.* At the left end of the continuum in Figure 7.2, the web product is intended to develop specific skills in the most efficient way possible. For example, after a study of recycling methods, a class might produce a web project explaining how to create and manage a compost heap. Such a presentation would probably follow a step-by-step format.

*Encouraging study of alternatives*

- *Teaching and education.* Experiences in the middle of the continuum try to encourage the viewer to consider an issue or topic, but are less directive in the conclusion the learner is to reach. For example, a web project might explain the snow goose crisis that you read about in Chapter 5 and present various possible strategies for solving this dilemma. The web pages would encourage the visitor to examine the issues, weigh the alternatives, and come to a personal conclusion.

*Collecting reference material*

- *Reference.* At the far right end of the continuum in Figure 7.2, the intent is to offer a collection of resources based on a central theme. For example, students might create a collection of web pages presenting local buildings of historical significance. Each page might include a picture of

**FIGURE 7.2** A continuum describing the possible educational purposes of web pages (based on Lynch & Horton, 1997).

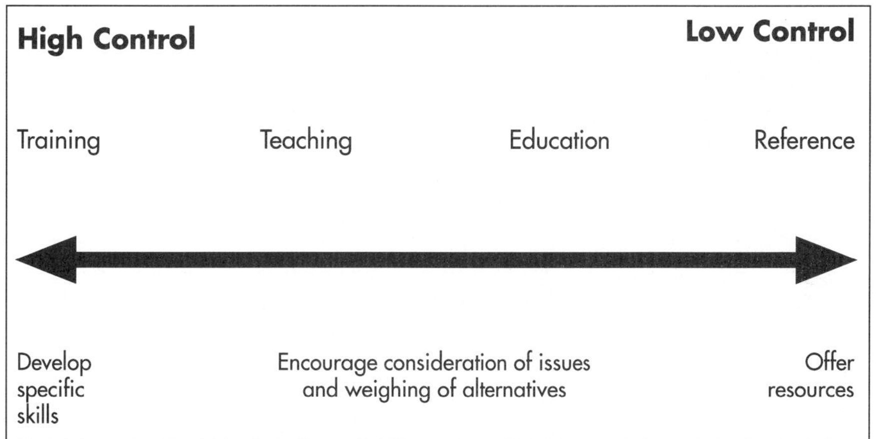

the building as it looks today, an earlier picture if available, and a paragraph explaining the significance of the building.

*How purpose influences choices*

Committing to a purpose will influence the information that students choose to present and the structure of the web site. For instance, for a training approach, they might give the web presentation a linear structure that leads the learner from one web page to another. For a reference page, on the other hand, they might choose a more complex structure in which the learner could choose a particular topic of greatest interest and branch off from the main page.

### AUDIENCE

*Adjusting presentation to the audience*

The *audience* is the group for which the web content is being prepared. The audience may consist of parents, other students from the school, students of a similar age at any school connected to the Internet, or any other such group. As web authors, students can attempt to adjust their presentation style, examples, and even the site appearance to appeal to their intended audience.

The target population can be defined in other useful ways as well (Lynch & Horton, 1997). Web "surfers," for example, can be distinguished from web users who are searching for specific information. Web surfers are simply exploring, more or less at random; if they are the audience, a major design goal is to capture their attention and lead them to dig deeper into the content a site offers. Attractive graphics and intriguing titles are frequent tactics for this purpose. On the other hand, experienced web users and those who return to a particular site are frequently looking for specific useful information and do not want to waste time with embellishments that detract from their purpose. These users value efficiency and clear communication.

*"Surfers" versus frequent users*

You and your students might consider these alternatives and the related design strategies and then discuss what the students' pages should look like. The somewhat conflicting goals of attracting casual browsers and serving those who want an efficient source of information will often spark a lively discussion.

## CONTENT ORGANIZATION

Content organization concerns the way individual web documents are connected. The Web, because it is a form of hypermedia, offers the designer many options for connecting one document to another.

As you have seen in earlier chapters, the designer connects various web documents through the use of *links.* The links allow a structure to be imposed on the total body of content. A structure of some sort exists in any medium. For example, in a typical textbook, the author creates a structure so that the reader encounters ideas in a certain order and interrelates them in a certain way. While the reader can override this structure by thumbing through the text or by searching for information using the index, the "built-in" structure encourages the reader to move from one page to the next.

*Options for structure*

A hypermedia application can promote this type of sequential structure, or it can facilitate other options. The purpose of the web page should influence the choice of structure. As a starting point, we suggest you think of the possible alternatives as *sequential, hierarchical,* and *web* structures, as illustrated in Figure 7.3. These options describe idealized forms. In practice, web projects are usually hybrids of these alternatives.

## SEQUENTIAL DESIGN

The most basic way to present information is with a **sequential design,** in which each element leads directly to the next in logical sequence, with no other options for the user. You are already familiar with this structure because it is typically used in print media to present short descriptions or explanations.

**FIGURE 7.3** Common organizational structures for web sites.

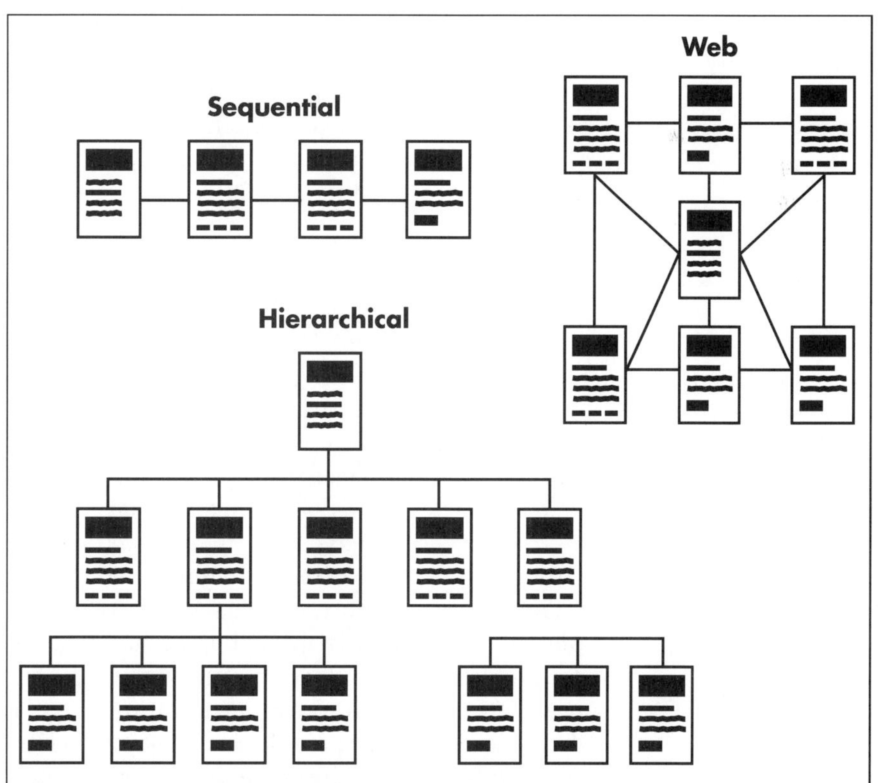

*Sequential design: Logical, simple*

The major advantage of a sequential design is simplicity. Users are familiar with this format, and it is also relatively easy for the designers, because there is no need to set up a complicated navigation system. This may be the best structure for younger or beginning designers. As we mentioned earlier, the sequential structure is especially useful when the purpose is to train the viewer in a specific skill.

If your students use a sequential design for a web project focused on a brief and well-defined topic, they can embellish the structure by adding a few links that expand key concepts, provide an opportunity to consider an interesting sidelight, or branch to related web sites developed by other authors. But the emphasis in sequential design is on the careful and systematic development of the main idea.

## HIERARCHICAL DESIGN

A **hierarchical design,** as you can see in Figure 7.3, organizes content as a system of categories and subcategories. A user interacts with information of this type by moving through a series of choice points—that is, branches. Each branch narrows the user's immediate focus in some way.

*Hierarchical design: Organizing by category*

The Yahoo! directory, described in Chapter 4 (pp. 118–119), is a good example of an extensive web project organized in this manner. One purpose of a hierarchical structure is to organize information so users can find what they need without inspecting all the available information. A hierarchical structure also allows users to reorient themselves if they become lost. When disoriented, it is a simple matter to move back up the hierarchy and gain a sense of the structure for the entire site.

## WEB DESIGN

*Web design: The full potential of hypermedia*

A **web design,** as Figure 7.3 illustrates, takes fuller advantage of the potential of hypermedia by creating a complex set of connections among web pages. The intent is to provide users as much freedom as possible to follow links that address their own interests and needs. Such structures are particularly common when the purpose of the web site falls toward the right side of the continuum in Figure 7.2—that is, when the site is intended to serve as a reference.

*Drawbacks of web design*

The learner-centered aspects of a web structure may seem attractive. Throughout this book we have argued for the benefits of allowing learners certain freedom to pursue their own interests. You may wonder, then, why your students shouldn't always build that potential into their own web sites. One problem is that web designs are not suitable for inexperienced users who are encountering completely novel information. Nor are they appropriate when the intent is to provide an efficient experience focused on learning a specific thing (the left side of the continuum in Figure 7.2). For your students' web projects, then, you will probably want to adopt design guidelines that discourage the widespread use of complex structures that are difficult for both the authors and the potential users to conceptualize (Lynch & Horton, 1997).

## NAVIGATION OPTIONS AND THE USER INTERFACE

As web page designers, your students should give some thought to the practical mechanisms by which potential users will interact with the web resources. Collectively, these mechanisms represent the **user interface.**

*Problem of passive experiences*

Despite all the recent developments in web technology, many people consider web experiences too passive. This is especially true when web pages are compared with the kinds of educational experiences available through CD-ROMs or through software that can be loaded on an individual computer or operated over a LAN. Some methods are emerging for making web pages more interactive, such as small programs written in Java (see the Afterword, pp. 299–300) and special programs that run on the web server. At present, we do not feel these extensions are practical for the kinds of student web projects we are proposing. If you are interested in greater interactivity, you might want your students to develop projects in a multimedia authoring environment such as HyperStudio, as described in Chapter 6 (pp. 188–189).

*The navigation system and interactivity*

At present, then, the most basic form of interactivity for web designers is the **navigation system**—that is, the ways the user can move about within the web site and connect to other sites. The main tools for navigation are the links that the web designer embeds on the page. Some links allow transitions to **anchors** that mark other spots on the same web page. Other links lead to different web pages within the same site, and some lead to pages on other sites.

*Hot spots and image maps*

Links are usually a word or phrase, an image, or a designated part of an image. When an individual image contains multiple **hot spots,** or links, the image is called an **image map.** Figure 7.4 contains an image map from a site

**FIGURE 7.4** An image map representing categories of historical artifacts. By clicking with the mouse on a particular segment of the image, the web user links to artifacts of a particular type. Clicking on the framed picture, for instance, takes the user to a collection of photographs.

called Grandparents' Attic, a history project that allows learners to explore historical artifacts organized around historical themes. The various artifacts include documents, sounds, old photographs, personal possessions, and pictures of objects. Clicking on different segments of the image in Figure 7.4 takes the user to different categories of artifacts (we will let you consider which parts of the image represent which categories). Later in the chapter we will look in more detail at the construction of image maps.

The following sections explore design principles for setting up individual links and for allowing collections of links to work together to provide a navigation system.

## GUIDELINES FOR INDIVIDUAL LINKS

Here are some simple suggestions for you and your students to follow in creating individual links:

*Checking for broken links*

- *Make sure the links work, and then check regularly to be sure they continue to work.* One of the most common and overlooked problems with web pages is links that do not function. **Broken links** can exist for many reasons. Changes to your web site or changes on other web sites can invalidate links. Errors in adding the address to a link may not be apparent when you test the links from the authoring program. Make certain to check links *after* the pages have been put on the server, and continue to check them periodically.

*Adhering to link conventions*

- *Change customary link characteristics only after careful thought.* Users rely on conventions to guide their use of web pages. They expect that text links will be underlined and appear in a particular color, and they anticipate that images serving as links will be indicated by a colored border. Be consistent in how links are indicated and alert users to departures from conventions.

*Making a link's function clear*

- *A link's function should be apparent from the link name or the context.* In other words, you want users to know what is likely to happen when a link is selected. The text phrase or the image to serve as a link should be carefully selected.

*Links as part of natural syntax*

- *When using text links embedded within a segment of text, the linked phrase should be a natural part of the text.* Don't say "*Click here* for more information on the 1971 law protecting wild horses." Instead, make use of the critical part of a meaningful sentence: "*A 1971 law* protected wild horses as part of the national heritage."

*Avoiding distractions*

- *Make sure your links are not too much of a distraction.* Why write something to inform and then fill it with a large number of invitations for the reader to go somewhere else? Embedded links should address only the most essential connections to other resources. In place of distracting links in the midst of your page, consider adding a list of additional resource links following the main body of content.

*Alerting the user to special conditions*

- *Links that may take a significant amount of time or that require special resources should be clearly designated.* For example, links to pages containing large graphic images might indicate the file size of the images in parentheses ("contains 3.5 MB graphic images"). This will alert the user that following that link will take some time. Likewise, links to pages requiring a special capability on the user's machine should indicate that capability and how the user might acquire it. You might annotate a link, "Requires QuickTime 4.0 plug-in," and then offer a separate link to a page where that plug-in can be downloaded.

## GUIDELINES FOR THE NAVIGATION SYSTEM

In designing the interface, it is important to provide users some overview of the information resources and to show them how to move efficiently among these resources. The user must know what actions are possible. At any point, the user must have some idea of where he or she is within the information and how to get to some other desired location. To put it simply:

*The "sense of place" in hyperspace*

- *When exploring a hypermedia system, users must have some sense of place (Lynch & Horton, 1997).*

*Site maps*

This general context can be provided in a couple of ways. Many projects supply an overview in the form of a site map. A **site map** can be a diagram that shows the organization of the site and the structure of links among the major parts. Or it can take the form of an outline that lists the major components and subcomponents of a site (Williams & Tollett, 1998). Usually, clicking on an element of the diagram or outline will take the user to that page of the project. The site map is usually available from the project home page.

*Site menus*

A second method provides context in the form of a visible menu. The menu may appear in a separate frame or in the cell of a table. A common technique is to use a narrow vertical column on the left-hand side of the display to present the menu and a broad area on the right-hand side to present the page content (see Figure 7.7 on page 207). A related approach makes use of a menu bar presented at the top or bottom of the page. The menu bar may take the form of a series of images, as shown in Figure 7.5. Or it may be an image map or a simple series of text links separated by vertical bars (such as *Home* | *Notes* | *Resources* | *News*). However the menu bar is constructed, the user can simply click on an item to move to the designated location.

**FIGURE 7.5** A simple menubar built from individual images.

Home Notes Resources News

Taking all these considerations into account, here are some basic suggestions for creating navigation systems:

*Tips for navigation systems*

- The navigation system should provide access to major choice points. Within a hierarchical structure, for example, that would mean access to the major divisions of the structure.
- The navigation system should provide an indication of the present location. Within the menu system, the choice corresponding to the page presently being displayed is typically marked or differentiated in some way.
- The navigation system should use a consistent approach throughout the project. For example, if a project has a number of chapters, the navigation system might consist of a link to the project home page followed by links to the major components of the chapter being examined. From any page, a user could move to a different component of the chapter or return to the project home page in order to select a different chapter.

## PAGE DESIGN

In designing web pages, you and your students will surely want them to look nice. But in addition to appearance, good page design optimizes the qualities of communication and interactivity.

*Reluctance to scroll*

Decisions about many aspects of page design depend on a careful consideration of the three elements we discussed earlier in the chapter: content, purpose, and audience. For example, it appears that casual web visitors rarely scroll down to view material that is not visible in the top portion of a page (Lynch & Horton, 1997). If you were interested in attracting random browsers, what would you do? Clearly, you would choose carefully what appeared in the top 4 or 5 inches of your web pages. You might use this space to try to make the visitors curious or capture their attention.

Now consider a different scenario. Assume that you want to provide biology teachers with some curriculum ideas on recycling, including some classroom experiments they can conduct with pop bottle composting. Your description of how to do pop bottle composting experiments is about five typewritten pages in length, and you have four pictures that help explain how to set up the apparatus. Would you simply put all this information on one page?

*Reading on screen versus printing*

Most web visitors prefer not to read more than three pages of text from the screen, and they will frequently print out longer documents. So, you might say, I can still put all the information on one page—let them print the descriptions out. But there are some other inherent design problems.

Assume that you decide to present some of the information in the form of a table (see the description of web tables in Chapter 6, pp. 182–183), because this technique allows you some control over how graphics and text will appear on different monitors and browsers. You set the width of the table at

600 pixels because this is the recommended width for the presentation of a web page on a standard monitor. Do you recognize any design problems yet?

*Width problems in printing web pages*

If not, take a sheet of typewriter paper and hold it up against a standard monitor. If you align the sheet of paper with the left-hand side of the monitor, you will notice that several inches of the monitor on the right-hand side are uncovered. Perhaps, in trying to print pages from the Web, you have already discovered the problem this presents. If what appears on the monitor extends beyond the width of the paper, part of the information does not print. (*Note:* If this does happen to you when you print from a web site, try setting your printer to "landscape" orientation. This will print pages sideways on standard sheets of paper, giving you extra width.)

These examples illustrate that page design can involve many different concerns. The following sections offer a number of suggestions for page layout and text presentation.

## PAGE LAYOUT

Objects on a web page should be placed and grouped in a way that facilitates the user's activities. (An object in this sense could be a segment of text, a picture, a link, a form field, or any multimedia element that can be presented on a web page.) From this general principle we can deduce a couple of more specific points:

*Basic principles of page layout*

- The placement of objects should be predictable.
- Objects important to the purpose of the page should be presented in a way that attracts the user's attention.

### Page Templates

One way to develop a strategy for pages of a certain type is to create a template (see Figure 7.6). A **page template** defines certain areas of the page and identifies the general type of information that is to appear in these areas. The simple template shown in Figure 7.6 would be appropriate for many student web projects. This template consists of three areas: navigation, content, and page footer.

#### *Areas of a Page Template*

*Navigation area*

- The *navigation area* is intended to provide a link back to the more general level of the site hierarchy (such as the school or class home page) as well as links to major pages of the project. In Figure 7.6 the navigation area appears at the left, with a gray background added.

*Content area*

- The *content area* (the blank area of 360 pixels in the figure) establishes a large space for present project information.

*Page footer*

- The *page footer* is an area for providing some important items of information: the date the page was created, the identity of the project, the host

**FIGURE 7.6** Example of a web page template. This template consists of two tables, each made up of three cells. The tables are separated by a horizontal rule. The dimensions are set so that the total width is less than 500 pixels, allowing the page to be printed on standard paper. The height of the page would vary depending on how much content was added.

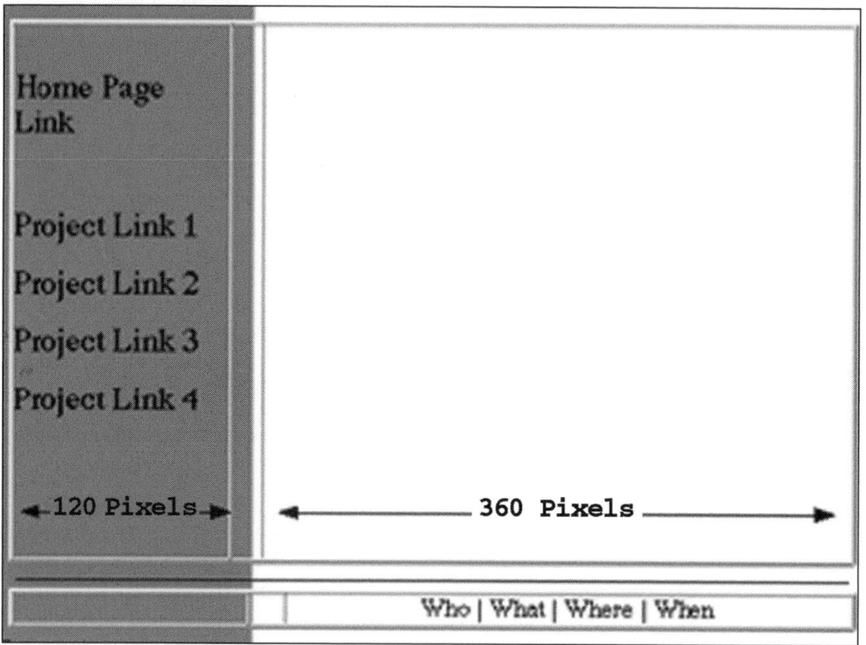


(school), and the author. In Figure 7.6 this is the bar at the bottom labeled "Who | What | Where | When." (*Note:* In many cases, it is inappropriate to use student names as the "authors," so a class project might use the teacher's name: "Mrs. Grabe's 4th Grade.")

*The template as an HTML file*

A page template can mean different things. It may be simply a sketch on paper that students use as a guideline in creating their own web pages. In the example used here, however, the template is an HTML file that establishes key areas of the page and includes some dummy text to indicate where critical elements are to be inserted. This file would be distributed to students, who would use it as a starting point for their own individual pages. This kind of template could be created using many different web page authoring programs now available in schools, such as the ones described in Chapter 6. You may find it very useful to construct an HTML template for your students. More advanced students could also create their own simple templates after some basic instruction in the use of a web authoring program.

Figure 7.7 shows a web page that students built using this template. In

**FIGURE 7.7** Example of a finished web page based on the template in Figure 7.6.

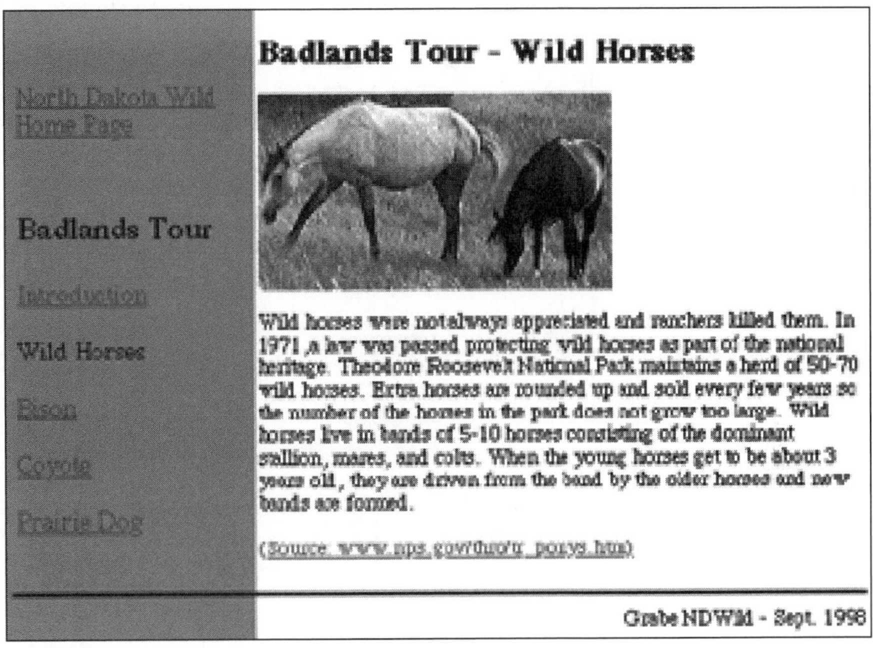


*A sample page designed with a template*

this case, the project involved a summary of observations made during a field trip to a national park. Some of the elements in the design are controlled by the template, and some represent conventions that were established so that each page would have a consistent appearance. Each page in this series includes a picture of one of the animals that was observed and some information about that animal gleaned from online resources. The title for each page includes the overall project title as well as the name of the particular animal. The animal names are also used as links in the navigation area of the page. For instance, by clicking on "Bison," users can go to a page about bison. (On screen, the link to the current page is clearly differentiated because it is in a different color from the other links and is not underlined.) At the bottom of the content area, the "Source" line provides a link to the online source from which the students drew their information.

## Additional Guidelines for Page Layout

To develop our suggestions a bit further, here are some specific guidelines for page layout:

*Consistency*

- Perhaps the most basic rule is consistency. Using a template is one way to gain consistency. If you don't use a template, try to maintain the same format throughout a page or sequence of pages.

**FIGURE 7.8** Methods for aligning objects on a web page. (a) Inconsistent alignment, which produces a jumbled appearance that makes the page hard to read. (b) A consistent left alignment, much clearer for the user.

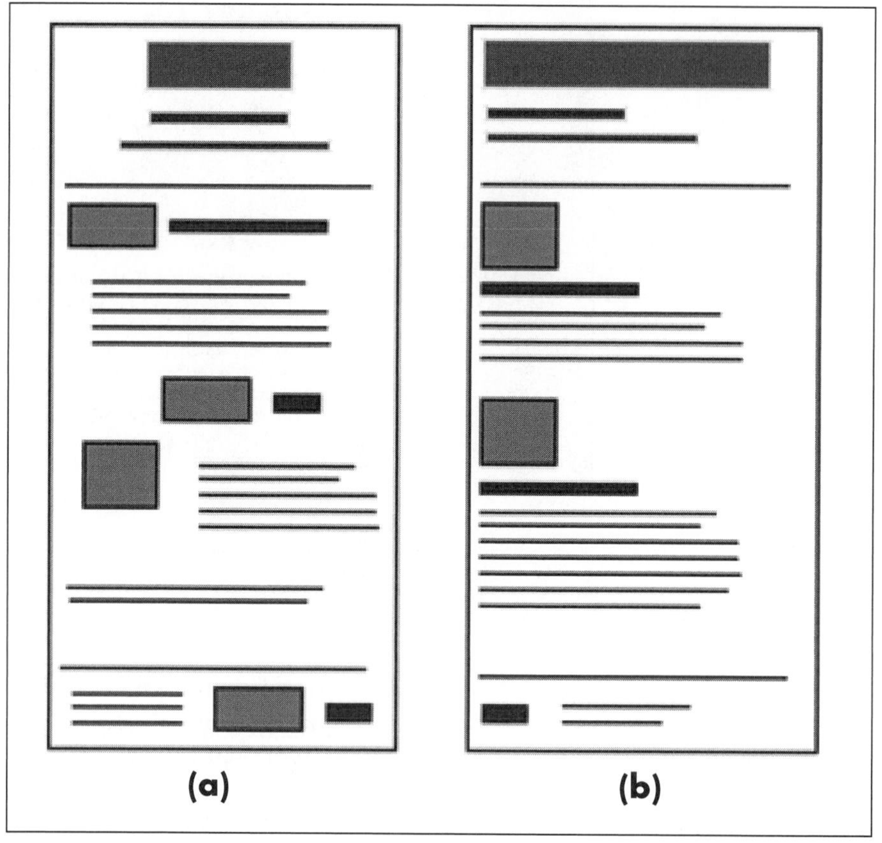


For instance, Lynch and Horton (1997) recommend that new designers stick to one method of alignment for all objects. For most purposes this would mean left alignment, the kind used in Figure 7.7. Do not mix centered titles or graphics with left-aligned headings and text. Figure 7.8 illustrates the jumbled effect that often results from inconsistent alignment.

*Using tables to control alignment*

- The appearance of web pages can vary based on the operating system and browser used to view the pages. If your pages require precise alignment, as might be the case when you want to align text to the left or right of an image, the best approach is to create a table and use the cells in the table to align related elements.

*Suggested page widths*

- Consider whether your pages are likely to be viewed from the screen or printed. The suggested width for screen pages is 600 pixels. The suggested width for pages likely to be printed is about 500 pixels. Page width is most likely to be an issue when using tables or frames.

### TEXT PRESENTATION

Typical guidelines for hypermedia recommend against the presentation of page after page of continuous text. Screens of solid text are difficult to read.

On the other hand, if the content contains a lot of text, the solution is not to ask users to move through many individual web pages consisting of a single paragraph. In fact, if the project consists of many pages of text, the usual recommendation is to present web pages containing at least three pages of text. You can then break up the extended text in a variety of ways. You can block text messages and surround them with space. You can use headings to organize and separate blocks of text. When possible, you can present your text information in the form of numbered or bulleted lists.

*Number of text pages per web page*

Here are some further guidelines for text design:

*Tips for text design*

- Avoid using background colors or graphics that make text difficult to read.
- Avoid colored text, and minimize the use of different text styles and sizes.
- Learn how to position a heading closer to the text it relates to than to the previous paragraph. There should be an empty line before headings, but not after. (Many authoring programs automatically insert the paragraph code <P>, which adds an extra empty line. Use the break code <BR> to eliminate this extra space.)

## USE OF GRAPHICS

A very high proportion of web pages includes graphics, and the ability to combine text and images had much to do with the early excitement the Web generated among the general public.

*Uses of images*

Images serve a variety of purposes on the Web. They can serve as attention grabbers. They can be used to efficiently describe complex processes or present information that is spatial in nature, such as maps. In some disciplines (molecular biology, astronomy, and art, for example), images may provide a more appropriate means of representation than pure text.

*Drawbacks of images*

On the other hand, images can be a distraction and a hindrance, especially when the user is attempting to navigate a web site using a low-bandwidth connection. Meaningless images simply annoy web viewers who are searching for specific information.

We feel that the use of images in student web projects has great potential benefits. An image can serve as the background for a web page, as a link or a container for a collection of links (image map), or as an element of information. But students probably have less experience in making decisions about the presentation of visual images than they have in presenting their ideas with text. In this section we comment on some design issues involving graphics and offer guidelines you can use with your students. Later in the chapter, we address methods for generating graphics and some of the technical issues involved in preparing them for use on a web page.

## IMAGE SIZE

*Image size related to file size*

The size of images raises a number of important issues. Image size tends to be related to file size. Larger files take longer to download, and a page with several large images may take several minutes to display when the data must be sent over a low-bandwidth connection. Large images also fill a large part of the limited viewing space on a monitor. Because casual visitors seldom scroll beyond what is first visible, placing large images at the top of a web page may lead many users to miss more important information on the rest of the page.

In some cases—for example, with complex maps or satellite photography—large images may be necessary. When possible, though, it is important to be efficient with respect to image size. Here are some suggestions:

### Guidelines for Sizing Images

*Thumbnails*

- Consider using thumbnails as an alternative to large images. A **thumbnail** is a small version of a large image. The smaller image provides an idea of what the larger one looks like and serves as a link to a page containing the full-size image.

*Dead pages*

- When using thumbnails, do not link to a **dead page** (a page with no return link) or a page containing only the image. Provide a return link to the main page, and either repeat or expand the original text to accompany the larger image.

*Interlaced format*

- If you are using large GIF images (described in the next section), save these images in the **interlaced format.** If you have noticed that some web images seem to fade in as a series of layers of increasing clarity, you are already familiar with the interlaced format. The rough outline of the image is first available, and then the image improves in quality.

  The benefit of interlacing is that the viewer can make decisions and do things while the images are loading. The initial version of the image may be all the viewer needs to see, and he or she may decide to move on. Or the viewer may scroll down and read the text while the interlaced images are loading.

*Saving images in desired size*

- Save images in the size you want them to appear on the screen. Save two images if you want to use both a thumbnail and a larger image.

  In some web authoring programs, images can be resized by simply dragging a corner. Web authors who prefer to write raw HTML can also specify the display size. However, a good case can be made for using the actual size of the image rather than modifying the original size. Changing the size of an image does not change the file size or its transfer time. It is most efficient to save the image as you want it to appear.

## GRAPHIC FILE FORMATS

One of the great things about the WWW is that it works so well on different kinds of computers and with different web browsers. In part, this is the case because web developers remain committed to a set of standards.

*GIF and JPEG*

Web graphics are a good case in point. Nearly all web graphics are sent over the Internet in one of two file formats: **GIF** (Graphic Interchange Format) or **JPEG** (Joint Photographic Experts Group). Web authors need to know how to convert existing images to these two formats; but once the conversion has been accomplished, compatibility problems are greatly reduced. The GIF and JPEG formats are designed to be **cross-platform**—that is, to work well on different types of computers.

Web designers do need to recognize that there are some important differences between the GIF and JPEG formats, and it is important to learn when to use each. The following points summarize some of the most important differences. See "Focus: Working with Color Graphics Files" for a related discussion.

### *Guidelines for Using GIF and JPEG Formats*

*Solid-color areas*

- The GIF format is most appropriate for images containing large areas of solid color, as might be the case in logos that appear at the top of web pages, simple illustrations, cartoons, or large decorative text.

*Number of colors*

- The GIF format works best when the designer can control the colors that will be used. This is easiest to do when the images are created on the computer rather than captured from some other source. GIF images must use no more than 256 colors, and distortions occur when other hues are converted to these basic colors.

*Transparency*

- Use the GIF format when you want an image to appear as an object against the background of the rest of the page, rather than in the shape of a rectangular box. GIFs allow **transparency.** That is, it is possible to select one color (any color) and set it to "invisible." If an image consists of an object surrounded by a solid color background, setting the solid color to invisible creates the appearance that only the object is present. This technique is easiest to use with simple images created specifically for the Web. With complex images, the color of the background may also appear in parts of the image.

*Complex images*

- The JPEG format is most appropriate for complex images such as photographs that contain many colors in complex patterns.

For both GIF and JPEG images, there are a couple of other practical suggestions to remember:

*Save the original version!*

1. It is always important to save the original version of the image. The generation of web graphics is a little unpredictable and may require experimentation. With graphic software, it is very easy to load an image, adjust the number of colors or select a file format, and resave the image. The problem

*Focus*

## Working with Color Graphics Files

As we have pointed out, the file size of web graphic images can be a problem because large files may take a long time to transfer. There are a couple of common ways to create smaller graphics files.

One method is to restrict the number of colors you use. Older monitors were limited to the display of 8-bit graphics; 8 bits is 2 to the 8th power, or 256, and this meant 256 possible colors. New monitors with more dedicated memory can now allow 16- bit or 24- bit graphics, offering thousands or millions of colors. But even if all users had access to these more powerful systems, displaying so many colors creates very large graphics files. Thus, for practical reasons, when you create art specifically for the Web, you will probably want to limit the number of colors you use.

In 256-color graphics, certain specific colors have to be designated as among the 256 colors that are available. The set of colors available within a particular computer system is called the **palette** (also called the **color lookup table** or **CLUT**). Unfortunately, the palettes for the Macintosh and Windows operating systems rely on slightly different sets of colors; only 216 of the 256 colors are the same. That creates a problem. When a computer is unable to generate a match for a requested color, it resorts to **dithering,** trying to simulate the color by mixing pixels of other colors. On close examination, dithered images appear spotty. To avoid such distortions, the conservative approach is to use just the common set of 216 colors.

**File compression** is the other common method for dealing with large graphic files. Compression methods attempt to improve the efficiency of information storage. Compressed files take less space and can be transmitted over the Internet more quickly. There are two basic types of compression:

- **Lossless compression** schemes rely totally on increased efficiency and generate a smaller file without a reduction in image quality.
- **Lossy compression,** in contrast, creates an even smaller file that approximates rather than exactly matches the original. With this type of compression, you lose some preciseness in the image, but you can reduce the file size even further and thus increase the transfer speed.

The two common file formats for web images, GIF and JPEG, both use file compression, but GIF uses a lossless technique and JPEG, a lossy method. Both have advantages and disadvantages.

GIF files require that images be converted to what is called **indexed color**—the colors of the system palette. When creating an image from scratch, this is not a problem. The image can be drawn or painted with the colors the palette makes available. But when an image is creating by digitizing an input—for instance, by scanning or video capture—the colors in the original image may not match the colors in the system palette. In that case, some distortion may occur when the image is digitized and converted to a GIF file.

The JPEG format allows more colors, and so this format is better suited to saving images when the specific colors cannot be controlled. But the lossy compression technique of the JPEG format creates a different problem. Although it allows a sizable reduction in file size, it introduces a small amount of visual "noise" into the image. When the image is complex (lots of colors and a complex pattern), the noise is difficult to detect. But when an image has large solid areas and a simple pattern, the distortions are noticeable. That is why we recommend the JPEG format for photographlike images and the GIF format for simple illustrations.✱

in doing this is that any distortion created cannot be reversed, and using the same name for the image file will eliminate the original. So be sure to save your modified images as new files, keeping your original version unchanged.

*View on different systems*

2. Whenever possible, view your web images using different computer systems. Because the cross-platform compatibility ideal has not been perfectly implemented, you may see distortions on a Macintosh that you did not see with a Windows machine, and vice versa. In this case you may have to make some adjustments in the image.

## POSITIONING GRAPHICS

In the earlier discussion of page design, we provided some general comments about the positioning of objects. There are some additional issues to consider in positioning graphics.

*"Inline" graphics*

Graphics that appear on a web page are technically called "inline" graphics. This means that the browser treats an image like a single giant letter. Text can precede or follow the image, but the default procedures allow only one line of text to be on the same "line" as the image. This hinders a web page designer from establishing the obvious connection between an image and its description. There are two ways to get around this limitation:

*Alignment in tables*

- The easiest way to align text and graphics is to create a table. One strategy is to generate a row of three cells: one for the graphic, one to serve as a spacer, and one for the text. You will also have to learn how to position the image and the text within the cell: left, center, or right justified; top, middle, or bottom aligned.

*Positioning images with HTML tags*

- You can also position a block of text beside an image by using HTML. The tag used to display images can contain additional codes that position the text to the left or right of the image and even create a space between the image and the text. Here is what this tag might look like:

  ▶ <IMG SRC="image.gif" align="left" hspace="5">

  This tag would be followed by text and then by the tag <BR CLEAR="ALL">. Text would appear to the right of the image and be separated from the image by an open space. The break tag <BR> tells the browser to stop trying to position text to the right of the image.

## CREATING INTERACTIVE WEB PAGES WITH IMAGE MAPS

An image map, as we mentioned earlier, is an image containing designated areas (hot spots) that serve as links. Image maps are useful in the creation of navigation systems and have many applications in the presentation of content. As a teacher you should learn about image maps because they are an easy way to make web content more interactive.

### Examples of Image Maps

*Image maps for self-tests*

As one possibility, you or your students can use image maps to create self-tests by combining the map with a request: "Click on the lobe of the brain that is responsible for vision." "Click on the part of the camera that is used to adjust focal length." The image map can be constructed so that correct responses take users to one web page and incorrect selections to another.

*Image maps to encourage exploration*

Image maps can also help you create an exploratory environment for users. For the OWLS project described at the beginning of this chapter, we have been working with students to create online representations of the small habitats that the students have been developing near their schools. The web pages allow students to share their experiences with other schools that are developing similar projects. The initial image map, which serves as a welcome to the web site, is created from a drawing or wide-angle photo of the habitat (see Figure 7.9). Clicking on part of the image moves the web visitor to another page that includes descriptive text about that portion of the habitat and another image providing greater detail. The visitor can move about the site—

**FIGURE 7.9** An image map for the OWLS project web page. Clicking on one of the outlined areas takes the viewer to a separate page that offers more information on that part of the habitat.

both the virtual site and the physical habitat—and learn what is occurring at each location.

### Types of Image Maps

As web authoring programs have become more powerful, image maps have become easier to construct. There are two kinds of image maps: server side and client side. The difference lies in which computer determines whether the user's click falls within a hot spot on the image.

*Server-side image maps*

The location of each click can be translated into specific coordinates on the screen. In a **server-side image map,** the coordinates are sent to the server and then passed along to a CGI (a second program running on the server), which evaluates the click and determines which new page should be sent. (Technically, CGI stands for Common Gateway Interface, a term that will be discussed further in Chapter 8.) Server-side image maps require that a file defining the area associated with each hot spot be stored on the server and that the CGI program be operating. School servers typically have the capability to run such programs, but the person responsible for the server has to make sure the program is available and running.

*Client-side image maps*

**Client-side image maps** embed the data defining the hot spots within the HTML page itself, and the user's browser evaluates the position of a click against these predefined areas. When it detects a click within one such area, the browser requests the page associated with that area. Earlier browsers were not capable of performing these functions. Now that browsers have improved, image maps are much easier to implement. There is no need to worry about what happens on the server.

### Advice for Using Image Maps

Here are two points to keep in mind when you and your students consider using image maps:

*Tips for wise use of image maps*

- Creating image maps is time consuming. Save this technique for situations in which image maps provide a unique advantage, such as a meaningful form of interaction.
- Follow image maps with text links that provide the same access to other web pages. Even if the text links are not used, they will help the user understand what links are available from the image. (Obviously, though, you would not want to do this when the image map functions as a test.)

## IMAGE GENERATION AND TRANSLATION

*Sources of images*

Images that appear on the web originate in many ways. They may be: (1) created from scratch on a computer, using a paint or draw program; (2) generated from an original page or object using a scanner; or (3) "captured" directly using a digital camera or indirectly by using the computer to digitize

Focus

## Capturing Images from a Video Input

The opportunity for students to "capture" images can play a prominent role in student web projects. Students can take a camcorder into their community to document local historic sites or industrial plants. Images captured during visits to nearby ponds, roadside ditches, parks, or even the schoolyard can become a part of ecology projects. Even within the

**FIGURE 7.10** The display screen and control panel from Apple Video Player

school building, opportunities for learning can be expanded through the use of image capture. For instance, physical education students could use a camcorder to generate a guide to proper weight training technique. To put such material on the Web, students need a cost-effective and efficient method for creating digital images or movie segments from what they have recorded with the camcorder.

The analog output from a typical camcorder, the same signal you would feed to your television to watch a video, can be processed in a computer by special hardware known as a video digitizing board or card. The cable from the "video out" connection of the camcorder brings a signal represented in terms of continuous values (analog) to the "video in" connection of the computer, where the digitizing board translates the continuous values into the discrete digital ones needed by the computer. This digital information can then be saved as a file. Many "multimedia" or "audiovisual" computers now come with this capability built in.

To perform video capture, you activate a software program that accesses the video digitizing board. The active digital image from the board appears within a window on the screen. The experience is very much like watching a small television screen within a section of your monitor. Actually, with the input from a television tuner, this is exactly what you would be doing.

The exact method for capturing an image varies with the hardware and software that are used. Figure 7.10 shows the display screen and control panel of the Apple Video Player, which comes as part of the system software on an AV Macintosh. To capture an image, you watch the video in the window and click the Freeze button when you see what you want. A still image stays in the window and in the computer's memory. If the image you see is something you would like to keep, you then click the Save button to name and save the image as a file. If the image is not worth keeping, clicking the Freeze button again returns the window to the live feed from the digitizing board. The process is extremely easy and within the capability of young students. This same equipment can be used to record short movie segments (QuickTime movies).✷

the input from a camcorder or videotape (see "Focus: Capturing Images from a Video Input").

Images generated in any of these ways can be stored in a bewildering variety of file formats. This variety exists for several reasons:

*Reasons for multiplicity of ffle formats*

1. Certain file formats are associated with different computer operating systems. For example, the *BMP* format is a common graphics format on Windows machines, and *PICT* is a common Macintosh format.
2. File formats may have different capabilities that are suited to different tasks. Some formats involve compression for more efficient storage, and some allow images to contain a greater number of colors.
3. Finally, many software applications have their own "native" formats that are in some way especially suited to those programs. For example, Photoshop and AppleWorks both default to a file format developed just for that program. AppleWorks cannot open a graphics file saved in the default

Photoshop format, and Photoshop cannot open a file saved in the default AppleWorks format. Fortunately, most programs with a native format also allow files to be saved in at least a few other formats.

*Translators*

As we mentioned earlier, web pages typically rely on just two graphic formats: GIF and JPEG. But what can you do if you have an image in PICT, for example, and you want to use it on a web site? In some cases, you may have to do very little to accomplish the necessary conversion. Many programs have built-in **translators**, small utilities that allow the program to open a variety of file types. For example, the web authoring programs discussed in Chapter 6 all do some translation.

*Usefulness of high-end graphics programs*

High-end graphics programs such as Photoshop provide the greatest flexibility, and we recommend that schools invest in this kind of software. Even if students rarely use it, such a program can open and save files in a variety of formats. For example, it can accept the file generated by scanning a student's drawing and then output the image in a format that can be used by a web authoring program.

## ASSESSMENT OF STUDENT WEB PROJECTS

After all we have said about student web projects in this chapter and the preceding one, we hope you feel knowledgeable enough to begin planning projects that involve your students in designing their own web presentations. In Chapter 8 we will go on to discuss working with your school server and perhaps creating a personal server of your own. First, however, there may be another important question on your mind: During and after an extended web project, how can I assess what my students have learned? What should I expect them to do, and how can I evaluate their performance?

*Informative, fair assessment*

For authentic tasks to achieve their potential benefits, student performance must be evaluated in ways that the students find both informative and fair. The specific components of an assessment device (some authors use terms like *assessment rubrics* and *analysis guides*) will have to vary with the nature of the project and with what you want to emphasize. Here, though, we can provide a model by describing a sample project.

Look back at the OWLS project described at the start of this chapter. The web portion of the activity might be presented to students in this manner:

*Sample presentation of the OWLS web project*

> *Task:* Each group will develop at least two web pages to describe the work it has done in developing an OWLS habitat.
>
> In constructing your group web pages, be sure to (1) explain the characteristics of the habitat you are working on and (2) describe the work you have done to develop the habitat. Each page should contain one informative pic-

ture created by videotaping and then digitizing images using video capture. Your pages should be linked to the school OWLS home page, to each other, and (if helpful) to no more than two external web pages.

Assume that visitors to your web pages are your age or older, but have no knowledge of the habitat you are studying. You will be evaluated on the appearance of your web pages, the informativeness of your text and pictures, the quality of your writing, and how you work as a team to complete this assignment.

*A generalized assessment form*

For the scoring guidelines or rubric, we can use several continua of descriptors. That is, for each competence area in the assessment process, we define specific levels of accomplishment along a continuum from lesser competence to greater (Tierney, Carter, & Desai, 1991). To implement this approach, it is useful to begin with a general form for describing the assessment guidelines. Table 7.1 shows an example of such a form.

*Specific project guidelines*

Now let's develop specific continua of descriptors for our sample project. (In practice, we urge you to develop these assessment devices in collaboration with your students.) We probably want to evaluate at least three general areas: domain knowledge and effective communication, design skills, and team skills. Specific competencies could involve content coverage, page layout, graphics, navigation, and the involvement level of team members. Each area of competency could then be defined in terms of concrete levels of accomplishment. The form built from these continua might look something like Table 7.2.

Using assessment methods of this type—especially ones developed in collaboration with your students—you can feel as comfortable in assessing their web design efforts as you do in evaluating traditional written products, such as reports and essays. Establishing guidelines will alert students to areas you will be looking at most carefully in evaluating their work and will also help you take a systematic approach to grading.

**TABLE 7.1**
A Generalized Form for Developing Assessment Guidelines

| PROJECT TITLE | | |
|---|---|---|
| **NEEDS IMPROVEMENT** | **ADEQUATE** | **STRONG PERFORMANCE** |
| Descriptor 1A | *Competency 1*<br>Descriptor 1B | Descriptor 1C |
| Descriptor 2A | *Competency 2*<br>Descriptor 2C | Descriptor 2C |
| Descriptor 3A | *Competency 3*<br>Descriptor 3B | Descriptor 3C |
| | *Competency 4 . . .* | |

**TABLE 7.2**
Assessment Guidelines for the Web Assignment in the OWLS Project

| HABITAT WEB PAGES | | |
|---|---|---|
| **NEEDS IMPROVEMENT** | **ADEQUATE** | **STRONG PERFORMANCE** |
| | *Information* | |
| The information is poorly written, inaccurate, or too brief. | The information is adequately presented with few spelling or grammatical errors. | The information is interesting to read and contains very few errors. |
| | *Page Layout* | |
| The pages are difficult to read, and the layout is disorganized. | The pages are adequately designed, and the text is readable. | The pages are particularly well organized and attractive. |
| | *Links/Navigation* | |
| The links are missing or do not work. | The links all work, but labels are unclear. | The links work, and link purpose is clearly communicated. |
| | *Graphics* | |
| There are no images, or the images are not appropriate to demonstrate the characteristics of a habitat or a method of construction. | The images are appropriate but of poor quality. | The images are appropriate and of high quality. |
| | *Cooperation* | |
| The group has obvious difficulty getting along, and the members allow or require one student to do most of the work. | Each group member contributes, but group interaction is limited. | All group members contribute, and the group works together to improve the quality of the final product. |

## SUMMARY

◆ This chapter describes a fairly minimalist approach to web page design—one appropriate for most student designers. First of all, in planning web projects, students should consider the content they have to offer, the audience they want to reach, and the purpose this audience might have for visiting the site.

◆ In organizing their site, the student designers can choose a sequential, hierarchical, or web design, or an amalgam of the three types. For the navigation system, they should consider the function and characteristics of links as well as methods of orienting the viewer (for instance, a site map or menu). Decisions about page design should be based on the content, purpose, and audience of the site, and a page template is often a useful guide.

◆ Because image capture and manipulation provide new learning opportunities, we think students should acquire the basic skills for preparing images for web pages. That is, students should gain some understanding of GIF and JPEG formats and when to use them, ways to convert one format to another, and methods for positioning images on a page. Image maps can increase the interactivity of a web page, but they require time to create and should probably be used only when they provide a distinct advantage.

◆ For assessing student web projects, you can create a general format that describes levels of accomplishment along multiple continua from lesser competence to greater. Then, for each project, you can develop specific descriptors for each appropriate type of competency.

## REFLECTING ON CHAPTER 7

### Activities

1. Plan a student web project, specifying the content, purpose, and audience.
2. Conduct a web search for the phrase "site map." What different approaches to site maps have been taken by the designers of commercial web sites?
3. Propose a "makeover" for an existing web page. Print the existing page and then show how you would rework the page according to the guidelines provided in this chapter.
4. Go back to the outline for a web project that you developed in the first activity above. Set up a scoring rubric (continua of descriptors) appropriate to this project.

### Key Terms

anchor *(p. 201)*
broken link *(p. 202)*
client-side image map *(p. 215)*
color lookup table (CLUT) *(p. 212)*
cross-platform *(p. 211)*
dead page *(p. 210)*
dithering *(p. 212)*
file compression *(p. 212)*
GIF *(p. 211)*
hierarchical design *(p. 200)*
hot spot *(p. 201)*
image map *(p. 201)*
indexed color *(p. 212)*
interlaced format *(p. 210)*
JPEG *(p. 211)*
lossless compression *(p. 212)*
lossy compression *(p. 212)*
navigation system *(p. 201)*
page template *(p. 205)*
palette *(p. 212)*
sequential design *(p. 199)*
server-side image map *(p. 215)*
site map *(p. 203)*
thumbnail *(p. 210)*
translator *(p. 218)*
transparency *(p. 211)*
user interface *(p. 201)*
web design *(p. 200)*

### Resources to Expand Your Knowledge Base

**Classroom Assessment**

Tierney, R., Carter, M., & Desai, L. (1991). *Portfolio assessment in the reading-writing classroom.* Norwood, MA: Gordon Publishers.

### Using Video

Herrell, A., & Fowler, J. (1998). *Camcorder in the classroom: Using the videocamera to enliven curriculum.* Columbus, OH: Prentice Hall.

### Web Design Principles

Siegel, D. (1997). *Creating killer web sites* (2nd ed.). Indianapolis, IN: Hayden Books.

Williams, R., & Tollett, J. (1998). *The non-designers web book.* Berkeley, CA: Peachpit Press.

# Chapter 8

# Working with Your School Internet Server

## ORIENTATION

In this chapter you will learn about the operation of a server. At a general level, you will learn what a server does and become familiar with its software, hardware, and personnel requirements. Two types of servers are described: large-capacity servers appropriate for an entire school or school district and smaller servers appropriate for a classroom. We expect you will be especially interested in what you can do with an ordinary computer in your own classroom. Finally, this chapter presents some of the factors to consider for productive use of a school web site.

As you read, look for answers to the following questions:

**FOCUS QUESTIONS**

- What are the necessary components in the operation of any server?
- What are three ways a school might establish a web presence?
- How could you as a teacher establish a server in your own classroom?
- What are some situations that might warrant spending more money on a more powerful server system?
- What is a CGI, and how does it extend the capabilities of server software?
- What are some of the more common categories of web content present on school servers?

## WHAT IS A SERVER?

As you learned in Chapter 1 (p. 16), a **server** is simply a computer that makes resources available to other computers. You may think that the workings of a

*Why you should learn about servers*

server can safely be left to the technicians—the computer specialists who hang out in the lab and indulge in incomprehensible techno-speak. But understanding the way a server works can help you provide better Internet experiences for your students. Besides, as you will see later in the chapter, there are servers simple enough for you to operate yourself, and they can have an immediate impact on your teaching.

All Internet servers rely on the same fundamental set of components: a computer, a connection to the Internet, software to implement the TCP/IP protocol, and server software. Systems integrating these components can be assembled by using very inexpensive or free software and hardware in the $1,000 to $1,200 range or by spending thousands of dollars on software and tens of thousands of dollars on hardware. Even at the low end, a system could be assembled to serve basic web content (web server), files (FTP server), and e-mail. Some of the variables that differentiate low-end from high-end systems include:

*Factors distinguishing high-end from low-end systems*

1. The computer operating system (typically UNIX, Macintosh OS, Windows 98, or Windows NT).
2. The power and capacity of the computer, including the speed of the *central processing unit (CPU)*, the quantity of *random access memory (RAM)*, and the amount of available disk space.
3. The sophistication of the server software; for instance, can it share information with support software running on the same system, and does it offer ways to extend basic HTML?
4. The variety and sophistication of support software. For example, some software can accept a query from a user or search a database and return the results to the user.

*How expensive a system do you need?*

These variables combine in various ways to influence the number of simultaneous users who can be accommodated, the speed with which information can be served, the number of services that can be offered, and the complexity of tasks that can be accomplished. More expensive systems have the potential to do a lot of sophisticated things for a lot of people very quickly. But whether such systems are necessary depends on what the school and the teachers hope to accomplish. Will it be a major problem if users are occasionally unable to connect? How important is it to impress the people who use your system? Is it necessary to create an environment in which users can submit information?

This chapter will describe several options available for your school and for your own classroom. As an educator, you should understand the resources you can use to accomplish your purposes.

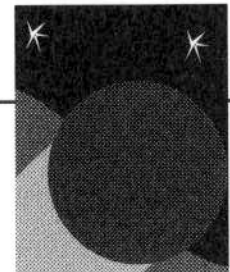

## OPTIONS FOR SERVING INTERNET RESOURCES

A school can establish an Internet presence in at least three different ways:

*Three basic options*

- Using equipment and services from outside the school district.
- Using a school or district server.
- Using personal servers within individual classrooms.

*An outside server*

In the first case, the school can serve Internet content by using equipment, software, and expertise not maintained by the district. For example, many commercial Internet service providers (ISPs) offer users the opportunity to establish a home page and make available a limited amount of content on it. The same ISP that provides a school with its Internet connection may offer space for web pages. In addition, many other businesses and organizations operate servers, and some of them allow individuals or schools to buy space on these machines. In a few situations, businesses or organizations are willing to donate server space to educational institutions. Although schools or classrooms can make do with these opportunities, many of the web activities we have described are more practical to implement when schools have direct control over the server.

*A school or personal server*

If a school has a direct Internet connection, it is quite feasible for the school to operate its own server, which is usually a better option than using a server not controlled by the school. In the following sections, we will describe two levels at which this might be accomplished: a school server and a personal server. Each of these methods has advantages and disadvantages.

To keep the discussion focused, we will proceed as if a *school server* means a powerful computer situated outside of the classroom and a *personal server* means a more typical computer located in the classroom. In many schools the situation is actually more complex. For example, a school may combine the two methods, operating both a main server and multiple personal servers.

Most of what we say about school servers will also apply to district-level servers. Again, though, some districts will have a more complex arrangement: for instance, a district may use one machine to handle e-mail and another for web pages.

## FUNDAMENTALS OF A SCHOOL SERVER

By a **school server,** we mean an Internet server dedicated to use by a particular school. A number of factors affect the operation of a school server and the way you as a teacher will interact with it. In the following sections, we explain the most important factors.

## PHYSICAL RESOURCES REQUIRED TO OPERATE A SCHOOL SERVER

A school server requires an Internet connection, relatively high-level hardware, and a collection of appropriate software.

### Internet Access

*Varieties of Internet connections*

An Internet connection is a basic requirement for all servers. However, connections to the Internet differ in capacity. Within a district the connection from the ISP may be split to go to particular schools and split again to go to individual rooms or offices. For a school's server to be high capacity, it usually needs to be connected at a point *before* the line has been split many times.

### Hardware

*Type of machine needed*

A school server is likely to be a powerful machine. To satisfy the heavy demands that can be placed on it, it may be a different type than the other computers in the school. It may be, for example, a Sun or IBM minicomputer rather than an ordinary PC or Macintosh, and it may use a different operating system such as UNIX or Windows NT. While most computers could function in a limited way as servers, the machines that computer companies label as servers tend to have a faster CPU, a more substantial amount of RAM, and larger-capacity hard drives than standard computers.

### Software

School servers typically offer multiple applications. Most commonly, e-mail and the World Wide Web are available. Many schools also use FTP and some RealAudio, RealVideo, or CU-SeeMe applications. If teachers are allowed to add pages to their own web sites, FTP would probably be required so that HTML pages and related image files could be uploaded to the server.

*Varieties of software*

Although there are inexpensive or free versions of each of these software types, schools can spend several thousand dollars to operate more powerful versions of the software. Additional programs are also required to take advantage of interactive World Wide Web applications that allow users to submit requests or data that are then interpreted and acted upon.

## HOW ACCESS, HARDWARE, AND SOFTWARE QUALITY AFFECT PERFORMANCE

What are the advantages to a school of investing in more powerful and expensive Internet access, hardware, and software? Generally a more powerful and integrated server system allows the provider to respond to more users simultaneously, to serve resources more quickly, and to provide more sophisticated services.

## Darin King, Technology Administrator

As the director of technology for the Grand Forks, North Dakota, school district, Darin King operates the district's servers. You first met Darin in Chapter 1. He was responsible for the "flood cam" and many of the other curriculum projects created in response to the natural disaster that struck the community in which he works. This interview should give you some insight into what it takes for a school district or a school to operate a server.

*Would you describe the Internet applications you are responsible for and the equipment you use to provide these services?*

The district has its own e-mail system, web server, and White Pine Reflector Site, an application that allows multiple CU-SeeMe users to connect to the same live audio/video source. We also operate our own domain name server (DNS) because we want to be able to assign names to the hundreds of computers in our schools and do not want to have to rely on the ISP to take care of this.

Our primary computer is presently a UNIX machine. When we started providing e-mail access, the UNIX platform was the most mature. We have recently added both Macintosh and Windows NT servers for some applications, and we will gradually move toward relying on these machines because they are easier to operate.

*Whom do you define as the primary audience for your server services, and what do you presently consider your best applications for these groups?*

We consider the teachers and students from our district to be our primary audience. We would like to grow toward becoming an information source for the community, but I think you need to focus initially on your teachers and students.

I would say our best application at present is an online registration service that teachers use to sign up for after-school technology in-service sessions. We use web pages to describe the different sessions we intend to offer, and teachers complete an online form to indicate their interest. Sessions tend to have enrollment limits, so the first responses we receive are given priority. Because we are trying to reach teachers in many different buildings in a timely manner, this system has worked very well.

I think some of our student and teacher web projects have also been impressive. We have pockets of production rather than general involvement in web projects, but some of the projects are very nice.

*How have you defined your role as "webmaster"?*

I want to be involved in shaping what appears on the school web site. I attempt to promote ideas I get from looking at other schools' web sites—ideas that I feel justify the time and expense those schools have had to invest.

Teachers or students sometimes come to me with ideas that I do not have time to help them develop. I sometimes redirect the orientation of the project toward something that can be done more easily, but I also try to keep track of the original ideas and will come back to them when possible. The development of a virtual tour of the Airbase school for students coming into the community was an idea of this type. The school district operates schools on a military base, and students often come and go as their parents are assigned to new duty stations.

Students are not allowed to have their own web pages at this point. I would rather have students work on class projects or work on a project they arrange through a teacher. Our system is set up to allocate space for teachers to have their own web pages within their own accounts.

We have just started thinking about web publishing guidelines. We presently define appropriate content as content related to a class. We expect the people responsible for web pages to be committed to the maintenance of that content so we do not accumulate material that is no longer useful. Pages should be updated or removed as they become outdated.

Our expectations for mandatory design elements are minimal. Pages should provide a link back to the district home page and should contain an e-mail address indicating the person responsible for the page. I prefer to look at the pages that are created and make suggestions rather than attempt to dictate design requirements.

*Do you make an effort to provide interactivity in your web services?*

The teacher registration pages I described allow teachers to submit information through web pages that are stored by the server. I wrote the online registration application using Applescript. We are moving toward "out of the box" solutions to provide greater interactivity. The newer tools are nice and easy to work with, and meet most of our needs. The combination of FileMaker and HomePage, a database and web authoring program, seems very useful.

*What role do you see the resources you have described playing within the curriculum?*

We are trying to provide the resources and prepare teachers so that student web projects can be part of the curriculum. We offer web publishing classes as an in-service opportunity for teachers, and approximately sixty teachers completed these classes last year. Our technology training staff also promotes and helps with some classroom projects. I think the skill of making web pages is less of an issue than coming up with good ideas for projects; the technology skills we can work to develop, but we need to have teachers come up with quality applications.

As a district, we have promoted multimedia projects using programs like HyperStudio and Kid Pix for many years, and now student web authoring is a new variation. The Web offers a similar experience with a bonus—students must think carefully in order to create their web pages, and then there is the opportunity for others to examine what the students produce and perhaps to respond.

There is a learning curve in getting teachers into the creation of their own web projects. They have to invest some time in learning the skills. Past the point of understanding some of the basics of using the tools, they have to make personal judgments about investing time. The time issue always comes up with curriculum development, and not just when technology is involved. We have long recognized this issue, and the district does have summer curriculum money that has been used in some cases. The technology staff has also written and received funding for some state block-grant money that has been applied to curriculum projects. When we secure grant money, we have asked teachers to submit their own grant proposals to us, so that we can evaluate their projects and perhaps fund the equipment and time that will be required.

When it comes to helping teachers develop curriculum projects, we rely on our entire technology staff. The teachers we fund within buildings, curriculum integration specialists, are the first point of contact. Requests for assistance that cannot be handled in the buildings come to the Technology Facilitators, staff members working full time to provide inservice experiences and technology support, and finally to me. We have invested heavily in making personnel available to support the teacher and curriculum activities.

*Could the school district justify a full-time webmaster?*

I think so. Some districts "outsource" their web needs, paying an outside consultant to operate the server. If a larger district wants to make heavy use of a server for student projects and to support general curriculum needs, I think the money invested in a designated person makes some sense.

## Number of Simultaneous Users and Speed of Transmission

*A server's hit rate*

Active web servers may be asked to send hundreds of thousands of files a week, and at peak times they may be in the process of sending a hundred files in any given second. In the jargon of the web, the activity level of a server is often called the **hit rate,** and each time the server is asked for a file is called a

**hit.** While school servers accumulate a very small number of hits in comparison to those operated by other types of institutions, there are still times when the request for resources can easily overrun the capabilities of the system.

You can understand this problem by recalling what you have already learned about how web servers and clients operate. First, remember that the display a user experiences is actually assembled by the web browser (client) from multiple components. A web page containing three images requires that the server send the HTML file and three separate image files (4 hits). Because images tend to be large files, it may take several seconds to transmit each of the images.

Now consider the following situation. A teacher takes a class of twenty-five students to the computer lab to work on an assignment she has already prepared as a web page and stored on the server. The web page contains three images. The teacher gives some introductory comments and then asks the students to load the page she has created. Even if no one else were using the server at this time, this situation would result in a peak load of between 50 and 100 hits a second!

*Effects of server overload*

In this case, it is helpful to imagine that each client creates four active connections with the server—one for the HTML file and three for the image files. Each connection remains active until the entire file has been sent and received. As more and more students ask for the files, more and more connections are established. The server operates by rotating among the active connections; it sends a specific amount of information to one connection and then moves on to the next. This means that as more and more users connect, individual students have to wait longer and longer for the data they need.

*Timing out*

To keep the server and the connected browsers from becoming hopelessly bogged down, the software has built-in safeguards that at some point cause the system to "give up." You have probably experienced this situation, which is called **timing out.** Most likely you have seen it when you fail to receive some images on a web page. When the transfer of a web page times out, the browser displays a default image to act as a placeholder (Figure 8.1).

**FIGURE 8.1** Placeholder image resulting from a time out.

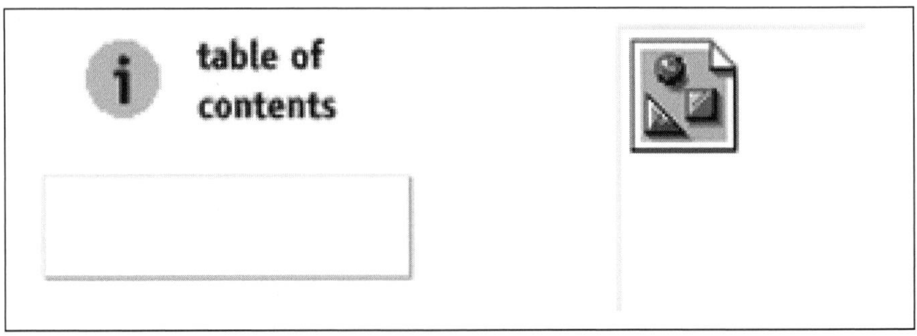

*The webmaster's choices*

A web site that frequently fails to deliver all parts of requested web pages is very frustrating for users. One preventative measure is to limit the number of connections the server will accept at any one time. If a **webmaster**—the person in charge of the web site—must choose between (1) asking some users to wait and (2) sending only partial web pages, the former is usually considered a better option. For that reason, in the school situation we have described, some of the students would likely get a message that the server was "busy."

*Advantages of a powerful system*

A more powerful server system helps reduce this kind of problem. The faster each individual file can be transferred, the more quickly the server can concentrate on new connections. And the transfer speed is affected by the three physical components we have described: the quality of the Internet connection, the CPU speed of the computer, and the quality of the server software. A higher-capacity Internet connection allows the files to move more quickly. Servers with more powerful CPUs can complete more tasks in the same amount of time. Finally, higher-quality software operates more efficiently so that the same tasks are completed in a shorter time.

As you have probably gathered, transfer speed and the number of users who can be served are interrelated. When the server system is operating efficiently, the webmaster can set the server software to allow more users to connect. So the same factors that influence transfer speed influence the number of users who can be served.

## Number of Server Applications and Sophistication of Interactivity

*Running programs simultaneously*

More powerful hardware and software allow other advantages as well. One important advantage of powerful hardware is that a computer with more memory and a faster CPU allows more programs to operate simultaneously. A powerful computer has the capacity to have an e-mail, web, and FTP server active at the same time. If schools want to offer a number of services, they must either operate a powerful computer or use several computers.

*Greater interactivity*

Higher-end resources are also necessary to operate the more interactive kinds of web pages. A typical server program has a very limited capacity to respond to users. It can send the pages a user requests, but it does little else. For a more substantial type of interactivity, the server must pass information back and forth to additional programs that are running simultaneously—a capability that requires a powerful server.

*CGI*

The additional programs generally rely on two elements. First, web *forms* (discussed in Chapter 4) allow users to submit information by entering text or numerical values into fields, by clicking on buttons, or by selecting items from a menu. Second, the **Common Gateway Interface (CGI)** allows the server software to extend what it can accomplish by calling on external programs. Some of the more typical applications of CGI are described in "Focus: Common CGI Applications."

Focus

## Common CGI Applications

Here are some examples of CGI applications. You may recognize them from your own experiences exploring the Web.

1. *Integration of a database and web server.* Users are able to interact with a database through web pages. Most web users have encountered this capability when using a web search engine. When the user enters search parameters in a web form, any records within the database that match those parameters are returned to the user as web pages. In some applications, users can also add a new record to a database by entering information in a web form. For example, a recent project in our region encouraged students to submit information on deformed frogs. Students filled out a web form to record data from their observations, and the information submitted was automatically entered into a database.
2. *Form processing.* Many types of web-based form processing do not involve interaction with a database. The information submitted in a form is transferred to a second program, which then acts on that information in some fashion. A very simple action might be to save the information in a file or add an entry to an existing HTML document. For instance, many web pages ask visitors to sign a guest book. When the form is completed, the information is automatically integrated into an existing web page—the guest book. In a related technique offered by some services, a home page is constructed for the user on the basis of information that the user submits through a form.
3. *Interface with external devices.* Computers can be connected to a variety of external devices. In some cases, the devices feed data into the computer: images from a digital camera, for instance, or data from sensors measuring variables such as temperature and barometric pressure. In other cases, the computer feeds data to an external device, such as a robot. When such operations are linked with server software, Internet users can gain access to the data and exercise control over the devices. An example combining both access to data and control of an external device is a controllable *web camera* (or web cam for short). A device of this type can be manipulated remotely (zooming in or out, panning to focus on different objects) by clicking on buttons representing the different actions. The camera then sends the user the video or still images it captures.

   The software involved in this example has to be able to accomplish some other challenging tasks. Consider what might happen if an entire class or even several classes connected to the same web cam at the same time. Without some method for assigning control of the camera, there would be chaos. The software typically allows the first connected user to control the camera as long as commands continue to arrive within predetermined intervals. When the user stops sending commands, control is passed to the next user who has connected. Meanwhile, all those who are connected can view what is going on.
4. *Interpretation of responses to an image map.* As you saw in Chapter 7, a server-side image map requires the server to run a CGI pro-

gram to determine whether a user's click is within one of the "hot spots" on the image.

5. *Access control.* There are times when a webmaster might want to limit access to specific web content. Perhaps the webmaster has created a portion of the web site just for teachers working within the district. Perhaps some of the material available from the server is to be viewed only from machines operated within the school buildings. A second program interacting with the web server can require and check a password before requested web pages are sent. A second program can also identify the IP number of the computer submitting a request and determine if the number is on an approved list.✷

## PERSONNEL ISSUES

One issue that seems to surface time and time again is that schools fail to adequately consider the personnel requirements for a particular application of technology. Operating a school Internet server or servers is no exception. The following list identifies some of the tasks that may be involved. As you read, think of a school with which you are familiar and ask yourself who handles these tasks or who may handle them in the future.

*Identifying the personnel: who will handle these tasks*

### Tasks for School Server Personnel

- *System operation and maintenance.* A connection must be established between the server and the Internet; the server software must be installed and customized; supporting software (such as CGI applications) must also be installed and customized; the content to be served must be loaded to the computer; and an organization system must be developed for maintaining this content.
- *System security.* The contents of the server must be protected from computer viruses and various forms of vandalism. Often, password-protected accounts must be established. Just keeping track of passwords for those who forget them can be demanding.
- *Technical support and instruction.* Teachers and students may need assistance in taking advantage of server functions. For example, users may require instruction in using FTP software to upload content to the server.
- *Policy development and administration.* A wide variety of policies and issues will need to be addressed: basic design requirements for web pages, copyright standards, responsible and approved use of resources, content emphasis. Someone must take the lead in establishing the policies, preparing documents to communicate them, and, when necessary, taking the appropriate action when policies have been violated.
- *Vision.* Frequently, someone must help other educators make adjustments and set priorities. All of the areas listed here are constantly

changing; new capabilities are emerging, interesting new implementations are demonstrated, and new regulations are established. Bringing such changes to the attention of the appropriate individuals in a tactful manner is a very helpful contribution.

*Need for attention to personnel issues*

In all these areas, the specific requirements for the individual or individuals responsible for the server will depend on the complexity of the server and the software and on the tasks the server is supposed to accomplish. Our general point here is that many issues may be involved, and the time and skill it takes to accomplish some of the more sophisticated server functions should not be underestimated. Personnel issues require serious consideration. Even before people start to work on the server, the school or district may need to generate job descriptions, provide release time for specific duties, and prepare written policies.

## SETTING UP A PERSONAL SERVER

*Nondedicated computer as a personal server*

We define a **personal server** as a low-cost server application designed to operate on a nondedicated and low-cost computer. By *nondedicated* we mean that the server software can operate in the background while the computer is used for another purpose such as word processing. If you have a computer in your classroom with an Internet connection, you have the hardware you need to operate a personal server.

The companies developing personal server software have promoted it primarily as a tool that allows members of organizations to share documents and engage in collaborative projects. Schools are probably not the target audience, but teachers and their students are ideally suited to take advantage of personal servers. Nearly all of the web activities we have described in this book could be implemented from a classroom computer.

If these inexpensive and convenient applications offer such a fine opportunity, why are relatively few educators making use of them? The answers may include the following:

*Why do many teachers neglect opportunities?*

- Lack of familiarity with the opportunities offered by personal servers.
- General lack of interest in offering web resources.
- Perceived limitations in the technical skill necessary to set up and operate a personal server.
- Resistance from administrators who fear yielding control of Internet resources to individual teachers.
- Concerns related to liability and supervision.

In this section we will attempt to deal with as many of these perceived problems as possible. In "Resources to Expand Your Knowledge Base" at the end of the chapter, you can find information about several personal servers.

As we discuss what classroom teachers can do with personal servers, we hope you will be encouraged to look into acquiring one to use with your students.

## BENEFITS OF PERSONAL SERVERS

*Surprisingly low cost*

First of all, why would you even want to consider operating a personal server? Our answers to this question involve issues of cost, convenience, and control.

### Cost

If a classroom has an existing dedicated Internet connection, the cost of a personal server is negligible. The server software can typically be obtained free of charge from a major company or as a very inexpensive shareware product (less than $20). Hardware costs are also negligible, because a personal server is designed to operate on a low-end computer and to function in the background. Operating in the background means the server can do work when the computer is not actively processing information for some other program. For example, when the computer is being used for word processing, there are free times when the writer is thinking. Even when the writer is typing at a rapid rate, the computer's capacity is probably not fully engaged.

Cost also involves training and support, of course, but we believe that teachers can learn to operate a server of this type by spending a little time on their own or with a relatively limited amount of instruction. In contrast, accomplishing web projects on a school server requires both more highly trained personnel and in some cases greater effort from the classroom teacher.

### Convenience

*Hands-on access*

A server that is immediately and personally accessible to you is going to be convenient to operate. Typically, people think of a server as something to be accessed only through another computer. But personal servers encourage hands-on access. If you have a personal server in your classroom, there is no need to send web pages that you and your students have created to another machine—you can create them and store them on your own computer. Making the pages available to others becomes as simple as moving the HTML file and any related image files into a designated folder. If students create pages on another computer, the files can easily be transferred to the server, using a disk.

*Useful page templates*

Personal servers are also designed to offer other conveniences. For example, many come with page templates that make it easy to create basic web pages (see the discussion of templates in Chapter 7). The page displayed in Figure 8.2 was created using the software from Microsoft's Personal Web Server. This software provides a very automated approach to the construction of a home page. It prompts you to enter specific categories of information (name, e-mail address, favorite web addresses, and so forth), allows you to paste in pictures, and then uses the resources you have provided to generate a web page.

**FIGURE 8.2** A home page generated with Microsoft's Personal Web Server template.

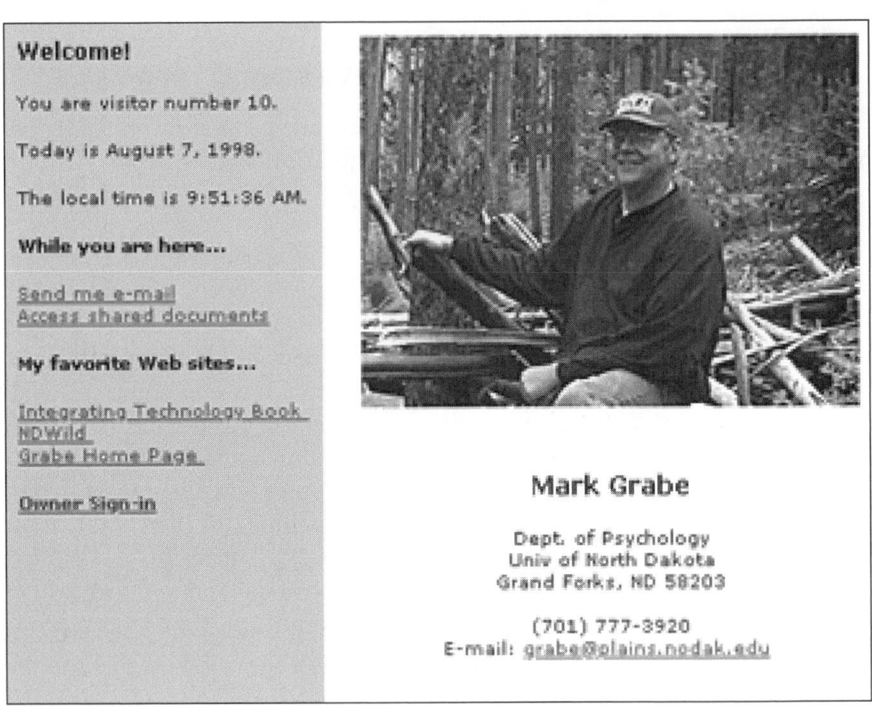


## Control

When you have personal control of a server, you have the flexibility to do things you probably could not do with a school server. You can experiment, you can be spontaneous, and with the proper skills, you can offer unique experiences to your students and to those who visit the site.

*Boosting student motivation*

Immediate access to a server can add important motivation to class projects. Students working on collaborative projects can load their own web pages to the server and ask for an immediate response from partners through e-mail or chat. Watching the hits accumulate is also exciting. The opportunity to publish web resources in a very direct fashion provides the autonomy that is such an important motivator in teaching and learning.

In some cases students themselves may take most of the responsibility for operating the server. For example, the middle schools in our community offer a nine-week course in technology applications. What better way to learn about the Internet than to set up a functioning server? It would not be practical or advisable to allow middle-school students full control of the school's main server, but operating a smaller and simpler server can be quite informative.

*Need for clear policies*

Greater control will likely bring added responsibility. Teachers and students alike must understand the policies that their schools have established, and teachers may have to create additional policies unique to the circumstances of their classrooms. Because adding new material to a site powered by a personal server is such an easy task, it may be appropriate to require that the teacher give approval before any new pages are added.

Similarly, some policies may be needed to govern the way teachers themselves use these resources. Would you consider it appropriate for a teacher to advertise a summer house-painting service as part of a personal information page? Personal freedoms involve complex issues, and the potential and power of the Internet only add to these complexities. Our advice would be to anticipate as many issues as possible and discuss them before controversies arise.

## OPERATING A PERSONAL SERVER: AN EXAMPLE

We want you to feel confident in your ability to set up and operate a personal server. If your classroom computer already has a continuous connection to the Internet—that is, if you can operate a web browser without the use of a modem—you should be able to add a functioning web server to that same machine.

*Microsoft Personal Web Server*

The Microsoft Personal Web Server is a good example of personal server software. The following description is based on a Macintosh, but the software is also available for the Windows operating system. The server is operated from a Control Panel that offers four options: Main, About Me, Web Site, and Advanced. We will take you through some of the basic functions.

*Using the templates*

Personal Web Server creates a home page based on information the user provides in response to the About Me and Web Site options. In the About Me template (Figure 8.3) you enter personal information, and in the Web Site template (Figure 8.4) you can add links from the home page to other web pages. You simply type or paste the information into the fields of the template, and the home page is automatically assembled. To better understand how this works, examine the entries in the template fields in Figures 8.3 and 8.4 and then look back at the home page generated from this information in Figure 8.2.

*Ease of creating a class home page*

Creating and serving a class home page is one obvious way for a teacher to use a personal server. Because the server is easy to set up and operate, and because the page served is easy to modify, a great deal can be accomplished without ever directly creating an HTML page or uploading resources to a school server. For example, you could readily describe a student assignment and offer links to web sites you would like students to examine. A WebQuest (see Chapter 5, pp. 150–152) could be easily implemented from a classroom computer.

Personal servers also provide the opportunity to serve web resources

**FIGURE 8.3** The Personal Web Server About Me template.

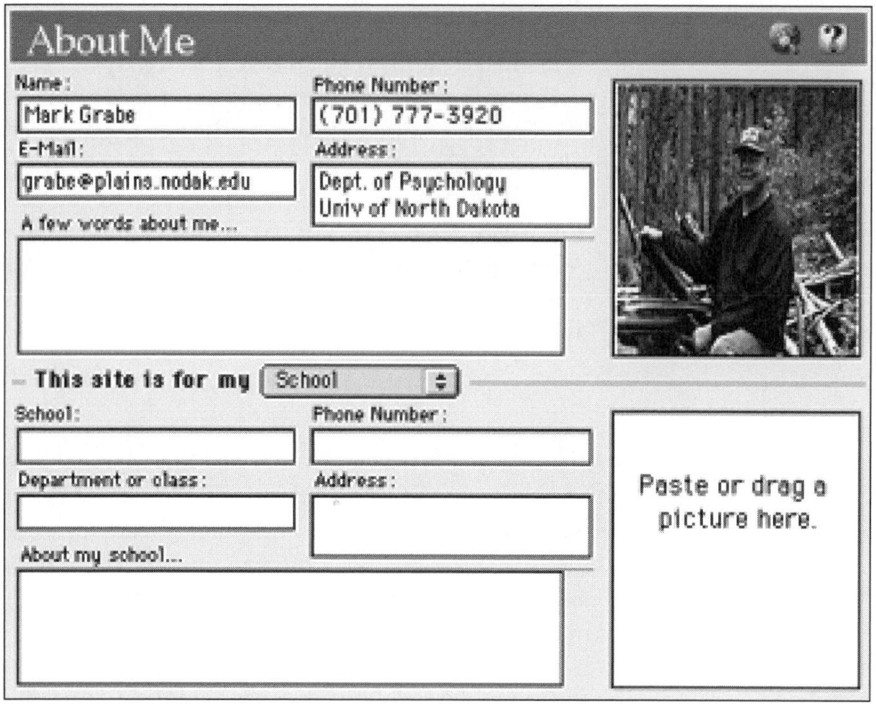

Screenshot reprinted by permission from Microsoft Corporation.

*Publishing students' products*

created in more traditional ways. A classroom server is a perfect way to publish the final products from student projects. Once files have been generated with other programs, the only challenge is putting these files in the place where the server expects to find them. The folder where Personal Web Server expects to find files is indicated on the Main Page (Figure 8.5).

The Main Page is important for a couple of other reasons. This is where the server is activated and deactivated. Basic information about how busy the site has been also appears here.

You may be wondering how readily you can generalize from this description of Microsoft's Personal Web Server to other personal servers. We think you would not find it at all difficult. You would just need to obtain the information to answer the following questions:

## Where Do I Put the Files I Want to Serve?

*Where to store files*

If you or your students prepare web pages using the methods described in Chapter 6, you will need to know where to store the files so that the server can

**FIGURE 8.4** The Personal Web Server Web Site template.

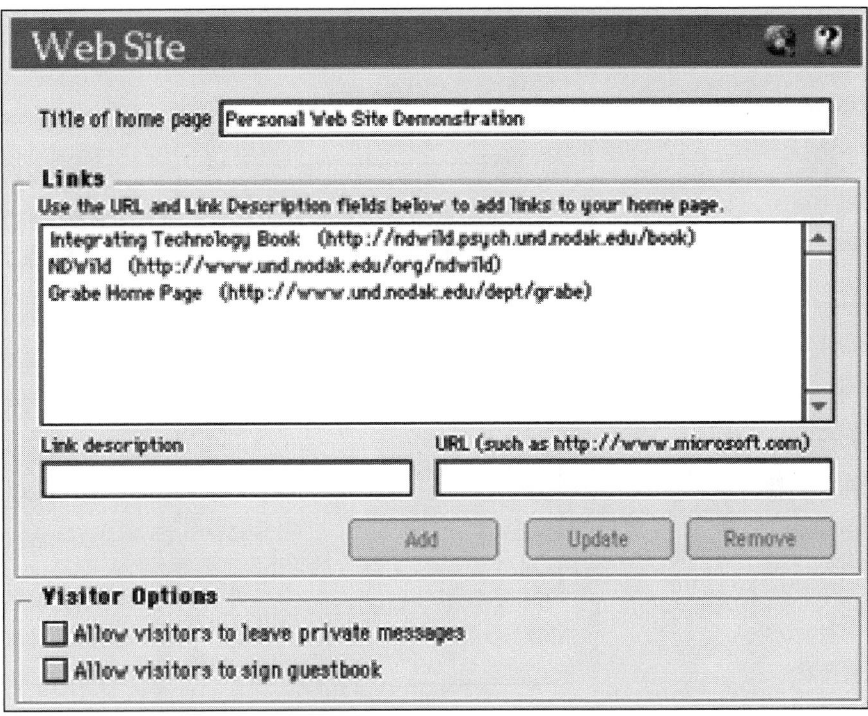


Screenshot reprinted by permission from Microsoft Corporation.

find them. Each server has a location where it expects to find files—the default folder.

## How Do I Activate the Server?

First, the computer must be running. This probably means you will leave your computer on continuously. Instead of turning your computer off when no one is using it, you will turn your monitor off and leave the computer on.

*Running server software: foreground versus background*

The server program must also be running. Personal server software can run in the foreground or the background. You will have the server program in the foreground when you set up the server and when you perform other operations such as checking how many users have downloaded pages from your site. When it is operating in foreground mode, the controls for the server are available from the screen. Once the server is operating the way you want, you will likely switch to background mode. When the server is operating in the background, it will not be obvious from the screen that a server even exists. The idea is to have a server functioning on a machine that is regularly used for other classroom tasks.

**FIGURE 8.5** The Personal Web Server Main Page.

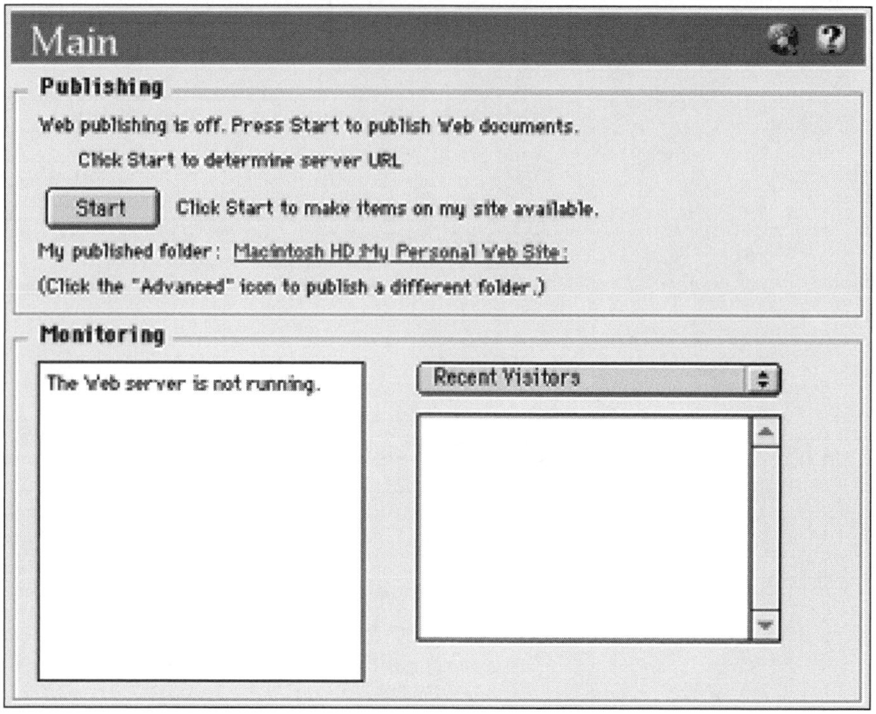

Screenshot reprinted by permission from Microsoft Corporation.

Personal server software is often designed so that outside access to the server can be turned on and off. For example, if you needed to modify the information on your home page template, you could turn off the outside access to the server and then turn it back on when you were finished.

## What Is the Address for My Server?

Other users need to know the address (URL) to connect to the server, and you need to know the address if you want to create web pages on other machines with links to the classroom machine.

*Establishing a server name*

As we mentioned in Chapter 1, a server is identified on the Internet by its IP number, which consists of four numbers separated by periods (such as 134.129.172.88). You seldom enter the IP number when connecting to a server because a name has usually been established as equivalent to that number. To set up a name for your server, you will likely call on a person with technical expertise affiliated with your school or your ISP. A server can operate without being assigned a name, but it cannot operate without a valid IP number.

Focus

### Steps in Activating a Personal Server

1. Connect computer to the Internet (done by technical person).
2. Install personal web server software.
3. Add some files to be served to the appropriate file folder. For instance, create a file using a template, or create files with other programs and move files to this folder.
4. Start the server software.
5. Allow access to the server.
6. Move server to the background (optional).
7. Test the arrangement by attempting to connect to the server.

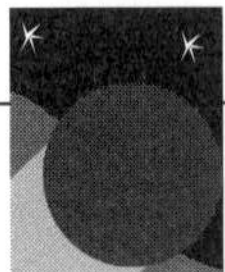

## HOW CAN K–12 INSTITUTIONS USE WEB SITES MOST PRODUCTIVELY?

Before ending this chapter, we want to broaden the focus once more to look at the ways schools can use their web sites. For you as a teacher, it will help you to have an overview of what the school as a whole is doing with its site.

*Variety of school uses*

Individual schools use their sites in very different ways. While our emphasis has been on curriculum-related uses of technology, a school web site often satisfies a much wider range of objectives. Table 8.1 offers a summary of what we have gleaned from examining quite a few school sites. We encourage you to conduct your own analysis by exploring as many school web sites as you can. The web addresses for directories of K–12 web sites appear in "Resources to Expand Your Knowledge Base" at the end of the chapter.

*Beginning with simple objectives*

We would suggest that educators who want to develop a school web site have a general familiarity with educational resources on the Internet and then spend some time examining what other schools are trying to accomplish. While successful web sites tend to grow more and more complex, it is typically impractical to begin with a complex venture. Attempting too much, too soon, will burn out key participants and fail to deliver a quality experience to those who visit the site. It is better to choose a single set of focused activities that have a high likelihood of success. A successful venture will persuade administrators to provide more resources, motivate new groups to contribute, and cultivate a loyal audience.

*A model for planning*

Here is one model that might guide the initial planning process. In the early stages of developing a school site, it is helpful to identify the *purpose* the site is to serve, the intended *audience* for site content and experiences, the *tasks* required to develop site content and maintain both the content and the server, and the *personnel* willing, available, and capable of accomplishing

**TABLE 8.1**
Typical Topics Addressed on School Web Pages

I. Information About School and School Programs

This category includes resources that allow the web visitor to learn about the school, the school's personnel, and the academic and extracurricular activities the school sponsors.

- General description
  - Location
  - Grade level
  - Enrollment
  - Faculty
    - Number
    - Personal descriptions
  - Images of facilities
  - Course descriptions
  - Description of unique programs
  - Student honor roll
  - Featured student or faculty member of the week
- Philosophy, mission, guidelines
  - Administrator message
  - Mission statement
  - Student handbook
- Schedules, calendars, deadlines
  - School year—dates and events
  - Student activity schedules—athletics, music, etc.
  - Bus schedules
  - Lunch menu
- Student activities
  - Description of student organizations
  - List of faculty advisors, sponsors, coaches
  - Required qualifications, tryout information
  - Scheduled events, meeting times
  - Event outcomes: scores of games, awards achieved, pictures, etc.

II. Curriculum Pages Prepared for Classrooms of Host School

This category includes resources that are potentially involved in learning and instruction.

- Integrated curriculum materials
  - Guided Web activities; WebQuests
  - Online instructional materials
- Student-authored projects
  - Projects prepared for Web
  - Projects repurposed for Web
    - Scanned student artwork
    - Student poetry

III. Curriculum Pages with a General Focus

- Hotlists of Internet resources
  - List of search engines and directories
  - Useful web sites
- Guidelines for using technology tools
- Lesson plans or online content-area activities
- Information resources
  - Local landmarks, informal educational opportunities
  - Community events

IV. Opportunities for Interaction

- E-mail addresses for administration and staff
- Project-related discussion
- Form to enroll teacher for in-service activity

necessary tasks. These four factors should be considered in combination (see Figure 8.6), and all elements must be in place for success.

## Purpose

*Specifying what you hope to accomplish*

In Chapter 2 we suggested that the Internet could be used as a tool for communication, inquiry, or construction. These broad categories can be used to identify various purposes for a web site. The site could provide an opportunity

**FIGURE 8.6** Factors to consider in planning a school web site.

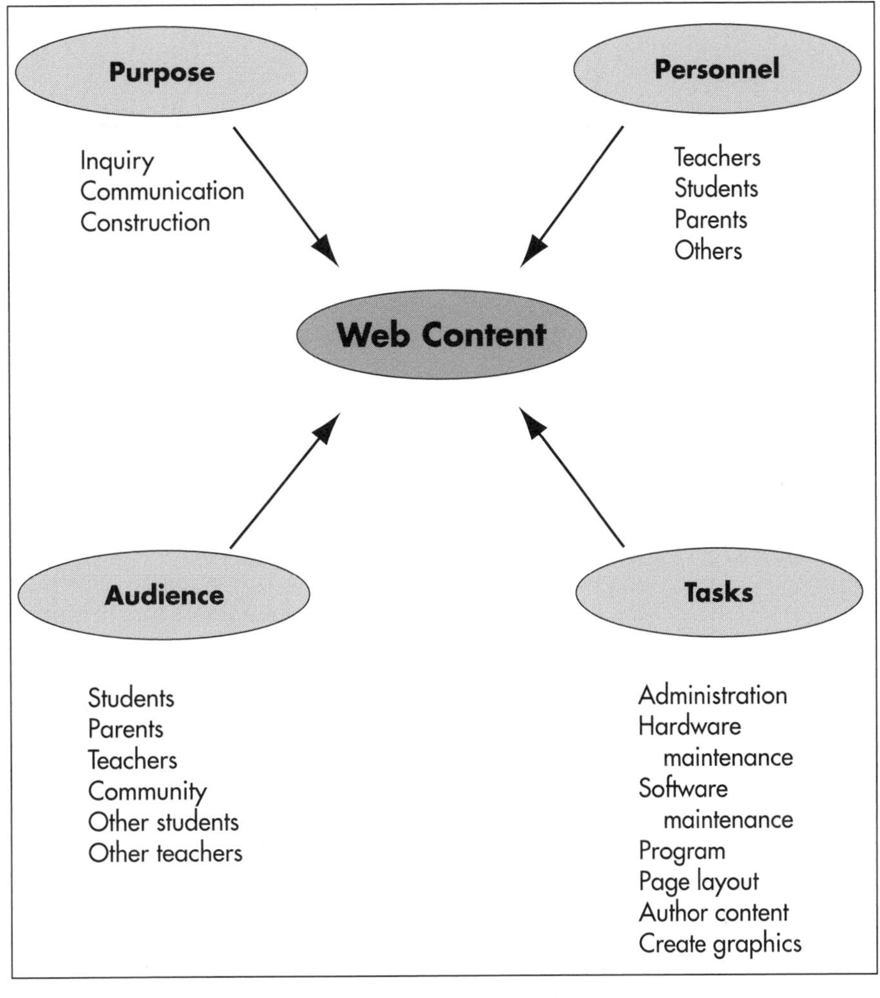


for interaction (communication), access to useful information (inquiry), an outlet for creative products (construction), or a combination of all of these.

## Audience

*Defining your audience*

Resources placed on an Internet server are potentially available to any connected user, but to maintain a focus it helps to have a particular group or groups in mind.

## Tasks

*Identifying the tasks*

Accomplishing any significant server project involves completing a variety of tasks. These tasks range from technical chores involved in operating the server, tweaking the server software, and programming CGIs to the supervision and instruction of teachers and students who want to make their work available on the server.

### Personnel

*Considering the personnel*

Finally, it is important to consider what personnel will be involved in school web projects and what roles different individuals will play. Is the necessary expertise available, and are the people motivated to participate? Will the expectations placed on key individuals become unfairly burdensome over time? Who will be allowed to participate, and who will make key decisions?

## SUMMARY

- ◆ All Internet servers rely on the same set of components: a computer, connection to the Internet, TCP/IP software, and server software. But systems integrating these components can differ greatly in price and power.
- ◆ There are a number of ways in which a school might gain access to a server. A school might make use of space on a commercial server, perhaps one maintained by the same ISP that provides the school's Internet connection. A school might also invest in the equipment and software necessary to operate its own server. Such a server might be a high-capacity system designed to provide for the needs of the entire school (or district) or a smaller system suitable for operation within individual classrooms. Which system a school should use depends on the tasks to be accomplished and the resources available for supporting the system. More powerful systems are necessary to serve many users simultaneously and to support web experiences that allow a substantial amount of interactivity.
- ◆ Personal servers, low-cost server applications that can run on a classroom computer, offer many interesting opportunities for student projects. Such servers have the advantages of low cost, great convenience, and individual control. These products have been designed so users can create and serve basic web pages in relatively simple ways.
- ◆ Schools need to give some thought to what they want to accomplish in establishing their own web sites. Educators should consider the purposes, the intended audience, the full range of tasks involved, and the personnel available to perform these tasks.

## REFLECTING ON CHAPTER 8

**Activities**

1. Conduct a survey of school web sites to determine the types of resources that are emphasized. Using the list of common web page topics in Table 8.1 or a system of your own creation, summarize the types of resources you find. Then combine the data from all participants in your class. How frequently do student projects appear? Are teachers using the web to present learning activities to their students?

2. The senior class sponsor has proposed that each senior be allowed to create a personal home page. Take a position for or against this proposal as an appropriate use of the school server.

3. If your institution (either a college or a K–12 school) has direct Internet connections in individual rooms (such as dormitory rooms or classrooms), ask the appropriate administrator if personal servers are allowed. Present the administrator's response and explanation to the class.

## Key Terms

Common Gateway Interface (CGI) *(p. 231)*
hit *(p. 230)*
hit rate *(p. 230)*
personal server *(p. 234)*
school server *(p. 225)*
server *(p. 223)*
timing out *(p. 230)*
webmaster *(p. 231)*

## Resources to Expand Your Knowledge Base

### Lists of K–12 Schools Operating Servers

Gleason Sackman maintains a *Hotlist of School Web Sites* for the Global School Network: **http://www.gsn.org/hotlist/index.html**

Stephen Collins at the University of Minnesota maintains the *Web66 School Web Site Registry:* **http://web66.umn.edu/schools.html**

### Information on Operating a School Server

*Web66: A K12 World Wide Web Project,* maintained at the University of Minnesota by Stephen Collins, provides basic instructions on the operation of a Macintosh or Windows server for K–12 schools: **http://web66.umn.edu/**

### Personal Servers

*Microsoft Personal Web Server* is a product of the Microsoft Corporation for Windows and Macintosh computers. This product can be downloaded at no charge from the Microsoft web site (**http://www.microsoft.com**; use the search feature to locate PWS).

*NetPresenz,* developed by Peter Lewis, is a $10 shareware server providing FTP, Gopher, and WWW applications for Macintosh computers. This product can be downloaded from a number of shareware sites.

*Personal Web Sharing* is a product of the Apple Computer Corporation for Macintosh computers. Personal Web Sharing has been included as part of the system software since version 8.0. Information about Personal Web Sharing can be obtained from the Apple web site (**http://www.apple.com**; use the search feature to locate Personal Web Sharing).

PART FOUR

# Issues of the Internet as an Emerging Medium

# Chapter 9 Responsible Use of the Internet

## ORIENTATION

This chapter discusses three topics related to responsible use of the Internet: equity, copyright law, and the protection of students from inappropriate content and experiences. After you have completed your study of this chapter, you should be able to explain important issues associated with each of these areas of concern and list some concrete suggestions that teachers and schools might follow to assure that students will use the Internet in a responsible manner.

As you read, look for answers to the following questions:

**FOCUS QUESTIONS**

- What inequities exist in student access to the Internet and in the learning activities that students experience? What factors appear responsible for these inequities?
- What adaptations can be implemented for students with special needs?
- What is copyright law designed to protect? What are the key guidelines that determine what can be taken from the Internet and what can be placed on the Internet?
- What are some safety guidelines that all Internet users should know?
- What options can schools use to protect students from inappropriate Internet content?

The areas of responsible use that we discuss in this chapter represent challenges that must be met in order for Internet applications to find broad success in classrooms. We must find ways for *all* students to take advantage of what the Internet can offer, provide appropriate recognition and copyright protection for those who create these resources, and make certain that students have experiences that are safe and productive.

## EQUITY OF EDUCATIONAL OPPORTUNITY

We believe that technology already plays an important role in K–12 education and that it will play an increasingly important role in the future. Clearly, technology has become an indispensable part of the way we live and work, and our educational system must accept some responsibility for preparing students for this reality.

*Effects on students' future lives*

▶ *Students who move through the educational system without having access to technology not only are limited in the ways they can approach traditional academic subjects; they are also missing out on experiences that would enhance their future ability to work and learn in a world more and more dependent on technology.*

*Recent technology trends*

To gain some perspective on equity issues, think of the technology trends of the past two decades. The 1980s were largely a time when schools became involved with computers and various computer peripherals. The 1990s served a similar function for the Internet. Early in each decade, funding for the newer forms of technology was fairly experimental, and some districts moved ahead more quickly than others. As computer or Internet applications became more commonplace, lack of access to these opportunities came to be seen as a liability. Lack of access was viewed with particular alarm when it perpetuated or exacerbated existing inequities.

*Focus on SES*

A number of descriptive studies have attempted to identify inequities in technology access. They examine whether variables such as student-to-computer ratios and classroom Internet access can be associated with factors like gender or the proportion of minority students. Some focus on links with low **socioeconomic status (SES),** a measure of prestige based on income, education, and occupation. We will offer some numbers generated by these studies, but we will focus more on trends than on the numbers themselves. Variables such as student-to-computer ratios and classroom Internet access change quickly; the overall trends are of much more lasting significance.

### EQUITY AND SES

A number of resources must be present before students are likely to have the communication, inquiry, and construction experiences we have described in this book. Simplistically, the schools these students attend have to:

1. Invest in the necessary hardware and software.
2. Connect computers to the Internet.
3. Furnish teachers with the background and support necessary to provide students with meaningful learning experiences.

*Uneven advances*

These areas of emphasis have not been developed in a coordinated manner. Schools have been spending money on computers for years. More recently, attention has shifted to providing Internet access. Teacher support and training have traditionally lagged behind (Jerald, 1998a).

*Inequities in speed of progress*

One simple way to describe equity issues is to suggest that schools with a higher proportion of advantaged and majority students seem to have progressed through this list—from computers to Internet access to teacher training and support—at a more rapid pace. Here are some of the findings that support this notion:

*Access to computers*

- Access to computers in schools, usually measured as the ratio of students per computer, once showed sizable differences when schools with high proportions of students from low-income families were compared with schools with low proportions of such students. Now, though, the differences have narrowed substantially (Panel on Educational Technology, 1997; Wenglinsky, 1998).

*Access to the Internet*

- Schools with a low percentage of low-income students (defined as less than 11 percent receiving free or reduced-priced school lunches) have greater access to the Internet than schools with a high percentage of low-income students (defined as more than 70 percent receiving free or reduced-priced school lunches). The data, gathered in 1997, are summarized in Figure 9.1.

*Teacher training and support*

- Schools with a low percentage of low-income students are more likely to have a full-time computer coordinator. Using the same designations based on the proportion of reduced-cost lunches, the figures for the two most extreme groups are 39 percent versus 26 percent (National Center for Education Statistics, 1998). Socioeconomic status differences in schools are also a predictor of whether teachers report receiving professional development in the use of computers in the past five years (Wenglinsky, 1998).

*Resources at home*

Technology access in school is not the only issue of concern. The resources available outside of school influence the skills students bring to school and the academic work students can do on their own. Here the trend is more discouraging. The difference in the likelihood of access between low- and high-income families is actually *increasing* (National Center for Education Statistics, 1998).

Are these differences important? Logically, we think so. Students with fewer technology-related experiences will be less prepared to use technology

**FIGURE 9.1** Differences in Internet access, by percentage of low-income students in the school. The left pair of bars compares Internet access in individual classrooms; the right pair, access in the school as a whole. Although the specific numbers change year by year, low-income students tend to be consistently shortchanged.

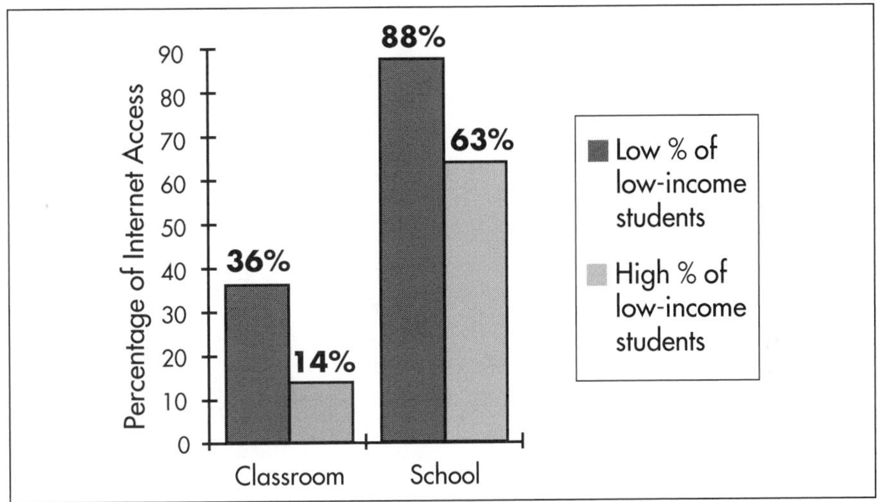


*Source:* Based on data from National Center for Education Statistics (1998).

in future work and learning settings. Lack of experience may also narrow a student's range of vocational aspirations. Of course, we also assume that lack of access will affect students' academic performance.

Is there more to offer on this subject than logical arguments? Yes: A considerable body of research supports claims that student use of technology is beneficial. However, as we explained in Chapter 2, there is considerable controversy surrounding this research. A recent major study avoids some of the areas of controversy and also provides an interesting perspective on some of the equity issues we have just outlined. The next section examines this study and its results.

## The Educational Testing Service Mathematics Study

The Educational Testing Service (ETS) mathematics study (Wenglinsky, 1998) was based on data gathered from fourth and eighth grade students who took the 1996 National Assessment of Educational Progress (NAEP) exams in mathematics. This research is unusual because it relates achievement data gathered using a major standardized test and a national sample of students to variables providing information about the students' schools and the students' uses of technology. The students and their schools supplied information about

Focus

## The E-rate as an Aid for Disadvantaged Schools

The **e-rate,** a subsidy for the costs of providing Internet connection to schools and libraries, was established by the Telecommunications Act of 1996. The more general purpose of this law is to assure "universal telecommunication and information services" to all citizens of the country regardless of income or location. Elementary and secondary schools, health care providers, and libraries are specifically targeted within this legislation for access to "advanced telecommunications services." (Federal Communications Commission, 1997).

The e-rate is funded by charges to the telecommunications industry. Some argue that this charge represents a "back-door tax" levied without providing citizens the opportunity to approve it or control how the money is spent. Supporters argue that the intent was not to have the telecommunications industry pass the costs on to consumers, but to have the industry absorb these additional costs out of the savings allowed by regulatory changes that reduced access charges previously paid by long-distance companies. Thus the funding mechanism for the e-rate is controversial, and the future of the program is somewhat uncertain (Department of Education, 1998).

The e-rate is intended to provide discounts on hardware and services essential to the transmission of information. The e-rate can be used to fund:

- Telephone connections.
- Wiring for ethernet connections.
- Internet access charges through dial-up or leased line connections.
- Hardware required for Internet connections—routers, hubs, computers used as servers.

Schools are eligible for subsidies ranging from 20 percent to 90 percent depending on the proportion of low-income students attending the school. Schools receiving the lowest reduction (20 percent) have less than 1 percent of the student body eligible for reduced-price lunches. Those schools eligible for the 90 percent reduction must have more than 75 percent of the students eligible for reduced-price lunches. Rural schools are eligible for slightly higher discounts because their telecommunications costs tend to be higher. Through the end of 1998, the e-rate transferred a total of $427 million to schools.

The e-rate is administered for the Federal Communications Commission (FCC) by an organization called the Universal Service Administration Commission. This organization receives applications and decides how the available money will be awarded. Applying for e-rate money is not a trivial exercise. Schools need to file a technology plan that explains how the e-rate money will be used to improve educational services. This plan must include an assessment of communications needs, provisions for staff development, and a strategy and budget for maintenance. A school must also take steps to show that eligible vendors will have an opportunity to compete to provide the services that the school is requesting (Department of Education, 1998).✷

*Variables in the ETS mathematics study*

- How frequently technology was used in the study of mathematics.
- Student access to technology.
- The professional development of teachers.
- What students did with technology that was relevant to the study of mathematics.
- The social environment of the school.

Several of these variables (access, student use, professional development, and social environment) are similar to ones we have already emphasized. The ETS study identifies equity differences similar to those mentioned earlier, but more importantly, the study provides some possible connections between these equity issues and student achievement. The fundamental conclusion was that the most significant inequities did not lie in how frequently computers were used, but in what students did when they used the computers:

*Inequities revealed*

- Mathematics achievement benefited when eighth graders used computers to work on content-area-appropriate "simulations and applications." Mathematics achievement suffered when students used computers to work on drill-and-practice activities.
- Students in schools with a higher proportion of less affluent students or more minority students were more likely to use computers to work on drill activities.
- Teachers in schools with a higher proportion of less affluent students had received fewer professional development experiences with technology.
- Teachers with fewer professional development experiences were more likely to emphasize drill and practice.

*Interpreting the ETS results*

The fact that several variables are interrelated does not necessarily demonstrate a causal relationship among them. Even when we take this caution into account, however, one way of interpreting the ETS mathematics data is clear: Some students do not do as well in mathematics because teachers engage them in less powerful uses of technology, and one reason why teachers are likely to use less powerful methods is the lack of appropriate professional development experiences. In addition, this lack of teacher preparation is a greater problem in schools with higher levels of low-income and minority students. These data also suggest that what students do with the technology available to them is a more serious equity issue than differences in how much time students spend using technology.

## The Role of Educators' Perceptions

Other studies have also found that what students are asked to do with technology is related to the students' economic background (see, for instance, George, Malcolm, & Jeffers, 1993; Sutton, 1991). However, teacher preparation is not the only explanation provided for why student experiences differ.

A second interpretation focuses on educators' perceptions of the type of learning experiences that would be most helpful to students. According to this view, educators working with large numbers of students from less affluent backgrounds assume that these students lack basic skills and fundamental knowledge. Therefore, the educators conclude, the most productive use of school time and resources is to focus on the remediation of such fundamentals. The assumption is that problem solving and authentic student projects must build on basic skills and will not be useful until students have first developed an adequate background.

*Educators who focus on remediation*

It is indeed possible that this view is held by many educators and that it may explain the classroom activities they emphasize. Yet this hierarchical view of classroom tasks is not universally accepted. Many educators believe that, even for students lacking in certain basic skills, a more productive approach is to embed the practice of academic skills within activities that students find to be personally meaningful. As you have seen in this book, using technology to facilitate activity-centered projects in content-area instruction is one way to provide such experiences. Students can be inspired by the opportunity to use technology in interesting and challenging ways, and it would be a shame to limit the involvement of any student who could profit from this source of motivation (Laboratory of Comparative Human Cognition, 1989).

*Educators who focus on meaningful activities*

## Equity and the Classroom Teacher

The research on technology and equity that we have just described did not focus specifically on how teachers and students make use of the Internet. Comparable data for Internet use have yet to emerge, so we are asking you to consider how Internet activity will resemble other instructional uses of technology. Think about the possible connections among such variables as student background, teacher training, teacher beliefs about what is best for students, variations in access to technology, and variations in how students use technology. All of these may affect your students and the way you teach in your classroom.

For classroom teachers, two issues particularly concern us:

1. Learning experiences of the type we have described in this book—inquiry and construction experiences in which students use technology to go beyond passive reception of information—may be less frequently available to some students because their teachers do not have the training and support necessary to guide them. One solution might be to provide practicing teachers with ongoing opportunities for professional development, perhaps through interaction with a full-time computer coordinator. Unfortunately, without external support, this is just the resource that is least likely to be available in school districts in low-income areas. Perhaps our observation that investments tend to move from computers to Internet access and then to professional development will hold true, and eventually the support for staff development will be improved.

*Teacher training and support: A financial problem*

*Focus of teaching: A problem you can address*

2. Our second concern is that teachers will focus disadvantaged students exclusively on the accumulation of information. The solution to this challenge is not financial; it is something you can address. Throughout this book we have encouraged you to consider applications that lead students to evaluate information thoughtfully and to use it to address personally meaningful problems. So the matter is in your hands as a teacher. We hope the activities outlined in this book will provide you with some ideas.

## GENDER EQUITY

In addition to inequities related to SES, there are others that cannot be explained in terms of differences in access or teacher preparation. Males and females have different experiences with technology, and these differences in experience may limit future academic or vocational opportunities (Weinman & Haag, 1999). Here is a sample of the type of indicators that concern some educators:

*Gender differences*

- Differences exist in the technology-related courses that males and females select. Females dominate courses focused on clerical skills, which are regarded as being associated with careers that are less technologically advanced.
- A very small proportion of high school females take the computer science advanced placement examination.
- Only about 25 percent of college undergraduate computer science degrees are awarded to women.
- Females rate themselves as having lower computer abilities than males and are less likely to believe that computer skills help them do better in school (American Association of University Women Educational Foundation, 1998).

Why might males and females have such different experiences, and why might they feel differently about themselves as potential users of powerful applications of technology? Several factors frequently appear as explanations:

*Potential explanations*

- Stereotypes of computer use and computer users are perpetuated in popular media. Males are commonly represented as "power users."
- Recreational software that may interest people in computers is strongly slanted toward males.
- The computer is viewed as a tool for math, science, and programming—subjects that, sadly, may be of less interest to many females than to males.
- The more aggressive nature of young males may offer an advantage in gaining access to computers or the Internet when there is not enough equipment for everyone.
- Some computer tasks emphasize mastery rather than social motives and may therefore be more likely to appeal to males (Sanders & McGinnis, 1991; Weinman & Haag, 1999).

In contrast to past classroom applications of technology, however, communication, inquiry, and construction activities associated with the Internet may offer some advantages in involving students in a more equitable fashion:

*How Internet applications can reduce gender inequity*

1. Internet applications exist for all disciplines and offer the opportunity to engage all students.
2. Internet applications can offer opportunities for collaboration and social interaction as well as opportunities for independence and competition.
3. Development of skills associated with Internet applications can lead students toward vocational opportunities.

Again, we hope the broad range of classroom activities we have described in this book will offer opportunities for both male and female learners.

## ADAPTING TECHNOLOGY FOR EQUAL ACCESS

This book is based on the premise that the Internet can provide meaningful learning experiences for the benefit of *all* students. However, more than 50 million Americans have some type of disability that restricts their ability to take advantage of what technology has to offer.

*Types of impairments that affect technology use*

These individuals may have mobility impairments that make it difficult to operate a mouse or use a keyboard. They may have visual impairments that restrict their use of a computer monitor. Learners may also have auditory impairments or learning disabilities that present special challenges for technology use. As we have observed before, the computer and the Internet can provide great independence and compensate for many traditional obstacles. However, without meaningful access, technology can also impose new barriers.

For these reasons, educators must seek ways to adapt technology to individual needs. This is a topic with many important subissues, and some of the more important ones are explored in the following sections.

### Adaptations for Mobility Impairments

Mobility impairments make it difficult for learners to interact with technology. The problem may involve difficulties in manipulating input devices (keyboard, mouse) or even basic physical tasks associated with operating a computer or peripheral device (turning on the computer, inserting a diskette or CD). Here are some ways to respond to mobility impairments:

*Potential solutions for mobility problems*

- A power strip can be used to turn all equipment on and off with a single switch.
- Alternative keyboards position the keys farther apart and disable repeat keys so that users with slower and less precise movements have less difficulty.
- Special software allows the cursor to scan across a screen representation or across program choice buttons, permitting users to make selections

simply by controlling a switch. The switch can be operated in any number of ways—with the knee, mouth, or head, for instance.

## Adaptations for Visual Impairments

Visual impairments should not hinder learners from taking advantage of technology. Some of the following adaptations can be made:

*Potential solutions for visual problems*

- Though most blind individuals can use a standard keyboard, Braille key labels may be helpful for some users.
- Special **screen reader** software "reads" the screen to the learner (earphones can be used to reduce the distraction to others). Basic speech synthesis from text is fairly standard, but screen reader software can also "describe" menus, windows, and screen icons.
- Special software can allow magnification of the screen image for learners with limited vision. Some programs allow screen content to be enlarged sixteenfold.

## Adaptive Web Page Design

The adaptations we have described so far address the general use of computers, and they would certainly apply in helping students make use of the Internet. In practice, though, challenges and solutions are often unique to a particular combination of learner limitation and computer application. The use of the Web by blind students offers a good example.

For blind students to use the Web, adaptations we have already discussed, such as screen reader software, are essential. However, there are some other challenges that cannot be met through modifications in the software or hardware used by the student. The way that web pages themselves are designed is important.

*Need for designers to recognize user limitations*

Consider the issue from the perspective of the designer. Most web designers recognize the need to accommodate limitations such as older versions of browsers and relatively slow modems. But designers often forget that some Internet users face very different challenges. Visually impaired students cannot read a web page or scrutinize images and illustrations. Less obviously, these students cannot use the mouse to point at a text link or click on a hot spot in an image map.

*A basic question*

Some basic design suggestions can make a big difference, and web designers of any age can implement many of these features (Adaptive Computer Technology Centre, 1998; World Wide Web Consortium, 1999). Often it is helpful to begin with the question: Could the web page be interpreted totally by listening? This question does not imply that a web author must create an audio version of each web page; rather, the page design should allow the user's special software to "read" the screen to the user. Here are some principles to follow:

*Text alternatives to graphics and video*

1. If some page information is not presented as text—for example, if important content information is contained in images, illustrations, or video—consider offering alternative sources of information. An image

Keeping Current

## Adaptations Allowed by Newer Versions of HTML and New Software

The Hypertext Markup Language continues to offer more features as newer versions of HTML are released. One aspect of this evolution is the introduction of new tags and tag attributes. Think of these as the commands that allow new functions. Some of these new functions allow greater flexibility in the way a browser can interpret the information the web page contains.

The idea in newer approaches is to separate content and structure and to allow the user greater control over how a personal browser will structure the presentation of content. The details of this concept are beyond the scope of this book, but a simple example may be helpful. Consider a web page that includes a two-column table presenting a segment of text. Older screen readers for the visually impaired attempt to read the entire page from left to right, which results in confusion. The older system cannot separate the content (the entire segment of text) from the structure (a two-column table). More sophisticated browsers will interpret the structure of the table and present the contents in a more comprehensible manner.

Here are some examples of features in HTML version 4 that could be very helpful to a browser configured to be sensitive to the needs of visually impaired learners.

1. The new *tabindex* and *accesskey* attributes added to the anchor tag for links allow greater control of page functions with the keyboard rather than the mouse. Tabindex allows options (such as links to other web pages) to be ordered, so that pressing the Tab key allows the user to jump from link to link in the specified order. Pressing the Return key when a desired link is selected then causes the browser to load the requested page. Accesskey allows the assignment of browser actions to keyboard actions. For instance, the "H" key might be designated as a way to return the user to the home page.
2. The *longdesc* attribute allows a long segment of text to be attached to a graphic. The longdesc attribute points to a text file that might be sent on request to provide information in place of the visual information offered by the graphic file.
3. The *summary, caption,* and *table header* attributes allow the author to describe a table and label the cells within the table. A summary would allow a screen reader to offer a comment explaining that the following information is contained within a table. The screen reader could also use the caption and header to label entries within the table as they are read. If a table displayed the present standings in the National Basketball Association, for example, it might consist of multiple rows, each consisting of three cells—: team, games won, and games lost. If properly labeled, a row from the table might be read as "Team: Utah Jazz," "Games Won: 34," "Games Lost: 17."

As we write this chapter, the web authoring programs we described in Chapter 6 do not offer easy methods for including HTML 4.0 tags and attributes, and the older browsers available on many computers cannot implement them. This situation will change rapidly.

To comprehend web content and make effective use of the navigational and interactive elements built into web pages, visually impaired users need more than a spoken version of web page text. They also need to hear a description of other elements appearing on a page; they need to know when text segments serve as links; and they need access to some of the alternative descriptive information that may not be automatically displayed. If the page author has done a conscientious job, all of this information is embedded in one way or another within the raw HTML, so what is required is a different way of interpreting the HTML and presenting information to the user.

*Home Page Reader* is an example of a program that extracts and presents such supplemental information. This product:

- Reads text in a male voice and text links in a female voice.
- Reads ALT text and HTML 4.0 information provided by web page authors.
- Describes tables, frames, and forms.
- Summarizes page links and allows selection of links using the number keypad.
- Allows visually impaired users to create "readable" bookmarks.

In these ways, advances in HTML and software are coming together to allow visually impaired users to benefit from web resources.✱

map should be accompanied by text links that can be used as alternatives to the map's hot spots. A link to a separate page containing a text segment can be offered as an alternative to an explanatory illustration. Video can be supplemented with an audio track to provide descriptive information.

2. Take advantage of the built-in opportunities to provide redundant information. HTML offers various ways to include supplemental information, but designers frequently ignore these opportunities. Imagine, for example, that a web page uses a graphic "forward" arrow as a link to the next page in a sequence. Many visually impaired students, who have no use for graphics, set their browsers to avoid loading graphic images. Fortunately, the designer can use the ALT attribute to specify text that will appear as a replacement for an image. In this case, specifying ALT="Next Page" would allow the text phrase "Next Page" to appear in place of the arrow.

*Adding supplemental information: The ALT attribute*

   This kind of supplemental information is very easy to add when using a web authoring program. With all the authoring programs we described in Chapter 6, you can open a dialogue box and manipulate various attributes of the image, including the ALT label. (See the "Keeping Current" feature for more options available with newer versions of HTML.)

3. Information presented in tables or multiple columns can be confusing when "read" by older screen reader programs, because the reader attempts to follow the text horizontally across the entire page. We do advocate the use of tables as a way to structure web pages, but tables with

*Alternatives to tables*

side-by-side columns of lengthy text are especially problematic for users dependent on a screen reader. The best solution may be to insert a link at the top of the page providing access to a single-column, alternative version of the page.

*Using punctuation*

4. Remember to use punctuation. Screen readers identify punctuation marks, and these can be critical for a user's understanding of the content. On many web pages, items in lists do not end with punctuation marks, and this lack of punctuation can make them more difficult to interpret.

## COPYRIGHT LAW AND RESPECT FOR INTELLECTUAL PROPERTY

All educators would like a clearly written explanation of what copyright law has to say about various educational uses of the Internet. Unfortunately, this is much easier to wish for than to achieve. Our own work sometimes involves advising others on such issues, so we are careful to review as many sources as we can, and in doing so we have noticed an interesting phenomenon. Nearly every expert is careful to state that what he or she has written should not be accepted as legal advice. Each expert includes a disclaimer, and most urge anyone who has concerns about a specific activity to contact a lawyer. Needless to say, this is not very practical advice for an average teacher.

The lack of commitment on the part of experts does have an explanation, which is relevant to our discussion. But we hope you are not disappointed that we first offer our own disclaimer. The information that we provide here is intended to acquaint you with copyright law, but should not be treated as legal advice. You should be aware that personal interpretation of copyright law can result in violations and that the safest approach is to contact the copyright holder and request permission before you copy anything.

*Laws lag behind behavior*

One reason that even experts offer disclaimers is that copyright law is very likely to lag behind practice. This means that people have the ability to do things before there are specific laws to govern their behavior. Laws are established through the political process, and the interests of many groups often must be considered. It sometimes takes some time before pressure builds to the point at which additions to the law are written.

This does not mean that you can do what you feel like doing until a law is written to forbid it. You are obliged to follow certain general principles established in existing law. What is or is not allowed is likely to depend on several criteria that are open to interpretation. You are entitled to your interpretation, but the same is the case for the holder of the copyright. The final ruling may end up being rendered by a judge in court.

For our purposes, let's begin with a wish list. What are the fundamental questions that should be answered to guide classroom teachers?

*A wish list: Four questions to answer*

### Questions About Internet Copyright Law

- Can students and teachers take resources from web sites for use in learning and instructional activities?
- Can students and teachers use the material developed by others on their own web pages?
- Can teachers post student work on the Web?
- What should teachers do if they want to protect online resources they have developed?

Keep these questions in mind as you read the following material. We will attempt to answer the questions, but please remember our previous caution that definitive answers may require a formal legal opinion.

## EDUCATION AND COPYRIGHT: ISSUES AND PROBLEMS

All teachers need to be aware of their personal obligations regarding copyrighted materials, and they also need to teach their students to respect the intellectual property of others. It may be helpful to think of these responsibilities as interrelated. A powerful way to develop any behavior in your students is to model this behavior yourself.

*Importance of copyright questions in education*

Copyright is such an important issue in education because the process of education relies heavily on instructional materials (including textbooks, films, and computer programs) and on other resources that can serve an educational purpose (newspapers, television programs, videotapes, music CDs, reference books). We now must add Internet resources as a new option for both instructional material and general information. It is very important to recognize that these essential information resources were purposefully created through the intellectual efforts of others—often as a way for these individuals to make a living. If we want creative individuals to spend their time preparing instructional materials, it is essential that they be compensated when their materials are used.

*Teachers who violate copyright*

Without dwelling on the subject, we will simply state that some educators violate copyright law. The music teacher may copy orchestra sheet music so each child can take a copy home to practice. The biology teacher may develop a personal collection of informative television programs for use in class. The English teacher who has purchased a new word processing program may copy it to all three computers in his room. A college professor may print out an article from a subscription Internet information service, make copies, and distribute them to her students. The list of common violations could go on and on.

*Desire to help students*

Because teachers are not, as a rule, prone to breaking the law, why do they sometimes violate copyright law? Some may want to help students but lack the resources they feel are necessary to do so. We certainly cannot provide easy remedies for all types of educational copyright abuse when money is short, but we do feel the issues involving Internet resources will not usually fall within this category.

*Easy access to copying methods*

A second reason may result from a combination of easy access to the means for making copies and sketchy knowledge of when copying is appropriate. Nearly every teacher has access to a photocopy machine, tape recorder, video recorder, scanner, and computer with blank disks. These are available in schools and in most public libraries. Most users of the Internet probably realize that if you hold down the mouse button while clicking on a web page image (or click with the right button when working on a Windows machine), the browser will ask you if you would like to save a copy of the image. If it were illegal to copy documents, TV programs, computer programs, web images, and the like, would the methods and equipment for doing so be so readily accessible?

*Available≠legal*

The answer is yes. The methods and materials are available even though some of the copying for which they are used is illegal. Of course, schools, libraries, and the companies creating products that enable copying are not advocating theft of intellectual property. These organizations assume that those who use their products and resources are aware of situations in which copying is appropriate and in which it is not. When violations occur, it is sometimes because teachers or students assume the opportunity to copy something implies more than it does. In this situation, teachers and students need a better understanding of what is appropriate.

*Free≠unprotected*

For the Internet in particular, one final problem may be caused by a different set of false assumptions. Access to a tremendous amount of Internet material is free, and often there are no obvious indicators such as a copyright symbol or a statement that the material is protected. Can you steal something that has no posted price and for which no one has openly spoken? Again, the simple answer is yes, for these reasons:

- The assumption that you are not taking revenue away from an author by copying content from a web page may be wrong. The individual responsible for the web content may be paid by others—advertisers, for example—when the information on the page is accessed. If your behavior prevents others (such as your students) from visiting a web page, you may be limiting the income of the web site author.
- The intent to make money is not necessary for intellectual property to be protected. The author has the right to control who displays what he or she has created.
- Finally, the absence of a copyright statement is not an indication that the author has given up his or her rights.

Again, teachers and students may simply need a better understanding of what is appropriate.

Our goal in the following sections is to make you aware of some of the general issues involved in copyright and then to take a more specific look at issues pertaining to the Internet.

## THE COPYRIGHT LAW

*Constitutional basis of copyright*

The government's authority to develop copyright law is established in the Constitution of the United States in Article I, Section 8, which grants Congress the authority "to promote the progress of science and useful arts, by securing for limited times to authors and inventors the exclusive right to their respective writings and discoveries." This section of the Constitution is responsible for what we know as copyrights and patents.

The current copyright law was written in 1976 and has since been amended to make the law more specific. But it does not yet directly address many issues raised by the Internet. Concern has been expressed that the Internet's uniqueness requires more explicit guidance than the existing law offers.

*"Any tangible medium"*

On the basis of existing law, it appears that teachers and students should treat Internet resources in the same way that they treat other materials for which the guidelines are more commonly known. The original law, written to be very open-ended, defines as copyrightable "original works of authorship fixed in any tangible medium of expression, now known or later developed" (Copyright Act of 1976, Title 17 of the U.S. Code, Section 102, included in Salpeter, 1992). Thus "fixing" a creative product in digital form results in the same protection afforded other forms of intellectual property (Major, 1998).

*Value of copyright protection*

It is easy for educators to see only one side of copyright law: copyright law just tells teachers what they cannot do. However, if you read and think carefully about the statement from the Constitution authorizing copyright laws, you may gain a different perspective. Copyright law is intended to encourage "the progress of science and useful arts." In other words, if educators expect others to create and improve instructional materials, educators should also expect that mechanisms must be put in place to allow these individuals to make a fair profit on their work. For example, if subscription-based web services become perceived as a market prone to frequent copyright violations, commercial developers will not put effort into creating high-quality products for that market.

## ESTABLISHING A COPYRIGHT

How exactly does a work's creator establish copyright under the current law? In fact, the creator does not need to take any specific steps to claim copyright.

▶ *Any author's work is automatically protected from the time it is created.*

This principle applies not only to written works but also to music, photographs, artwork, and so on.

*Copyright notice and registration*

An author can provide notice of copyright with a notation in the following form: © year name; for example, © 1999 Cindy Grabe. The word *copyright* can also be used in place of the copyright symbol. You are probably aware that there is a U.S. Copyright Office and that authors can register their works with this office. But the fact that a work has not been registered or even that it does not carry a notice of copyright should not be interpreted as a waiver of copyright.

## RIGHTS, LICENSES, AND PERMISSIONS

Copyright law grants authors or owners five basic rights:

*The five basic rights of copyright*

1. *The right to make copies.* If you are the creator of the work, you can make as many copies as you want.
2. *The right to create derivations.* A derivation is an adaptation of the original. For example, a painter might create prints from an original painting, or an author might create a movie script based on a book.
3. *The right to sell or distribute copies.* The author can make a profit by copying and selling works to others.
4. *The right to perform a work in public.* Generally the author of a work controls the presentation of the work to the public. The performance right covers, for instance, live performances of music and the presentation of a play.
5. *The right to display a work in public.* This right covers situations like the display of a painting or the presentation of original artwork on the Internet.

*Transferring rights*

The author or creator of a work can transfer some or all of these rights to others. If the copyright itself is assigned to someone else, that means that all rights are transferred. For example, a large software company may pay an independent developer a large sum of money to be assigned the copyright for a computer program the developer has written. From that point on, the company can do whatever it wants with the program.

*Licenses*

In an alternative arrangement, the granting of a **license,** only the rights specified in the agreement are transferred (Fritz, 1992). Although the term *license* may not always be used, this is a common type of agreement, and it may or may not involve money.

*Site licenses*

Examples of license agreements in education are common. You may have heard of a software **site license,** which allows a school or other organization to make copies of software it has purchased. The license may limit the number of copies, or it may allow unlimited copying as long as the software is used on a machine owned by the school. A license of this type does not allow the school to distribute copies outside the site. A site license offers some advantages to both parties. The school is allowed to purchase the software for less than the standard price per copy. The company selling the software usually saves on packaging and manuals.

*Asking for permission*

When you ask a copyright holder for permission to copy a work in a specific way for a certain context, you are in effect applying for a mini-license. For example, you may ask an artist for permission to scan a painting or drawing to include it in a classroom project. In instances of this sort, only very specific and limited rights are granted. For advice on acquiring permission, see "Focus: Obtaining Permission to Copy."

## Obtaining Permission to Copy

The first step in obtaining permission is to determine who owns the copyright. With books, journals, and documents, the copyright notice usually appears very near the front of the publication. Also check the acknowledgments page. Pay special attention to information about multiple copyrights. With music, the lyrics and musical score may be protected separately. This is also frequently the case with the text and illustrations in documents. Web sites may include a "Terms and Conditions" statement that explains the author's position on the use of site contents.

Following is a list of items to include in your request for permission. This list assumes that you want to copy material from a document, and some of these items may need to be modified slightly if another type of material is involved. Circumstances may also require that the form of the letter or e-mail message be modified. In general, however, be sure to include these items:

- The full name of the author or artist responsible for the work you propose to copy.
- The exact reference for the source material.
- The page number(s) or the URL (for web content) for the material you want to copy.
- The number of copies you propose to make.
- A full description of how the copied material will be used, including:
  - — The nature of the project.
  - — Whether the material will be used alone or combined with materials obtained from other companies.
  - — Who will assemble the project.
  - — Who will view the finished project.
  - — How long the materials will be kept and what will happen to the project after the intended academic task has been completed.
- A description of the course in which the material is to be used.
- Your name, position, institutional affiliation, full address, and telephone number.

Some companies may expect you to pay a royalty fee for using their material. You may feel it is appropriate to acknowledge that this is a possibility and ask what the fee will be. For example, you might say, "If a royalty fee applies to copying the material that has been described, please notify me so that I can determine whether funds are available."

It is important to allow several weeks for your request to be considered. It may take a month to process your request, and you will want to allow time to develop an alternate plan in case your request is denied.

Remember to be courteous. What you are requesting is a privilege. (*Source:* Based on suggestions provided by Long, Risher, and Shapiro [1997]. We have added suggestions based on our own experiences.)✷

## FAIR USE

As we noted earlier, libraries provide easy access to photocopy machines, so it is very easy for you to copy material from books, journals, and magazines. This does not mean that all types of copying are legal; yet, since libraries do not want to promote copyright violations, there must be some situations in which material can be copied without seeking permission from the author or creator.

*The concept of fair use*

In fact, you are allowed to make photocopies in the library because of a provision called **fair use,** defined in Section 107 of the copyright law. The guidelines governing fair use can be confusing, and it is important for you as a teacher to understand what they involve. Essentially, Section 107 provides some exceptions to the general principle that the creator of the work holds exclusive rights to copy and distribute it.

For purposes like teaching, scholarship, and research, Section 107 specifies four "factors to be considered" in determining whether a particular act of copying represents fair use:

*Factors determining fair use*

- *Purpose of the use.* Generally, copying is more acceptable if it is for nonprofit purposes than if it is done for profit.
- *Nature of the copyrighted work.* The copying of factual material, such as a summary of historical events, is more likely to be fair use than the copying of original poetry or fiction.
- *Amount and substantiality of the portion used.* Copying a small part of the original is more likely to be tolerated than copying the entire work.
- *Impact on commercial value.* Copying should not harm the commercial value of the original or deprive the creator or publisher of permission fees. For instance, copying of workbooks is not considered fair use because workbooks are intended to be purchased and used only once. A related consideration, for many kinds of material, is the number of copies made; obviously, a large number of copies would have a greater impact on a work's commercial value than a small number.

These four factors were intended to be balanced against one another in particular cases. The overall intent was to create a law that was flexible and applicable to many situations, reflecting the great variety of copyrighted material and the equally great variety of possible uses. For many educators and other professionals, however, the result has been uncertainty about what they can and cannot do.

To make matters even more complicated, the meaning of "fair" in fair use sometimes varies with the medium (Major, 1998; Martin, 1994; Salpeter, 1992). As for the Internet, fair use practices—like the Internet itself—are still evolving (see "Focus: Fair Use on the Internet"). Without specific guidelines for Internet materials, the reasonable approach is probably a conservative one, drawing on existing policies that apply to other media.

Focus

### Fair Use on the Internet

What is meant by "fair use" is open to interpretation. When parties disagree, it may be necessary for the legal system to make a final decision. Here is an example of a legal case involving the Internet—a case that may have implications for what schools can post on their web sites (eSchool News Staff, 1998).

The Free Republic (**http://www.FreeRepublic.com**), an online site focused on current events, is the target of a copyright lawsuit brought by the *Los Angeles Times* and the *Washington Post.* The site has posted many complete news stories taken without permission from the newspapers' own web sites. The Free Republic contends its practices are legal, under the principle of fair use, because it is a noncommercial site that encourages discussion and criticism. The major newspapers argue that the availability of their material on another server limits their advertising revenue, which is based on the number of hits on their home sites.

The papers suggest that a more appropriate approach would be for the Free Republic to provide links to articles on their sites. This is regarded as a significant case for schools because it may be viewed as a test of whether the universal access allowed by the Internet eliminates certain applications that might otherwise be allowed under the guidelines of fair use.

What do you think?✷

*Attempts to clarify remaining issues*

Because of the matters left unresolved by the copyright law, there have been various attempts to bring interested parties together to negotiate more specific guidelines. One of the earliest such negotiations focused on the issue of photocopying of printed works, and a set of guidelines was worked out specifically for that medium. Let's look at what those rules entail. A key point to remember is this:

▶ *The guidelines that apply to copying material for your own professional use differ from the guidelines for preparing multiple copies for your students.*

## Copying for Your Own Use

*Liberal allowances for personal photocopying*

In general, as an individual, you are allowed to copy rather extensively in preparing for your classes or in conducting scholarly work. For example, your college or university library will likely allow you to copy an entire journal article or book chapter as part of your research for a paper. The same is true when you are doing research to prepare for teaching a class. Fair use guidelines for individual scholarship are fairly liberal.

This does not mean, however, that there are no limits. For example, when Mark Grabe's university library honors his request to copy a chapter from a book, the library records his name and the book title. The library will not allow him to copy a second chapter from the same book. This is the point at which the library feels copying might be perceived as a substitute for purchasing the book.

### Making Multiple Copies for Classroom Use

Guidelines for making multiple copies for class use are much more conservative than those controlling personal use. For books and periodicals, the multiple-copy fair use guidelines include these points:

*Guidelines for multiple photocopies*

- *Brevity.* A teacher is allowed to excerpt and distribute 1,000 words or 10 percent, whichever is less, from a written document. Similar guidelines have been set for other media, as we describe in the next section.
- *Spontaneity.* Copying a particular work must be the "inspiration" of the teacher who wants to use the work. For example, a librarian is not supposed to collect material for a teacher. The decision to use the work must occur so close in time to its actual use that it would not be practical to obtain permission.
- *Cumulative effect.* Material is to be copied for a single course, and the time period during which the material may continue to be used is restricted. To control the cumulative effect of the copying, limits are placed on how many items may be taken from the works of a single author or artist.

Again, these are the guidelines that were developed to contend with the technological innovation called the photocopier. Now let's consider what headway has been made in dealing with more recent advances in multimedia and distance education.

## GUIDELINES FOR CREATING MULTIMEDIA AND FOR DISTANCE EDUCATION

*CONFU*

In recent years, individuals from various parties with a vested interest in fair use (such as the U.S. government, publishing companies, the Software Publishing Association, and the Association for Educational Communications and Technology) have met to propose guidelines for technological applications in educational contexts. These meetings evolved into the **Conference on Fair Use** (commonly referred to as **CONFU**). After two years of work, CONFU's suggestions for teacher- or student-created multimedia and for distance education were finalized in 1997. The full text of the documents prepared by this committee is available on the Internet (CONFU, 1997a, 1997b), and the preamble to each document includes a good discussion of fair use in general.

The CONFU guidelines still do not provide the focus on Internet resources or issues that we would prefer. When the CONFU meetings occurred, only a few colleges and schools were beginning to explore uses of the World Wide Web for teaching their students. Another attempt to deal with emerging copyright issues, the Digital Millennium Copyright Act, became law in late 1998. This law includes a provision (Section 403) directing the Copyright Office to work with educators, nonprofit libraries, and publishers to submit a proposal to Congress concerning distance education and digital technology. While this addition to copyright law is welcome, it, too, does little to answer questions related to fair use in educational applications of the Internet.

*Digital Millennium Copyright Act*

For the moment, then, the CONFU guidelines are the most applicable ones, and they are worth examining in more detail.

## The CONFU Guidelines

The Conference on Fair Use offered guidelines concerning (1) distance learning and (2) educational multimedia. The multimedia guidelines have received widespread acceptance, whereas the ones for distance education have prompted much disagreement. For any of these guidelines, though, it is important to understand that they are not legally binding; rather, they are in the nature of proposals.

*Guidelines for distance learning*

The suggestions for distance learning apply to telecommunications applications, such as teaching a class via videoconferencing. Generally they allow a teacher to read, display, or perform copyrighted works in a distance education setting in the same way that the teacher might do in face-to-face instruction. The teacher can read a poem aloud, for example. But an entire work or "a large portion thereof" can be transmitted only once for a particular course. The transmission must be over a secure system so that only eligible students have access to it. Although the institution that receives the transmission can record or copy it, the recording can be saved for only 15 consecutive class days without obtaining permission.

*Guidelines for multimedia*

The guidelines for multimedia may be more relevant to most of the applications described in this book. CONFU's multimedia guidelines address student use of copyrighted work as part of course-related multimedia projects and teacher use of copyrighted work in the creation of "noncommercial" multimedia for instructional purposes. They attempt to suggest the applications, time frame, copying, distribution, and portion limits that would comply with established fair use standards.

### Application Limits

- *Students.* Students may create and present multimedia projects containing copyrighted material for educational purposes within the course for which they were created, and they may save these projects as examples of their academic work for future job or academic interviews.

- *Teachers.* Teachers may use multimedia including copyrighted material conforming to fair use for purposes of: (1) face-to-face instruction, (2) student self-study, (3) remote instruction to enrolled students on a network providing controlled access, or (4) evaluations of teaching performance or job interviews.

### Time, Copying, and Distribution Limits

- *Time.* Teacher-created multimedia may be used in instruction for up to two years. (*Note:* If the teacher cannot prevent duplication of copyrighted material, the material can remain available for only 15 days.)
- *Copying and distribution.* It is suggested that only two copies, the original and a backup, should be created. Only one copy should be available to users, and students should not be allowed to make personal copies. In those situations in which the product has been the result of a collaborative effort, each participant may keep a copy for archival purposes.

The portion limitations define the amount of material that may be taken from a copyrighted work. These limits apply cumulatively to projects created by students or teachers. For example, a teacher who creates multimedia resources to be used in conjunction with daily lectures must consider the total material used in all lectures in determining what resources may be taken from a given source. The allowable portions vary according to the media used.

### Portion Limits

- *Video.* Users are allowed to use up to 10 percent, or 3 minutes, whichever is less, of material from a video work.
- *Text material.* Users are allowed to use up to 10 percent, or 1,000 words, whichever is less, from a text work. Poetry represents a special category. A poem of 250 words or less may be used in total, but no more than 3 poems by one poet, or 5 poems from a published anthology, may be used.
- *Music.* Users may use 10 percent, or 30 seconds, whichever is less, from an individual musical work.
- *Photographs and other illustrations.* No more than 5 images by an artist or photographer may be used. For images from a collection (such as a book), the limit is 10 percent, or 15 images, whichever is less.

*Additional guidelines*

There are some additional expectations. Students and educators are required to carefully cite all sources when using copyrighted material. Providing credit includes listing a full citation for the original work and including any copyright notices displayed in the original source. With the exception of copyright information related to images, this information may be consolidated in a single section within the multimedia product (for instance, it may appear as a list at the end). For images, however, information about the source and copyright should accompany each individual image. Finally, students and teachers should include in the introduction to their multimedia product a statement indicating that material is incorporated in this product under the fair use exemption of the U.S. copyright law and is restricted from further use.

## Gaps in the Guidelines

As you can see, both the existing law and the guidelines developed by the Conference on Fair Use have gaps where teachers want answers. For example, the CONFU participants provided suggestions for what teachers can use in their classrooms and with locally based students, but they stated clearly that these guidelines do not apply to students involved in distance education. Nor do the separate guidelines for distance education answer many Internet-related questions that teachers will have. We certainly cannot assume that teachers are free to do online the same things they can do with in-class multimedia. The gap in the guidelines remains even when the teacher can guarantee that access is limited by a password protection system.

*Unresolved questions*

Another important uncertainty involves the use of web resources in the creation of student or teacher multimedia. For example, the CONFU guidelines make clear suggestions about the use of images from a book or part of a song from a CD. But there is no clear statement about using an image or part of a song copied from a web page.

You can probably see other gaps in the guidelines that may apply to your own classroom situations. Within a few years, the copyright rules for Internet educational uses should become clearer, through new laws or negotiated policies. In the meantime, as we suggested earlier, a conservative approach is advisable.

## Using Student Work on Web Sites

*Can students claim copyright?*

Before we sum up our outlook on copyright issues, there is one more area we want to address. It is common to view student work on school web sites. But do students have rights as authors? Copyright law is clear on the issue of ownership. Unless a student has been hired to create material and is operating under a formalized work-for-hire agreement, a student owns any work he or she has created.

*Restrictions on use of student work*

Does this mean that the teacher cannot keep or make copies of a student's work? According to one opinion (Burke, 1993), a teacher may have an implicit license to make copies to be used as an example for later classes. For example, teachers sometimes save outstanding research papers so that students in later classes can see what the teachers expect. However, the instructor would not have the right to use student material in a derivative work—something like a book authored by the teacher in which the student work appears as an example. Because placing work on a web site can clearly be considered a form of distribution, web publication of a student's work raises similar concerns.

Therefore we make this recommendation,

> *The best policy is to treat student work in the same way you would treat the work of any artist or author; that is, request signed permission to use the work.*

*Permission from students and parents*

Note that, because K–12 students are minors, certain situations may also require permission from a parent or legal guardian. Often the best option is to work out the publication arrangements at the beginning of a project, obtaining the necessary consent from both students and parents.

Recognizing student work in this manner helps the student understand the concept of authorship. It also develops an appreciation for the rights accorded those who produce intellectual and creative works.

## RULES OF THUMB: SUGGESTED ANSWERS FOR THE COPYRIGHT QUESTIONS

We have told you as much as we can about how copyright and fair use apply to the Internet. Obviously, these are complex topics without definitive answers. Still, educators do want guidance, and if definitive answers are not available, they need rules of thumb. Returning to the four fundamental questions that we posed at the beginning of this discussion, here are our suggested answers:

*The four questions answered*

- *Can students and teachers take resources from web sites for use in learning and instructional activities?*
  Check the web site itself for terms and conditions governing usage. In the absence of guidelines on the site itself, a convenient way to think about fair use has been provided by Georgia Harper (1997), who recommends that educators follow the suggestion of "small parts, limited time, and limited access." The CONFU guidelines may provide a way to interpret this suggestion.
- *Can students and teachers use the material developed by others on their own web pages?*
  We feel the use of copyrighted resources on web pages without permission is questionable and should be avoided. Certainly, the activities we have emphasized in this book do not require this type of material. The Golden Rule provides a useful way to think about this issue. As a teacher, would you want other teachers to "borrow" some of your best lesson plans or classroom materials without at least asking?
- *Can teachers post student work on the Web?*
  We encourage schools to use the Web to present student work, but to do so in a way that recognizes the creative talents of the student. In any decision to publish student work, the students and parents should be involved.
- *What should teachers do if they want to protect online resources they have developed?*

> There is no guaranteed way to protect your work once it is online. What you can do is to indicate that you regard your work as copyrighted and that it should not be used without your permission. (Be aware, however, that in some cases the institution you work for, such as your school or school district, may believe that it owns the rights. You may want to check your district's policies.)

If your work is intended for a specific audience, such as students involved in a distance education experience, you can limit access through the use of password protection.

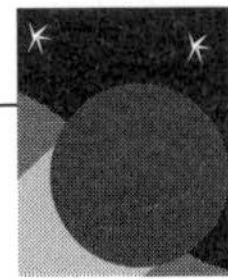

## PROTECTING STUDENTS FROM INAPPROPRIATE MATERIAL AND EXPERIENCES

*The Internet compared to other information systems*

Educators must recognize that the Internet does not exist specifically to support educational goals. In this regard, the Internet is similar to other information systems we encounter in our daily lives. Cable television has the capacity to bring sporting events, congressional testimony, educational programming, and sexually explicit content into our living rooms. The telephone can be used to chat with Grandma about Thanksgiving dinner or with a psychic about your future. For adults, all are acceptable forms of "information." If we want to benefit from powerful communication systems, we must both recognize and find ways to adjust to the multiple purposes and audiences the Internet serves.

It is true that there are risks in allowing students to use the Internet. Both educators and students must recognize these risks so that protective measures can be taken. In this section we will explore the dangers and outline what we consider reasonable responses to them.

### POTENTIAL DANGERS AND REASONABLE PROTECTION

What are the possible risks of Internet access? Students may encounter the following (Magid, 1998):

*Types of risk from Internet access*

- *Inappropriate content.* Students using the World Wide Web may encounter material displaying sexual acts and violence, promoting the hatred of specific groups, or encouraging dangerous or unlawful activities.
- *Physical molestation.* Students using e-mail or chat areas may encounter individuals who wish to do them harm, such as pedophiles. Some individuals, often representing themselves deceptively, use Internet communication tools to become acquainted with students and eventually attempt to arrange a meeting.

- *Harassment.* Students using e-mail or chat areas may be subjected to harassment, becoming the target of demeaning or threatening messages.
- *Legal and financial threats.* Students may knowingly or unknowingly become involved in situations with legal or financial consequences. For example, an attempt may be made to deceive students into providing a credit card number.

## Balancing Freedom and Protection

In light of these potential dangers, the general public and educators are justifiably concerned about abuses of the Internet. However, proper caution and paranoia are two different reactions. There is some level of potential danger involved in openness to any means of communication. Pornography, hate literature, descriptions of how to create explosive devices, and the open discussion of drug use certainly exist, and educators cannot guarantee that students won't find such material on the Internet. But educators also cannot guarantee that such materials are not being stashed in some student's locker and passed around during school. Likewise, there is a small number of individuals who seek to take advantage of young people through Internet conversations, but such individuals may also hang out near play areas after school.

*Putting the danger in context*

*A clash of ideals*

One issue that educators face in trying to regulate students' Internet access is a clash between the democratic ideal of a right to personal expression and the desire of parents and educators to protect young people from harmful experiences. At least on an abstract level, most people would agree that both personal expression and individual safety are fundamental rights. The challenge is to create an Internet environment that does not impose censorship and yet allows adults to control what minors in their care experience.

Conflicts of this type are often resolved without major difficulty in other situations. For example, our local grocery store and gas station carry magazines containing nudity. Publishers have a right to sell this material, and adults have a right to purchase it. The solution: the magazines are enclosed in plastic envelopes that cannot be opened until the magazine has been purchased, and the business establishments will not sell the magazines to minors. In this situation, reasonable measures have been taken to satisfy the conflicting values.

In the case of Internet use, how can educators provide a similar balance between freedom and protection? What would constitute reasonable measures? To answer this question, consider a parallel situation.

*A parallel situation*

We, the authors of this book, have always allowed our children to answer the telephone even when we are not at home. The telephone is a valuable communication tool, and we recognize that our children have friends to whom they want to talk. We certainly want them to answer when we're calling them. On the other hand, we do recognize that there are possible dangers. We cope with these dangers in the following ways:

- *Technology.* One of our responses is technological: we have caller ID and voice mail. Our children can see who is calling or allow the caller to record a message. If we are calling from a phone that is not recognized by caller ID, our daughter may pick up the phone when she hears us talking to the voice mail system.
- *Instruction.* We supplement the technology with instructions we have given our children. For example, if a strange caller asks for one of us, our daughter is not supposed to say that her parents are not home. Instead, she says that they can't come to the phone right now and asks that the caller leave a message or call back in a little while.

*A three-pronged response*

The Internet presents a different set of challenges, but the goals are basically the same, and a similar combination of measures can be used. Educators can (1) direct students toward safe areas of the Internet; (2) take advantage of filtering systems that screen Internet content; and (3) directly intervene with students through supervision, instruction in safety guidelines, and the administration of an acceptable use policy. We will discuss each of these areas in turn. We believe that educators need to consider all of these methods rather than assuming that a single approach will be sufficient.

## SAFE AREAS OF THE INTERNET

Internet sites that have been screened and that operate under supervision may be thought of as "safe areas." We have mentioned several such resources throughout this book, and we will attempt to organize and summarize our comments here. Additional information about any resource mentioned here is provided at the end of the chapter.

These are some ideas for identifying and using safe areas:

*Guidelines for finding and using safe areas*

- Search for web sites using a directory that rates web sites and that will allow searches to be limited to sites approved for students and younger users (see Chapter 5). A good example of a directory of this type is Yahooligans, an offshoot of Yahoo! The searchable Yahooligans database provides links only to sites appropriate for student exploration. Magellan takes a different approach, allowing "safe sites" to be set as one of the search criteria.
- Focus most student web experiences on well-tested curriculum projects. For example, Pacific Bell sponsors Blue Web'n, a very large, annotated, online database of educational web sites. The subscription curriculum projects we described in Chapter 5 would also include only carefully reviewed web material.
- Use chat services that provide supervision. For example, Kidlink, a service that establishes communication opportunities among students (see Chapter 3), sponsors supervised chat areas.

- Emphasize e-mail or CU-SeeMe projects that are organized through other teachers.

## FILTERING

*Three approaches to filtering*

**Filtering** allows a more proactive approach to controlling what Internet users are able to access. Filtering is accomplished in different ways, but the basic idea is to block access to material and activities that have been judged to be inappropriate or dangerous. We will describe three approaches schools might consider: a firewall, commercial stand-alone filtering software, and filtering tools built into the most recent versions of the Netscape and Microsoft browsers.

### Firewall

A **firewall** is basically a computer and sophisticated software that control the flow of data between two networks. A firewall might be used to separate the Internet and the network connecting the computers within a school district. In such a situation, the barrier created by a firewall could serve two functions:

*Uses of a firewall*

- The firewall could protect the information maintained by the district's computers from being damaged or accessed from any computer external to the district network.
- The firewall could determine what someone within the district could request from the Internet.

Data flow across a firewall can be filtered on the basis of either IP address or protocol. This means that students can be prevented from downloading information from certain designated web sites (identified by IP address) or from using specific services such as Internet relay chat or e-mail (identified by protocol). A firewall is also capable of gathering information on attempted external breaches of the security system or keeping a record of the web pages requested by each computer in the district. A district firewall would be managed by an individual with advanced technical skills.

### Stand-alone Filtering Software

*How filtering software works*

Commercial stand-alone software has been around for several years and is popular for both schools and homes. This software works primarily by refusing to accept material sent from certain targeted sites. The companies selling these products continually update their lists of sites that provide offensive material, and they make these lists available to those who own copies of the software.

These systems do not offer perfect protection. Offensive material can be added to an existing site at any time, and new servers are always being connected to the Internet. However, this kind of software does provide a reasonable means of protection from established sites that offer material not appropriate in a school environment.

Filtering programs offer some other interesting strategies for controlling access:

*Options available with filtering software*

- Several companies offer those who purchase their filtering software lists of disapproved and approved sites. Using a list of approved sites would offer protection against inappropriate material contained on new servers.
- Some filtering programs can also keep track of which sites students have visited. The intent is not to punish those students who ignore school policies (actually, it is the identity of the computer that is stored, not that of the user), but to make school personnel aware of which sites have been visited. If necessary, the school can use this information to add sites to the disapproved list.
- One filtering program, Cyber Patrol, offers some protection against another concern: young people's revealing personal information to strangers during chat sessions. School personnel or parents can enter protected words (names, phone numbers, addresses, credit card numbers) into a file. If a student types one of the protected words during a chat conversation, a series of Xs will be substituted. Although it would not be appropriate or practical to store all of these items of information on school computers, a subset of the items might be entered.

Public concern has encouraged the continued development of filtering software. Local and nationwide Internet service providers, such as America Online and WebTV, often offer filtering software free or at a nominal cost to their customers. A list of the more popular commercial filtering programs is included at the end of the chapter.

## Browser Filtering

Recent versions of the two major browsers have built-in filtering options. These filters are possible because the World Wide Web Consortium (W3C), an oversight committee that attempts to guide the technical development of the Internet, created a protocol referred to as the **Platform for Internet Content Selection (PICS).**

*How PICS tags work*

You may encounter references to PICS-formatted ratings or PICS-compatible browsers. Just think of PICS as allowing an extension of HTML. A special tag, inserted at the top of a web page, contains information about the type of information and images contained on that page. When a browser that has been prepared to receive PICS information encounters this tag, it checks the information carried by the tag against settings established by the person responsible for the browser. The rest of the page is displayed only if the comparison indicates the content is allowable.

*The RASCi system*

There are several different rating schemes based on the PICS protocol (see additional information at the end of the chapter). The simplest one, the Recreational Software Advisory Council on the Internet (RASCi) system, will serve as our example. The RASCi system is based on four categories: nudity, sex, language, and violence. Each category is assigned a rating based on guidelines from 0 to 4. For example, a level 0 nudity rating indicates that the web site contains no nudity. A level 4 rating indicates that the site contains provocative frontal nudity.

Web authors who want to have their sites carry RASCi ratings connect to the Recreational Software Advisory Council web site and provide information about their sites (see "Focus: Self-Rating a Web Site"). The process of self-rating concerns some people, who wonder whether it provides adequate safeguards; but self-rating does represent one way to address the clash between personal freedoms and the need to protect young people from inappropriate content.

In the Netscape browser (Navigator 4.5), the special tool for setting and modifying filtering categories is called Netwatch. Microsoft Internet Explorer 4.0 enables screening from the Ratings preference option. The terms and methods associated with filtering preferences may vary in future versions of the software. At this point, however, the process of setting up a browser to screen requested web sites is fundamentally the same for both browsers; it requires that the person responsible for the browser do the following:

*Steps in setting the browser for filtering*

1. Enable (turn on) the filtering function.
2. Select the "level" of material that will be allowed in several different categories (see Figure 9.2).
3. Indicate whether web sites that do not carry a rating will be allowed.
4. Enter a password.

*Use in a school library*

Consider how this procedure might be used for computers in a school library. The school computer coordinator might take responsibility for setting the filtering categories according to established school policy. Students then would be shielded from most objectionable sites. Most likely, however, the password would be made available to the librarian because there would be circumstances in which the filtering system would need to be disabled. For example, a teacher might want her class to examine a particular web site although the author of that site had not taken the trouble to enroll with a rating service. Using the password, the librarian could temporarily disable filtering and the students would be able to view the site.

The use of browser filtering assumes that web authors will support this approach and make the effort to label their material accurately. This approach has been endorsed as a reasonable one for protecting the needs of most citizens (Center for Democracy and Technology, 1997).

## SAFETY GUIDELINES, ACCEPTABLE USE POLICIES, AND SUPERVISION

Schools cannot rely totally on technological mechanisms to control how students will use the Internet. Technological mechanisms are not foolproof. Preparing students to be responsible users of the Internet also involves helping them learn what is safe and appropriate behavior.

*Focus*

## Self-Rating a Web Site

Both the Recreational Software Advisory Council on the Internet (RSACi) and the SafeSurf rating systems are based on labels provided by web publishers. With RSACi, the system works like this:

A web publisher visits the RSACi web site (**http://www.rsac.org**) and completes a form that includes the site URL and basic information about the publisher (name, address, phone, e-mail address). The publisher then goes through a series of descriptive phrases relevant to each of the four RSACi categories and provides a response indicating the most extreme behavior that may be present on the site. Ultimately the publisher receives a RSACi rating that ranges from 0 to 4, with 4 representing the greatest potential danger to a user.

Earlier in the book we used the North Dakota Project Wild site (NDWild) as an example (see Figure 6.3 on page 183). This site, sponsored by the North Dakota Game and Fish Department, promotes the educational exploration of the North Dakota outdoors. The RSACi standards were applied to this site. As you might expect, the site does not depict nudity or sexual acts, so in those categories it received a 0, the most inoffensive score. It also received a 0 in the language category. But one option in the RSACi violence category contains the phrase "death of non-human beings resulting from natural acts," and this seemed a possible way to describe hunting or fishing. So the NDWild site received a rating of 1 for violence.

Once the necessary information has been entered in the RSACi forms, the site records the information and generates some HTML code (a special META tag). The web publisher must insert this code in the heading section of site pages. The information in the tag is used by the web browser to determine if the site is acceptable on the basis of the standards stored within the browser software. Here is the HTML code for the NDWild site:

<META http-equiv="PICS-Label"
content='(PICS-1.1 "http://www.rsac.org/
ratingsv01.html" l gen true comment
"RSACi North America Server" for
"http://www.und.nodak.edu/org/ndwild"
on "1999.01.15T14:46-0800" r
(n 0 s 0 v 1 1 0))'>✷

### Safety Rules

*The need for clear rules*

Students need to know that inappropriate material exists on the Internet and that it is possible someone might attempt to exploit them through Internet conversations. They need to know what content and situations they are to avoid. It is especially important that younger students be informed in concrete terms of behaviors they should avoid.

For a summary of some common rules as they might be presented to younger students, see "Focus: Rules for the Safe and Appropriate Use of the Internet." Classroom teachers should take the time to present and explain guidelines of this sort. In addition, it is helpful to post them in a visible location.

**FIGURE 9.2** Netscape Netwatch allows use of the RSACi Rating System.

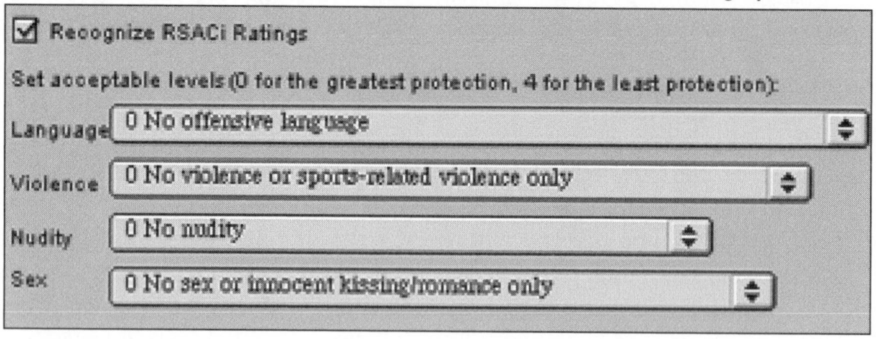

☑ Recognize RSACi Ratings

Set acceptable levels (0 for the greatest protection, 4 for the least protection):

Language: 0 No offensive language

Violence: 0 No violence or sports-related violence only

Nudity: 0 No nudity

Sex: 0 No sex or innocent kissing/romance only



## Acceptable Use Policies

Schools need to establish clear standards that go beyond a simple list of rules. It is useful to formalize such guidelines in a written document, often called an **acceptable use policy (AUP).**

*The AUP*

An AUP typically establishes expectations for how students and sometimes faculty will use school resources, procedures they are expected to follow, and consequences when expectations and procedures are violated. If you are presently a student, we suggest you search through your room to find your institution's guidelines for student behavior. This document may be referred to as the "Code of Student Life" or some similar title. Somewhere within this document you will find policies relating to the use of computer and Internet resources and a general explanation of various actions the institution can take against you for violating these and other stated policies.

An AUP for a K–12 institution accomplishes similar goals, but with these differences:

1. It is likely to exist as an independent document.
2. It will emphasize instructional as well as regulatory goals.
3. It will recognize that K–12 students are minors.

Rather than reproducing a complete AUP, we will outline some of the issues that typical AUPs address. Finding real examples of AUPs is easy: they are commonly included as web pages within school web sites. Use any search engine and request "Acceptable Use Policy," and you will find many examples.

AUPs usually address the general use of technology in schools. Here we will focus just on issues concerning the Internet. Typical AUPs treat the following subjects:

*Internet issues covered in a typical AUP*

1. *Student learning as the reason the school provides access to technology.* Many AUPs explain that access to the World Wide Web, e-mail, and other Internet tools is provided to help students learn. This statement of purpose establishes boundaries that can then be used to set priorities or exclude certain activities. Playing online games, for instance, may be

*Focus*

## Rules for the Safe and Appropriate Use of the Internet

Below are some sample rules for Internet use, worded as they might be presented to students. The wording could be adjusted depending on the age of the students.

1. I will not reveal personal information in e-mail or chat messages. Personal information includes:
   - My home address
   - My home phone number
   - The names of my parents, my teacher, and other students in my class
   - The name and address of my school

   (Note: Schools may also decide that students should not reveal their own names, perhaps using only a first name and last initial, such as "Cindy G.")
   If I am asked for any item of personal information, I will ask my teacher what I should do.
2. I will never agree to talk on the telephone or meet in person with anyone I met through chat or e-mail without first talking with my teacher.
3. I will tell my teacher if I find any information that I should not see or that makes me feel uncomfortable.
4. I will not share my e-mail password with anyone, including my best friends.
5. I will not make fun of other students in e-mail messages. If anyone sends me an e-mail message that makes me feel uncomfortable or angry, I will not respond. I will report e-mail messages that make me feel uncomfortable to my teacher.
6. I will not visit web sites that are inappropriate for school use. If I accidentally load this kind of site, I will leave it immediately. If I have questions about whether or not I should be looking at certain web sites, I will ask my teacher or librarian. I understand that viewing inappropriate sites may result in the loss of Internet privileges. (*Source:* Based on L. Magid [1998], *Kids' Rules for Online Safety* [On-line]. Available: http://www.safekids.com/kidsrules.htm)✱

perfectly good fun, but such behavior would be outside the established priorities.

After connecting Internet resources with valued educational experiences, the statement of purpose often continues by explaining that certain rules and regulations are necessary to assure that learning occurs in a safe and productive environment.

2. *Access to services.* Most AUPs explain the services the district provides and what is necessary for students to use these services. For example, the school may make the web available to all students, but students in the elementary grades may have access to e-mail only through a common class account. Middle-school and high school students might be given

individual e-mail accounts provided the student and parents sign a user agreement form.

3. *Unacceptable behaviors.* After making the point that many uses of technology are a privilege and not a right, most AUPs list behaviors that are not allowed and indicate sanctions that may be applied if students engage in unacceptable behavior. The common areas of concern include personal safety; violations of system security or attempts to purposefully damage system functions or online content; academic violations such as plagiarism; purposeful efforts to view online materials identified as inappropriate; and harassment of other people. Sanctions typically involve loss of access privileges, but in severe cases they may include more severe punishment, such as suspension or even criminal prosecution.
4. *Position on privacy.* Will school officials examine student or faculty e-mail, monitor web sites that have been visited from a particular computer, or open data files saved in student accounts? If such practices are regarded as necessary, the AUP should state clearly that all accounts are considered school property and may be examined to assure safe and responsible use.

### Supervision

*Monitoring as a function of active participation*

Finally, the clear statement of rules and careful documentation of policies are not enough. Classroom teachers, libraries, and other school staff members need to be willing to monitor students' use of computers and the Internet. We have frequently argued in this book that teachers should participate actively when students work with technology. Supervision is yet another reason to remain involved, not sit at a desk while students under your charge do their work.

This combination of honest concern, clear standards, and appropriate supervision is how schools customarily teach and maintain appropriate behavior. Although absolute protection cannot be guaranteed, these measures do seem a reasonable response to the potential dangers posed by Internet use.

## SUMMARY

◆ This chapter examines several issues under the general heading of the responsible use of technology. Accepting responsibility is a matter of acknowledging, understanding, and meeting obligations to the laws of our society, to parents and students, and to our colleagues.

◆ Educational equity involves educators' responsibilities for providing fair and equal experiences for all students. At present, not all students have equal opportunities to use technology. Many schools with a large number of less affluent students have less Internet access than affluent schools and engage students in fewer technology-supported learning experiences. Federal programs are beginning to address the issue of access, but access alone will not provide equal experiences. Teacher preparation and support are vital. So are educators' assumptions about the types of experiences students from less affluent homes require. If teachers focus disadvantaged students strictly on the accumulation of information, rather than on meaningful activities of inquiry and construction, technology access may have little impact.

◆ Equity concerns also include the differences in how males and females are involved with technology in educational settings. The communication, inquiry, and construction tasks the Internet allows may contribute to an improvement in female interest in technology.

◆ Students with physical, sensory, or cognitive limitations may also be at a disadvantage in taking advantage of Internet resources and experiences. In many cases, adaptations in hardware and software can provide improved access and opportunity. A more thoughtful approach to web design can also be helpful.

◆ Another responsibility that educators must accept is to respect copyright law. Both teachers and students need to know what resources they can take from online sources or present online as part of instructional or learning activities. Understanding fair use guidelines is not always easy, but a responsible user should be familiar with general principles and be willing to seek permission from copyright holders.

◆ Finally, educators must accept the responsibility of protecting students from the potential dangers of Internet access. Educators can direct students toward safe areas of the Internet, employ filtering systems that provide barriers to the display of inappropriate materials, and directly intervene with students through supervision and instruction in safety guidelines.

## REFLECTING ON CHAPTER 9

### Activities

1. Write a "Responsible User" contract that students and parents must sign before the student will be allowed an e-mail account.
2. Try the following as a simulation of what visually impaired students experience when they use the Internet. First, modify the browser so that it does not display images. Second, use only the keyboard to explore the Web (use a Windows machine and the Tab and Return keys to select and follow links). Did you encounter pages that you could not comprehend? Were there situations in which you were unable to navigate?
3. Several software products are sold for the purpose of downloading individual pages or entire web sites. Using your interpretation of fair use, argue for or against the legality of using this software to collect resources for (a) personal scholarship, (b) access by your class within your classroom, and (c) worldwide access from a server located in your school.

### Key Terms

acceptable use policy (AUP) *(p. 280)*
Conference on Fair Use (CONFU) *(p. 268)*
e-rate *(p. 252)*
fair use *(p. 266)*
filtering *(p. 276)*
firewall *(p. 276)*
license *(p. 264)*
Platform for Internet Content Selection (PICS) *(p. 277)*
screen reader *(p. 257)*
site license *(p. 264)*
socioeconomic status (SES) *(p. 249)*

## Resources to Expand Your Knowledge Base

### Gender Equity

The *American Association of University Women* promotes education for gender equity (**http://www.aauw.org**).

### Adaptive Software

*JAWS,* a screen reader for the Windows operating system available from Henter-Joyce, Inc., is one of the most popular products for personal computers (**http://www.hj.com/Index.html**).

*Home Page Reader,* a screen reader with special capabilities for Internet tasks, is available for the Windows operating system from IBM (**http://www.austin.ibm.com/sns/hpr.html**).

### Guidelines for Accessible Web Pages

World Wide Web Consortium (1999). Techniques for web accessibility initiative page author guidelines. Online Available: **http://www.w3.org/TR/WD-WAI-PAGEAUTH** (February 1999).

### Safe Areas of the Internet

***Directories*** *Magellan*'s search service (**http://www.mckinley.com/**) allows users to search for key words within what are designated as "green sites" (containing no objectionable content).

*Yahooligans* (**http://www.yahooligans.com/**) was created by Yahoo! as a specialized and separate directory of sites for younger web users.

***Educational Content Database*** *Blue Web'n,* a database of "blue ribbon" educational learning sites sponsored by Pacific Bell, provides access to reviewed, high-quality educational sites (**http://www.kn.pacbell.com/wired/bluewebn/**).

***Supervised Chat Environments*** The *Kidlink* organization (**http://www.kidlink.org**) matches students from all over the world for e-mail and chat. The chat rooms are supervised.

### Filtering Internet Content

***Explanation of Filtering Tools*** Center for Democracy and Technology (1997). Internet family empowerment white paper: How filtering tools enable responsible parents to protect their children online. Online Available: **http://www.cdt.org/speech/empower.html** (January 1999).

***Internet Filtering and Control Products*** *Cyber Patrol* is available for the Windows and Macintosh platforms from Microsystems Software (**http://www.cyberpatrol.com**).

*CYBERsitter* is available for the Windows platform from Solid Oak Software, Inc. (**http://www.cybersitter.com**).

*Net Nanny* is available for the Windows platform from Net Nanny Software International, Inc. (**http://www.netnanny.com**).

*SurfWatch* is available for the Windows and Macintosh platforms from Spyglass, Inc. (**http://www.surfwatch.com**).

***The Platform for Internet Content Selection (PICS) and PICS Rating Systems***

*The World Wide Web Consortium* (W3C) was responsible for developing the PICS protocol (**http://www.w3.org/PICS/**).

*The Recreational Software Advisory Council on the Internet* (RASCi) (**http://www.rsac.org/**) is a nonprofit organization that promotes the rating of Internet resources using the PICS protocol. The RASCi rating system can be implemented in newer Netscape and Microsoft browsers.

The *SafeSurf Rating Service* is provided by SafeSurf Wave Inc. (**http://www.safesurf.com**) and applies a rating system using the PICS protocol. The SafeSurf rating system can be implemented in newer Netscape and Microsoft browsers.

### Acceptable Use Policies

The National Education Association has developed suggestions for the development of school acceptable use policies. The present version of the policy can be found at **http://www.nea.org/cet/briefs/12.html.**

*Afterword*

# Some Concluding Thoughts about Current and Future Uses of the Internet

We hope that your study of this book and the experiences provided by your instructor have given you the background and interest necessary to make productive use of Internet resources in your classroom. We feel the Internet already provides many exciting opportunities for communication, inquiry, and construction that you will be able to apply with students.

It is probably also fair to say this: we haven't really seen anything yet! The Internet has generated tremendous excitement and encouraged a great deal of exploration and experimentation. It has caused people in many fields to ask serious questions about how things are presently done. This is clearly the case for educators, and we hope you will become an active participant in the discussion about future directions for your chosen field.

*Rapid change to be expected*

The Internet and rapid change are nearly synonymous. This means that what the Internet has to offer and the tools you might use to take advantage of these new opportunities will evolve over the course of time during which this book is available. While you may implement the ideas in this book with newer tools, we feel confident that the basic instructional strategies will continue to be useful. We do have some thoughts, though, about how the Internet will evolve in the next few years. Please stay with us for a few more pages as we speculate about future developments that may influence you as an educator.

## PURCHASE OF EDUCATIONAL INTERNET RESOURCES

Prediction: Quality educational Internet resources and services will increasingly be purchased by schools or students.

The continued development of Internet-based instructional resources, primary information sources, and educational services such as direct instruction and administrative support will require that educational institutions—and in some cases individual learners—accept greater financial responsibility. More and more, K–12 institutions will purchase online curriculum materials for classroom use as well as information services that extend the print resources presently available in libraries.

*Budgeting for online resources*

The key word in this prediction is *purchase.* While schools are already making some investments in such resources (see the lists of subscription information resources and structured Internet activities provided at the end of Chapter 5), budgeting for online resources will become a more serious matter. As a teacher, you may be asked to suggest online resources you would like to use. Perhaps, too, you will serve on a curriculum committee that makes decisions about how online instructional units will replace more traditional classroom activities. In this case, the issue of cost—what was spent on traditional resources versus the cost of Internet replacements—will be a matter your committee will have to consider.

What we are proposing is that the cost of Internet resources and services will be shifting, moving actually toward more traditional funding sources. As we see it, there are several ways in which Internet content and services might be supported:

*Possible means of supporting Internet resources*

- Government subsidies, such as grants.
- Industry, foundation, or individual subsidies and donations.
- Cooperatives of educators.
- User payment for services—that is, a commercial system.

We believe the final option is the one that will become increasingly dominant. To explain why, we will consider the various alternatives in turn.

### GOVERNMENT AND PRIVATE SUBSIDIES

Much of what exists on the Internet now has probably originated from the first two categories of providers: subsidies from government or from private donors. Government grants have funded major curriculum development projects. Other government organizations, such as NASA, have been active in producing online instructional materials, and many nonprofit organizations, such as the National Audubon Society, offer information and instruction re-

**TABLE A.1**
Some Government and Nonprofit Organizations Offering On-line Educational Resources

|  |  |
| --- | --- |
| Audubon Online (National Audubon Society) | **http://www.audubon.org/** |
| The Exploratorium: The Museum of Science, Art and Human Perception | **http://www.exploratorium.edu** |
| NASA's Education Program (National Aeronautics and Space Administration) | **http://www.hq.nasa.gov/office/codef/education/index.html** |
| Smithsonian Institution | **http://www.si.edu** |
| U.S. Fish and Wildlife Service | **http://www.fws.gov/** |

lated to their areas of interest. (Table A.1 lists a few web sources of these types.) Various commercial organizations, such as newspapers and magazines, also offer important resources.

*Continued subsidies unlikely*

However, it does not seem likely that these sources can be counted on—or would be desirable—as the only sources for schools. Private organizations have vested interests and cannot be expected to provide the broad perspective necessary for general educational goals; instead, they should be regarded as a source for occasional supplements. The government's most productive role is probably to encourage continued development and innovation.

## COOPERATIVES OF EDUCATORS

*Educators' collaborations take time*

Some learning opportunities will continue to originate from the cooperative efforts of groups of educators. These educators might organize themselves through their local districts or through state or national professional organizations (see, for instance, the discussion in Chapter 5 of the curriculum development efforts by teachers in Bellingham, Washington). We encourage such collaborative efforts, but it is important to recognize that educational experiences developed in this manner are not free. These curriculum development activities clearly extend beyond traditional expectations for how teachers will spend their time—and that time is valuable.

## COMMERCIAL PROVIDERS

Our logic thus brings us to the conclusion that institutions and learners are going to be spending more money to secure educational resources and ser-

## Chris Moggia, Director of Online Teacher Education, OnlineLearning.net

OnlineLearning.net (**http://www.onlinelearning.net/**) delivers over 400 online courses in several different disciplines throughout the world. This interview provides a brief look at the company and some of its policies as explained by Chris Moggia, Director of Online Teacher Education. Dr. Moggia is most directly involved with online course delivery to teachers, and his comments should help you understand how online education may have a direct influence on your own professional development.

*OnlineLearning.net is a private company that is responsible for online courses through UCLA Extension [the division of the University of California, Los Angeles, that offers extension courses]. Many people are probably unfamiliar with this type of arrangement. Please describe OnlineLearning.net and explain how the arrangement with UCLA Extension works.*

OnlineLearning.net was formed as a private company to help institutions of higher learning develop distance learning opportunities for working professionals. In 1994 we arranged a partnership with UCLA Extension to begin the process of porting their existing courses over to a distance learning format.

The partnership is beneficial in a number of ways. First, UCLA Extension retains the rights to hire instructors, develop curriculum, etc. Basically it continues to do what it has always done effectively; namely, all of the teaching and university responsibilities associated with college courses. OnlineLearning.net performs essentially two roles: customer support and marketing.

OnlineLearning.net assumes all of the technological responsibilities, e.g., setting up servers and web pages, training instructors and students to use the online software, providing twenty-four-hour technical support, etc. We also are the marketing arm of UCLA Extension outside of Los Angeles County. We promote the online courses over the Internet, through our printed catalog, and at national educator conferences.

*What is your role within this company?*

As the Director of Online Teacher Education, my role is to facilitate the development of online courses, determine areas of need, train instructors to use the computer-mediated format, and establish partnerships with educational organizations and school districts. I have a background as an elementary educator and teacher technology trainer.

As an advocate of technology in education, I was attracted to the field of distance education because of the opportunities it opens up for nontraditional learning and advanced professional development.

One of the things I have been working on recently is a partnership with the California Teachers Association to offer online courses that meet the unique professional development needs of their teachers and faculty. We are currently working on creating courses online to train teachers to work successfully with English language learners in the classroom.

*A page you developed for the OnlineLearning.net web site explains that changes in California law have approved online courses as a way for teachers to meet professional growth requirements. What aspects of the expectations for practicing teachers have changed?*

Because most of the courses offered by UCLA Extension are described as "continuing education," few courses transfer to undergraduate degree courses. UCLA Extension does, however, offer courses that lead to the completion of several sequenced certificate programs such as the Cross-Cultural, Language, and Academic Development certificate or the Online Teaching Program. Recently the need to prepare teachers more effectively has become an important aspect of the standards movement. I think the availability of online courses provides just another way for teachers to access quality professional development that is ongoing, interactive, relevant, and helps in their understanding of technology issues as well.

*We live in North Dakota, where teachers who want a professional development course may be more than a hundred miles from the nearest university. It doesn't seem that California teachers would face this problem. Why do the teachers you work with take advantage of online courses?*

Actually many teachers here do face those same inconveniences of distance, inaccessible classes, etc. In a recent class I taught online, my students lived in both northern and southern California, Ohio, Texas, and even Sweden! The reasons they enrolled varied, but many mentioned the fact that they lived more than fifty miles away from a major university. Some had teaching or coaching responsibilities in the evenings that precluded them from participating in traditional courses, and some simply had family or other personal issues that made online courses more appealing for one reason or another.

*In looking through the qualifications of your course instructors, it is apparent that your instructors have impressive credentials. However, many do not work in academic institutions, and some work at academic institutions outside your state. How do you recruit your instructors, and what are the skills you look for?*

The quality of our instructors is paramount, since the courses are taught by individual instructors and are highly engaging and interactive. Unlike some computer-based training models in which students simply interact with a computer simulation or software program, all UCLA Extension online courses are taught by instructors in classes that usually have twenty or fewer students in them.

Traditionally UCLA Extension has hired instructors who lived within driving distance of the campus. Now, however, with the advent of online courses, no one is hindered by geographical restrictions. We are currently conducting a national recruitment effort for instructors and are hiring individuals who teach from other states and some from other countries.

*We would like the students reading our book to have some understanding of what it would be like to take a course online. What are some of the experiences that tend be commonly included in OnlineLearning.net courses?*

That's the one-million-dollar question! With such a diverse student population and so many different courses currently being offered online, I doubt that many common experiences exist.

I can tell you from personal experience that my initial concerns about a "lack of contact" between instructors and students (because we never actually come face to face) were alleviated the very first time I taught online. Because the online medium allows you to send much more information across the network than would be permissible in a one- or two-hour weekly class, I actually ended up knowing more about my students' personal and professional backgrounds than I did in the traditional courses I teach. One of the first activities we do in each class is to post a one-page note about who we are, where we teach, etc. From this a sort of "cyber community" emerges, in which students begin to have private conversations with other students, create their own study groups, etc. The hardest part is when the course is over and everyone still wants to communicate! People usually end up sharing e-mail addresses with each other so they can keep talking with one another.

vices from commercial providers. The commercialization of Internet-based educational resources and services could take many forms. For K–12 institutions, we anticipate immediate growth in online subscription information resources (such as EBSCO Information Services and SIRS Researcher) and supplemental virtual learning experiences (for example, OnlineClass).

*Cost-effective commercial resources*

These resources provide cost-effective access to primary sources and to well-organized and stimulating curriculum units. We have listed a few examples in

"Resources to Expand Your Knowledge Base" at the end of the Afterword, and more are listed in Chapter 5.

Our prediction that K–12 institutions will make greater use of such commercial providers in no way assumes that the total cost of education will increase. We presume that high-quality resources and services obtained from the Internet will replace ones those that schools or learners already purchase. If all factors are considered (including travel expense and time), it is very possible that in many situations the cost will be reduced, either for the institution, for the individual learner, or for both.

## COMPETITION TO PROVIDE EDUCATIONAL RESOURCES

Prediction: The Internet will encourage greater competition to provide educational resources. Alternatives will become more plentiful.

We initially intended to fold this prediction into our comments on purchasing online resources. Clearly, revenue opportunities encourage competition. However, we felt it would be useful to recognize separately that more and more organizations and companies are offering educational resources and services.

*Internet-based extension courses*

In some cases, traditional organizations like colleges and universities are shifting to the Internet as a way to deliver instruction and instructional materials. For years, many institutions of higher education with extension programs have asked faculty to teach courses at remote sites or have delivered instruction through correspondence study. Now, Internet-based courses are recognized as a different way of serving the same students and perhaps even extending the institution's reach to new students. While Although extension activities are not new, it seems that more institutions are becoming involved with an increasing number of courses, many of which target new categories of learners.

*Publishing ventures online*

The shift to the Internet is accelerating in other areas as well. Consider the new ventures undertaken by publishing companies that already have a major focus on the education market. Traditionally, publishing companies have sold study guides as supplements to textbooks. The same companies have also provided resources to instructors, such as overheads, lecture outlines, and resource lists. Many of these companies now offer Internet sites to provide the same services.

Not all such changes will be limited to higher education. As an elementary school student, you probably read the *Weekly Reader*. The *Weekly Reader* now has an online presence (**http://www.weeklyreader.com/**).

*More options for learners*

The potential of the Internet will increasingly attract the attention of existing companies and institutions and motivate the formation of new ones. Learners, as well as traditional institutions that serve them, clearly have more choices than in the past, and this trend seems destined to continue. We explore some of these options and related issues in the following sections. Though the distinction may be a bit arbitrary, we first consider supplemental resources (information sources and instructional materials) and then larger-scale educational experiences, such as online courses and learning modules.

## SUPPLEMENTAL RESOURCES

One area of change will be in the provision of Internet-based resources that supplement or replace instructional materials such as textbooks, videotapes, and traditional library resources. The competition in providing these resources will likely come from the following types of organizations:

*Likely competitors*

- Publishing companies with a longstanding interest in the educational market.
- Organizations with an existing investment in information resources, such as major newspapers and television companies.
- Organizations with an existing commitment to informal education (major museums, zoos, and so on).
- Companies involved in the field of entertainment that believe that their experience, resources, and popularity will allow them to create educational materials with special appeal to learners.
- Companies that have previously focused on instructional software.
- New organizations formed specifically to offer online educational resources.

*Developing the entire continuum of resources*

What will these different organizations offer? In Chapter 5, we proposed a continuum of Internet resources that includes primary sources, instructional resources, and online tutorials. We anticipate development in all these areas. Access to primary sources in school libraries is already fairly common; for example, text and image resources from major news companies and articles from popular and scholarly periodicals are available as large, searchable databases. Instructional resources (learning materials that depend on a local teacher for classroom implementation) and online tutorials (which do not depend on the local presentation of information) are also becoming more popular. To provide students with resources of these types, schools will likely reassign funds used for instructional software or for traditional instructional materials.

## LARGE-SCALE EDUCATIONAL EXPERIENCES

A more difficult question is what other educational experiences will be delivered on a large scale via the Internet. Schools and teachers can probably accept a different source for supplemental materials and experiences. But what about more challenging possibilities, such as high schools' outsourcing to Internet-based providers entire classes they feel they cannot teach efficiently? Or what about virtual universities that award traditional degrees, even though they operate independently of traditional institutions of higher education? (To explore some current examples of such developments, see the links in the section "Courses and Degrees on the Internet" in the "Resources to Expand Your Knowledge Base" at the end of the Afterword.)

*Outsourcing courses and degree programs*

We see the most immediate signs of this Internet-based competition in higher education. Without travel or with only short-term visits to a physical campus, college students can take courses and even complete degrees at a large number of traditional and nontraditional institutions. Practicing K–12 teachers will be commonly involved in programs of this type as they pursue advanced degrees and professional development experiences. After all, teachers exemplify many of the characteristics that create the demand for such new approaches and delivery systems:

*Distance learning for teachers*

- Teachers are commonly required to undertake continued training for professional development.
- They need to fit their educational experiences around their work requirements.
- They often do not live or work near an educational facility.

When such needs exist, there are tremendous opportunities for organizations to offer learning opportunities from a distance, and we expect more and more competition to do so.

Although adult learners offer the most immediate growth area, we see the competition in distance education spilling over to K–12 schools in a number of ways:

*Effects on K–12 education*

- Outside agencies may increasingly bring vocational training programs into high schools.
- Introductory college courses may be brought into high schools through early enrollment or **dual-credit arrangements,** in which a course taken from a high school counts for both high school and college credit.
- Although a direct influence on more traditional K–12 courses will take a little longer to emerge, the potential for fundamental change exists, and it will likely be explored in some locations.

*Complex consequences*

When the issue involves alternative courses or degrees, the consequences of competition are complex. Competition can encourage creative approaches and greater efficiency, which result in more productive and less expensive learning opportunities. However, new players in a competitive setting may also be insensitive to complex arrangements that have bound past participants, and this insensitivity can end up having a disruptive influence.

## The Oversight Issue

*Stakeholders in education*

In some situations, there is a clear danger of disruption when new providers of educational services feel accountable only to learners. This statement is not as inflammatory as it first may seem. Contrary to surface appearances, formal education involves more stakeholders than students and the educators who are serving them. Employers and the public at large are also affected by educational policies and practices. So are other educational institutions that accept the students for subsequent programs. These institutions assume the students will possess certain knowledge and skills because they have completed certain courses, but if the Internet-based courses do not meet the usual standards, the system breaks down. This means that an educational agency and a student should not be able to define what constitutes an acceptable educational experience without expecting external scrutiny.

*Setting and enforcing standards*

The question at the core of the controversy is who will be allowed to serve in an oversight role. Are institutions able to rise above self-interest when evaluating transfer credits? Are accreditation bodies capable of formulating and enforcing meaningful standards? Who will judge whether an Internet course offered by a virtual university is equivalent to a similar campus-based course from traditional institutions?

Accreditation issues are not new, of course, and the presence of accreditation bodies has never been a protection against controversy. Multiple accreditation bodies already exist, and each serves a different constituency. Other interests are also represented in the public discussion. State and national teacher organizations take stands promoting the needs of their members. Legislative bodies intervene when educational costs seem too high or when standards seem to have slipped. All these organizations will interact to shape the boundaries within which education providers will operate.

*Reaction of traditional institutions*

Overall, we anticipate that more and more organizations will become involved in offering Internet-based learning resources and experiences. This trend is already developing. The issues that are less predictable at present concern the recognition of these learning experiences by traditional educational institutions and what will happen to traditional institutions as all learners have more options.

## MORE POWERFUL APPLICATIONS

Prediction: The Internet and Internet applications will become increasingly powerful.

As a general statement, a prediction of this type is not much of a risk. Early 1999 saw the launch of Internet2, an independent high-speed and high-bandwidth Internet connecting major research universities and industry partners (see the "Resources to Expand Your Knowledge Base"). The intent of this independent Internet is to stimulate research work focused on evaluating and developing prototypes for more powerful Internet applications. Immediate areas of interest are likely to include interactive video and the sharing of high-quality images (for instance, images needed for medical diagnosis). Projects of this type will eventually influence how the Internet will be used in classrooms.

*Internet2*

In addition, there are likely to be many advances not dependent on this new venture. A number are already very close to becoming mainstream. An immediate goal of many developers is to increase the power and interactivity of Internet applications—an area of great relevance for educators. The Internet is a great way to transmit information, especially text and simple graphics, but simply receiving information is not sufficient to encourage meaningful learning. True, teachers and classmates can help a learner think deeply about information received from Internet sources. But with more powerful applications, instructional designers will also be able to make a more meaningful contribution:

*Increasing power and interactivity*

*Likely benefits for users*

- More powerful applications will allow users to make choices and experience consequences.
- More powerful applications will store and analyze user input over an extended period of time.
- More powerful applications will perform complex calculations or evaluate complex rule systems in response to user actions.

Capabilities like these will eventually extend Internet experiences far beyond information presentation.

The following sections discuss three examples of such applications that have already emerged.

### DYNAMIC HTML

The most immediate advances in power will come by extending traditional HTML. **Dynamic HTML (DHTML)** basically adds dynamic (changing) features to otherwise static web pages. Generally DHTML is enabled by:

1. Fourth-generation or later browsers (Netscape or Internet Explorer 4.0 or later).

2. HTML tags.
3. JavaScript.

DHTML, in other words, is not an independent Internet format, and it does not require special software to create or use.

## Capabilities of DHTML

DHTML allows the web author greater control over:

1. How HTML tags display their content (including the use of style sheets).
2. The positioning and visibility of page elements.

*Standard HTML text appearance*

As an example of the first point, think about the text appearance of most web pages. The text tends to look pretty much the same: the font, the alignment, and the spacing (between words, between lines, within the boundaries of the page) are all very standardized. Some web pages look different, however, and their design and positioning of screen elements are more complicated and interesting.

*Changing appearance with style sheets*

The appearance of text is typically so standardized because HTML contains minimal information about text style. The default values you have set in your browser are applied to construct what you view on the monitor. One way to create web pages that more closely resemble magazine pages is with **style sheets** that override browser defaults. The older versions of HTML did not allow style sheets, but with DHTML they are becoming more and more common.

For a very simple demonstration of a style sheet, create a basic web page and include the following line of HTML code:

```
<P STYLE="text-indent: 2em; margin:0;">This is indented</P>
```

You will see something you are very used to seeing in print material but probably have not seen on earlier web pages that you created: an indented paragraph. Web browsers typically ignore multiple spaces that you might use to begin a paragraph. The introduction of this simple style overrides that convention. Of course, style sheets created in DHTML typically do more than create a single change in appearance. Typically, they establish multiple attributes that apply consistently throughout a document.

*Controlling object attributes*

In addition to text, web pages are built from objects such as links, frames, and images, and DHTML allows greater control over the attributes of all these objects. Look at the web page shown in Figure A.1. In the center of the page you will notice a small segment of text surrounded by multiple images. This particular segment of text appears when the cursor is positioned within the image of the mule deer. It disappears when the cursor moves outside the boundaries of that image. A different segment of text is displayed when the cursor points to a different image. Each small image is actually a link to another web page, and the text explains what the user will encounter if he or she clicks on the link. As you can see, this is truly a dynamic feature because the web page changes in response to the user's cursor movements. Again, this is just a simple instance of what DHTML can do.

**FIGURE A.1** A sample use of DHTML: a web page in which the user's actions dynamically control the text that is displayed. Positioning the cursor on the image of the mule deer brings up text about that animal, and the same is true for the other species pictured. Small JavaScript statements attached to each link control the text display.

## Using DHTML

*DHTML via authoring tools*

Some authoring environments, such as Macromedia Dreamweaver, and GoLive Cyberstudio, allow DHMTL capabilities to be added to web pages by selecting options with buttons or menus in a manner similar to the WYSIWYG editors described in Chapter 6 (p. 180). Even so, these applications are more complex than the authoring tools and page-development techniques we have described in this book.

What teachers and students do with DHTML is likely to follow the developmental pattern we have observed with HTML and web-authoring environments. Some DHTML functions will be added to newer versions of basic authoring programs, and these will be relatively easy to implement. However, the capabilities of these authoring programs will always lag behind what professional developers can do with their more advanced skills.

*Lack of consensus*

There are presently multiple versions of DHTML: the World Wide Web Consortium version, the Netscape version, and the Microsoft version. This lack of agreement is unfortunate because some of the unique features available for Netscape or Internet Explorer cannot practically be implemented because they will not function on the other browser. As work to improve the sophistication and interactivity of web presentations continues, we assume DTHML will become more standardized.

## JAVA

Some new developments related to the Internet involve a new kind of computer language. **Java** is a programming language with a number of exciting characteristics. Here we'll discuss two of them: cross-platform capability and thin client systems.

### Java's Cross-Platform Capability

Java works across platforms. This means that the same Java program will run on different types of computers using different kinds of operating systems—for instance, on Windows, Macintosh, and UNIX, as well as on unique machines built specifically for Java.

*Virtual machine*

For the same program to work on a variety of platforms, a Java virtual machine must be present on the computer. A **virtual machine** is a computer program, adapted to a particular hardware and operating system environment, which allows different machines to function as if they were equivalent. Once the virtual machine is in place, the different machines can run the same Java program.

### Thin Client Systems

*Simplified system*

Java is attractive as part of network computing because small segments of Java code can be downloaded from server to client as they are needed to perform a particular task. Therefore, theoretically, network-based Java programs make possible a thin client computer design. **Thin client** computers rely on a simplified operating system and do not need some of the hardware items found on traditional computers.

For example, if the programs that a computer runs come through an Internet or LAN connection, the computer may not need a hard drive. Simple versions of such computers for home use may focus specifically on browsing the World Wide Web and sending and receiving e-mail. They could consist of an inexpensive box and keyboard that connect to your television (like WebTV).

*Advantages for schools*

For the classroom or office, thin client machines will be more complicated than those just described, but still significantly different from traditional computers. The thin client design is expected to require less maintenance because the hardware is simpler and because there is no need to continually upgrade programs and operating systems on individual machines. In theory, the cost of operating such systems over a period of time should be significantly lower than the cost for regular computers, which would be great news for schools.

*School intranets*

Some of the content these machines would use would reside on the Internet. Other portions of the content (perhaps including traditional application programs) would reside on local, school-based servers that would provide resources on demand through an **intranet,** a local network intended to serve resources within a school or business. One model of commercial interest assumes that users would essentially rent their software. Because the client would download parts of programs as they were needed, the software would never really be saved on the computer. Instead of selling the software to the user, a commercial supplier would charge "rent" for its use.

### Emerging Java Applications

Java's cross-platform and thin client features work together to produce some interesting opportunities. It could be practical to supply programs entirely over the Internet, and all computers with an installed virtual machine could use them.

*Java applets in use*

Small Java programs, called *Java applets,* are already being used to extend traditional web pages, and it appears that this language will offer an approach for more sophisticated Internet applications.

## XML

Some developers feel that HTML is too inhibiting and that a new approach is needed. Applications built in Java, as described in the preceding section, would be an extreme example of using the Internet in a very different way, and some people will certainly pursue this method of providing learning experiences over the Internet. Another approach, however, is to develop a different kind of "markup" language.

*A new markup language*

**XML,** which stands for **extensible markup language,** appears to be an emerging alternative to HTML. "Extensible" implies that, if necessary, new markup commands can be created by the author. XML will probably will not replace HTML, but it may become popular for complex web sites that are very data oriented.

*User-defined tags for content structure*

XML maintains a stricter separation between content and presentation than HTML. In Chapter 9, when discussing the problems that blind learners experienced in using screen readers, we were essentially dealing with the significance of differentiating content from presentation. In XML, markup tags are used to indicate the logical structure of content, and they can be user defined.

*An XML example*

Imagine, for instance, an application intended to allow faculty members to obtain basic information on students. It might include an element called "student," containing other elements such as "name" and "grade." The element "name" might then be defined as containing the elements "lastname" and "firstname." Later in the XML document, these tags would be loaded with data:

```
<STUDENT>
    <NAME>
        <LASTNAME>Grabe</LASTNAME>
        <FIRSTNAME>Mark</FIRSTNAME>
    </NAME>
    <GRADE>Freshman</GRADE>
</STUDENT>
```

The basic approach might be compared to developing a database. In designing a database, the user first defines categories (such as name, home address, phone number) and then uses these categories as containers for information. To generate reports from a database, the user identifies the categories of information to be reported and how the data will be displayed. By changing the arrangement and selection of information categories, the same database can be used to generate reports differing in both content and appearance.

*Style sheets interpret tags for presentation*

XML makes possible a similar approach. Elements of information are tagged either with conventional tags like those in HTML or with tags assigned by the author. Presentation appearance is controlled through the independent generation of style sheets. The style sheets allow interpretation of the tags (the markup system assigned by the author) and tell the presentation system how to assemble the presentation.

We are purposefully using the phrase *presentation system* here rather than *browser,* because one of the goals of XML is to allow authors to create content a single time for presentation in multiple ways. One presentation system would be some form of web browser. Another might be printed pages.

Browsers capable of interpreting author-generated XML tags are still being developed. What XML hopes to add to web presentations is much greater sophistication. The likely initial advantages of this type of change will appear in the quality of presentations students experience from commercial providers.

## TECHNOLOGY INTEGRATION SKILLS

Prediction: Skills involved in the integration of technology into learning will receive considerable attention.

This prediction is more than a reference to the title of this book. It calls attention to the development of skills among both teachers and students.

### TEACHER COMPETENCIES

*Emphasis on technology training for teachers*

Increasingly, the background of teachers—their preparation and continued development—is seen as an important limiting factor for students' use of technology. It is difficult for students to do sophisticated Internet projects if the teacher struggles to differentiate the hard drive from the floppy. Although this basic fact has been known for some time, it seems to be receiving new emphasis both from researchers (such as Wenglinsky, 1998) and from policy advocates (CEO Forum, 1999), who recommend that schools concentrate a little less on the acquisition of hardware, software, and Internet access and more on the preparation and continued development of teachers.

*Changing requirements*

What will it take to ensure that teachers have the necessary skills to bring appropriate technology experiences to their students? For new teachers, responsibility must rest on colleges of education. This responsibility will take shape in accreditation standards and certificate requirements demanding not only that future teachers complete a course on technology, but that they have additional technology-integration experiences in methods courses and student teaching. A few states already require that future teachers submit a portfolio with examples reflecting their ability to integrate technology in their teaching. Required documentation of technological proficiency is likely to become more common (CEO Forum, 1999; Moursund, 1999).

The skills of practicing teachers will probably be advanced as federal money is targeted toward this area of need. Accountability through certification will also likely become more prevalent for practicing teachers. Our state is presently considering a three-level technology certificate system based on demonstrated competencies.

### STUDENT COMPETENCIES

*Guidelines for student competency*

Establishing expected student competencies is another way to highlight the need to integrate technology in learning. Present standards promote the same communication, inquiry, and construction activities we have emphasized. As guidelines like the National Educational Technology Standards (ISTE, 1998) filter down to be recognized at the state and district level and are revised to be content-area specific, benchmarks for integrated applications will provide instructional and evaluation guidelines for teachers.

## ONLINE PUBLISHING

Prediction: Textbooks will continue to exist, but book authors and publishing companies will use the Internet to supplement what traditional books offer.

You might wonder if book authors feel threatened by the Internet. Our personal feelings are mixed.

Focus

## eBooks: Traditional Books on the Screen

One way of adapting traditional books to technology and to the Internet is to digitize books for reading from the screen. There are two important barriers to this approach:

- First, a traditional computer is not the ideal device for presenting large amounts of information. Reading extended material from a computer screen is tedious. A computer, even a laptop, also does not allow you to be mobile in the way you are with a traditional book.
- Second, there is the important question of how publishers will make a reasonable profit. If books can be downloaded, how can the publisher prevent the downloaded material from being copied and passed around? (Of course, a traditional book can be passed around as well, but not at electronic speeds!)

A possible solution comes from the eBook and eBook reader. An **eBook** is a document prepared specifically to be read from a handheld electronic device. This device, the *eBook reader,* resembles a tablet and is designed specifically to present formatted text and graphics. For mobility, it is smaller and lighter than even a notebook computer, and to minimize cost it is built around a minimal number of components.

Books or other documents are downloaded from the Internet, either directly into the eBook reader or into a computer for transfer to the reader. The documents are stored in a proprietary file format so that they can be interpreted only by the reader. For the user's convenience, the eBook reader typically allows searching as well as a form of highlighting or underlining.

The eBook is not completely futuristic. There are several readers already available (see the examples in the Resources to Expand Your Knowledge Base), and the popular online book providers are already selling eBook content. It is interesting to compare the prices of traditional books with eBooks. At present there does not appear to be the kind of cost advantage you might expect for the eBook, but this will change if eBooks become more popular and the cost of transforming content into the eBook format can be spread across more customers.✷

At one level, an author has information to offer, and the form in which the information is communicated is not critical. We must hedge here a little bit, because different presentation formats require different writing skills. However, what you read in a book or on a web site is really the result of a team effort. Authors work with talented editors who help them present information. Specialists in web design are available to help authors adapt their message to web presentation.

In some ways, though, the Internet seems threatening to us as authors of a traditional book. Web-based information can be prepared for readers with

*The web's speed advantage*

greater speed and then updated with greater ease. The time required to write the various drafts of a textbook and prepare the book for actual publication is better described in years than in months. Once in print, a book has to be used with minimal modifications for a number of years in order to generate a reasonable profit for the textbook company and the author. Moreover, unlike the books you use in your college courses, K–12 books are purchased mostly by schools rather than by students and are used for much longer periods of time. Schools typically use books for many years to optimize their cost-effectiveness, and this can mean that the information in the books is far from current. Any method that would make the most current information available in a cost-effective manner has some obvious advantages over traditional textbooks.

*The book-web hybrid*

Given this situation, we feel that publishing companies will increasingly deliver what might best be described as hybrid products. The foundation for this hybrid will be the traditional textbook, but the book will be supplemented with online resources. The online resources will allow the authors and the company to:

1. Update the book content to reflect new developments in the field.
2. Provide additional content or experiences that cannot be included in the book, either for reasons of cost or because they are best presented in another way.
3. Develop a community of learners with ties to the book.

*Join us at our web site!*

We are trying to participate in the trend we have just described. You can connect to our web site at **http://ndwild.psych.und.nodak.edu/book.** We are using this site to update information in this book as it becomes dated and to offer other information that we hope will encourage your own use of the Internet. We encourage you to connect and explore these resources.

## Key Terms

dual-credit arrangement *(p. 294)*
dynamic HTML (DHTML) *(p. 296)*
eBook *(p. 303)*
intranet *(p. 300)*
Java *(p. 299)*
style sheet *(p. 297)*
thin client *(p. 299)*
virtual machine *(p. 299)*
XML (extensible markup language) *(p. 300)*

## Resources to Expand Your Knowledge Base

### Online Subscription Services

Information subscription sources mentioned in this chapter include

*EBSCO Information Services*: **http://www.ebsco.com/**

*SIRS Researcher on the Web*: **http://www.sirs.com/**

*OnlineClass* delivers what the company describes as interactive Internet-based teaching units for K–12 classrooms. See the company web site at **http://www.onlineclass.com/**.

### Courses and Degrees on the Internet

The *Distance Education and Training Council* is a nonprofit organization that provides information about distance education, institutions involved in distance education, and accreditation issues. The Council's web site can be found at **http://www.detc.org**.

Information about *Western Governors University,* which offers online degree programs, can be found at **http://www.wgu.edu**.

### New Internet Developments

***Internet2.*** Information about *Internet2* can be found at **http://www.internet2.edu/**.

***Authoring Environments with DHTML Capabilities.*** *Macromedia Dreamweaver* is a product for the Windows and Macintosh operating systems from Macromedia, Inc., **http://www.macromedia.com**.

*GoLive CyberStudio* is a product for the Macintosh operating system from GoLive Systems, Inc., **http://www.golive.com**.

***Companies Developing eBook Readers.*** Here are two types of eBook readers. Each has a different format.
The *Rocket eBook* reader is a product of NuvoMedia, Inc., **http://www.rocket-ebook.com/**.
The *SoftBook* eBook reader is a product of SoftBook Press, **http://www.softbook.com/**.

# Teacher's Handy Reference

## Useful Internet Sources

The following list is a compilation of most of the Internet resources mentioned in this book. Some sites may appear in more than one category if they have multiple uses. For further ideas and updates, check our web site for this book at **http://www.hmco.com/college** (and select "Education") or at **http://ndwild.psych.und.nodak.edu/book**.

| **Name** | **Internet Address** |
|---|---|
| **Online Discussion Forums** | |
| Apple Learning Interchange (p. 79) | http://ali.apple.com |
| Kidlink (pp. 80, 95, 284) | http://www.kidlink.org |
| Talk City EduCenter (p. 79) | http://www.jamz.com/ |
| Teacher Chat (p. 79) | http://www.realkids.com/tlchat.shtml |
| Women in NASA (p. 79) | http://quest.arc.nasa.gov/webchat/won-chat.html |
| **Curriculum Materials and Student Projects** | |
| Audubon Online (p. 288) | http://www.audubon.org/ |
| Blue Web'n (p. 284) | http://www.kn.pacbell.com/wired/bluewebn/ |
| Classroom Connect (p. 158) | http://www.classroom.com |
| The Exploratorium (p. 288) | http://www.exploratorium.edu |
| GlobaLearn (p. 161) | http://www.globalearn.org/ |
| Global Grocery List (p. 161) | http://www.landmark-project.com/ggl.html |
| Global SchoolNet Projects (p. 95) | http://www.gsn.org/project/index.html |
| Judi Harris's Network-Based Educational Activity Collection (p. 95) | http://lrs.ed.uiuc.edu/Activity-Structures/Harris-Activity-Structures.html |
| I-Kid-A-Rod (p. 167) | http://www.grand-forks.k12.nd.us/~wilder/iditarod.html |
| JASON Project (p. 161) | http://www.jasonproject.org/ |
| The Journey North (p. 161) | http://www.learner.org/jnorth/ |
| KidChronicles (p. 161) | http://www.gsn.org/project/newsday/index.html |
| Kidlink (pp. 80, 95, 284) | http://www.kidlink.org/ |
| Learning Circles (p. 77) | http://www.iearn.org/iearn/circles/lc-home.html |
| NASA's Education Program (p. 288) | http://www.hq.nasa.gov/office/codef/education/index.html |
| NASA's Quest Project (pp. 95, 162) | http://quest.arc.nasa.gov/ |
| North American Quilt (p. 162) | http://www.onlineclass.com/NAQ/NAQhome.html |
| One Sky, Many Voices (p. 162) | http://onesky.engin.umich.edu/ |
| OnlineClass (p. 304) | http://www.onlineclass.com/ |
| Project FeederWatch (p. 52) | http://birdsource.cornell.edu/features/pfw/ |
| Smithsonian Institution (p. 288) | http://www.si.edu |
| ThinkQuest (p. 162) | http://io.advanced.org/ThinkQuest/ |
| U.S. Fish and Wildlife Service (p. 288) | http://www.fws.gov/ |
| The WebQuest Page (p. 161) | http://edweb.sdsu.edu/webquest/webquest.html |
| Weekly Reader Galaxy (p. 293) | http://www.weeklyreader.com/ |

| Name | Internet Address |
|---|---|

## Educational Issues: Mailing Lists, Newsgroups, and Related Professional Development Resources

| Name | Internet Address |
|---|---|
| American Association of University Women (p. 284) | http://www.aauw.org |
| Copyright Questions | http://www.nacs.org/info/copyright/ <br> http://www.publishers.org/home/issues/index.htm |
| Cyber Fiber (p. 32) | http://www.cyberfiber.com |
| Distance Education and Training Council (p. 305) | http://www.detc.org |
| Educast (pp. 23, 32) | http://www.educast.com/ |
| Educational Administration (p. 76) | listserv@suvm.syr.edu |
| Educational Web Discussion (p. 76) | listproc@kudzu.cnidr.org |
| Forum on Educational Reform (p. 76) | listserv@lsv.uky.edu |
| Free Republic News Forum (p. 267) | http://www.FreeRepublic.com |
| Integrating Technology in Schools (p. 76) | listserve@unm.edu |
| International Classroom Connect (p. 76) | iecc-request@stolaf.edu |
| Internet Family Empowerment White Paper (p. 284) | http://www.cdt.org/speech/empowerment.html |
| Internet in the Classroom (p. 76) | listproc@schoolnet.carleton.ca |
| Internet2 Project (p. 305) | http://www.internet2.edu/ |
| The Lizst of Newsgroups (p. 32) | http://www.liszt.com/news |
| Liszt, The Mailing List Directory (pp. 76, 95) | http://www.liszt.com/ |
| Middle School Topics (p. 76) | listserv@postoffice.cso.uiuc.edu |
| OnlineLearning.net (p. 289) | http://www.onlinelearning.net/ |
| Publicly Accessible Mailing Lists (p. 95) | http://www.neosoft.com/internet/paml/default.html |
| The Recreational Software Advisory Council on the Internet (RSACi) (pp. 279, 285) | http://www.rsac.org/ |
| SafeSurf (p. 285) | http://www.safesurf.com |
| SAMI: Science and Math Initiatives | http://www./learner.org/sami |
| Teacher Education Station (p. 103) | http://www.hmco.com/college/education/station/index.html |
| Telecommunications in Education (p. 76) | listserv@unmvma.unm.edu |
| Tile.Net Lists (pp. 76, 95) | http://www.tile.net/listserv/ |
| Topics in Educational Technology (p. 76) | listserv@msu.edu |
| Web66: A K12 World Wide Web Project (p. 245) | http://web66.umn.edu/ |
| World Wide Web Consortium (pp. 284, 285) | http://www.w3.org/ |

## E-mail Connections

| Name | Internet Address |
|---|---|
| Intercultural E-mail Classroom Connections (pp. 19, 95) | http://www.stolaf.edu/network/iecc |
| Keypals International (p. 52) | http://www.collegebound.com/keypals/ |
| Kidlink (pp. 80, 95, 284) | http://www.kidlink.org |
| Yahoo! People Search (p. 66) | http://people.yahoo.com/ |

## Information and Reference Resources

| Name | Internet Address |
|---|---|
| EBSCO Information Services (pp. 161, 304) | http://www.ebsco.com/ |
| The Electric Library (p. 161) | http://www.elibrary.com |
| Encarta OnLine Library (p. 161) | http://www.encarta.msn.com/library/intro.asp |
| Library of Congress American Memory Digital Library (p. 52) | http://memory.loc.gov/ammem/ |
| *New York Times* (p. 161) | http://www.nytimes.com/ |
| Project Gutenberg (pp. 23, 32) | http://promo.net/pg/ |
| ProQuest Direct (p. 161) | http://www.umi.com/proquest/ |

| Name | Internet Address |
|---|---|
| **Information and Reference Resources** | |
| SIRS Researcher on the Web (pp. 161, 304) | http://www.sirs.com/ |
| *Wall Street Journal* (p. 161) | http://www.wsj.com/ |
| *Washington Post* and *Los Angeles Times* (p. 161) | http://www.newsservice.com/ |
| **Reviewed Web Sites** | |
| Blue Web'n (p. 284) | http://www.kn.pacbell.com/wired/bluewebn/ |
| Lycos (pp. 147, 160) | http://point.lycos.com/ |
| Magellan (pp. 133, 146, 160, 284) | http://magellan.excite.com/ |
| Yahooligans (pp. 147, 160, 284) | http://www.yahooligans.com/ |
| **School Web Sites** | |
| Hotlist of School Web Sites (p. 245) | http://www.gsn.org/hotlist/index.html |
| Web66: International School Web Site Registry (p. 245) | http://web66.umn.edu/schools.html |
| **Search Engines and Directories** | |
| AltaVista (p. 133) | http://www.altavista.com/ |
| HotBot (p. 133) | http://www.hotbot.com/ |
| Lycos (pp. 147, 160) | http://www.lycos.com/ |
| Magellan (pp. 133, 146, 160, 284) | http://magellan.excite.com/ |
| MetaCrawler (p. 133) | http://www.metacrawler.com/ |
| Northern Light (p. 133) | http://www.northernlight.com/ |
| SavvySearch (p. 133) | http://guaraldi.cs.colostate.edu:2000/ |
| Yahoo! (p. 133) | http://www.yahoo.com/ |
| Yahoo! People Search (p. 66) | http://www.people.yahoo.com |
| Yahooligans (pp. 147, 160, 284) | http://www.yahooligans.com/ |
| **Software** | |
| Adobe PageMill (p. 191) | http://www.adobe.com |
| AppleWorks (p. 191) | http://www.apple.com/appleworks/ |
| ConferWeb (p. 96) | http://www.caup.washington.edu/software/ |
| CU-SeeMe (newer commercial versions) (p. 96) | http://www.wpine.com |
| CU-SeeMe (older versions) (p. 96) | http://cu-seeme.net/ |
| Cyber Patrol (p. 285) | http://www.cyberpatrol.com |
| CYBERsitter (p. 285) | http://www.cybersitter.com |
| Eudora Light (Qualcomm) (p. 95) | http://eudora.qualcomm.com/products/<br>http://www.eudora.com/ |
| Filemaker Home Page (p. 191) | http://www.filemaker.com/ |
| GoLive CyberStudio (p. 305) | http://www.golive.com |
| Home Page Reader (p. 284) | http://www.austin.ibm.com/sns/hpr.html) |
| HyperStudio (p. 191) | http://www.hyperstudio.com |
| Internet Explorer (Microsoft) (p. 132) | http://www.microsoft.com/ie/ |
| JAWS screen reader (p. 284) | http://www.hj.com/Index.html |

| Name | Internet Address |
|---|---|
| **Software** | |
| Juno (p. 96) | http://www.juno.com/ |
| Macromedia Dreamweaver (p. 305) | http://www.macromedia.com |
| Microsoft FrontPage (p. 191) | http://www.microsoft.com/frontpage/ |
| Microsoft Office (p. 191) | http://www.microsoft.com/office/ |
| Microsoft Personal Web Server (p. 245) | http://www.microsoft.com |
| Myrmidon (p. 191) | http://www.terrymorse.com |
| Net Nanny (p. 285) | http://www.netnanny.com |
| Netscape Communicator and Navigator (pp. 132, 191) | http://www.netscape.com/ |
| Netscape Composer (pp. 132, 191) | http://www.netscape.com/ |
| Outlook Express (Microsoft) (p. 95) | http://www.microsoft.com/msdownload/ |
| Personal Web Sharing (p. 245) | http://www.apple.com |
| PopMail/Lab (p. 96) | http://www.shareware.com/ |
| RealPlayer (RealNetworks) (p. 132) | http://www.real.com/products/player/index.html |
| SurfWatch (p. 285) | http://www.surfwatch.com |
| Web Workshop (p. 191) | http://www.sunburst.com |
| WordPerfect Suite (p. 191) | http://www.wordperfect.com |
| **Streaming Audio and Video** | |
| Audionet (p. 32) | http://www.audionet.com |
| National Public Radio (p. 32) | http://www.npr.com |
| RealGuide (p. 32) | http://realguide.real.com/ |
| **Videoconferencing** | |
| CU-SeeMe Network (p. 96) | http://cu-seeme.net/ |
| CU-SeeMe Schools (pp. 83, 96) | http://www.gsn.org/cu/index.html |
| NASA Television (p. 96) | http://btree.lerc.nasa.gov/NASA_TV/ |
| Rice University's "Ask the Scientist" (p. 96) | http://space.rice.edu/hmns/ask.html |

# Glossary

**acceptable use policy (AUP)** Written guidelines defining how students (and sometimes faculty) will use school resources such as computers with Internet access; the guidelines typically specify procedures to follow and consequences for violation.

**active learners** Learners who make the effort to build on what they know in order to interpret and respond to new experiences. The term relates to the general theoretical position that meaningful learning results from the mental activities of the learner.

**address book** A feature of many e-mail clients that allows the storage of e-mail addresses for easy access.

**administrative address** The mailing list address that is used to execute administrative functions such as joining and leaving the list.

**analog** Expressed as a continuously varying signal rather than as discrete steps; in computer terms, the opposite of *digital.*

**anchor** A specific place on a web page that can be accessed quickly by using a link.

**applet** A small program that operates within a browser.

**ASCII** Short for American Standard Code for Information Interchange; refers to plain text files that use standard characters without special attributes or graphics.

**asynchronous communication** Communication in which a message is sent at one time and received or read at a later time (for instance, e-mail).

**attachment** A file sent as an independent addition to an e-mail message.

**authentic activity** A learning activity that allows students to apply their knowledge and skills in practices similar to those they will encounter in daily life.

**bandwidth** Literally the range of frequencies used by an electromagnetic signal; in common use, the amount of information that can be moved in a fixed amount of time over a transfer line.

**Big Six** A series of six activities involved in solving an information problem: (1) task definition, (2) information seeking, (3) locating and accessing, (4) use of information, (5) organizing and communicating, and (6) evaluation.

**binary** Based on the binary number system, which uses no numbers except 1's and 0's; computers and other digital systems work in binary code.

**BMP** Acronym for bit-mapped, a common graphics format on Windows machines.

**bookmarks** A list of web page addresses stored in a browser (Netscape).

**Boolean search** A search based on a logical combination of multiple keywords, using special operators like AND and OR.

**bounce** To be returned to the sender; used for e-mail that cannot be delivered.

**broken link** A web page link that fails to function.

**browser** Software used to connect to World Wide Web servers and to display information on the local (client) computer.

**CC** Short for "carbon copy"; the function of an e-mail client that allows the user to send copies of a message to one or more people besides the recipient.

**chat** On-line, text-based communication in which messages are exchanged in real time rather than being stored for later reading; a form of synchronous communication over the Internet.

**client** A computer (or its software) that connects to a server to access resources.

**client-side image map** The browser interprets the user's response to an image map and assigns the URL for the requested link.

**cognitive** Related to the mental process of learning or knowing.

**cognitive apprenticeship** Learning of a skill within a relationship with a more expert practitioner.

**color lookup table (CLUT)** The set of colors available within a particular computer system; same as *palette.*

**Common Gateway Interface (CGI)** A system that allows server software to extend what it can accomplish by calling on external programs, such as a database application.

**computer-mediated communication (CMC)** A form of communication that requires the exchange of information by computer, usually through the Internet.

**Conference on Fair Use (CONFU)** A series of meetings on copyright issues that produced guidelines in 1997 for teacher- or student-created multimedia and for distance education.

**constructivism** Theory proposing that students create a personal understanding (construct their own knowledge) by interpreting their experiences.

**cooperative learning** A setting in which students work together to accomplish an instructional goal.

**critical thinking** Solving problems by gathering and interpreting information; as an instructional approach, it emphasizes the development of analytical skills that can be applied to a wide range of subject matter.

**cross-platform** Capable of functioning on computers with different operating systems, for instance Windows and Macintosh computers.

**CU-SeeMe** Videoconferencing software developed originally at Cornell University.

**dead page** On a web site, a linked page that has no return link.

**dedicated connection** A connection to the Internet that is designed explicitly for that use and is always open; compare *dial-up connection.*

**design** In educational theory, the process by which active and motivated students create personal understanding, especially through projects that culminate in a student-created product such as a web site.

**dial-up connection** A connection to the Internet that operates through regular telephone lines.

**digital** Expressed as discrete steps that can be represented by numbers, especially by binary numbers; opposite of *analog.*

**discovery learning** A form of learning in which students discover important principles on their own.

**distance learning** Learning in which technology links students and instructors who are separated geographically.

**dithering** A process by which a computer tries to simulate a color by mixing pixels of other colors.

**domain name** A name that indicates a computer's address on the Internet; an easier-to-remember equivalent of the IP number.

**download** To transfer files from a server to a client over the Internet.

**dual-credit arrangement** An arrangement in which a high school course counts for both high school and college credit.

**dynamic HTML (DHTML)** A combination of JavaScript and HTML options, available in HTML version 4, that allows greater control over page appearance and greater interactivity.

**eBook** A document prepared specifically to be read from an eBook reader, a hand-held electronic device.

**e-mail** A method for sending a message over the Internet directly to the account of another Internet user.

**e-rate** A subsidy for the costs of providing Internet connections to schools and libraries, established by the Telecommunications Act of 1996.

**Ethernet** A physical medium for transmitting local area network data at speeds up to 10 megabits per second.

**Ethernet card** The hardware device that connects a computer to the Ethernet.

**facilitator** The term frequently used to describe the teacher's role when students are engaged in active, self-regulated learning.

**fair use** Copying of someone else's intellectual property that is within the parameters allowed by copyright law.

**favorites** A list of web page addresses stored in a browser (Internet Explorer).

**file compression** Reducing the size of an electronic file so that it can be stored more efficiently and transmitted over the Internet more quickly.

**File Transfer Protocol (FTP)** A standard allowing the transfer of a file to and from a host computer.

**filtering** Controlling what Internet users are able to access by blocking content that is deemed inappropriate.

**firewall** A computer and software that control the flow of data between two networks—for example, between a school's internal network and the Internet.

**flame war** An on-line exchange of insults.

**form** A special web page capable of accepting information from the user and transferring this information to the server.

**frame** A subdivision of the content window on a web page that can be changed independently of the other parts; often used on the left of the screen to provide menu selections that control the display on the right.

**generative learning** A theory emphasizing the student's active search for meaning through the integration of new experiences with existing knowledge or the generation of inferences.

**GIF** Acronym for Graphic Interchange Format, a lossless technique of file compression for graphic files that relies on indexed color.

**group investigation** Cooperative learning method in which group members develop a project focused on an assigned theme.

**guided discovery** A modified version of discovery learning in which the teacher plays a more purposeful role.

**header** In an e-mail message, the top portion that contains, at a minimum, the address for the sender, the address for the receiver, and a topic for the e-mail.

**helper application** An application that processes files that cannot be processed by a browser.

**hierarchical design** A form of web site design in which the content is organized as a system of categories and subcategories.

**hit** An individual visit to a web page; more exactly, each time the server is asked for a file is a hit.

**hit rate** The activity level of a server, often expressed as the number of hits in a certain period of time.

**home page** The initial display when a user connects to a particular World Wide Web site.

**hot spot** A portion of a web page image that functions as a link.

**hypercomposition design model** An educational strategy in which students undertake projects in hypercomposition design as part of their content area learning.

**hypermedia** Multimedia that can be examined in a nonlinear manner. The user can typically move at will from one information source to several others.

**hypertext markup language (HTML)** The basic coding language used in the creation of web pages; specifically, the tags inserted in a document that inform the web browser how to display hypermedia elements (such as images) and how to take specific actions (such as branching to other web pages).

**hypertext transfer protocol** The protocol used by the World Wide Web for transmitting pages; abbreviated as "http" at the beginning of a web site address.

**image map** A web page image in which designated areas function as independent links to other web pages.

**indexed color** A color system that uses the colors available in a particular system's palette.

**inert knowledge** Knowledge that exists but is not applied when it could be useful.

**inquiry** The process of finding sources of information appropriate to a task, working to understand those sources, and applying this understanding in a productive way.

**instructional resources** Information resources that have been prepared specifically for an instructional purpose.

**interlaced format** A graphic format that renders an image by means of layers of increasing clarity, so that a rough outline appears first, then sharper versions.

**Internet** An international collection of computer networks.

**Internet relay chat (IRC)** A chat format that can be used by anyone with Internet access and IRC client software.

**Internet service provider (ISP)** A commercial or publicly funded company that provides connectivity to the Internet.

**Internet2** An independent high-speed and high-bandwidth Internet connecting major research universities and industry partners.

**intranet** A local network intended to serve resources within a school or business.

**IP number** For every computer with a permanent connection to the Internet, the number designating its precise Internet address.

**ISDN (integrated services digital network)** A digital technology for carrying data at relatively high speed over a standard copper telephone wire.

**Java** A programming language that allows cross-platform and thin client applications.

**jigsaw** A form of cooperative learning in which each member of the group becomes an "expert" in a particular subtopic and teaches it to the other members; thus each person makes a unique and essential contribution to the accomplishment of the group task.

**JPEG** Acronym for Joint Photographic Experts Group, a lossy technique of file compression for graphic files that is especially useful for photographs.

**killer application** An application so powerful and popular that it eliminates earlier applications and attracts new users to the technology.

**knowledge as design** Knowledge constructed by the individual to accomplish a particular purpose.

**learning circle** A group of classes that agree to develop projects focused on a common theme and share their projects with each other.

**learning community** A group of students, teachers, and other adults who cooperate to create learning experiences that encourage communication among the participants and access to real-world examples.

**leased line** A dedicated telecommunications circuit (private line) between any two locations.

**license** An agreement that grants specific rights concerning the copying or reproduction of copyrighted material.

**lifelong learning** Learning continuously throughout one's life span as life presents new challenges; an idea promoted by those who believe that learners in the contemporary world will be unable to limit their learning to a designated period.

**link** Connection between two web pages.

**listserv** An alternative term for a mailing list.

**list server** The computer or site from which a mailing list originates.

**local area network (LAN)** A set of interconnected computers in one location, such as a school building or office.

**lossless compression** File compression that relies totally on increased efficiency, generating a smaller file without reduction in image quality.

**lossy compression** File compression that approximates rather than exactly matches the original; produces a smaller but less precise file than lossless compression.

**lurking** Observing an e-mail or chat session without participating.

**mailing list** A on-line discussion group in which all messages are sent to a common e-mail address, which then forwards the message to all members of the list.

**meaningful learning** Learning in which new experiences are linked with information already stored in memory.

**metacognition** Knowledge about one's own thinking and learning.

**modem** A device that connects a computer (or network) to a telephone line.

**multimedia** A communication format that integrates several media (such as text, audio, and visual).

**navigation system** The methods by which a user can move about within a web site and connect to other sites.

**netiquette** Conventions for appropriate on-line conduct.

**newbies** Individuals new to an activity; for instance, new members of a mailing list.

**newsgroup** A topical discussion group in which messages (articles) are posted to an on-line server, where they can be accessed by any member of the group.

**newsreader** The client application needed to read articles of a newsgroup.

**page** A single World Wide Web document. Pages are connected by links.

**page template** In web page authoring, a pattern or model that defines certain areas of the page and identifies the general types of information that are to appear in these areas.

**palette** The set of colors available within a particular computer system; same as *color lookup table.*

**personal server** A low-cost server application designed to operate on a nondedicated and low-cost computer.

**PICT** A common Macintosh format for graphics.

**Platform for Internet Content Selection (PICS)** A web protocol, useful for filtering purposes, that allows each web page to carry a tag designating its type of content.

**plug-in** An application that works within a browser to process certain types of files.

**point-to-point connection** A temporary link established between two computers.

**Point to Point Protocol (PPP)** One of the standard protocols used for modem transmissions over the Internet.

**primary source** A general information source prepared without consideration for student needs.

**protocol** A set of rules and conventions governing how devices on a network exchange information.

**pull technology** A system by which the user continually selects the next information source to access; the user must deliberately "pull" in each new resource.

**push technology** A system by which new information on a particular subject is automatically delivered to a user's computer account; for example, a web site that the user can instruct to deliver daily weather reports for Chicago or Santa Fe.

**query** A request made to a search engine.

**QuickTime** A format that allows digital movies and sounds to be compressed, edited, and played on a computer.

**RSACi rating system** A system, developed by the Recreational Software Advisory Council, for rating the potential offensiveness of web site content on the basis of nudity, sex, language, and violence.

**reception learning** A method in which concepts, principles, and rules to be learned are presented directly to the student; contrast *discovery learning.*

**reflector site** A site that feeds a CU-SeeMe signal to multiple other sites.

**rote learning** Learning with little attention to meaning.

**router** A system for making decisions about which of several paths network traffic will follow.

**scaffolding** External support for learning or problem solving; especially applied to a teacher's deliberate structuring of a learning experience so that students receive assistance at appropriate points until they develop their own skills.

**school server** An Internet server dedicated to use by a particular school; generally a powerful computer situated outside of the classroom.

**screen reader** Software that "reads" the screen to the learner, synthesizing speech from the text and also describing menus, windows, and screen icons.

**search engine** A program, used by a search service, that checks a user's request against the database of web pages maintained by the service and returns a list of matches.

**self-regulated learning** Strategic student behavior involving planning, evaluation, and appropriate adjustment of learning.

**sequential design** A form of web site design in which the content is organized so that each element leads directly to the next in logical sequence.

**server** A computer that makes a resource available to other computers.

**server-side image map** The server interprets the user's response to an image map and assigns the URL for the requested link.

**shareware** Software that is available free for evaluation but that must be purchased if used after the evaluation process.

**signature** A concluding part of an e-mail message that is automatically added by the sender's e-mail software; typically it includes the sender's name and whatever other information the sender wishes to provide.

**site license** A license for copyrighted material that offers certain privileges to users at a specific site; for instance, an agreement allowing a school to copy particular software for use on the school's computers.

**site map** A diagram or outline that shows the organization of a web site.

**SLIP (Serial Line Internet Protocol)** One of the standard protocols used for modem transmissions over the Internet.

**socioeconomic status (SES)** A measure of prestige based on income, education, and occupation.

**streaming** A web-based technology allowing the continuous reception of audio and/or video information.

**streaming audio** A method by which audio can be played continuously rather than being transferred as a file and then played.

**streaming video** A method by which video can be viewed continuously rather than being transferred as a file and then viewed.

**style sheet** The set of information defining how a tag or tags will be applied throughout a web site; essentially, a method for controlling how text will appear.

**subject field** A field in which the sender of an e-mail message enters a phrase intended to describe the purpose of the message.

**submission address** The mailing list address that is used when a message is to be sent to all members of the list.

**synchronous communication** Communication in which a message is sent and received almost simultaneously (for instance, chat).

**tag** An HTML command; see *hypertext markup language.*

**TCP/IP protocol** Short for transmission control protocol/Internet protocol, the standard protocol for connecting computers via the Internet.

**Telnet** A means of logging in to a remote computer and using it as though it were a local computer.

**thin client** A computer that contains minimal hardware components; it runs programs transferred across an intranet or Internet connection.

**thread** A series of linked messages consisting of replies to previous messages.

**thumbnail** A small version of a larger image, often used on the web as a link to a page containing the full-size image.

**timing out** Exceeding the time limit allowed for a transfer of information over the Internet, so that the system stops trying to complete the transfer.

**Transparency** A special characteristic of a GIF image allowing the designation of one color or transparency. The appearance of the next layer is visible through the transparent area.

**Universal Resource Locator (URL)** An address for an FTP or WWW file on the Internet.

**user interface** The methods provided to allow a user to interact with a computer program or web site.

**videoconferencing** Synchronous video and audio communication over the Internet.

**virtual learning community** An on-line learning community; a cooperative learning group that uses the Internet for communication among members.

**virtual machine** A system- and hardware-specific program that allows a computer to run programs written in the Java language.

**web, the** Shorthand term for the *World Wide Web.*

**web authoring program** Software that allows the user to create web pages without writing directly in HTML code.

**web design** A form of web site design that establishes a complex set of connections among web pages.

**webmaster** The person in charge of a web site.

**WebQuest** A type of structured Internet problem-solving activity developed by Bernie Dodge.

**World Wide Web (WWW)** A system that allows access to Internet resources that include multimedia and hypermedia. A single web *site* can include a number of *pages.*

**WYSIWYG** An acronym for "what you see is what you get"; used for computer software that displays text and other objects as they will actually appear in the final product.

**XML (extensible markup language)** An alternative to HTML that allows user-defined markup tags.

# References


Adaptive Computer Technology Centre. (1998). *Accessible web page design* [On-line]. Available: http://www.aspbc.org/gen/webaccess.html (May 1999).

Alessi, S., & Trollip, S. (1991). *Computer-based instruction: Materials and development* (2nd ed.). Englewood Cliffs, NJ: Prentice-Hall.

Althaus, S. (1997). Computer-mediated communication in the university classroom: An experiment with on-line discussions. *Communication Education, 46*(3), 158–174.

American Association of University Women Educational Foundation. (1998). *Gender Gaps: Where Schools Still Fail Our Children.* Washington, DC: Author.

American Psychological Association Board of Educational Affairs. (1995). *Learner-centered psychological principles: A framework for school redesign and reform.* Washington, DC: American Psychological Association.

Anderson, T., Anderson, R., Dalgaard, B., Paden, D., Biddle, W., Surber, J., & Alessi, S. (1975). An experimental evaluation of a computer based study management system. *Educational Psychologist, 11,* 184–190.

Andres, Y. (1996). Elements of an effective CU-SeeMe videoconference. *Connections: Special Interest Group of Technology Coordinators, 12*(4), 28–29.

Ausubel, D. (1963). *The Psychology of Meaningful Learning.* New York: Grune and Stratton.

Baker, L. (1985). Differences in the standards used by college students to evaluate their comprehension of expository prose. *Reading Research Quarterly, 20,* 297–313.

Bandura, A. (1977). *Social Learning Theory.* Englewood Cliffs, NJ: Prentice-Hall.

Berkowitz, B. (1997). Student self-assessment skills: Focus on success. *The Big 6 Newsletter, 1*(2), 4–5.

Beyer, B. (1988). *Developing a Thinking Skills Program.* Boston: Allyn and Bacon.

Black, S., Levin, J., Mehan, H., & Quinn, C. (1983). Real and non-real time interaction: Unraveling multiple threads of discourse. *Discourse Processes, 6,* 59–75.

Branscomb, L. (1995). Balancing the commercial and public-interest vision of the NII. In B. Kahin & J. Keller (Eds.), *Public Access to the Internet* (pp. 24–33). Cambridge, MA: MIT Press.

Bransford, J. D., Brown, A. L., & Cocking, R. R. (Eds.). (1999). *How People Learn: Brain, Mind, Experience, School.* Washington, DC: National Academy Press.

Brown, A. (1992). Design experiments: Theoretical and methodological challenges in creating complex interventions in classroom settings. *Journal of the Learning Sciences, 2*(2), 141–178.

Brown, A., & Campione, J. (1994). Guided discovery in a community of learners. In K. McGilly (Ed.), *Classroom lessons: Integrating cognitive theory and classroom practice* (pp. 229–270). Cambridge, MA: MIT Press.

Brown, J., Collins, A., & Duguid, P. (1989). Situated cognition and the culture of learning. *Educational Researcher, 18,* 32–42.

Bruce, B., & Levin, J. (1997). Educational technology: Media for inquiry, communication, construction and expression. *Journal of Educational Computing Research, 17*(1), 79–102.

Burke, E. (1993). Copyright catechism. *Educom Review, 28*(5), 46–49.

Butler, D., & Winne, P. (1995). Feedback and self-regulated learning: A theoretical synthesis. *Review of Educational Research, 65,* 245–281.

Center for Democracy and Technology. (1997). *Internet family empowerment white paper: How filtering tools enable responsible parents to protect their children on-line* [On-line]. Available: http:www.cdt.org/speech/empower.html (January 1999).

CEO Forum. (1999). *Professional development: A link to better learning* [On-line]. Available: http://www.ceoforum.org/ (February 1999).

Champagne, A., Gunstone, F., & Klopfer, L. (1985). Instructional consequences of students' knowledge about physical phenomena. In L. West & A. Pines (Eds.), *Cognitive structure and conceptual change* (pp. 163–188). Orlando, FL: Academic Press.

Champagne, A., Klopfer, L., & Anderson, J. (1980). Factors influencing the learning of classical mechanics. *American Journal of Physics, 48,* 1074–1079.

Christmann, E., Badgett, J., & Lucking, R. (1997). Progressive comparison of the effects of computer-assisted instruction on the academic achievement of secondary students. *Journal of Research on Computing in Education, 29,* 325–336.

Clement, J. (1983). A conceptual model discussed by Galileo and used intuitively by physics students. In D. Gentner & A. Stevens (Eds.), *Mental models* (pp. 206–215). Hillsdale, NJ: Erlbaum.

Cognition and Technology Group. (1992). The Jasper series as an example of anchored instruction: Theory, program description, and assessment data. *Educational Psychologist, 27,* 291–315.

CONFU. (1997a). *Educational fair use proposals for distance learning* [On-line]. Available: http://www-ninch.cni.org/issues/copyright/fair_use_education/confu/distancelearning.html (January 1999).

CONFU. (1997b). *Fair use guidelines for educational multimedia* [On-line]. Available: http://www-ninch.cni.org/issues/copyright/fair_use_education/confu/multimedia.html (January 1999).

Department of Education. (1998). *Discounted telecommunication services for schools and libraries* [On-line]. Available: http://www.ed.gov/Technology/comm-mit.html (May 1999).

Descy, D. (1996). Evaluating Internet resources. *TechTrends, 41*(4), 3–5.

*Digital Millennium Copyright Act* [On-line]. Available: http://lcweb.loc.gov/copyright (January 1999).

D'Ignazio, F. (1996). Minimalist multimedia: Authoring on the World Wide Web. *Learning and Leading with Technology, 23*(8), 49–51.

Dodge, B. (1995). *Some thoughts about WebQuests* [On-line]. Available: http://edweb.sdsu.edu/courses/edtec596/about_webquests.html (January 1999).

Dodge, B. (1998). *The WebQuest page* [On-line]. Available: http://edweb.sdsu.edu/webquest/webquest.html (January 1999).

Duffy, T., & Bednar, A. (1991, September). Attempting to come to grips with alternative perspectives. *Educational Technology, 32,* 12–15.

Dunkin, M., & Biddle, B. (1974). *The study of teaching.* New York: Holt, Rinehart & Winston.

Eisenberg, M., & Berkowitz, R. (1990). *Information Problem-Solving: The Big Six Skills Approach to Library & Information Skills Instruction.* Norwood, NJ: Ablex Publishing.

Eisenberg, M., & Johnson, D. (1996). *Computer skills for information problem-solving: Learning and teaching technology in context.* ERIC Digest ERIC Clearinghouse on Science & Technology. [On-line]. Available: http://ericir.syr.edu/ithome/digests/computerskills.html (May 1999).

Ennis, R. (1987). A taxonomy of critical thinking dispositions and abilities. In J. Baron & R. Sternberg (Eds.), *Teaching thinking skills: Theory and practice* (pp. 9–26). San Francisco: Freeman.

eSchool News Staff. (1998, November). Newspaper "fair use" challenge could limit what schools and others post on the web. *eSchool News,* 11.

Federal Communications Commission. (1997). *Report & Order in the Matter of Federal-State Joint Board on Universal Service* [On-line]. Available: http://www.fcc.gov/ccb/universal_service/fcc97157/97157.html (February 1999).

Flanders, N. (1971). *Analyzing teaching behavior.* Reading, MA: Addison-Wesley.

Fletcher-Flinn, C., & Gravatt, B. (1995). The efficacy of computer-assisted instruction: A meta-analysis. *Journal of Educational Computing Research, 12*(3), 219–242.

Flower, L., & Hayes, J. (1981). A cognitive process theory of writing. *College Composition and Communication, 32,* 365–387.

Fritz, M. (1992). Be juris-prudent. *CBT Directions, 5*(2), 6, 8–10.

Gage, N. L., & Berliner, D. C. (1998). *Educational Psychology* (6th ed.). Boston: Houghton Mifflin.

Gay, G. (1986). Interaction of learner control and prior understanding in computer-assisted video-instruction. *Journal of Educational Psychology, 78*(3), 225–227.

George, Y., Malcolm, S., & Jeffers, L. (1993). Computer equity for the future. *Communications of the ACM, 36*(5), 78–81.

Glenberg, A., Sanocki, T., Epstein, W. & Morris, W. (1987). Enhancing calibration of comprehension. *Journal of Experimental Psychology: General, 116,* 119–136.

Global Reach. (1998). *Global Internet statistics: By language* [On-line]. Available: http://www.euromktg.com/globstats/ (May 1999).

Glover, J., Ronning, R., & Bruning, R. (1990). *Cognitive psychology for teachers.* New York: Macmillan.

Gordin, D., Gomez, L., Pea, R., & Fishman, B. (1997). *Using the World Wide Web to build learning communities in K-12* [On-line]. Available: http://www.ascusc.org/jcmc/vol2/issue3/gordin.html (May 1999).

Grabe, M., & Grabe, C. (1998). *Integrating technology for meaningful learning* (2nd ed.). Boston: Houghton Mifflin.

Grabe, M., Petros, T., & Sawler, B. (1989). An evaluation of computer assisted study in controlled and free access settings. *Journal of Computer Based Instruction, 16,* 110–116.

Guthrie, J., & Dreher, M. (1990). Literacy as search: Explorations via computer. In D. Nix and R. Spiro (Eds.), *Cognition, education, multimedia: Exploring ideas in high technology* (pp. 65–113). Hillsdale, NJ: Erlbaum.

Habib, D., & Balliot, R. (1998). *How to search the World Wide Web: A tutorial for beginners and non-experts* [On-line]. Available http://www.ultranet.com/~egrlib/tutor.htm (May 1999).

Harasim, L. (1990). Online education: An environment for collaboration and intellectual amplification. In L. Harasim (Ed.), *Online education: Perspectives on a new environment* (pp. 39–64). New York: Praeger.

Harper, G. (1997). *Copyright law and electronic reserves* [On-line]. Available: http://www.utsystem.edu/ogc/intellectualproperty/ereserve.htm (January 1999).

Harris, J. (1995). Curricularly infused telecomputing: A structural approach to activity design. *Computers in the Schools, 11*(3), 49–59.

Harris, J. (1997). Wetware: Why use activity structures? *Learning and Leading with Technology, 25*(4), 12–17.

Hayes, J., & Flower, L. (1980). Writing as problem solving. *Visible Language, 14,* 388–399.

Healy, J. (1998). *Failure to connect: Why computers are damaging our children's minds.* New York: Simon and Schuster.

Hirsch, E. (1988). *Cultural literacy: What every American needs to know.* New York: Vantage Books.

International Society for Technology in Education. (1998). *National Educational Technology Standards for Students.* Eugene, OR: Author. Available online: http://cnets.iste.org (March 1999).

Jansen, B., & Culpepper, S. (1996). Using the big six research process. *Multimedia Schools,3*(5), 32–38.

Jerald, C. (1998a). Below full capacity. *Education Week, 18*(5), 106–107.

Jerald, C. (1998b). By the numbers: Student access to classroom technology is increasing dramatically. *Education Week, 38*(5), 102–105.

Johnson, D., & Johnson, R. (1989). Social skills for successful group work. *Educational Leadership, 47*(4), 29–33.

Johnson, D., & Johnson, R. (1999). *Learning together and alone* (5th ed.). Boston: Allyn and Bacon.

Johnson, D., Johnson, R., & Holubec, E. (1991). *Cooperation in the classroom* (rev. ed.). Edina, MN: Interaction Book Company.

Jonassen, D. (1991, September). Evaluating constructivistic learning. *Educational Technology, 32,* 28–33.

Jonassen, D., & Grabinger, R. (1990). Problems and issues in designing hypertext/hypermedia for learning. In D. Jonassen & H. Mandl (Eds.), *Designing hypermedia for learning* (pp. 3–25). New York: Springer-Verlag.

Jones, B., & Maloy, R. (1996). *Schools for an information age: Reconstructing foundations for learning and teaching.* Westport, CT: Praeger Publishers.

Kersch, B. (1978). The adequacy of meaning as an explanation of superiority of learning by independent discovery. *Journal of Educational Psychology, 49,* 282–292.

Kiesler, S., Zubrow, D., Moses, A., & Geller, V. (1985). Affect in computer-mediated communication. *Human Computer Interaction, 1,* 77–104.

Kirk, E. (1996). *Evaluating information found on the Internet* [On-line]. Available: http://milton.mse.jhu.edu:8001/research/education/net.html (January 1999).

Knapp, L., & Glenn, A. (1996). *Restructuring schools with technology.* Boston: Allyn and Bacon.

Koschmann, T. (Ed.). (1996). *Computer-supported collaborative learning.* Mahwah, NJ: Erlbaum.

Kraut, R., Patterson, M., Lundmark, V., Kiesler, S., Mukopadhyay, T., & Scherlis, W. (1998). Internet paradox: A social technology that reduces social involvement and psychological well-being? *American Psychologist, 53*(9), 1017–1031.

Kulik, C., & Kulik, J. (1991). Effectiveness of computer-based instruction: An updated analysis. *Computers in Human Behavior, 7,* 75–94.

Laboratory of Comparative Human Cognition. (1989). Kids and computers: A positive vision of the future. *Harvard Educational Review, 59,* 73–86.

Lawless, K., & Kulikowich, J. (1996). Understanding hypertext navigation through cluster analysis. *Journal of Educational Computing Research, 14*(4), 385–399.

Lawless, K., & Brown, S. (1997). Multimedia learning environments: Issues of learner control and navigation. *Instructional Science, 25*(2), 117–131.

Lawrence, S., & Giles, C. (1998). Searching the World Wide Web. *Science, 280*(3), 98–100.

Lehrer, R. (1993). Authors of knowledge: Patterns of hypermedia design. In S. Lajoie & S. Derry (Eds.), *Computers as cognitive tools* (pp. 197–227). Hillsdale, NJ: Erlbaum.

Lehrer, R., Erickson, J., & Connell, T. (1994). Learning by designing hypermedia documents. *Computers in the Schools,* 10(1/2), 227–254.

Leiner, B., Cerf, V., Clark, D., Kahn, R., Kleinrock, L., Lynch, D., Postel, J., Roberts, L., & Wolff, S. (1997). *A brief history of the Internet* (Version 3.1) [Online]. Available: http://www.isoc.org/internet-history (May 1999).

Li, X., & Crane, N. B. (1996). *Electronic styles: A handbook for citing electronic information.* Medford, NJ: Information Today.

Linn, M. (1986). Science. In R. Dillon & R. Sternberg (Eds.), *Cognition and instruction* (pp. 155–197). Orlando, FL: Academic Press.

Locatis, C., Letourneau, G., & Banvard, R. (1990). Hypermedia and instruction. *Educational Technology, Research and Development, 37*(4), 65–77.

Long, D., Risher, C., & Shapiro, G. (1997). *Questions and answers on copyright for the campus community.* Oberlin, OH: National Association of College Stores.

Loving, C. (1997). From the summit of truth to its slippery slopes: Science education's journey through positivist-postmodern territory. *American Educational Research Journal, 34*(3), 421–452.

Lynch, P., & Horton, S. (1997). *Yale Center for Advanced Instructional Media style guide* [On-line]. Available: http://info.med.yale.edu/caim/manual/contents.html (May 1999).

Lynch, P., & Horton, S. (1998). Refining web pages: Effective design strategies for educators. *Syllabus, 11*(6), 39–43.

Maddux, C., & Johnson, D. (1997). The World Wide Web: History, cultural context, and a manual for developers of educational information-based web sites. *Educational Technology, 37*(5), 5–12.

Magid, L. (1998). *Child safety on the Information Highway* [On-line]. Available: http://www.safekids.com/child_safety.htm (May 1999).

Major, A. (1998). Copyright law tackles yet another challenge: The electronic frontier of the World

Wide Web. *Rutgers Computer and Technology Law Journal, 24*(1), 75–105.

Market Data Retrieval. (1998). *High-tech schools: A profile of the leaders.* Shelton, CT: Author.

Markman, E., & Gorin, L. (1981). Children's ability to adjust their standards for evaluating comprehension. *Journal of Educational Psychology, 73,* 320–325.

Martin, J. (1994). Are you breaking the law? *MacWorld, 11*(5), 125–129.

McCloskey, M. (1983). Naive theories of motion. In D. Gentner & A. Stevens (Eds.), *Mental models* (pp. 71–94). Hillsdale, NJ: Erlbaum.

McComb, M. (1994). Benefits of computer-mediated communication in college courses. *Communication Education, 43*(2), 159–170.

McGinley, W. (1992). The role of reading and writing while composing from sources. *Reading Research Quarterly, 27,* 227–248.

McGrath, J. (1990). Time matters in groups. In J. Galegher, R. Kraut, & C. Egido (Eds.), *Intellectual teamwork: Social and technological foundations of cooperative work* (pp. 23–61). Hillsdale, NJ: Erlbaum.

McKenzie, J. (1997a). Making the net work for schools: Online research modules. *From Now On: The Educational Technology Journal, 7*(1). [On-line]. Available: http://fromnowon.org/sept97/online.html (January 1999).

McKenzie, J. (1997b). Telling questions and the search for insight. *From Now On: The Educational Technology Journal, 7*(1) [On-line]. Available: http://fromnowon.org/sept97/telling.html (January 1999).

Means, B., Blando, J., Olson, K., Middleton, T., Morocco, C., Remz, A., & Zorfass, J. (1993). *Using technology to support educational reform.* Washington: Government Printing Office.

Moran, S. (1997). Services rush to stamp out vexing e-mail blackouts. *Web Week, 3*(12) [On-line]. Available: http://www.webweek.com/97Apr28/webweek.html (May 1999).

Moursund, D. (1999). *Will new teachers be prepared to teach in a digital age?* [On-line]. Available: http://www.milkenexchange.org/research/iste_results.html (March 1999).

Murray, B. (1998). Data smog: Newest culprit in brain drain. *American Psychological Association Monitor, 29*(3), 1, 42.

Naisbitt, J. (1984). *Megatrends: Ten new directions transforming our lives.* New York: Warner Books.

National Center for Education Statistics. (1997). *Advanced telecommunications in US public elementary and secondary schools, 1996.* Washington, DC: U.S. Department of Education.

National Center for Education Statistics. (1998). *The condition of education 1998* [On-line]. Available: http://nces.ed.gov/pubs98/condition98/c9803a01.html

Netcraft. (1998). *The Netcraft Web Server Survey* [On-line]. Available: http://www.netcraft.com/Survey (May 1999).

Olaniran, B., Savage, G., & Sorenson, R. (1996). Experimental and experiential approaches to teaching face-to-face and computer-mediated group discussion. *Communication Education, 45*(3), 244–259.

Oliver, K. (1997). Getting online with K–12 Internet projects. *Techtrends, 42*(6), 33–40.

Oppenheimer, T. (1997). The computer delusion. *Atlantic Monthly, 280*(1), 45–62.

Palincsar, A., & Brown, A. (1984). Reciprocal teaching of comprehension-fostering and comprehension-monitoring activities. *Cognition and Instruction, 1,* 117–175.

Panel on Educational Technology, President's Committee of Advisors on Science and Technology. (1997). *Report to the president on the use of technology to strengthen K–12 education in the United States* [On-line]. Available: http://www1.whitehouse.gov/WH/EOP/OSTP/NSTC/PCAST/k-12ed.html (May 1999).

Paris, S., & Lindauer, B. (1982). The development of cognitive skills during childhood. In B. Wolman (Ed.), *Handbook of developmental psychology* (pp. 333–349). Englewood Cliffs, NJ: Prentice-Hall.

Perkins, D. (1986). *Knowledge as design.* Hillsdale, NJ: Erlbaum.

Pressley, M. (1995). More about the development of self-regulation: Complex, long-term, and thoroughly social. *Educational Psychologist, 30,* 207–212.

Pressley, M., Snyder, B., Levin, J., Murray, H., & Ghatala, E. (1987). Perceived readiness for examination performance (PREP) produced by initial reading of text and text containing adjunct questions. *Reading Research Quarterly, 22,* 219–236.

Quinn, C., Mehan, H., Levin, J., & Black, S. (1983). Real education in non-real time: The use of electronic message systems for instruction. *Instructional Science, 11,* 313–327.

Riel, M. (1993). *Learning circles: Virtual communities for elementary and secondary schools* [On-line]. Available: http://lrs.ed.uiuc.edu/Guidelines/Riel-93.html (May 1999).

Riel, M. (1997). *The Internet: A land to settle rather than an ocean to surf and a new "place" for school reform through community development* [On-line]. Available: http://www.gsn.org/teach/articles/netasplace.html (May 1999).

Ross, J. (1996). The influence of computer communication skills on participation in a computer conferencing course. *Journal of Educational Computing Research, 15*(1), 37–52.

Salpeter, J. (1992). Are you obeying copyright law? *Technology and Learning, 12*(8), 14–23.

Sanders, J., & McGinnis, M. (1991). *Computer equity in math and science: A trainer's workshop guide.* Metuchen, NJ: Scarecrow Press.

Sharan, S., & Shachar, H. (1988). *Language and learning in the cooperative classroom.* New York: Springer-Verlag.

Sharan, Y., & Sharan, S. (1992). *Expanding cooperative learning through group investigation.* New York: Teachers College Press.

Shea, V. (1994). *Netiquette.* San Francisco: Albion Press.

Sheingold, K. (1991, September). Restructuring for learning with technology: The potential for synergy. *Phi Delta Kappan,* 28–36.

Shenk, D. (1997). *Data smog: Surviving the information glut.* San Francisco: Harper.

Shipstone, D. (1988). Pupils' understanding of simple electrical circuits. *Physics Education, 23,* 92–96.

Slavin, R. (1990). *Cooperative learning: Theory, research, and practice.* Englewood Cliffs, NJ: Prentice-Hall.

Slavin, R. (1991). *Student team learning: A practical guide to cooperative learning* (3rd ed.). Washington, DC: National Education Association.

Slavin, R. (1996). Research on cooperative learning and achievement. *Contemporary Educational Psychology, 21*(1), 43–69.

Smilowitz, M., Compton, D., & Flint, L. (1988). The effects of computer mediated communication on an individual judgment. *Computers in Human Behavior, 14,* 311–321.

Sutton, R. (1991). Equity and computers in schools: A decade of research. *Review of Educational Research, 61*(4), 475–503.

Thomas, J., & Rohwer, W. (1986). Academic studying: The role of learning strategies. *Educational Psychologist, 21,* 19–41.

Tierney, R., Carter, M., & Desai, L. (1991). *Portfolio assessment in the reading-writing classroom.* Norwood, MA: Gordon Publishers.

Tobin, K. (1986). Effects of wait time on discourse characteristics in mathematics and language arts classes. *American Educational Research Journal, 23,* 191–200.

Tobin, K. (1987). The role of wait time in higher cognitive level learning. *Review of Educational Research, 57,* 69–95.

Vygotsky, L. (1978). *Mind in society: The development of higher mental processes.* Cambridge: Harvard University Press.

Weinman, L. (1996). *Designing web graphics: How to prepare images and media for the web.* Indianapolis: New Riders.

Weinman, J., & Haag, P. (1999). Gender equity in cyberspace. *Educational Leadership, 56*(5), 44–49.

Wenglinsky, H. (1998). *Does it compute? The relationship between educational technology and student achievement in mathematics* [On-line]. Available: http://www.ets.org/research/pic/dic/techtoc.html (March 1999).

Wheatley, G. (1991). Constructivist perspectives on science and mathematics learning. *Science Education, 75,* 9–21.

Whitehead, A. (1929). *The aims of education.* Cambridge, England: Cambridge University Press.

Williams, R., & Tollett, J. (1998). *The non-designer's web book.* Berkeley, CA: Peachpit Press.

Wittrock, M. (1974a). A generative model of mathematics learning. *Journal for Research in Mathematics Education, 5,* 181–197.

Wittrock, M. (1974b). Learning as a generative process. *Educational Psychologist, 11,* 87–95.
Wittrock, M. (1989). Generative processes of comprehension. *Educational Psychologist, 24,* 345–376.
Wittrock, M. (1992). Generative learning processes of the brain. *Educational Psychologist, 27,* 531–541.
World Wide Web Conseortium. (1999). *Web Accessibility Initiative page author guidelines* [On-line]. Available: http://www.w3.org/TR/WD-WAI-PAGEAUTH/ (February 1999).
Zinsser, W. (1988). *Writing to learn.* New York: Harper and Row.

# Index

# Quick Reference Guide

## *Keeping Current* Index

Throughout the text, this feature helps keep teachers up to date with the latest technology developments.



These special sections provide extended detail on high-interest topics.

## *Focus* Index